Ephraidge A. T. Rinomhota

ON

E.W. FACT PROFESSIONAL STUDIES SERIES (ACCA)

ADVANCED TAXATION

Finance Act 1989 Edition

Douglas Beardon MA FCA FCCA FCollP

Principal Lecturer in Taxation,
North East London Polytechnic

General Editors

Emile Woolf FCA FCCA FBIM
Suresh Tanna BSc (Hons) FCA
Karam Singh BTech MBA FCA

Hutchinson Business Books

Copyright © Emile Woolf Publications 1988, 1989, 1990

The right of Douglas Beardon to be identified as the author of
this work has been asserted by them in accordance with the Copyright, Designs and Patents Act, 1988

Published in Great Britain by Hutchinson Business Books Limited
An imprint of Century Hutchinson Limited
20 Vauxhall Bridge Road, London SW1V 2SA

Century Hutchinson Australia (Pty) Limited
20 Alfred Street, Milsons Point, Sydney
New South Wales 2061, Australia

Century Hutchinson New Zealand Limited
PO Box 40-086, 32-34 View Road, Glenfield
Auckland 10, New Zealand

Century Hutchinson South Africa (Pty) Limited
PO Box 337, Bergvlei 2012, South Africa

First published in Great Britain 1985
Second Edition 1986
Third Edition 1986
Fourth Edition 1988
Fifth Edition 1989
Sixth Edition 1990

Printed and bound in Great Britain by
Richard Clay Limited, Bungay, Suffolk

British Library Cataloguing in Publication Data
A CIP catalogue record for this
book is available from the British Library
ISBN 0-09174498-9

Ephraidge A. T. Rinomhota

Part 1 IT
2 CT
3 CGT
4 VAT
5 IHT

Contents

PART TWO: CORPORATION TAX

APPENDICES

CHAPTER ONE

History and Administration of Taxation

1.0   INTRODUCTION

Income tax in its present form was introduced by William Pitt the Younger in order to provide funds for the Napoleonic wars. It superseded an ineffective system of direct taxation largely based on property, e.g. the Window Tax. It remained at extremely low rates, rarely more than 5p in the pound, up to the end of the nineteenth century. It was originally intended to be a temporary measure only, but with the expansion of national income, receipts from the tax even at the low level of rates then in force proved too attractive to dispense with altogether. Over the years a marginal rate of 1p in the pound has crept up to one of 40p in the pound today!

All the other taxes are far more recent in origin. Corporation Tax and Capital Gains Tax were introduced in the Finance Act 1965; Value Added Tax and Capital Transfer Tax (now Inheritance Tax) in the Finance Acts 1972 and 1975 respectively.

In addition to the taxes considered above both central and local government have other ways of raising revenue. These include customs duties, local and water rates, social security contributions, car taxes etc. Whether these are 'taxes' in the true sense of the word is open to debate.

This book is concerned with three major areas of tax:

(a)   Direct Taxes - Income Tax, Corporation Tax, Capital Gains Tax and
      Inheritance Tax;

(b)   Indirect Taxes - Value Added Tax.

(c)   Social Security Taxes - National Insurance.

Direct Taxes are administered by the Board of the Inland Revenue; Value Added Tax by the Commissioners of Customs and Excise and National Insurance by the Department of Social Security.

2.0 THE ORGANISATION OF THE INLAND REVENUE

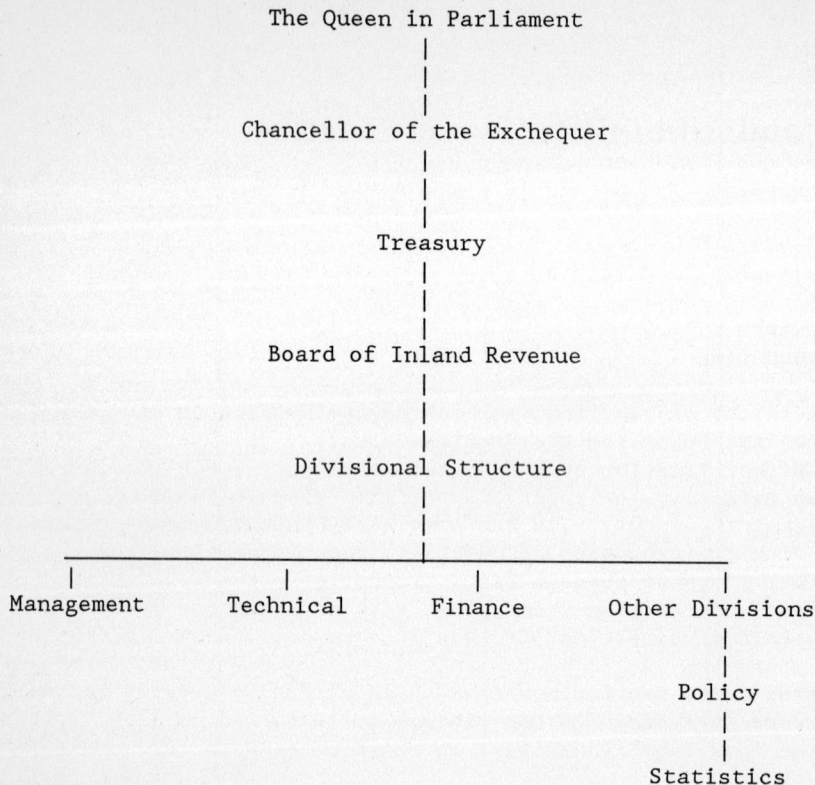

```
                    The Queen in Parliament
                              |
                              |
                              |
                    Chancellor of the Exchequer
                              |
                              |
                              |
                           Treasury
                              |
                              |
                              |
                    Board of Inland Revenue
                              |
                              |
                              |
                      Divisional Structure
                              |
                              |
                              |
        _____|_____
        |           |           |               |
   Management    Technical    Finance     Other Divisions
                                                 |
                                                 |
                                              Policy
                                                 |
        Fig.1                                    |
                                             Statistics
```

2.1 The Queen in Parliament

Tax law is derived from a number of Acts of Parliament. These include:

(a)   Income and Corporation Taxes Act 1988;

(b)   Capital Allowances Act 1968;

(c)   Taxes Management Act 1970;

(d)   Capital Gains Taxes Act 1979;

(e)   Value Added Taxes Act 1983;

(f)   Inheritance Tax Act 1984;

(g)   Annual Finance Acts.

Each year the tax proposals included in the budget become the subject of the annual Finance Act. This also empowers the Government to tax income, as the power to levy income tax must be renewed annually. The Provisional Collection of Taxes Act 1968 enables the Government to collect income tax on the basis of the budget resolution between the beginning of a fiscal year - 6th April - and the time that the Finance Act becomes law, provided that is no later than the following 5th August.

In addition to the above, there are other sources of 'legislation' deriving from the Inland Revenue directly. Whilst these have no legal effect they assist in the smooth running of the system. Critics, however, point out that it is undesirable that the Revenue can operate a quasi-legislative function in a largely unsupervised way. These sources include:

(a) Extra-statutory concessions - these mitigate a charge to tax despite the operation falling within the provisions of a taxing statute;

(b) Statements of practice - these broadly state how the Inland Revenue view the tax treatment of a particular operation;

(c) Advance rulings and clearances - these allow the Inland Revenue to comment on the tax implications of a particular transaction. The clearance procedure is specifically provided to avoid subsequent difficulties where a transaction, e.g. a demerger, can have dramatic tax implications if not carried through in the right form.

2.2 The Chancellor of the Exchequer

He is responsible to Parliament for the conduct and efficiency of the Inland Revenue. He reviews all proposals for legislation and through the Treasury may issue instructions to the Board of Inland Revenue concerning the administration of the Revenue service. He is assisted by the Financial Secretary to the Treasury.

2.3 The Commissioners of Inland Revenue

The Commissioners of Inland Revenue, known as the CIR, are full-time civil servants responsible to the Chancellor of the Exchequer. They consist of a Chairman, two Deputy Chairmen, two Directors General and two other Commissioners. The junior commissioners normally have a specific executive function within the Revenue such as responsibility for the establishment etc. The functions of the Commissioners are:

(a) to implement all Acts of Parliament relating to the Inland Revenue;

(b) to give advice and information to the Chancellor of the Exchequer and the Treasury concerning Revenue matters. In particular to provide statistical information;

(c) to exercise overall control of the various divisions of the Inland Revenue Service.

2.4 The Management Division

This is the largest division of the Inland Revenue. It is concerned with all aspects of the functional operations of the Revenue including personnel and training, general organisation and the operation of income and capital taxes. The

UK is divided into approximately 600 districts each under the charge of a
district inspector - often a law graduate with an expert knowledge of taxation.

The size of the district offices varies from a small country district to the
large 'London Provincial' offices responsible for several million taxpayers.
Special offices deal with civil servants and members of the armed forces. The
functions of the Inspectors of Taxes include:

(a) to issue return forms;

(b) to receive and examine completed returns;

(c) to obtain additional information if required;

(d) to make assessments;

(e) to receive notices of appeal against assessments;

(f) to negotiate settlements;

(g) to represent the Revenue at appeal hearings;

(h) to make repayments

(i) to conduct correspondence and liaise with taxpayers generally as regards
     their taxation liabilities.

In recent years there has been considerable activity in the ascertainment and
prevention of tax evasion. Whilst much of the work in this area is dealt with in
the district offices, specialist units also make significant contributions.
These include:

(a) the Enquiry and Investigation Offices which deal with cases of fraud;

(b) Special Offices which deal with types of case which a district could find
     difficult to manage;

(c) Audit Units dealing with PAYE compliance etc.

2.5 The Technical Division

This deals with the technical operation of the Revenue. It formulates advice on
the operation of legislation and the prevention of elaborate tax avoidance
schemes.

2.6 The Finance Division

This division deals with the accountancy of the Inland Revenue, including the
collection of tax, estimates of tax yields and the payment of Revenue salaries
and expenses. It operates as far as the collection is concerned through a number
of collection offices.

2.7 Interpretation of tax legislation

In many cases tax legislation is difficult to understand and, in some cases, almost incomprehensible. Rules of statutory interpretation have been evolved, and in these the courts have tried to blend consistency with the recognition that the taxing Acts are a rather special form of statute demanding a strict or predictable form of interpretation. Over the years certain broad principles have been laid down:

(a) The words of the Act must be given their natural meaning.

The taxpayer, when interpreting the taxing statutes, is entitled to assume a literal construction of the provisions in the Act even in those cases where the result is unusual. In **Rennell v. IRC (1962)**, Lord Justice Donovan said:

'Nevertheless in the end, one simply has to look at the words of the statute and construe them fairly and reasonably, and, if such a construction yields anomalous results in particular cases, it is a commonplace that they must be accepted, whether it be the Crown or the taxpayer who is thereby advantaged.'

(b) Where there is doubt as to meaning of a statutory provison, the taxpayer must be given the benefit of the doubt.

This principle states that where there is doubt, the taxpayer must be the one to benefit from it. In **IRC v. Ross and Coulter (1948)**, Lord Thankerton observed:

'...if the provision is reasonably capable of two alternative meanings then the courts will prefer the meaning more favourable to the subject.'

(c) The tax must be clearly imposed on the taxpayer by the terms of the statute.

This principle establishes that an individual cannot be liable to tax unless the words of the taxing statute unambiguously impose the tax upon him. In **Ayrshire Employers Mutual Insurance Association Limited v. IRC (1946)**, Lord Normand stated:

'In the end, I seem to be driven to the last refuge of judicial hesitation when faced with a difficulty of interpretation, the doctrine that no tax can be imposed on the subject without words in an Act of Parliament clearly showing an intention to lay a burden upon him...'

(d) There is no equity in taxation.

Lord Cairns, L.C. in **Partington v. Attorney General (1869)** said:

'..because, as I understand the principle of all fiscal legislation, it is this: if the person sought to be taxed comes within the letter of the law he must be taxed, however great the hardship may appear to the judicial mind to be.'

This leads to the presumption that the courts will adopt a literal approach to the interpretation of tax statutes without speculating on the probable opinions or motives of those who drafted the legislation, and without attempting to remedy deficiencies in drafting:

'It is not the function of the court to give words a strained and unnatural meaning which, had the legislature thought of it, would have been covered by appropriate words.'

per Lord Simmonds in **IRC v. Wolfson (1949)**.

Nor will the courts attempt to deal with suggestions that they should exercise a moral judgment. This, according to Lord Normand in **Vestey's Executors v. IRC (1949)**, would have been an undesirable first step down a very slippery slope.

"...the court will not stretch the terms of taxing statutes in order to improve on the efforts of Parliament and to stop gaps which are left open by the statutes. Tax avoidance is an evil, but it would be the beginning of a much greater evil if the courts were to subject to taxation people of whom they have disapproved."

In recent years the House of Lords has considered as an aid to interpretation the substance of the transaction. Although it can be said that the controversy of form over substance and vice versa is really concerned with the interpretation of the transaction as opposed to the interpretation of the statute, it is nevertheless of valid interest.

In looking towards the substance of a transaction, the courts take an overview of the intention and effects of a transaction rather than looking merely towards the relevant documentation. In the late nineteenth and early twentieth centuries there were several cases which intimated that this was the correct approach, e.g. **A-G v. Partington (1869)** and **Secretary of State for India v. Scoble (1903)**. Later cases, in particular **IRC v. Duke of Westminster (1936)** 19 TC 490 have disagreed with this approach:

'If all that is meant by the doctrine (the substance) is that having once ascertained the legal rights of the parties you may disregard mere nomenclature and decide the questions of taxability and non-taxability in accordance with the legal rights, well and good...If, on the other hand, the doctrine means that you may brush aside deeds, disregard the legal rights and liabilities arising under a contract between parties and decide the question of taxability or non-taxability upon the footing of the rights and liabilities of the parties being different from what in law they are, then I entirely dissent from such a doctrine.'

per Lord Russell of Killowen.

In the case of **IRC v. Plummer (1979)** it was held that separate transactions which are interlinking and mutually interdependent can be considered as a whole:

'The plan now involved was explained by the brokers in great detail and its intended accomplishment set out, with timetables in almost military precision. This...entitles and requires us to look at the plan as a whole. It does not entitle us to disregard the legal form and nature of the transactions carried out.'

per Lord Wilberforce.

The cases of **WT Ramsay Ltd. v. IRC (1981)** and **IRC v. Burmah (1982)** have extended this position still further. It appears that although an avoidance scheme consists of documentation and transactions which are genuine per se it will not preclude a different finding as to the effects of the scheme as a whole particularly when the following features are present:

> "i) On completion of the scheme the taxpayer is in the same financial position as he was at the beginning;
>
> ii) The clear and stated intention of the parties is that the scheme should proceed through its various steps to completion;
>
> iii) The taxpayer is not required to use his own money for the purpose of the scheme;
>
> iv) The whole and only purpose of the scheme is the avoidance of tax."

per Lord Wilberforce.

This emphasis on a new and radical approach was formalised by the House of Lords in **Furniss v. Dawson (1984)**. Broadly, in this case Dawson wished to sell shares to a UK company (WB Ltd.); to defer a liability to CGT the shares were first sold to a newly incorporated Isle of Man company (G Ltd.), in return for shares in that company. The Isle of Man company then sold the shares to WB Ltd. Throughout, the price charged and paid for the shares was £152,000. As a result of this:

(a) there was no liability to CGT on the disposal to G Ltd. - share for share exchange;

(b) there was no liability on the disposal from G Ltd. to WB Ltd. bought and sold for £152,000.

In the judgment of Lord Brightman:

> 'The whole process was planned and executed with faultless precision. The meetings began at 12.45 p.m. on 20th December at which time the shareholdings of the operating companies were still owned by the Dawsons...they ended with the shareholdings in the ownership of Wood Bastow.'

His Lordship held that the courts could ignore the parts of the operation which had no commercial purpose. Thus by excluding G Ltd. the position was a simple sale by the Dawsons to Wood Bastow Ltd.

Many commentators have stated that the **Furniss v. Dawson** decision raises more questions than it resolves, in particular:

(a) Will the presence of a commercial motive exclude the principle and what, in any case, is a commercial motive?

(b) Can the taxpayer apply the Ramsay principle against the Revenue?

(c) How will the principle operate when there is an express statutory defence?

The danger of these cases in the matter of interpretation is that an even greater level of judicial discretion has been introduced into the law. The fact that the transactions fall within the letter of the law will not preclude the court from ignoring this and looking to the end effect.

3.0 RETURNS AND ASSESSMENTS

A person chargeable to tax must make a return of his income and capital gains to the Inland Revenue. Even if he is not sent a return form he must notify the Revenue if he has received any income within one year from the year of assessment in which it is received. A year of assessment runs from 6th April to the following 5th April; the year from 6th April 1989 to 5th April 1990 is known as the year 1989/90. A return must include a declaration by the person making it that it is, to the best of his knowledge and belief, complete and correct and it must be submitted to the Inspector of Taxes 30 days after issue though, in practice, further time is allowed. Where the taxpayer's only income is from an employment, the Inspector may not issue him with a return form each year and in this case the taxpayer should ensure that the Inspector knows immediately about any changed circumstances.

Companies must make returns in respect of their accounting periods.

Assessments to tax are made by the Inspector of Taxes. They must show the following:

(a) the type and amount of income assessed,
(b) the date issued, and
(c) the time limit for making appeals.

The taxpayer may request the Inspector to send a copy of any assessment to his agent. Estimated assessments may be made when no return of income is submitted to the Inspector or where he is not satisfied that the return is full or complete.

A person who has been assessed to tax may apply for relief against any over-assessment due to an error or mistake in any return made to the Inland Revenue. This must be claimed within six years from the end of the relevant year of assessment. No relief is available if the income was assessed in accordance with the law existing at the time of assessment.

4.0 APPEALS

If a taxpayer objects to the amount of income tax assessed upon him, he can appeal against it. Appeals are initially heard by either the General or the Special Commissioners. To be effective the appeal must be:

(a) in writing, stating the grounds of the appeal,

(b) signed by the taxpayer or his agent,

(c) lodged within 30 days of the date of issue of the assessment.

A late appeal may be accepted by the Inspector if there is reasonable excuse for the delay. If he does not accept it, it must be referred to the Commissioners for their decision.

4.1 The General Commissioners

The General Commissioners are appointed locally for divisions. They are
appointed by the Lord Chancellor and in some ways, such as non-payment for
services, resemble the lay magistrates. They generally have no special
qualifications in tax or accounting and a clerk, often a local solicitor,
accountant or ex-Inspector of Taxes is appointed to assist them and to deal with
the administrative arrangements. The quorum required to hear an appeal is at
least two Commissioners.

4.2 The Special Commssioners

The Special Commissioners are full-time civil servants appointed by the Lord
Chancellor. They consist of barristers or solicitors with considerable
experience of Revenue law. Certain appeals such as those against inheritance tax
assessments can only be heard by them. The normal quorum is one Commissioner
unless the Presiding Commissioner decides otherwise.

Whilst Special Commissioners go on circuit to major provincial towns, their base
is London and most appeals can be heard there if desired.

Appeals are normally heard by the General Commissioners unless they involve
difficult questions of law when they are usually brought before the Special
Commissioners. Appeals can, by agreement, or by direction, be transferred from
one body to another.

4.3 The conduct of an appeal before the Commissioners

At the hearing of the appeal before the Commissioners, the taxpayer may be
represented by either a solicitor, barrister or member of an incorporated body of
accountants. The burden of proof is on the taxpayer and he or his
representatives will be asked to make the opening address and to call and examine
his witnesses who may be cross-examined by the Inspector or the other
representative of the Revenue. The Revenue then present their case and witnesses,
who are available for cross-examination by the taxpayer. The Commissioners may
examine witnesses on oath and may impose penalties for non-attendance. After
hearing all the evidence, the Commissioners may retire to consider their
decision. The Inspector of Taxes may not retire with them. The Commissioners
decide by a majority and if evenly divided the practice is to discharge the
assessment. The Commissioners have no power to award costs.

4.4 Appeals to the courts

Appeals fall into two main classes, fact or law; a Commissioners' determination
on a question of fact is normally final. The taxpayer or the Revenue may appeal
to the High Court on a question of law. This right can only be exercised if the
party concerned expresses dissatisfaction immediately upon receiving the
Commissioners' decision. The procedure is initiated by giving notice in writing
to the clerk to the Commissioners within 30 days after the decision requesting a
case to be stated for the opinion of the High Court. The fee for this is £25.
Once the case has been stated it must be sent by the appellant to the High Court
within 30 days of receipt. The appeal will be heard in due course in the Chancery
Division by a single judge. The court may confirm, amend or reduce the assessment
as appropriate; it may also award costs. Further appeals lie to the Court of

Appeal (Civil Division) and thence, with leave, to the House of Lords. Under
certain circumstances it is possible to take appeals directly from the High Court
to the House of Lords, omitting the Court of Appeal.

CHAPTER TWO

Income Tax

1.0 LIABILITY TO INCOME TAX

Broadly, income tax is chargeable on:

(a) All persons resident in the UK whether British subjects or not, and whether or not their income is derived from inside or outside the UK;

(b) Non-residents to the extent that they derive income from any property, trade, profession, vocation or employment in the UK.

Certain income derived from the UK may be exempt from UK tax in the hands of a non-resident, either under UK law (e.g. s.47 TA 1988) or under the terms of a double tax agreement.

The following are not liable to income tax on all or part of their income:

(a) limited companies - they are chargeable to corporation tax;

(b) Ambassadors, High Commissioners and Ministers of any foreign state, together with their staff;

(c) visiting armed forces and staffs of allied headquarters;

(d) officials of the United Nations;

(e) local authorities;

(f) approved pension funds;

(g) certain organisations such as charities, hospitals, trade unions, etc. on specific types of income.

2.0   INCOME LIABLE TO INCOME TAX

All income is liable to income tax with certain exceptions including the following:

(a)   National Savings Bank Ordinary Account interest not exceeding £70;

(b)   National Savings Certificate and SAYE scheme interest;

(c)   repayment supplements on overpaid tax;

(d)   certain benefits in kind to employees, other than directors, earning less than £ 8,500 pa provided the benefit cannot be converted into money or money's worth;

(e)   certain scholarships;

(f)   income support, family credit, child benefit and certain other social security benefits;

(g)   income from Personal Equity Plans;

(h)   wound and disability pensions;

(i)   War Widows' pensions, pensions for victims of Nazi persecution, etc;

(j)   annuities to holders of the George Cross, Victoria Cross, Edward Medal or Albert Medal, and additional pensions payable to the holders of such awards;

(k)   certain payments under divorce and separation agreements.

3.0   THE SCHEDULAR SYSTEM

Income is classified according to its source under one of five schedules. Certain of these schedules are sub-divided into cases. Each schedule has its own rules as to the calculation of income and the deduction of expenses. The schedules are mutually exclusive which means that the Inland Revenue cannot assess to tax under one schedule income which properly belongs to another (**Fry v. Salisbury House Estate Ltd. (1930)**).

The income liable under the various schedules can be summarised as given in Fig.2.

Schedule A	Schedule B	Schedule D	Schedule E	Schedule F
Income from land and buildings in UK Normal basis of assessment: actual	Interest out of public revenue paid through a UK paying agent Normal basis of assessment: actual	See below	Remuneration from unemployment Normal basis of assessment: actual	Taxed icome and dividends Normal basis of assessment: actual

Case I	Case II	Case III	Case IV	Case V	Case VI
Profit from trade and businesses	Profit from professions and vocations	Untaxed interest in the UK	Foreign securities	Foreign possessions	Miscellaneous

Normal basis of assessment: preceding year

Normal basis of assessment: actual

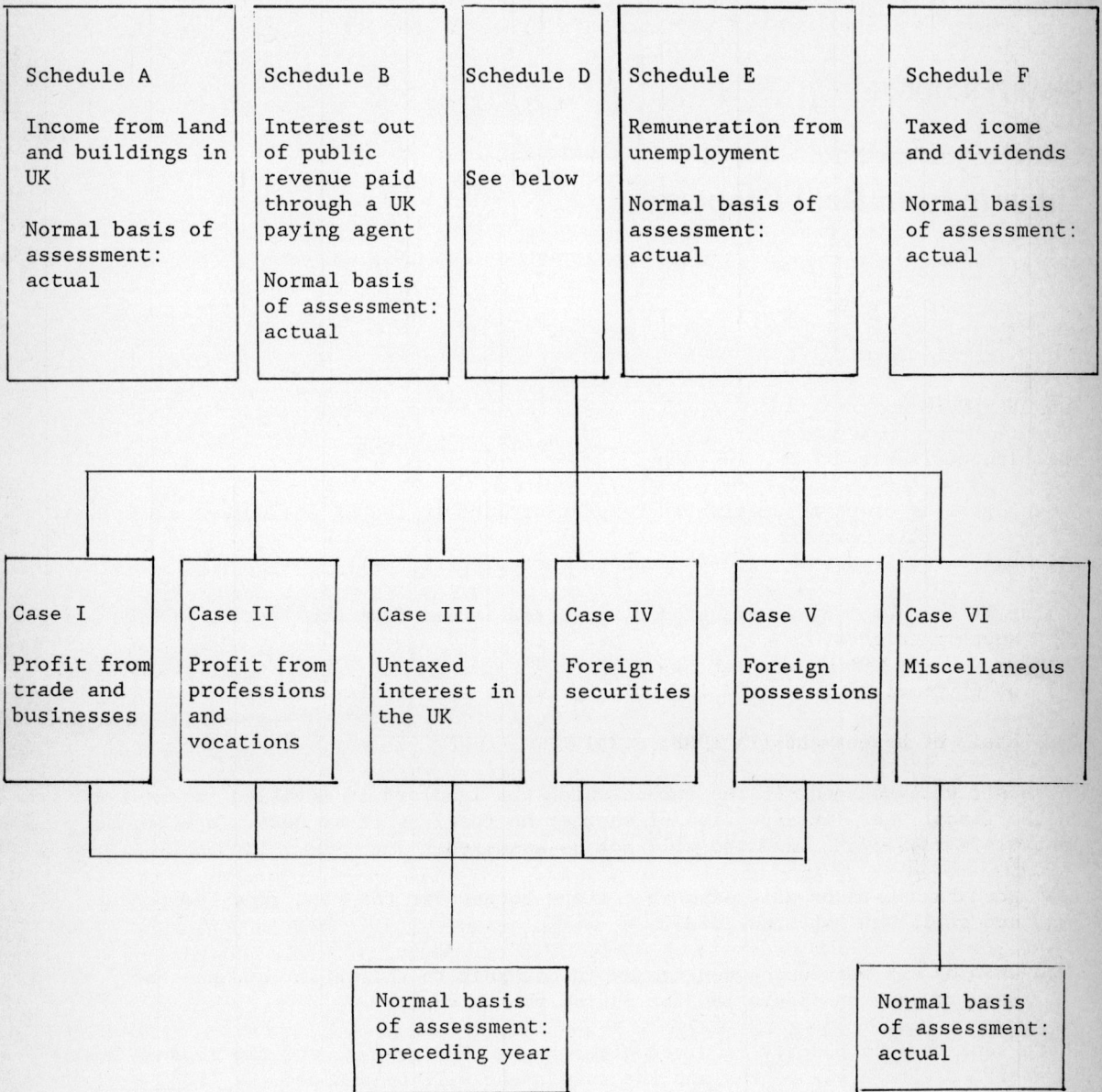

Fig.2   Summary of the Schedules and Cases

CHAPTER THREE

Income from Real Property

1.0 SCHEDULE A

1.1 Income liable

Annual profits or gains arising in respect of land in the UK including:

(a) rents received from land and unfurnished property;

(b) rent charges, wayleaves, ground rents and income from the letting of sporting rights;

(c) other receipts from land including premiums and similar receipts.

1.2 Basis of assessment (TA 1988, s.25)

The basis of assessment is the income which the landlord is entitled to receive in the fiscal year, irrespective of whether he receives it or not. To mitigate possible hardship the landlord will not be assessed:

(a) when he has taken all reasonable steps to recover the rent from the tenant, and still has not succeeded;

(b) when he has waived the rent to avoid hardship to the tenant and has not received any consideration for making the waiver.

Where rent is subsequently received after relief has been given, the Revenue must be notified within six months and the assessment will be amended (TA 1988, s.41).

Where rent has been paid in advance and the property is sold, the advance rent will be apportioned between buyer and seller (TA 1988, s.40).

Illustration
A let property for the first time on 24th June 1989 He has agreed a rent of £1,000 per annum payable by the tenant either:

(a)   annually in advance,
(b)   annually in arrears,
(c)   quarterly in advance, on the usual quarter days,
(d)   quarterly in arrears, on the usual quarter days.

The usual quarter days are:

24th June, 29th September, 25th December, 25th March.

Advise A in respect to the 1989/90 liability.

	(a) £	(b) £	(c) £	(d) £
24th June 1989	1,000	-	250	-
29th September 1989	-	-	250	250
25th December 1989	-	-	250	250
25th March 1990	-	-	250	250
	1,000	-	1,000	750

1.3 Deductible expenses

To be deductible, expenses must generally satisfy four basic criteria:

(a)   they must relate to the property;
(b)   they must relate to the period of ownership;
(c)   they must be reflected in the rent;
(d)   they must not be capital.

In detail, the expenses that may be deductible include:

(a)   interior and exterior repairs and redecorations. This only gives relief for current dilapidations and not for expenditure incurred in remedying preacquisition defects (TA 1988, s.25(3)).

(b)   the upkeep of gardens;

(c)   the wages of porters, cleaners and persons concerned in estate management;

(d)   insurance premiums, and valuation fees for insurance;

(e)   rates and rents payable to a superior landlord;

(f)   the cost of rent collection, but not rents stolen by an agent;

(g)   capital allowances on plant and machinery used in the maintenance and repair of the property;

(h)   payments of other services and amenities to tenants, of a revenue nature;

(i)   legal and accountancy costs for preparing accounts and tax computations.
Loan or mortgage interest for the purchase or improvement of the property is not treated as an expense in arriving at the assessment but as a deduction from the

assessable income.

To be allowed, the property must be let at a commercial rent for more than 26 weeks out of any 52-week period falling wholly or partly in the fiscal year, and during any period in which it is not let it must be:

(a)   occupied by the landlord as his main residence; or
(b)   available for letting; or
(c)   be incapable of being let because of repairs etc.

The interest payable may be relieved not only against the assessable income that it relates to but also against income from other properties, including those let furnished.   Unrelieved interest may be carried forward to be offset in future years.

Expenses are deductible in the fiscal year in which they are paid (TA 1988, s.25).

Illustration

On 1st December 1988 B purchased a freehold block of flats for £200,000. All the flats were let through letting agents on monthly tenancies at rack rents. All rents had been paid to 30th November 1988 prior to the purchase.
In the period to 5th April 1990 his receipts and payments were:

	1st Dec 1988 to 5th April 1989	Year ended 5th April 1990
Receipts:	£	£
Rents	4,760	14,950
Wayleaves	3	10
Contributions from tenants towards repairs	-	642
	4,763	15,602
Payments:		
Agents' commission (10% on rents)	476	1,495
Repairs and maintenance	218	1,748
Caretaker's wages	260	780
Outgoings on caretaker's flat	85	270
Insurance and incidentals (all allowable)	162	225
Construction of swimming pool - 31st May 1989	-	1,600
Rates on outbuildings	14	44
Purchase of motor mower - 1st January 1989	160	-
Professional charges	1,242	123
Mortgage interest	1,800	5,400
	4,417	11,685

	1st Dec 1988 to 5th April 1989		Year ended 5th April 1990
	£	£	£
(1) Rents received comprised:			
Rent owing at beginning of period	-		240
Rents due	5,000		15,520
	5,000		15,760
Less: Rent owing at end of period	240	540	
Rents lost through defaulting tenants.		270	
			810
	4,760		14,950

(2) Repairs and maintenance were made up as follows:	£	£
Garden maintenance	40	120
Lift maintenance	36	108
Normal decorations and incidental repairs	142	420
Asphalting drive (in April 1989), (the drive was in a dangerous state at the time of purchase)	-	1,100
	218	1,748

(3) The contributions from tenants towards repairs were deposits against work to be done in the summer of 1990.

(4) Professional charges comprised:	£	£
Legal charges re defaulting tenant	-	50
Accountancy	37	42
Valuation for insurance purposes	-	31
Valuation for mortgage	1,205	-
	1,242	123

(5) The swimming pool was constructed at the request of the tenants who agreed to higher rents having regard to this facility. HM Inspector of Taxes admitted a claim for capital allowances on 50% of the cost.

REQUIRED: Compute the amount of the Schedule A assessment for 1988/89 and 1989/90 making such assumptions as you consider necessary.

Schedule A assessments	1988-89		1989-90	
	£	£	£	£

Rents receivable		5,000	15,520
Less: Irrecoverable			270
			15,250
Wayleaves		3	10
		5,003	15,260
Less: Expenses:			
Repairs and maintenance	218		648
Insurance and incidentals	162		225
Agents' commission	476		1,495
Caretaker's wages	260		780
Outgoings on caretaker's flat	85		270
Rates on outbuildings	14		44
Professional charges	37		123
Capital allowances	40	1,292	230 3,815
Schedule A		3,711	11,445
Mortgage interest deducted from			
Schedule A assessments		1,800	5,400
		1,911	6,045

Capital allowances are claimed as follows:

1988/89	£		£
Motor Mower - cost	160		
WDA - 25%	40		40
	120		
1989/90			
Swimming Pool	800		
½ x £1,600			
	920		
WDA - 25% x 920	230		230
c/f	690		

No allowance can be given for expenditure unless incurred.

1.4 Classification of leases

There are two main classifications of leases:

(a)   leases at a full rent;
(b)   leases at a reduced rent.

Leases at a full rent

These can be defined as leases from which, taking one year with another, the landlord expects to recover his expenses. There can be two types of lease at full rent:

(a)   landlord repairing lease - a lease under which the landlord is required to maintain the property;

(b)   tenant repairing lease - a lease under which the tenant is responsible for all or substantially all the repairs to the property.

Leases not at a full rent

These are defined as leases from which taking one year with another the landlord does not expect to recover all the expenses relating to the lease.

The reason for the subdivision of leases relates to relief for excess expenses.

1.5 Relief for excess expenses

Relief for excess expenses depends on the type of lease:

(a)   **Landlord repairing lease (LRL)**

Surpluses and deficits on individual leases are pooled. Overall surpluses are assessed, overall deficits are carried forward to offset against future surpluses in the pool.

(b)   **Tenant repairing leases (TRL)**

Each lease is treated individually; surpluses are assessed; a deficit is either:

i)   carried forward against a surplus under the same or future leases of the same property;

ii)   set against available surpluses in the pool of landlord repairing leases of the same or future fiscal years.

(c)   **Leases at a reduced rent (LRR)**

Each lease is treated individually: surpluses are assessed, deficits are carried forward and offset against future surpluses under the same lease.

Illustration

C had several properties. You are provided with the following information for
the fiscal year 1989/90:

Property	Type	Profit £	Loss £	Loss b/f £
A	LRL	500		
B	LRL		120	
C	TRL	190		30
D	TRL		170	
E	LRR	60		80
F	LRR	15		

Losses brought forward in the pool of LRL are £100.

Schedule A assessable income 1989/90

	£	£	£

LRL
A	P 500		
B	L (120)		
	———		
		380	
Loss b/f		(100)	
		———	
		280	

TRL
C	P 190		
Loss b/f	(30)		160
	———		
D		L (170)	
		———	110

LRR
E	P 60		
Loss b/f	(80)		
	———		
	c/f (20)		
	==		
F			15
			———
			£285
			===

In general it will be advantageous to offset the loss on any TRL against profits
in the pool of LRL to obtain the earliest possible relief.

1.6 Void periods

There may be periods during the ownership of property where expenses are incurred but no income is being received. Relief is available to a landlord for this expenditure provided it is incurred in a void period. A void period occurs when the property is not occupied and which either:

(a)   begins with the acquisition of the property and is followed by a lease at a full rent; or

(b)   follows a lease at a full rent.

A lease at a full rent may be either landlord or tenant repairing.

Expenses incurred in a void period may be offset against income from the property in the fiscal year in which they are paid. Excess expenses may be carried forward and offset against further income from a lease at a full rent.

It is important to appreciate that a period of landlord occupation in the void period or the presence of a lease at a reduced rent, may negate the deduction of expenses in the void period.

1.7 Premiums (TA 1988, s.34)

(a)   General

A premium receivable by the landlord under a lease granted <u>not</u> assigned for a term not exceeding 50 years is treated as additional rent and taxable in the fiscal year in which it is received. The amount taxable is the amount of the premium less a deduction of 2% of the premium for each year of the life of the lease other than the first. Only complete years of the life of the lease are taken into account.

Illustration

D grants to E a lease for ten years on payment of a premium of £5,000.

		£
Premium		5,000
Less: 2(10 - 1)% x £5,000		900
		4,100

(b)   Duration of the lease

Whilst there is normally no doubt as to the duration of the lease <u>TA 1988, s.38</u> provides that full account may be taken of commercial reality. Thus where the landlord grants a lease which is likely to terminate before the end of its life either:

i)   because of a premature right of formal determination by the
      landlord, or

ii)   because of an informal right as, for example, having the right to
      increase the rent tenfold every five years but allowing the tenant
      to surrender the lease if wished,

then the duration of the lease will be from granting to the earliest date on
which it is likely to be determined (which is generally the earliest
possible date).

Illustration

F grants to G a lease for 60 years on payment of £10,000. The lease can be
terminated at the landlord's option at the end of the 7th or 35th year.

	£
Premium	10,000
Less: 2(7 - 1)% x £10,000	1,200
	8,800

(c)   Premiums paid by instalments

Where a premium is received by instalments, and provided that the taxpayer
can satisfy the Revenue that it would cause him undue hardship to pay tax on
the whole premium at once, the taxpayer may pay the tax by instalments over
a period not exceeding:

i)   eight years, or
ii)   the period during which the instalments are received, if less.

(d)   Other forms of premium

As a result of the high liability to tax on premiums, attempts were made to
avoid tax by either giving the premium a different name or putting it into a
form other than cash.

i)   A payment for the variation of the terms of a lease will be treated as
      a premium. The "duration" of the lease is the period for which the
      variation is effective.

Illustration

H grants to J a lease for ten years. The terms are that J uses the property
for offices. H grants to J a licence to use part of the building for
industrial purposes for a period of four years on payment of £1,000.

	£
Premium	1,000
Less: 2(4 - 1)% x £1,000	60
Assessable	940

ii) A requirement of the lease that the tenant carries out capital work on the property, the cost of which would not have been allowed as a Schedule A if incurred by the landlord, will mean that the landlord is deemed to have received a premium. The value of the premium is the difference between the values of the reversionary interest:

   (1) assuming that the lease did not require the carrying out of the capital work, and

   (2) assuming that it did require the carrying out of the work.

The valuations are to be made as at the date the lease was granted.

Illustration

C grants to D a lease for 16 years. A condition of the lease is that D will erect an extension to the office. It is estimated that this will increase the value of the landlord's reversion by £10,000.

	£
Premium	10,000
Less: 2(16 - 1)% x £10,000	3,000
Assessable	7,000

iii) Where the terms of a lease permit the lessee to surrender it on payment of a lump sum, that sum is treated as a premium when received by the landlord. The "duration" of the lease is the period of the lease from the date of surrender to the normal expiry date.

Illustration

E had a lease of 40 years under which he paid F his landlord £1,000 p.a. rent in arrears on 31st December annually. He found alternative premises at a rent of £ 200. On 31st December 1989 he paid F £5,000 to terminate the lease. It then had 30 years to run.

	£
Premium	5,000
Less: 2(30 - 1)% x £5,000	2,900
Assessable	2,100

(e) Relief for premiums paid

There are two basic forms of relief for a premium paid on the granting of a lease:

i)   against trading profits or rents received if a sublease is granted;
ii)   against premiums received if a sublease is granted.

Calculation of relief:

i)   Against trading profits and rents received:

$$\frac{\text{Premium assessed on superior landlord}}{\text{Duration of the lease}}$$

ii)   Against premiums received on a sublease:

$$\text{Premium assessed on superior landlord} \times \frac{\text{Duration of sublease}}{\text{Duration of head-lease}}$$

Illustration

G grants to H a lease for 20 years on payment of a premium of £10,000.

The amount of relief that H can get by deduction against trading profits (if he occupies the premises himself) or against rents received (if he grants a sublease) is:

Premium assessed on superior landlord:

	£
Premium	10,000
Less: 2(20 - 1)% x £10,000	3,800
	6,200
Relief 6,200/20 =	310 p.a.

If the premium was paid during an accounting period, the relief for that year is reduced on a time basis.

Alternatively, if H grants to J a six-year sublease for a premium of £6,000, the relief is:

	£
Premium received	6,000
Less: 2(6 - 1)% x £6,000	600
	5,400
Less: £6,200 x 6/20	1,860
Assessable	3,540

If the deduction for the premium paid exceeds the premium received the excess may be offset against rents received from the sublease. Thus if the premium received on the sublease was only £1,000 the position would be:

	£
	f
Premium received	1,000
Less: 2(6 - 1)% x £1,000	100
	900
Less:	1,860
Assessable	-

Relief against any annual rents received:

$$£960/6 = £160 \text{ p.a.}$$

It appears that where a sublease is granted at both a premium and a rent, the offset is first against the chargeable amount of the premium received and secondly against any rents.

Where only part of premises are sublet, an appropriate part of any premium paid may be deducted. In general, floor area is an appropriate criterion to apply.

(f) Date of payment of the tax

The tax due under Schedule A is payable on 1st January in the year of assessment. Provision is made for the assessment to be based initially on the income of the preceding year with a revision to the actual assessable income once the final details are known. If the income of the preceding year includes rents in respect of properties now sold or premiums in respect of leases, these may be eliminated by the Inspector provided that an application is made prior to 1st January.

Where rents are paid to an agent, the agent will be responsible for accounting for tax to the Revenue. There are powers in TA 1988, s.23 which allow the Revenue to direct the lessee of a property to pay part or all of the rent due, to the Revenue on account of the tax liability of the landlord.

2.0 SCHEDULE D CASE VI - INCOME FROM FURNISHED LETTINGS

2.1 Income liable

Income from furnished lettings is assessable under Schedule D Case VI. The computation follows the same general structure as for Schedule A except that income should strictly be calculated on the accruals basis. In practice, however, the Schedule A entitlement basis is commonly used. The expenses deductible will include:
(a) repairs
(b) rents payable
(c) rates
(d) management and letting expenses

(e) insurance
(f) capital allowances on furniture etc.

As an alternative to claiming capital allowances the taxpayer may claim a
deduction for wear and tear based on a fixed percentage of the gross rents, which
is normally ten per cent.

An Inland Revenue Statement of Practice of October 1977 indicates that rates or
other payments for services which are normally a tenant's burden should be
deducted from the rent, in arriving at the allowance for wear and tear, if they
are paid by the landlord.

Illustration

D owns a house in Ramsgate which he lets furnished at £50 per week.   During
1989/90 he incurred the following expenses:

	£
Rates	420
Outside painting	210
Furniture repairs	40
Commission	250
Garden upkeep	300
Insurance: Building	25
Contents	70
Accountant's fee	30

The Schedule D Case VI assessable income is as follows:

	£	£
Rent £50 x 52		2,600
Less: Rates	420	
Exterior painting	210	
Furniture repairs	40	
Garden upkeep	300	
Insurance: (£25 + £70)	95	
Commission	250	
Accountancy	30	
Wear & tear 10% x £2,180	218	
(£2,600 - 420)	___	1,563
Case VI		1,037

Where the taxpayer wishes, he may, by election made within two years of the end of the year of assessment, have the income from the property split - the rent applicable to the structure being assessed under Schedule A and that applicable to the contents under Schedule D VI. Expenses will be split in an appropriate manner.

Thus if D has unrelieved losses in 1989/90 from unfurnished property let at a full rent, amounting to £400, he should elect to split his Case VI assessment, in order to maximise the use of such losses. For this purpose the rent is agreed as £2,080 relating to the building and £520 relating to the contents. The computation is then:

		Building		Contents
	£	£	£	£
Rent		2,080		520
Less: Rates	420		-	
Exterior painting	210		-	
Furniture repair	-		40	
Garden upkeep	300		-	
Insurance	25		70	
Commission	200		50	
Accountancy	24		6	
Wear and tear	-		218	
	___	1,179	___	384
		901		136
Less: Loss under Schedule A		400		
		___		_
Schedule A		501	Case VI	136

Where the letting of the property involves a considerable degree of service, e.g. the providing of meals, cleaning etc., the profits may be treated as earned income assessable under Schedule D Case I.

2.2 Date of payment

The tax due is payable on 1st January in the year of assessment. Similar provisions apply to the making of estimated assessments and subsequent revision to actual as for Schedule A.

2.3 Furnished holiday lettings

General

Income from furnished holiday accommodation is assessable under Schedule D VI, subject to the right of the landlord to elect that the proportion of rent attributable to the structure be assessed under Schedule A. In most cases it was assessable on the recipients as earned income. However the case of **Griffiths v. Jackson (1983)** held that even if organised on proper business lines this type of activity could not constitute a trade. Amendments introduced in 1984 now permit such an activity to be treated as a trade whilst leaving the income assessable under Schedule D VI.

To qualify for this treatment, the lettings must be on a commercial basis and:

(a) the property must be available as holiday accommodation for at least 140 days in the fiscal year and be actually let for at least 70 days;

(b) for a period of at least 7 months (including the period in (a)) it is not normally in the same occupation for a continuous period exceeding 31 days.

It is possible to average the letting periods of two or more units of accommodation in order to achieve the aggregate of 70 days per unit required under (a) above. A claim must be made within two years of the end of the year of assessment or accounting period in the case of a company.

Illustration

A, an individual, has three flats in Hastings which are available for letting throughout the fiscal year 1989/90. The periods of holiday letting in that year are:

Flat 1   150 days
Flat 2   80 days
Flat 3   40 days

At present flat 3 would not qualify as it has not been let for at least 70 days. If, however, A elects no later than 5th April 1992, the periods of letting can be averaged, i.e.

150 + 80 + 40 = 270 ÷ 3 = 90 days.

Therefore all the properties qualify as furnished holiday accommodation.

The tests mentioned above to determine whether a property qualifies for relief will be made by reference to a year of assessment. On a commencement, however, the tests will be applied to the twelve-month period starting with the date on which it was first let furnished, and in the year of cessation the relevant period will be the twelve months ending on the date on which it ceased to be let furnished.

Illustration

B acquired furnished holiday accommodation on 30th June 1989 and let it furnished for the first time on 1st September 1989. To qualify the relevant periods are:

```
1989/90          1.9.1989 - 31.8.1990
1990/91          6.4.1990 -  5.4.1991
1991/92          6.4.1991 -  5.4.1992 etc.
```

For a company the conditions must be satisfied for the accounting period.

If the conditions are satisfied the following taxation advantages are available:

(a)   Expenditure is allowable if it satisfies the Schedule D I expenses rules; the full range of loss reliefs available for a normal trade are generally available;

(b)   the profits are treated as earned income, qualify for personal pension contributions and have the tax paid in two equal instalments on 1st January in, and 1st July following, the year of assessment;

(c)   relief is available for pre-trading expenditure;

(d)   capital allowances are available;

(e)   for CGT purposes, the following reliefs are available:

    i)   rollover;
    ii)   'retirement';
    iii) gifts;
    iv)   relief for losses on loans to trades.

Specific rules deal with the situation where holiday accommodation becomes the taxpayer's private residence.

3.0   SCHEDULE B

3.1   Occasion of charge

Tax was levied under Schedule B on the occupier of woodlands situated in the UK, managed on a commercial basis and with a view to the realisation of profit. The charge under Schedule B has been abolished from 6th April, 1988.

3.2   The normal basis of assessment

The assessment was based on one-third of the annual value of the property. The annual value was the rent that would have been received had the land been let in its natural state, (i.e. without the timber), with the landlord paying repairs and insurance and the tenant paying rates. There was no additional charge to tax on the sale of timber.

3.3 The alternative basis - the charge under Schedule D Case 1

The occupier of woodlands could elect within two years from the end of the year of assessment to be assessed under Schedule D Case I instead of Schedule B. Once the election had been made it continued until there was a change of occupier. Under normal circumstances a taxpayer would be advised to elect to be assessed under Schedule D Case I whilst the timber is growing, thus obtaining capital allowances on plant and utilising any losses against other income.

Although commercial woodlands have effectively been removed from the tax charge, those taxpayers who have elected for the alternative basis of charge will continue to obtain relief for expenses and interest paid up to 5th April 1993.

CHAPTER FOUR

Income from a Trade or Profession

1.0   WHICH CASE?

Schedule D Case I assesses the profits of a trade carried on in the UK or elsewhere.
Case II charges income tax on the profits of a profession or a vocation. A profession was defined by Scrutton LJ in **IRC v Maxse (1919)** as an occupation requiring either purely intellectual skill or manual skill directed by the intellectual skill of the operator. A vocation was described by Denman J in **Partridge v. Mallandaine (1886)** as the way in which a person passes his life. A dramatist, jockey and a racing tipster have all been held to be carrying on a vocation.

2.0   THE MEANING OF TRADE

The term trade is not precisely defined. TA 1988, s.832(1) provides that it includes:

> 'every trade, manufacture, adventure or concern in the nature of trade'.

In general, judicial definition adds very little to this unsatisfactory state of affairs. **In Erichsen v. Last (1881)** Sir George Jessel MR said:

> 'There is not, I think, any principle of law which lays down what carrying on a trade is. There are a multitude of things which together make up the carrying on of trade, but I know of no one distinguishing incident, for it is a compound fact made up of a variety of incidents'.

In **Ransom v Higgs (1974)** Lord Reid said that the word is used to denote:

> 'Operations of a commercial character...'

Broadly the question of whether a trade is carried on is one of fact. This means that the courts will be unwilling to interfere with the findings of the Commissioners unless there are overriding reasons for doing so. In reviewing the relevant case law it is important to appreciate that many of the cases were decided before the introduction of capital gains tax. Before 1965 there was no liability to tax on capital gains and thus if the Revenue wanted to assess a particular profit it was necessary to class it as a trading operation.   It is fair to say that had there always been a capital gains tax in operation, many of the cases on trading would never have been heard.

In 1955 the Royal Commission on Taxation attempted to classify trading under a number of indicators or 'badges' of trading. It is opportune to use these as main headings in reviewing the relevant case law:

(a)   The subject matter of the realisation

In general any item can be bought or sold but some items are more likely to be dealt in, in the course of trade than others.

In **Rutledge v IRC (1929)** the taxpayer, whilst in Germany on business, purchased one and a quarter million toilet rolls. Shortly after his return to England he sold them making a profit of £10,000. Held to be trading.

In **Martin v. Lowry (1927)** an agricultural machinery merchant purchased from the Government its entire stock of aircraft linen amounting to almost 45 million yards. He had hoped to sell the linen to manufacturers but instead was forced to sell it through an extensive retail operation direct to the public. He made a profit of almost £2,000,000. Held to be trading.

(b)   The length of the period of ownership

An item purchased as an investment is often held for a long period of time. Items bought as trading stock are generally intended to be kept for as short a period of time as possible.

In **Wisdom v. Chamberlain (1969)** the taxpayer had, with borrowed money, purchased silver bullion as a hedge against a possible devaluation. After about a year he sold it making a profit, after expenses, of approximately £48,000. Held to be trading, per Harman LJ:

> 'this was a transaction entered into on a short term basis for the purpose of making a profit ... and if that is not an adventure in the nature of trade, I do not really know what is'.

(c)   The frequency of a number of similar transactions

Broadly, the more often that a taxpayer has entered into a particular transaction, the greater the presumption of trading. In **J Bolsom & Son Ltd. v. Farrelly (1953)**, Harman J said:

> 'A deal done once is probably not (trading). Done three or four times it usually is'.

In **Pickford v. Quirke (1927)**, the taxpayer was one of a syndicate who purchased the shares of companies, liquidated them and sold the assets at a profit. The taxpayer had entered into four transactions each resulting in a profit. Held to be trading.

(d)   Supplementary work

Whether the transaction is trading or capital may depend on the way in which the product was handled or treated by the taxpayer.

In **Cape Brandy Syndicate v. IRC (1921)**, three individuals in the wine trade purchased 10,000 gallons of South African brandy. This was blended, bottled and sold to over 100 separate purchasers over a period of about 18 months. Per Rowlatt J, they had

> '... bought it with a view to transport it, with a view to modify its character by skilful manipulation, by blending with a view to alter...'

In **IRC v. Livingston (1927)**, a syndicate purchased a cargo vessel with a view to converting it into a steam drifter and selling it at a profit. They had never previously done this. Held to be trading.

(e)   Circumstances responsible for the realisation

> 'Some explanation such as a sudden emergency or opportunity calling for ready money, negatives the idea that any plan of dealing prompted the original purchase'.
>   Royal Commission on Taxation, 1955

There have been few cases on this point. In **Page v. Pogson (1954)** the taxpayer built a house for himself and sold it six months after completion. He then built another one but had to sell it when his employment moved to another part of the country. Held by the Commissioners to be trading and Upjohn J felt unable to reverse their finding whilst doubting whether he would have reached that conclusion himself.

(f)   Intention

Intention to trade is clearly trading. Intention to make a profit may not necessarily be so.

In **IRC v. Reinhold (1953)** the taxpayer bought four houses admittedly for resale. Held not to be trading. Per Lord Keith:

> 'It is not enough for the Revenue to show that the subjects were purchased with the intention of realising them some day at a profit. This is the expectation of most, if not all, people who make investments.'

Conversely, the intention not to make a profit will not necessarily mean that a trade is not being carried on.

In **Grove v. YMCA (1903)** the canteen of a YMCA made a surplus. The organisation was a non-commercial one. Held the profits were trading profits.

The fact that the profits are to be used for a particular purpose or even applied to the common good will not mean that they escape tax, **Mersey Docks & Harbour Board v. Lucas (1883)**.

The question of whether a trade is being carried on or not, often, in the minds of the Revenue, will depend on the results of the transaction. In **Salt v. Chamberlain (1979)** a number of speculative transactions in investments by an individual was not held to be the carrying on of a trade, thus denying him loss relief against income.

3.0   SPECIAL TYPES OF TRADING

3.1 Mutual trading

A basic rule of taxation is that a person cannot trade with himself. That means for example, that if a person decorates a room and as a reward to himself pays himself £10 for doing it, that amount is not taxable income. This concept, called the 'mutuality principle', also applies to the situation where two or more persons join together in some form of association, e.g. a sports or social club and contribute to a common fund for their joint benefit. Any surplus received by the members on division of the fund is free of tax, as it is really nothing more than a return to the members of the association of their own money. Where the mutual association trades with outsiders, the amount of profits relating thereto will be taxable **(NALGO v Watkins (1934))**. Similarly, mutuality must be genuine, the courts will not recognise elaborate shams designed to avoid tax **(Fletcher v. Income Tax Commissioner (1972))**.

3.2 Illegal trading

In general the profits from illegal activities are liable to tax. In **Partridge v. Mallandaine (1886)** the profits of a bookmaker from illegal betting contracts were taxable and in **Mann v. Nash (1932)** the profits of illegal fruit machines were similarly charged. One important factor may be that where there is, for example, a burglary then the 'profits' would not be chargeable as there would be a civil liability to restore the goods to their rightful owner. If there is no obligation on, or ability of, the person who receives these profits to restore them to the persons from whom they derive, then he will not be able to rely on their incidental illegality to avoid tax.

4.0   THE COMPUTATION OF ASSESSABLE PROFITS

4.1   General

Accounts of both individuals and companies will need to be 'adjusted' in order to arrive at the taxable profit. Certain income is not assessable to income tax and certain expenses are not allowable. Some items, such as a proportion of the premium paid on the acquisition of a lease, are allowable even though they are not an expense incurred in the particular accounting period.

4.2 Income not taxable under Schedule D Cases I and II

(a)   Income taxable under another Schedule or Case. Income from property would be taxed under Schedule A; income received as enterprise allowances is taxable under Schedule D Case VI;

(b)   Income which has already suffered tax by deduction at source such as dividends and certain interest payments;

(c) Income not liable to tax at all. This very restricted class comprises certain compensation payments, other isolated non-trading receipts, and interest on delayed tax repayments.

In **Murray v. Goodhews (1976)**, Watneys, the brewers, did not renew the tenancies of the tenants of a number of public houses that they owned and in order to protect their good name paid compensation to the tenants. It was not held to be a trading receipt as it was in the form of a testimonial or payment for other personal qualities. In **McGowen v. Brown and Cousins (1977)**, however, a payment to an estate agent for the loss of the opportunity to earn professional fees was held to be taxable, notwithstanding that it was made in consequence of a moral rather than a legal obligation.

A payment made to a trader for agreeing not to carry on his trade may be capital (as in **Higgs v. Olivier (1952)** where Sir Laurence Olivier was paid £15,000 not to make any films for an 18-month period) or revenue, as in **Thompson v. Magnesium Elektron Ltd. (1944)**, where ICI sold chlorine cut-price and made a capital payment to Magnesium Ltd., to prevent them making their own chemicals, which would compete with those of ICI.

4.3 The calculation of income and post-cessation receipts

Income is normally included in the accounts and taxed on the accruals basis. Thus a trader will be taxed on the amounts earned in the accounting period rather than on the amounts actually received. In the case of certain professions (particularly barristers), the Inland Revenue may allow profits to be calculated on the basis of the actual cash received in the accounting period provided that the person concerned undertakes to render bills promptly. Apart from barristers the cash basis will not normally be allowed in the first three accounting periods on a commencement or in the last period. Once an assessment for one of the intervening years has been made on the cash basis, the Inland Revenue cannot adjust it to an earnings basis **(Rankine v. IRC (1952))**.

If after a taxpayer has ceased to trade he receives income which was omitted from his last accounts either because they were prepared on a cash basis or because the debtors were incorrect, this income is assessable as earned income under Case VI. Post-cessation expenses may be deducted from such income, as may any unused losses or capital allowances of the trade. If the taxpayer wishes he can elect to have such income, which is received during the six years following cessation, added to his last profit.

4.4 Allowable and disallowable expenditure

Certain expenditure is specifically allowed or disallowed by statute. Other expenditure has been found to be allowable or disallowable through the procedure of being tested in the courts.

The basic rule for the deductibility of expenses is contained in TA 1988 s.74 - the Schedule D I and II expense rule. It states that no expenditure shall be allowed which is not:

'wholly and exclusively laid out or expended for the purposes of the trade, profession or vocation'.

In **Strong & Co. of Romsey v. Woodifield (1906)** Lord Davy said that it was not just sufficient that the expense was incurred for the purposes of the trade. It must be incurred:

> 'for the purpose of enabling a person to ... earn profits'.

The words 'wholly and exclusively' are interpreted strictly. In **Mallalieu v. Drummond (1983)**, a lady barrister bought dark clothing for her use in court. If she had not worn suitable clothing she would not have been allowed to appear as an advocate. This was held not to be enough, she needed the clothes for other purposes. Per Lord Brightman:

> 'it is inescapable that one object ... was the provision of clothing she needed as a human being.'

Where expenditure is incurred exclusively for business purposes but gives a coincidental private advantage to the trader then it will not necessarily preclude the exclusivity of the business purpose. Thus if a person went abroad on business and the taking of a holiday overseas was a reason, no matter how subordinate, no deduction could be claimed. However, if the holiday was a coincidental effect of the business trip then the whole of the expenditure will be allowed.

In **Caillebotte v Quinn (1975)** a self employed carpenter spent 40p per day on his lunch whilst working away from home but just 10p whilst eating at home. Held the excess 30p per day was not deductible, it was wholly devoted to giving the taxpayer a private advantage.

Certain items of expenditure have detailed rules:

(a) Appropriations of profit including:

    i)   transfers to reserve;

    ii)   salaries of a proprietor or partner;

    iii) interest on capital,

    are not allowed.

In **Owen v. Southern Railways of Peru (1956)** the company made reserves for compensation due to their Peruvian employees on the termination of their contracts. Held that there was no rule of law prohibiting the deduction of a potential future liability but it must be a 'measured provision rather than a rough reserve'.

(b) UK income tax on profits is not allowable.

(c) VAT will be allowable as a trading expense when it cannot be recovered because the trader is exempt or partly exempt or where he is not liable to VAT because of the smallness of his turnover.

(d) Depreciation is not an allowable deduction for tax purposes. It is replaced by a standardised depreciation known as capital allowances.

(e)   The cost of maintaining a trader's family or of providing them with private accommodation or services is disallowed.

Wages or salaries paid to his family will be disallowed to the extent that they exceed a reasonable commercial rate.

In **Copeman v. Flood (1941)** a pig breeder paid salaries to his son and daughter of approximately £2,500 per annum each. They were in their late teens or early twenties. Held that the Revenue could enquire as to whether they were wholly and exclusively incurred.

Goods taken by a trader from stock must be charged at full retail price.

In **Sharkey v. Werhner (1956)** Lady Zia Werhner owned a stud farm assessed as a trade and also racing stables which were admitted to be purely recreational. She transferred five horses from the stud to the stables. Held that the transfer should be at market value.

In **Mason v. Innes (1967)** the author Hammond Innes transferred the copyright in an unpublished novel as a gift. Held that **Sharkey v. Werhner** only applied to stock in trade and that the rights in a novel could not be so classified.

(f)   Capital expenditure is not allowable whilst revenue expenditure is.

In **British Insulated and Helsby Cables v. Atherton (1926)** Lord Cave said:

> 'When expenditure is made, not once and for all, but with a view to bringing into existence an asset or advantage for the enduring benefit of a business, I think that there is very good reason to treat such expenditure as capital'.

Thus a lump sum payment of £30,000 to form the nucleus of a pension fund was held to be capital expenditure.

The courts tend to look to an identifiable asset test - is there an asset in existence for which a payment was made?

In **Associated Portland Cement Manufacturers Ltd. v. Kerr (1945)**, lump sum payments were made to retiring directors on condition that they would not compete with the business. Held to be capital - the right of non-competition was being acquired.

Particular difficulty is often experienced in relation to repairs. In **Lurcott v. Wakeley and Wheeler (1911)**, Buckley LJ said:

> 'Repair is restoration by renewal or replacement of subsidiary parts of a whole. Renewal ... is the reconstruction of the entirety'.

In **O'Grady v. Bullcroft Main Collieries (1932)**, a chimney used to carry away smoke and fumes from a furnace became unsafe. A new one was built. Held to be capital; the chimney was not part of the factory but an entirety on its own. (There was no evidence that the old chimney had been pulled down).

In **Samuel Jones & Co. (Devondale) Ltd. v. IRC (1951)** a chimney which was part of the main factory was dangerous. It was therefore demolished and replaced. Held to be repairs; it was only a replacement of part of the factory.

In **Phillips v. Wheldon Sanitary Potteries Ltd. (1952)** a substantial amount of expenditure on one large job was held to be capital; and thus the question of repair or renewal often appears to depend on the size and importance of the work carried out. One large job may be capital whilst a succession of smaller jobs may be revenue.

When an asset is acquired which requires substantial expenditure to be incurred on it before it can be used in the trade, this expenditure will be capital.

In **Law Shipping Co. Ltd. v. IRC (1924)** a trader purchased a ship in a severe state of disrepair. Considerable expenditure had to be carried out to obtain the Lloyds Certificate of Seaworthiness. Held that to the extent that this related to remedying pre-acquisition defects it was capital expenditure.

In **Odeon Associated Theatres v. Jones (1971)** the taxpayer acquired a cinema in 1945. Owing to the war it was in a state of disrepair and because of postwar restrictions it had been impossible to carry out work immediately. Some years later renovation work was carried out and the Revenue claimed that the cost of the work needed to remedy defects existing at the time of purchase were capital. Held they were revenue. The factors influencing this decision and distinguishing it from the **Law Shipping** case were:

i)   the cinema was in use throughout the state of disrepair; the ship could not be used;

ii)   the purchase price of the cinema had not been reduced by the amount of any disrepair;

iii) accountancy evidence was produced in the **Odeon** case that the charge to revenue was in accordance with the principles of commercial accountancy.

There appears to be some practical doubt about the precise extent of the **Odeon** decision.

Amounts paid to get rid of an unsatisfactory employee are revenue expenditure but if coupled with a non-competition covenant they are capital. A lump sum for the surrender of a lease is capital expenditure.

(g) A charge for bad debts will be allowed provided it is for:

i)   a trade debt written off, or

ii)   a specific provision against trade debts.

Staff bad debts will not normally be allowed unless they result from the carrying on of the taxpayer's trade.

Bad debts written off but subsequently recovered, and reductions in a provision for specific doubtful debts, will be taxable as trading receipts.

Illustration

A provides you with the following bad debts account:

	£	£		£	£
Trade debts written off		500	Provisions b/f:		
			Specific	100	
Provisions c/f:			General	200	
Specific	150			___	
General	300				300
	___	450	Profit and loss account		650
		950			___
		===			950
					===

The charge for tax purposes should be:

	£
Trade debts written off	500
Increase in specific provision	50
	___
	550
	===
Already allowed	650
Should be allowed	550
	___
Increase taxable profit by	100
	===

No allowance is given for the increase in the general provision.

Illustration

B also provides you with the following bad debts accounts. He is a toy manufacturer.

	£	£		£	£
Trade debts written off		600	Provisions b/f:		
			Specific	200	
Loan to supplier written off		200	General	250	
				___	450
Provisions c/f:			Trade debts recovered		100
Specific	150		Loan to customer recovered		50
General	300		Profit and loss account		650
	___	450			
		1,250			1,250
		====			====

The charge for tax purposes will be:

	£	£
Trade debts written off		600
Less: Decrease in specific provision	50	
Trade debt recovered	100	
		150
		450
Already allowed		650
Should be allowed		450
Increase taxable profit by		200

No allowance is given for the loan to the supplier as the business of B is not to make loans. Similarly, there is no charge in respect of the loan to the customer now recovered as, when it was incurred, it was not allowed as a bad debt.

The expenses of trade debt collection are allowable. Defalcations of an employee are generally allowable but not those of a person having control such as the proprietor or director.

In **Curtis v. Oldfield (1925)** the managing director of a company used cash of the company to pay bills relating to his personal expenditure.

Held the loss was not allowable but per Rowlatt J, losses due to the dishonesty 'of the subordinates' would be allowed.

(h) Subscriptions to trade associations are allowable, provided that the association has entered into the usual agreement with the Revenue to pay tax on its excess income. Charitable subscriptions, apart from small amounts to local charities, are not allowed. Direct donations to a political party are not allowable.

(i) Entertaining expenditure is not allowable unless it was incurred in entertaining:

i)   staff, though there may be a Schedule E benefit on the employee concerned if the amounts involved are excessive.

ii) a customer who is not ordinarily resident in the UK, or the agent, who is himself not ordinarily resident in the UK, of an overseas customer. For both these groups, expenditure is not allowed if incurred after 14th March 1988.

Such expenditure may be incurred by the proprietor or a member of his staff.

The cost of a gift is also disallowed unless:

i)   it bears a prominent advertisement for the donor, and

ii) the total value of such gifts in the year to any one customer does not exceed £10. Gifts of food, drink, tobacco are not allowed. The cost of trade samples, mainly for advertisement, is allowable.

Gifts to charities are not subject to the above restrictions; however, the expenditure must still satisfy the 'wholly and exclusively' condition.

(j) Legal and professional fees are normally allowable when they are connected with the following:

i)   **renewal** of leases with a life of less than 50 years (short leases);

ii) the preservation of existing trading rights,

iii) successfully refuting an allegation of breach of contract,

iv) termination of an onerous trading contract,

v)   audit and accountancy fees,

vi) contracts of employment for staff.

They are not normally allowable when they relate to:

i)   acquiring a new asset or a new right,

ii) professional and legal services in relation to a tax appeal or investigation, **Smith's Potato Estates v. Bolland (1948)**,

iii) preparing a partnership agreement.

Fines, costs and other penalties incurred for breaches of the law are not allowed. Where, however, they are paid on behalf of an employee and assessed on him as a benefit under Schedule E they will be treated as an allowable expense to the employer. Civil penalties, default interest, etc, incurred because of VAT offences are not allowed.

(k) The cost of hiring a motor car is restricted to the amount obtained by the formula:

$$\text{Hire charge} \times \frac{£8,000 + \frac{1}{2}(\text{Retail price of car} - £8,000)}{\text{Retail price of car}}$$

Illustration

C rented a car for £2,000 per annum. The retail price was £13,000.

$$\text{Amount allowable} = £2,000 \times \frac{£8,000 + \frac{1}{2}(£13,000 - £8,000)}{£13,000}$$

$$= £2,000 \times \frac{£10,500}{£13,000}$$

$$= \underline{£1,616}$$

The amount that must be disallowed is **£384**.

(1) Payments of fees to obtain and renew patents are allowable.

(m) Payments for technical education of staff are allowable.

(n) Remuneration of employees, and contributions to approved pension funds are allowable.

Where sole traders, partnerships or companies make the services of an employee available to charity, the expenditure attributable to the employee's employment is deductible as a Schedule D Case I or II expenses. The secondment must be of a temporary nature. Expenditure on retraining ex-employees or employees who will shortly cease employment will be allowed as a trade expense when incurred after 5th April, 1987.

(o) The cost of a shop front is capital; the cost of replacing it is revenue. (Any improvement element on a replacement would be capital).

(p) Payments made under deduction of tax are not allowable deductions. Where appropriate, however, they can be treated as a charge on the taxpayer's total income. This will be dealt with later.

(q) Incidental costs incurred in obtaining loan finance will be allowable. The costs referred to are expenditure on fees, commissions, advertising, printing, etc., wholly and exclusively incurred for the purpose of obtaining finance, whether obtained or not, or providing security for it, or repaying it. This does not include stamp duty. The finance must be by way of a qualifying loan or the issue of qualifying loan stock. For this purpose 'qualifying' means that the interest on the loan or loan stock is deductible for income tax or corporation tax purposes. For corporation tax purposes loan stocks which carry the right of conversion into ordinary shares or other non-qualifying loan stocks will be treated as qualifying, providing the conversion rights are not exercised within three years of the date of issue.

If the conversion rights are exercised within the three-year period then no part of the expenses of the issue will be allowed. If some of the rights are exercised within this period and some not then the expenses qualifying for relief are proportionately reduced.

(r) Expenditure incurred for the purposes of a trade before the trade commences will be allowable as a deduction where it is incurred not more than five years before commencement. It is treated as a loss incurred on the first day of trading.

(s) A person carrying on a trade or profession can claim a deduction from his total income of 50% of the final Class 4 National Insurance Contributions. No relief is available for the flat rate class 2 contributions.

(t) The costs of travelling in the course of the trade or profession are allowable. The costs of travel between home and work are not allowed. In **Newsom v Robertson (1952)** the travelling expenses of a barrister between home and work were not allowed. However, if a self employed person can establish that his home is also his place of business, then travel costs will be allowed.   In **Horton v Young (1971)** a self employed bricklayer was allowed the expenses of travelling between his home and the sites on which he worked because, on the facts, the business was operated from his home.

Similar rules apply to hotel and subsistence purposes.   The cost of overnight stays will normally be allowed, with no reduction for what would have been saved had the trader spent the night at home.

If the trader carries on a trade overseas then the costs of travel to and from the UK are allowable together with the costs of board and lodging.   If the trader is abroad for at least 60 consecutive days the travel costs of visits from his spouse and minor children are also allowed up to a maximum of two visits per fiscal year.

4.5   The format of the computation

The format of the computation is demonstrated below.   It commences with the net profit and proceeds to adjust it for tax purposes.   The final figure of **adjusted profits** represents the amount of trading profits liable to tax.

Illustration

H Beech, who has carried on a manufacturing business for many years makes up his accounts to 31st May each year.   The following is a summary of his profit and loss account for the year to 31st May, 1989:

	£		£
Salaries and wages	12,320	Gross profit	30,160
Rates and insurance	850	Bank interest	60
Light and heat	750	Profit on sale of car	40
Repairs	650	Dividend received (excluding	
Motor car expenses	280	tax credit)	45
Bank interest	170		
Loan interest	240		
Bad and doubtful debts	150		
General expenses	1,630		
Management salary: H Beech	1,200		
Net profit	12,065		
	30,305		30,305

Particulars of the accounts were as follows:

Repairs:	£
Additional toilet facilities for staff	200
Redecorations	400
Overhaul of machinery	50
	650

General expenses:	£
Printing and stationery	250
Legal costs: Debt collections	25
Agreements with staff	30
Loan agreement	28
Accountancy and audit fee	320
Annual payment under deed of covenant to	
trade benevolent association (gross)	35
Subscription: Trade association	20
Donation: Spastics Society	15
Entertaining and gifts	907
	———
	1,630

Entertaining expenses and gifts were made up as follows:

	£
Entertaining: UK customers	300
Foreign customers	400
London agent of foreign firm	25
Christmas gifts to London agent of foreign firm	20
Gifts of wine to UK customers	162
	———
	907
	===

The copy of the bad and doubtful debts account was:

	£		£
Trade debtors w/o	120	Balance 1st June 1988:	
Loan to customer w/o	80	Specific debt reserve	115
Balance 31st May 1989:		2% of debtors	200
Specific debt reserve	150	Debt recovered (previously	
2% of debtors	135	charged and allowed for,	
		Case I)	20
		Profit and loss account	150
	———		———
	485		485
	===		===

It has been agreed that one-third of the use of the car is for private purposes.

H BEECH
Computation of Adjusted Profit for the year ended 31st May 1989

	£	£
Net profit per accounts	12,065	-
Management salary: H Beech	1,200	
General expenses:		
Annual payment under deed of covenant	35	
Entertaining	907	
Bad and doubtful debts (Note 1)	15	
Motor car expenses (one-third)	93	
Repairs: Additional toilet facilities	200	
Donation to Spastics Society	15	
Bank interest		60
Dividend received		45
Profit on sale of car		40
	14,530	145
	145	
Schedule D I adjusted trading profits	14,385	

Note 1

	£
Doubtful debts:	
Trade debts written off	120
Increase in specific provision	35
c/f	155

	£
b/f	155
Less: Debt recovered	20
Allowable	135
Already allowed	150
Add back	15

5.0   THE BASIS OF ASSESSMENT

5.1 The normal basis (TA 1988,s.60)

The normal period of assessment for Schedule D Cases I and II is the adjusted trading profits of the accounting period of twelve months ended in the preceding year of assessment. Thus to find the profits that are assessable for a particular fiscal year it is necessary to find an accounting period of twelve months ended in the preceding fiscal year.

Illustration

G makes up accounts as under:

Year ended 31st December 1988
Year ended 31st December 1989

The adjusted profits of these years will be assessed for the fiscal years, 1989/90 and 1990/91 respectively. The year ended 31st December 1988 is said to be the **basis period** for 1989/90 and the year ended 31st December 1989 is the **basis period** for 1990/91.

5.2 The basis of assessment on the commencement of a trade

Special rules apply on the commencement of a business.

The normal basis (TA 1988,s.61)

Year of assessment	**Assessable Profit**
First year	Profits from date of commencement to 5th April following.
Second year	Profits of the first twelve months trading.
Third and subsequent years	Profits of the accounting period of twelve months ended in the preceding year of assessment.

Any apportionment of profits is made on a strict time basis.

Illustration

H commenced trading on 1st July 1988 and made up accounts to 30th June, each year. The profits, as adjusted for tax, were as follows:

	£
Year ended 30th June	
1989	4,800
1990	6,000
1991	9,800

The assessments will be:

		£
1988/89	(year in which trade commenced) 1st July 1988 to 5th April 1989 $\frac{9}{12}$ x £4,800	3,600
1989/90	First 12 months trading 1st July 1988 to 30th June 1989	4,800
1990/91	Preceding year basis Year ended 30th June 1989	4,800
1991/92	Preceding year basis Year ended 30th June 1990	6,000
1992/93	Preceding year basis Year ended 30th June 1991	9,800

The revised basis (TA 1988,s.62)

As the first three assessments are based on the profits of the first accounting period, it might prove a considerable disadvantage where the profits of that period were materially higher than those in future accounting periods. It is therefore provided that the taxpayer has the right to have the assessments for the second and third years of assessment calculated by reference to the actual profits of those years - TA 1988,s.62. The election, which must be made within 7 years of the end of the second year of assessment, covers both second _and_ third years. It may be revoked within 6 years of the end of the third year of assessment.

Illustration

If H in the above example made an election under TA 1988,s.62 for the second and third years, the assessments would become:

		£
1989/90	6th April 1989 to 5th April 1990	
	$\frac{3}{12}$ x £4,800 + $\frac{9}{12}$ x £6,000	5,700
1990/91	6th April 1990 to 5th April 1991	
	$\frac{3}{12}$ x £6,000 + $\frac{9}{12}$ x £9,800	8,850
		14,550

	Normal	Revised
	£	£
1989/90	4,800	5,700
1990/91	4,800	8,850
	9,600	14,550

In this case, it will not be beneficial to make the s.62 election.

If, when trying to find the assessment of the third fiscal year, there is no accounting period of 12 months ended in the preceding year of assessment, the normal practice of the Inland Revenue is:

(a)   if the first accounting period is less than 12 months, reassess the profits of the first 12 months of trading;

(b)   if the first accounting period exceeds 12 months, assess the last 12 months of the first accounting period.

Illustration

J commenced a music shop on 1st October 1987 and decided to make accounts to 30th June 1988. The results adjusted for income tax were as follows:

	£
9 months ended 30th June 1988	1,800
Year ended 30th June 1989	1,200
Year ended 30th June 1990	1,500

The assessments for the first 3 fiscal years would be:

Original assessment	£	Revised assessment	£

1987/88 1.10.87 to 5.4.88

$\frac{6}{9}$ x £1,800   1,200

1988/89 1.10.87 to 30.9.88
  (first 12 months)   6.4.88 to 5.4.89

£1,800 $+\left(\frac{3}{12} \times £1,200\right)$ 2,100 $\frac{3}{9}$ x £1,800 $+\left(\frac{9}{12} \times £1,200\right)$ 1,500

1989/90 1.10.87 to 30.9.88
  (first 12 months
   reassessed)   2,100   6.4.89 to 5.4.90

                                                   $\frac{3}{12}$ x £1,200 $+\left(\frac{9}{12} \times £1,500\right)$ 1,425

                            4,200   2,925

In this case the taxpayer will be advised to have his profits assessed on an actual basis.

Illustration

K commenced trade as a builder on 1st October 1987 and decided to make accounts to 31st December 1988 with the following adjusted results:

	£
15 months to 31st December 1988	20,000
Year ended 31st December 1989	16,800
Year ended 31st December 1990	18,000

The assessments are:

Original assessment	£	Revised Assessment	£
1987/88 1.10.87 to 5.4.88			
$\frac{6}{15}$ x £20,000	8,000		
1988/89 1.10.87 to 30.9.88		6.4.88 to 5.4.89	
$\frac{12}{15}$ x £20,000	16,000	$\frac{9}{15}$ x £20,000 + $\left(\frac{3}{12}$ x £16,800$\right)$	16,200
1989/90 1.1.88 to 31.12.88		6.4.89 to 5.4.90	
$\frac{12}{15}$ x £20,000	16,000	$\frac{9}{12}$ x £16,800 + $\left(\frac{3}{12}$ x £18,000$\right)$	17,100
	32,000		33,300

In this case there will be no revision to actual.

If the first accounting period straddles three fiscal years, then in the fourth fiscal year there will again be no accounting period of 12 months ending in the preceding year of assessment.   The normal practice of the Inland Revenue will be to:

(a)   In the third fiscal year - reassess the profits of the first 12 months trading.

(b)   In the fourth fiscal year - assess the profits of the last 12 months of the first accounting period.

Illustration

L commenced to trade on 1st January 1988 and made up accounts to 30th June 1989 and thereafter annually.   The adjusted profits are:

	£
18 months to 30th June 1989	9,000
Year ended 30th June 1990	12,000

The assessments on the normal s.61 basis are:

	£
1987/88 1.1.88 to 5.4.88	
$\frac{3}{18}$ x £9,000	1,500
1988/89 1.1.88 to 31.12.88	
$\frac{12}{18}$ x £9,000	6,000

```
1989/90 1.1.88 to 31.12.88
        12
        ── x £9,000                        6,000
        18                                 =====


1990/91 1.7.88 to 30.6.89
        12
        ── x £9,000                        6,000
        18                                 =====
```

5.3 Assessments on the cessation of a trade (TA 1988,s.63)

As with a commencement, there are special rules of assessment on the cessation of a trade.

Year of assessment   **Assessable Profits**

Ultimate year   Profits from 6th April preceding
                                      discontinuance to the date of discontinuance.

Penultimate year   Normal (preceding year) basis

Pre-penultimate year   Normal (preceding year) basis

Illustration

M ceased business on 30th September 1990 after trading for many years and making accounts up to 30th September each year. The assessable profits for recent years had been:

```
Year ended 30th September                                    £
1987                                                       9,600
1988                                                      12,000
1989                                                      18,000
1990                                                      16,800


1990/91 (ultimate year)                                      £
6th April 1990 to 30th September 1990
 6
── x £16,800                                               8,400
12                                                         ======


1989/90 (penultimate year)
Year ended 30th September 1988                            12,000

1988/89 (pre-penultimate year)
Year ended 30th September 1987                             9,600
                                                          ──────
                                                          21,600
                                                          ======
```

Just as when a taxpayer commences to trade he pays tax on the same profits more than once, so when he ceases, some profits will not be taxed at all. In the above illustration M would not pay tax on the profit for the year ended 30th September 1989 of £18,000 plus the time-apportioned profit for the six months to

5th April 1990 of £ 8,400. However, the Revenue have rights when there is a cessation of trade, similar to those of the taxpayer on commencement. If the total of assessments on an actual basis for the penultimate and pre-penultimate years is greater than those on the normal basis, they may adopt actual.

In the case of M, the Revenue would adopt an actual basis for 1989/90 and 1988/89 which in total amounts to £32,400 - greater than the preceding year basis total of £ 21,600:

	£
1990/91 (ultimate year)	
As before	8,400
	======
1989/90 (penultimate year)	
6th April 1989 to 5th April 1990	
$\frac{6}{12}$ x £16,800 + $\left(\frac{6}{12} \text{ x } £18,000\right)$	17,400
1988/89 (pre-penultimate year)	
6th April 1988 to 5th April 1989	
$\frac{6}{12}$ x £18,000 + $\left(\frac{6}{12} \text{ x } £12,000\right)$	15,000
	32,400
	======

5.4 Change of accounting date

For the normal preceding-year basis to apply, certain conditions must be complied with in relation to each accounting period:

(a) it must be a twelve-month period;

(b) it must end in the year preceding the year of assessment;

(c) it must be the only accounting period ending in that year.

Where these rules are not complied with, the Revenue, have the right to select any period of twelve months that ends in the year preceding the year of assessment and to base the assessment on the profits of those twelve months. The Revenue will adopt this procedure every time the rules are not complied with. They also have the right to determine the profits of another twelve-month period corresponding to the earliest period of twelve months they have had to determine. It should be noted that this second right, to compute the profits of a corresponding period, will amend an assessment for which there is already an otherwise acceptable twelve-month accounting period ended in the year preceding the year of assessment.

This procedure, if applied rigidly, is arbitrary in result and can be distinctly advantageous to either the taxpayer or the Revenue. To avoid inequity the Revenue have adopted a Code of Practice whereby they seek to average profits actually made over the years of assessment affected. Although the Code of Practice is not statutory, it has received judicial approval in the case of **IRC v. Helical Bar Ltd.**, (1972).

The calculations on a change of accounting date can be best explained by an
example.

Illustration

O Bow made up accounts to 30th September each year until 30th September 1989
when it was decided for stock-taking reasons to prepare accounts to 30th June in
future. The adjusted trading profits were:

		£
Year ended 30.9.1987		20,000
Year ended 30.9.1988		39,000
Year ended 30.9.1989		24,000
9 months ended 30.6.1990		16,000

Step 1

Allocate the basis periods to fiscal years:

Year to 30.9.87	£20,000	-	1988/89
Year to 30.9.88	£39,000	-	1989/90
Year to 30.9.89	£24,000	-	1990/91
9 months to 30.6.90	£16,000	-	1991/92

It can be seen that there will be difficulties with the fiscal year 1991/92 as
there is no accounting period of twelve months ended within the preceding year
of assessment. There will be the need to make up a new basis period for that
fiscal year and the normal practice of the Revenue will be to select a
twelve-month period ended on the new permanent accounting date.

1991/92   £

12 months to 30.6.90

$\frac{3}{12}$ x £24,000   6,000

9 months to 30.6.90   16,000
                                                            _____
                                                            22,000
                                                            ======

Step 2

Find whether there is a missing year. On occasions, because of the timing of
the changed accounting date, a fiscal year drops out with no basis period. These
calculations will be shown in a later example; however, the test is whether the
fiscal years in Step 1 follow sequentially. Here they do - there is no missing
year.

Step 3

Find the corresponding period. This is a period of twelve months immediately
preceding the earliest new basis period. In this example it is the twelve
months to 30th June 1989.

Corresponding period:

		£
12 months to 30.6.89		
$\frac{3}{12}$ x £39,000		9,750
$\frac{9}{12}$ x £24,000		18,000
		27,750

Step 4

Find how many fiscal years have been affected by the calculations in Steps 1 to 3 above. A fiscal year is affected if any of the profits of its basis period have been used.

In Step 1 the profits that have been used are:

(a) £16,000 - nine months to 30th June 1990, thus 1991/92 affected.

(b) Part of £24,000 - twelve months to 30th September 1989, thus 1990/91 affected.

In Step 3 the profits that have been used are:

(a) Part of £24,000 - twelve months to 30th September 1989, thus 1990/91 affected.

(b) Part of £39,000 - twelve months to 30th September 1988, thus 1989/90 affected.

Thus the fiscal years affected are:

                    1991/92, 1990/91 and 1989/90

Expressed in months this gives 36 months.

Step 5

Find how many accounting periods have been affected, by the calculations in Steps 1 to 3. Again, an accounting period is affected if any of the profits of that period have been used. Thus the accounting periods affected are:

          twelve months to 30th September 1988
          twelve months to 30th September 1989
          nine months to 30th June 1990

Expressed in months - a total of 33 months.

Step 6

Find out the total profits of the accounting periods in Step 5.

	£
12 months to 30.9.88	39,000
12 months to 30.9.89	24,000
9 months to 30.6.90	16,000
	79,000

Step 7

Find the revised profits of the fiscal years
affected. Here there are three fiscal years
affected - a total of 36 months; however,
there are profits of 33 months only. These
need to be upgraded to 36 months. Perform
the calculation:

$$\frac{\text{Fiscal years}}{\text{Accounting periods}} \times \text{Profits}$$

	£
$\frac{36}{33}$ x £79,000	86,182

Step 8

This represents the total profits of the three
fiscal years 1989/90, 1990/91 and 1991/92.
One of these years will be the variable year.
This will be the fiscal year for which the
corresponding period could have formed a basis
period. The corresponding period - the twelve
months to 30th June 1989 - could form a basis
period for 1990/91; this is the variable year.

Deduct the 'fixed' assessments for the other two
years:

	£	
1989/90	39,000	
1991/92	22,000	
		61,000

| This could be assessed for 1990/91   c/f | 25,182 |

$£$

Step 9   b/f   25,182

For this figure to be assessed for 1990/91
it must satisfy the intermediacy test. If
it does not, the Revenue will not allow the
averaging formula to be used. It will
satisfy the test if it lies between:

(a) the original assessment for 1990/91 -
£24,000

and

(b) the profits of the corresponding
period - £27,750.

In this case the test is satisfied.

Step 10

Deduct the original assessment
for 1990/91   24,000

Potential additional assessment   1,182
                                               ======

Any adjustment to the original assessment will only be made by the Revenue if it
is material. It will be immaterial where it is **both**:

(a) less than £1,000 and also

(b) less than ten per cent of the average of the original assessment of the
variable year and the assessment of the next following fiscal year.

Here, the adjustment is material as it exceeds £999 and therefore it is not
necessary to perform part (b). If this were done, however, the calculation
would be:

$£$

1990/91 original assessment   24,000
1991/92 assessment   22,000

46,000
======

Average   23,000
======

10% thereof   2,300
======

The final assessments will be:

		£
1988/89		20,000
1989/90		39,000
1990/91		25,182
1991/92		22,000

Illustration

B made up accounts to 30th September until she decided to change her accounting date to 31st March. Her adjusted results for tax purposes were:

	£
Year ended 30.9.1987	2,000
Year ended 30.9.1988	3,750
Year ended 30.9.1989	1,500
6 months to 31.3.1990	500
Year ended 31.3.1991	1,800

Step 1

Allocate the accounting periods to fiscal years:

	£	
Year ended 30.9.87	2,000	1988/89
Year ended 30.9.88	3,750	1989/90
Year ended 30.9.89	1,500	1990/91
6 months to 31.3.90	500	1990/91
Year ended 31.3.91	1,800	1991/92

There will be difficulties in the year 1990/91 as although there is an accounting period of twelve months ended in the preceding year of assessment 1989/90 it is not the **only** accounting period ended in that year. It will therefore be necessary to make up a new basis period of twelve months ended on the new permanent accounting date.

1990/91		£
12 months to 31.3.90		
$\frac{6}{12}$ x £1,500		750
6 months to 31.3.90		500
		1,250

Step 2

There is no missing year.

Step 3

The corresponding period is the year to 31st
March 1989.

		£
$\dfrac{6}{12}$ x £3,750		1,875
$\dfrac{6}{12}$ x £1,500		750
		2,625
		=====

Step 4

Fiscal years affected:
         Step 1   1990/91
         Step 3   1990/91 and 1989/90

Two fiscal years - 1989/90 and 1990/91 - equals 24 months.

Step 5

Accounting periods affected:

	£
12 months to 30.9.88	3,750
12 months to 30.9.89	1,500
6 months to 31.3.90	500
30 months	

Step 6

Profits of those accounting periods	5,750
	=====

Step 7

	£
$\dfrac{24}{30}$ x £5,750	4,600

Step 8

Deduct assessments for the fixed fiscal year
(the variable year will be 1989/90 as it is the
fiscal year for which the corresponding period
could have formed a basis period).

1990/91	1,250
Possible assessment 1989/90	3,350 c/f

		£
Step 9		3,350 b/f

This passes the intermediacy test as it lies
between:

	£
(a) the original assessment for 1989/90, and	3,750
	=====
(b) the profits of the corresponding period	2,625
	=====

Step 10

Deduct the existing 1989/90 assessment	3,750
	─────
Possible reduction in assessment	(400)
	=====

As this is less than £1,000 it satisfies the first test of immateriality. The
second test is whether it is also less than ten per cent of the average of:

	£
1989/90 original assessment	3,750
1990/91 assessment	1,250
	─────
	5,000
	=====
Average	2,500
	=====
10% thereof	250
	=====

Here it exceeds £250 and therefore the difference is material; the Revenue will
revise the 1989/90 assessment to £3,350.

The final assessments will be:

	£
1988/89	2,000
	=====
1989/90	3,350
	=====
1990/91	1,250
	=====
1991/92	1,800
	=====

Illustration

K made up accounts as under:

		£
Year ended	28.2.1987	9,000
Year ended	28.2.1988	8,400
Year ended	28.2.1989	7,200
16 months ended 30.6.1990		12,000

Step 1

Allocate the accounting periods to fiscal years:

		£	
Year to	28.2.1987	9,000	1987/88
Year to	28.2.1988	8,400	1988/89
Year to	28.2.1989	7,200	1989/90
16 months to	30.6.1990	12,000	1991/92

Make up a new basis period for 1991/92.

12 months to 30.6.1990

$\frac{12}{16}$ x £12,000   £9,000

Step 2

Here there is a missing year and it will be necessary to make up another new basis period for 1990/91. Following the normal practice of the Revenue, this will be the twelve months immediately preceding the first new basis period.

1990/91

Twelve months to 30.6.1989

	£
$\frac{8}{12}$ x £7,200	4,800
$\frac{4}{16}$ x £12,000	3,000
	7,800

Step 3

The corresponding period is the year to 30th June 1988.

	£
$\frac{8}{12}$ x £8,400	5,600
$\frac{4}{12}$ x £7,200	2,400
	8,000

Step 4

Fiscal years affected:

Step 1	1991/92
Step 2	1990/91 and 1989/90
Step 3	1989/90 and 1988/89

4 fiscal years affected - 1991/92; 1990/91; 1989/90 and 1988/89 - equal to 48 months.

Step 5

Accounting periods affected:

	£
12 months to 28.2.1988	8,400
12 months to 28.2.1989	7,200
16 months to 30.6.1990	12,000
40 months	

Step 6

Profits of those accounting periods   27,600

Step 7

$$\frac{48}{40} \times £27,600$$

£

33,120

Step 8

Deduct fixed assessments:	£
1991/92	9,000
1990/91	7,800
1988/89	8,400

25,200

Possible assessment 1989/90   7,920

1989/90 will be the variable year - it is the fiscal year for which the corresponding period could have formed a basis period.

Step 9

This passes the intermediacy test as it lies between:

		£
(a)	the original assessment for 1989/90	7,200
(b)	the profits of the corresponding period	8,000

Step 10

Deduct the existing 1989/90 assessment	7,200
Possible increase in assessment	720

As this is less than £1,000 it again satisfies the first test of immateriality. The second test is whether it is also less than ten per cent of:

	£
1989/90 original assessment	7,200
1990/91 assessment	7,800
	15,000
Average	7,500
10% thereof	750

As the possible additional assessment is less than £750 it will be immaterial and no adjustment will be made by the Revenue. The final assessments will be:

	£
1987/88	9,000
1988/89	8,400
1989/90	7,200
1990/91	7,800
1991/92	9,000

5.5 Date of payment

Tax due under Schedule D Cases I and II is due in two equal instalments on 1st January in the year of assessment and 1st July following the end of the year of assessment. This makes the choice of a suitable accounting date important and in general it is more beneficial to have an accounting period ending just after the end of a fiscal year rather than on or just before the end of the year. Assuming that there are two alternative year-end dates - 31st March or 30th April, the following points are relevant:

(a) the choice of the 30th April year end date gives the longest period of 'credit' for the payment of tax. The year to 30th April 1989 would be assessed for the fiscal year 1990/91 and tax would be paid on:

      1st January 1991
      1st July 1992

Periods of credit of 20 months and 26 months respectively. Conversely if accounts were made up to 31st March 1989 the assessment would be for the year 1989/90 with payment due on:

1st January 1990
1st July 1990

(b)   A 30th April year-end date will give a reasonably long period of time for the finalisation of accounts before submission to the Inland Revenue.

(c)   On cessation there will be a 'drop out' resulting in profits being earned which are not liable to tax. A 30th April accounting date will result in a far greater drop-out period than one ending on 31st March.

As can be seen in the second example dealing with changes in accounting date substantial tax savings may occur. This technique may not only be used to mitigate a tax liability but also to change an accounting date to an earlier part of the fiscal year and so secure the advantages referred to above.

6.0   RELIEF FOR FARMERS (TA 1988,s.96)

6.1   Nature of relief

Where an individual has been carrying on a trade of farming or market gardening in the UK, he may claim to have the adjusted profits from that trade for any two consecutive years of assessment averaged, so that the profits for each year equal one-half of the aggregate profits for the two years.

Relief will not be applicable if either year is the year of assessment in which the trade commenced or ceased, neither will relief be given in respect of any year which is before a year for which a claim has already been made,

To qualify for full relief the profits of one of the years must not exceed 70% of the profits of the other. Profits are defined as the Schedule D Case I assessment for the year of assessment before:

(a)   any deduction for losses;

(b)   any deduction or addition for capital allowances or balancing charges;

Illustration

D has been a farmer for many years and her adjusted profits for years ended 31st March 1989 and 31st March 1990 were £14,000 and £6,000 respectively. Capital allowances for 1989/90 are £1,600 and for 1990/91 £6,000. She has no other income.

Without an average claim the net assessments will be:

		£		£
Adjusted profit	1989/90	14,000	1990/91	6,000
Less: capital allowances		1,600		6,000
		12,400		NIL

Personal allowances for 1990/91 will be lost.

If an averaging claim is made the assessments become:

		£
1989/90	$\dfrac{(£14,000 + £6,000)}{2}$	10,000
Less: capital allowances		1,600
		8,400

	£
1990/91	10,000
Less: capital allowances	6,000
	4,000

Thus preserving some personal allowances.

Where one of the years concerned has a 'Nil' profit, because of an adjusted Schedule D Case I loss, the profit of that year is treated as Nil.

Illustration

R has been a farmer for many years and has adjusted results for the years ended 31st May 1989 and 31st May 1990 of £27,000 profit and £8,000 loss. Before averaging, the assessments will be:

1990/91	£27,000
1991/92	Nil

after averaging they will be:

1990/91	£13,500
1991/92	£13,500

Loss relief will be available for the £8,000 loss in the normal way. If s.380 relief is claimed it would be against the profits of 1990/91.

1990/91		£
DI	Year to 31.5.1989	13,500
s.380 relief	Year to 31.5.1990	(8,000)
		5,500

Successive claims to relief will give the effect of giving a moving average on a two-year basis. If in the first illustration D had profits of £20,000 for the year ended 31st March 1991 and a further claim was made, the assessments would become:

1990/91

DI $\dfrac{(£10,000 + £20,000)}{2}$ =   £15,000

1991/92

DI   =   £15,000

6.2 Marginal relief

If the profits of one year exceed 70% but do not exceed 75% of the other year, a marginal relief is available. This does not provide full averaging but does allow some of the profits of one year to be charged to tax in the other. This is computed as under:

$$3(PH - PL) - \frac{3}{4}PH$$

where PH is the higher profit
      PL is the lower profit.
The resulting figure is deducted from the higher profit and added to the lower.

Illustration

S had been a farmer for many years and had adjusted profits of £30,000 and £22,000 for the years ended 30th September 1989 and 30th September 1990.

The assessments are:

          1990/91   £30,000
          1991/92   £22,000

£22,000 is more than 70% of £30,000 but not more than 75% of £30,000.

Marginal relief gives:

$$3(£30,000 - £22,000) - \frac{3}{4} \times £30,000$$

£24,000 - £22,500 = £1,500

The assessments become:

          1990/91 (£30,000 - £1,500) = £28,500
          1991/92 (£22,000 + £1,500) = £23,500.

6.3   Effects of claim

Any adjustments made under these provisions have the effect of substituting the average assessment for all purposes of income tax except that:

(a)   any loss for a particular period of account will still qualify for relief in the normal way (see 6.1 above);

(b)   for the purposes of TA 1988,s.63 (adjustment of assessments on discontinuance of trade) the averaging adjustment will be ignored;

(c)   where a claim for averaging has been made, and either one or both of the years concerned are subject to an adjustment for any other reasons, the averaging claim will be treated as not having been made. It may, however, still be possible to make an averaging claim on the basis of the revised figures for the years concerned;

(d)   whilst averaging can reduce a tax liability or preserve personal allowances, it can also have the undesirable effect of accelerating the payment of tax; this potential danger should always be borne in mind.

6.4   Time limits

Any claim must be made by notice in writing to the Inspector of Taxes not later than two years after the end of the second year of assessment.

7.0   THE VALUATION OF STOCK

Trading stock can be valued on either a global or piecemeal basis at the lower of cost or market value. Where a trade is discontinued, stock can be valued on one of two bases:

(a)   where it is sold or transferred for valuable consideration to a person carrying on a trade in the UK who can deduct the cost as an expense for tax purposes, the stock is to be valued at sales price. To counter what appears to be an easy avoidance device it will be appreciated that the closing stock of one trade will be the opening stock of the successor;

(b)   in all other cases stock is to be valued at the open market price at the date of discontinuance.

8.0   SUCCESSIONS AND EXTENSIONS

A trader may carry on more than one trade and it is a question of fact whether a trader who starts a new activity expands his existing trade or starts a new one. The position is of some importance. If a new trade is started then the commencement rules will be applied to it, whereas if it is merely an extension of an existing trade the profits will start to be taxed on a normal preceding-year basis. In **Scales v. George Thompson & Co. Ltd. (1927)** Rowlatt J said:

> 'the real question is, was there any interconnection, any interdependence, any unity at all...'.

Illustration

A is a fishmonger. His profits for recent years have been:

	£
Year to 31.12.1988	10,000
31.12.1989	15,000
31.12.1990	14,000

On 1st January 1990, A acquired a fish and chip restaurant next door to his existing premises. The profit of that restaurant for the year to 31st December 1990 was £12,000.

If the acquisition is treated as the start of a new business:

	Continuing trade P/Y		New trade commencement		Total
		£		£	£
1989/90	Year to 31.12.88	10,000	1.1.90 - 5.4.90	3,000	13,000
1990/91	Year to 31.12.89	15,000	1.1.90 - 31.12.90	12,000	27,000
1991/92	Year to 31.12.90	14,000	Year to 31.12.90	12,000	26,000
					66,000

If it is treated as the expansion of an existing business:

		£		£	£
1989/90	Year to 31.12.88	10,000			10,000
1990/91	Year to 31.12.89	15,000			15,000
1991/92	Year to 31.12.90	14,000	Year to 31.12.90	12,000	26,000
					51,000

Once both trades are on the P/Y basis then they may be merged if they are absorbed together, otherwise they are kept separate for assessment of capital allowances and losses.

Where a person succeeds to a trade by acquisition from its former owner there will be a cessation on that latter person. He will not be able to transfer across unused losses to the new owner. A succession must be distinguished from an expansion of an existing business by the purchase of assets from another trader which in general will not mean the start of a new trade (unless the assets are used in a totally different business). Very often the distinguishing factor between acquisition of assets and the acquisition of an entire business is the treatment of goodwill.

Where two businesses merge and the proprietors agree to carry on in partnership then both businesses will normally cease and a new combined one will be considered to have commenced. This may be avoided by a continuation election under s.113(2) TA 1988.

9.0 NATIONAL INSURANCE

Self-employed persons aged over 16 are liable to Class 2 and Class 4 National Insurance contributions.

Class 2 contributions are a weekly amount of £4.25 for 1989/90. They can be paid by monthly direct debit or by buying a contribution stamp from a post office and which is fixed to a contribution card.

The following are not liable for Class 2 contributions:

(a)   A person whose income from self-employment is small (1989/90 - £2,350) provided a certificate of exemption is obtained;

(b)   Persons over retirement age - 65 males and 60 female;

(c)   Persons working overseas;

(d)   Certain married women.

Class 4 contributions are charged at a percentage rate on taxable profits, less capital allowances, between certain maximum limits. For 1989/90, the limits are:

> 6.3% on profits between £5,050 and £16,900

Class 4 contributions are collected by the Inland Revenue on the Schedule D I or II assessment. One-half of the contribution is allowed as a deduction from total income (see earlier in Section 4.4).

Illustration

	£
A's income for 1989/90 is:	
Schedule D I trading profits	
Year to 31.12.1988	16,000
Capital Allowances 1989/90	1,962
The Class 4 contributions would be:	
D I	16,000
Less: CA	1,962
	———
	14,038
	======
6.3% x £(14,038 - 5,050)	566.24
	======

Of this one-half - £283.12 - is allowed as a deduction from total income.

If the taxpayer claims loss relief then the losses are only set off against trading income for NHI purposes. Any loss offset against other income in a fiscal year will thus be carried forward into the next fiscal year and offset against trading profits of that year. Broadly the persons exempt from Class 4 contributions are the same as those for Class 2.

In the case of a partnership Class 4 contributions are calculated for each partner individually but collected on the partnership assessment.

CHAPTER FIVE

Capital Allowances

1.0   GENERAL

Depreciation of fixed assets is not an allowable deduction for taxation purposes. It is replaced by capital allowances which are a standardised system of depreciation for taxation purposes. Capital allowances are available in respect of a number of categories of assets, which include:

(a)   plant and machinery,

(b)   industrial buildings, hotels and dwelling houses let on assured tenancies,

(c)   agricultural buildings and works,

(d)   patents,

(e)   mines and oil wells,

(f)   scientific research,

(g)   know-how.

Capital allowances are normally given to a trader in respect of assets owned on the last date of an accounting period. For an individual they are not given for the accounting period itself but for the fiscal year for which the accounting period is the basis period. Thus the capital allowances based on the assets owned by a trader in the year ended 31st December 1988 will be given for the fiscal year 1989/90, for which the year ended 31st December 1988 is the basis period.

In the case of a non trader, such as a lessor of industrial buildings or a landlord claiming allowances on plant used for property maintenance, the allowances will be given in respect of the fiscal year for which the income is calculated.

In general an asset will qualify for capital allowances when the expenditure is incurred. This is the date on which the obligation to pay is unconditional irrespective of the date of payment though if the payment date is more than four months after the above date the expenditure will be treated as having been incurred on that later date.

Assets acquired before the commencement of trade will be deemed to have been acquired on the first day of trading. The rate of first year or initial allowances were, however, determined by the date on which the expenditure was incurred.

1.1 Relief for allowances

Relief for capital allowances can be given in two ways:

(a) in taxing the trade, or

(b) by discharge or repayment of tax.

1.2 Relief given in taxing the trade (CAA 1968,s.70)

In this case, the allowances are given as a deduction against the Schedule D Case I assessment. If they exceed the assessable income they can be used in a loss claim or carried forward without time limit and offset against future assessable profits of the same trade.

1.3 Relief given by discharge or repayment of tax (CAA 1968,s.71)

Relief in this case is given primarily from a specific class of income. If the allowances exceed the income, they may be carried forward and offset against income of the same class in future years without time limit. The main allowances dealt with in this way are:

(a) certain agricultural buildings allowances;
(b) allowances on certain leased assets.

Illustration

A is a farmer. His adjusted profits are:

	£	£
Year ended 31st December 1989	2,000	
Year ended 31st December 1990	14,000	

Agricultural buildings allowances from rented properties are:

	£
1990/91	7,800
1991/92	3,000

1990/91	£	
Year ended 31.12.1989 DI	2,000	
ABA 1990/91	7,800	
	NIL	5,800 c/f

1991/92
     Year ended 31.12.1990 DI   14,000
     ABA 1990/91 brought forward   5,800
        1991/92   3,000
                             8,800
                           5,200

Where the allowances exceed the specific class of income from which they are deducted, the taxpayer may elect to offset the excess against the other income of the fiscal year to which the allowances relate. As no specific order of deduction is laid down in s.71 the excess allowances can be deducted:

(a) from unearned income before earned income, or

(b) from earned income before unearned income,

as desired.

Illustration

A's other income for the fiscal year 1990/91 was:

	£
Salary as journalist	10,000
Dividends (gross)	9,000

The excess allowances for 1990/91 may be offset against the other income of that year as under:

	Earned		Unearned
	£	£	£
Salary	10,000		
Dividends			9,000
s.71 Relief for excess allowances			(5,800)
	10,000		3,200

                                13,200

Before 1984/85 this order of offset would have resulted in a saving of an additional tax on investment income - the investment income surcharge.

Where the excess allowances exceed the other income of the fiscal year to which they relate or exceed the other income of that year, the excess may be carried forward into the next fiscal year and offset against:

(a) income of the specific class,

(b) the other income.

If there are still excess allowances they may be carried forward without time limit against income of the specific class only. Where in the next fiscal year there are also similar capital allowances the order of utilisation is:

(a)   capital allowances brought forward,

(b)   capital allowances of that year.

Illustration

Information as before except that the ABA of 1990/91 were £70,000. The other income of 1991/92 was identical to 1990/91.

	£	£
1990/91		
DI - year ended 31.12.1989	2,000	
ABA 1990/91	70,000	(68,000)
	───────	
	NIL	
	───────	
Other income:		
Salary	10,000	
Dividends	9,000	
	───────	
	19,000	
s.71 Relief for excess allowances	(19,000)	19,000
	───────	───────
	NIL	(49,000)
	───────	
1991/92		
DI - year ended 31.12.1990	14,000	
ABA brought forward	(14,000)	14,000
	───────	───────
	NIL	(35,000)
	───────	
Other income as above	19,000	
s.71 Relief for excess allowances	(19,000)	19,000
	───────	───────
	NIL	(16,000)
	───────	══════

The £16,000 may be carried forward and offset against future agricultural income **only**. The ABA of 1991/92 may either be:

(a)   carried forward against future agricultural income, or

(b)   offset against other income of 1992/93 with any excess carried forward.

An election to offset against other income must be made within two years of the end of the year of assessment for which relief is claimed.

2.0   PLANT AND MACHINERY

2.1   The meaning of plant and machinery

There is no definition of plant and machinery in the Taxes Acts. The first
definition was given in 1887 by Lindley, L.J. in **Yarmouth v. France** (a workmen's
compensation case) when he said,

> '... in its ordinary sense (plant) includes whatever apparatus is used by a
> business man for carrying on his business - not his stock in trade ... but
> all goods and chattels, fixed or movable, live or dead which he keeps for
> permanent employment in his business'.

This definition is wide and a number of cases have excluded specific items from
relief. In general, if the item is of a durable nature, it may be plant, so in
Caledonian Railway Co. v. Banks (1880), railway engines and carriages were held
to be plant as were shoemaking knives and lasts in **Hinton v. Maden and Ireland
Ltd (1959)**. However, in **Earl of Derby v. Aylmer (1915)**, stallions for stud
purposes were held not to be plant and in **Norman v. Golder (1944)** similar
treatment was applied to the human body.

The definition of plant is not however restricted to items used physically. In
Munby v. Furlong (1977) the law books of a barrister were held to be plant; they
were, per Fox J:

> '... part of the apparatus used by a professional man for carrying on his
> profession'.

According to Lord Denning, they were part of 'the intellectual storehouse' of a
professional man.

More recent cases have drawn a distinction between an asset with which the
business is carried on and the setting in which it is carried on. In **Dixon v.
Fitch's Garage Ltd. (1975)**, Brightman J said:

> 'The proper test is whether the canopy had a functional purpose to enable
> the taxpayer company to perform the activity'.

It was not...

> '... whether the item in question is commercially desirable or necessary to
> enable the taxpayer to sell his (product)'.

This concept has been approved by Lord Reid in **IRC v. Barclay Curle & Co.Ltd.
(1969)**. In **St. Johns School v. Ward (1975)**, Templeman J applied the functional
test in considering the tax status of a prefabricated building at a school used
to accommodate a chemistry laboratory and held that as the building had no
function to perform other than to shelter the pupils they could not qualify as
plant and machinery. This may be contrasted with **Cooke v. Beach Station
Caravans Ltd. (1974)** where Megarry J held that a swimming pool in a caravan park
qualified as plant:

'Nobody could suggest that the principal function of the pool was merely to protect the occupants from the elements ... (it) is part of the means whereby the trade is carried on and not merely the place at which it is carried on'.

One particular difficulty in trying to draw a distinction between plant and setting is that the terms are not mutually exclusive. Electrical wiring and fittings have often been victims of this difficulty. The Revenue generally refuse to allow wiring as plant whilst light fittings will not be plant unless they are of a specialised nature **Cole Brothers Ltd. v. Phillips (1982)**.

Wimpy International Ltd v Warland (1988) normal expenditure on shopfronts, tiling and suspended ceilings was held not to be plant and machinery.

Details of important cases are:

Held to be plant and machinery:

The law books of a barrister	**Munby v. Furlong (1977)**
A swimming pool and paddling pool together with the appropriate landscaping	**Cooke v. Beach Station Caravans Ltd. (1974)**
Grain silos including bins and chutes	**Schofield v. R & H Hall Ltd. (1975)**
Decorative screens placed in the windows of a building society's offices	**Leeds Permanent Building Society v. Proctor (1982)**
Movable partitioning	**Jarrold v. John Good & Sons Ltd. (1963)**

Held not to be plant and machinery:

Prefabricated buildings used as a laboratory and gymnasium	**St. John's School (Mountford and Knibbs) v. Ward (1975)**
A canopy over the forecourt of a petrol station (The correctness of this decision has been recently doubted in **Cole Brothers Ltd. v. Phillips**, per Lord Hailsham LC).	**Dixon v. Fitch's Garage Ltd. (1975)**
A ship used as a floating restaurant	**Benson v. Yard Arm Club (1979)**
A stand for spectators at a football stadium	**Brown v. Burnley Football and Athletic Club (1980)**

In general, everything that would come within the normal meaning of plant and machinery including furniture, equipment, etc. will qualify for allowances as plant. Since 5th April, 1989 expenditure on equipment to improve the personal security of the trader or his employees qualifies as plant.

Certain expenditure, although not strictly incurred on plant and machinery, qualifies for capital allowances as if it was so incurred.   The expenditure includes:

(a) fire safety expenditure;

(b) industrial building heat insulation expenditure;

(c) sports stadium and sports ground expenditure, to comply with a safety certificate.

For items (a), (b) and (c), when the premises on which they are erected are disposed of, the deemed disposal proceeds is treated as nil.

2.2 The general scheme

(a) Pooling

Unless the plant comes within one of certain special cases, expenditure on plant acquired after 26th October 1970 is pooled.

The exceptions are expenditure on:

i)   motor cars;

ii)   motor cars costing more than £8,000;

iii) plant with an element of private usage by the proprietor;

iv)   short life assets acquired after 31st March 1986.

Apart from item (i) these will normally be treated individually with each asset forming a separate pool. Motor cars not falling into classes (ii) and (iii) will form a combined but separate pool.

(b) Allowances available

The allowances available for assets acquired after 26th October 1970 are:

i)   In the year of acquisition - a **First Year Allowance** (FYA) at the following maximum rates:

       Expenditure incurred between 27.10.70 and 19.7.71   60%
       Expenditure incurred between 20.7.71 and 21.3.72   80%
       Expenditure incurred after 22.3.72 up to 13.3.84   100%
       Expenditure incurred between 14.3.84 and 31.3.85   75%
       Expenditure incurred between 1.4.85 and 31.3.86   50%
       Expenditure incurred from 1.4.86   NIL.

       FYA was not available:

       (1) on motor cars (not lorries), capable of private use other than those:

        (a)   of a type unsuitable, and not commonly used as private
             vehicles, or

        (b)   provided wholly or mainly for a trade of public hire or
             conveyance;

    (2)   on assets acquired when the buyer and seller are "connected
        persons" unless the asset has not been used before;

    (3)   on expenditure in a period related to the permanent discontinuance
        of the trade.

First year allowances were available to the owner of plant and
machinery provided that the items belonged to him at some time in the
respective basis period.

The rates of FYA above were maximum rates; a claim could be made for
any amount up to the maximum.

ii)   In subsequent years, or in the current year when a first year allowance
is not available, writing down allowances (WDA) are available at the
rate of 25% on the balance of the amount in the pool at the beginning
of the accounting period, plus any additions, less the disposal
proceeds of any plant sold etc. in the accounting period. In the case
of motor vehicles costing £8,000 or more the annual writing down
allowance is restricted to £2,000 per annum per vehicle.

Where assets are acquired on hire purchase, the full cost of the asset will
qualify for capital allowances immediately provided the asset is brought into
use; the interest is treated as a trading expense.

Where a trader has previously acquired an asset for non-trading purposes and
subsequently commences to use it in the trade, he will be deemed to have
acquired it at its market value in the basis period in which it was first used
in the trade.

2.3 Disposals of plant

Where plant is disposed of in the accounting period, the disposal value (or
original cost if the disposal value exceeds the original cost of the asset) must
be deducted from the balance in the pool at the beginning of the accounting
period. Disposal value means the following:

(a)   where the sale is between unconnected persons, the sale proceeds;

(b)   where the sale proceeds are less than the open market value, the open market
valuation unless:

    i)   the buyer will be claiming capital allowances on the expenditure, or

    ii)   a charge will arise under Schedule E, when the actual sales proceeds,
        irrespective of market value, will be used;

(c)   where the asset is lost or destroyed, the compensation or scrap value
received.

If the sale proceeds exceed the balance of expenditure in the pool there will be
a profit known as a balancing charge. This will be assessed as a trading
receipt. There will, of course, be no unrelieved expenditure in the pool on
which writing down allowances may be claimed.

Where the asset forms a pool on its own, on its disposal there will be a profit
or a loss. The profit will be a **balancing charge** (described above), and the loss
a **balancing allowance**. A balancing allowance is given as a capital allowance of
the year.

The cost of assets less the capital allowances given on them to date is known as
the **tax written-down value**. This is normally described as the tax written-down
value at 5th April in the fiscal year for which the allowances are given.   Thus
if A makes up accounts to 31st December 1989, the capital allowances based on
that year are the allowances for 1990/91 and the tax written-down value is that
at 5th April 1991.

2.4 Expenditure qualifying as plant and machinery

Certain expenditure, although not strictly incurred on plant and machinery,
qualifies for capital allowances as if it was so incurred.   The expenditure
includes:

(a) fire safety expenditure;
(b) industrial building heat insulation expenditure;
(c) sports stadium and sports ground expenditure, to comply with a safety
        certificate.

2.5 Specimen capital allowances computation

	Pool		Car with private use	Separate pools		Total Allowances
	General	Cars		Car costing >£8,000	Car Costing >£8,000	
£	£	£	£	£	£	£
Brought forward	x	x	x	x	x	
Additions not qualify	x	x				
	-	-				
	x	x				
Disposal proceeds of assets	(x)	(x)		(x)		BC/BA
	x	x	x	x		
Writing down allowances	(x)	(x)	(x)		(x)Restricted	x
	x	x	x	x	x	
Less: Private use reductions						(x)
Add: balancing allowances						x
						x

Leased assets acquired after 31st March 1986 will normally enter the general pool. There are limited exclusions including assets leased to non-residents etc.

2.6 Assets with an element of private use

It has already been mentioned that expenditure on assets with an element of private use (almost invariably motor cars) forms a separate pool of expenditure. In addition, the capital allowances must be restricted by the amount of the private use. The amount deducted from the value of the asset, resulting in the tax written-down value, remains the same; the amount of the restriction is only deducted from the total allowances column. This only applies to private use by the proprietor; if the private use is by an employee full allowances will be given, with no private use restriction.

Illustration

B makes up accounts to 31st October annually. In the year to 31st October 1989 he bought a car costing £5,000. Private use was agreed at 20% per annum.

		Car £	Total Allowances £
1990/91	(Year ended 31.10.1989)		
	Cost	5,000	
	WDA	1,250	1,250
		3,750	
	Less: Private element - 20%		250
			1,000
1991/92	(Year ended 31.10.1990)		
	WDA 25%	937	937
		2,813	
	Less: Private element - 20%		187
			750
1992/93	(Year ended 31.10.1991)		
	WDA	703	703
		2,110	
	Less: Private element - 20%		141
			562

Should the car now be sold for £2,650 in the year to 31.10.92 there will be a balancing charge:

1993/94	(Year ended 31.10.1992)		
	Sales proceeds	2,650	
	Balancing charge	540	

To avoid an element of double taxation, this will be reduced by applying the private use percentage:

	£
Balancing charge	540
Less: 20% thereof	108
	432

This will be assessed as a trading receipt of the fiscal year 1993/94 (based on the year to 31st October 1992). In no case can the balancing charge exceed the allowances actually given.

In certain cases the element of private use can vary each year. If in the illustration the private use element was:

1990/91	20%
1991/92	50%
1992/93	30%

the abbreviated computation would be:

Year	Cost £	Restrict for private use	Allowance given £
1990/91			
31.10.89	5,000		
WDA	1,250	-20%	1,000
	3,750		
1991/92			
31.10.90			
WDA	937	-50%	468
	2,813		
1992/93			
31.10.91			
WDA	703	-30%	492
	2,110		1,960

Should the car now be sold, again for £2,650, the calculation of the restricted balancing charge is more complex. It is multiplied by the fraction:

$$\frac{\text{Allowances actually given}}{\text{Allowances that could have been given}}$$

	£
WDV (as above)	2,110
Sales proceeds	2,650
Balancing charge	540

Restricted to: $\dfrac{1,960}{1,250 + 937 + 703}$ x 540 = $\underline{\underline{366}}$

An alternative calculation to achieve the same adjustment is to restrict the balancing charge by the average business use:

$$540 \text{ x } \frac{0.8 + 0.5 + 0.7}{3} = \underline{\underline{360}}$$

If there is a balancing allowance it will be similarly restricted.

Where the plant is used for other purposes, i.e. there is some private use, then it will be deemed to be used in a separate trade placed in a separate pool and have any capital allowances restricted by reference to the non-business use. Where plant was originally used wholly for the purposes of the trade and is then only partly used for trading purposes, it will be transferred from the general pool to a separate pool at market value. Writing-down allowances will be restricted in the same way as before. This transfer is made at the beginning of the period in which the change of use occurred.

Illustration

X, a trader, bought a typewriter on 1st February 1986 for £1,000. It was wholly used for trading purposes up to 31st December 1987. On 1st January 1988 X started to use it privately. It was agreed that the private use was 50% and that the market value at the date of transfer was £600. Accounts are prepared to 31st December throughout and the tax-written-down value in the pool at 5th April 1987 was £8,000.

1987/88

Year to 31.12.1986		Pool £	Typewriter £	Allowances £
Brought forward		8,000		
WDA		2,000		2,000
	£	6,000		
Typewriter	1,000			
FYA - 50%	500			
		500		500
		6,500		$\underline{\underline{2,500}}$

1988/89

Year to 31.12.1987

WDA	1,625		1,625
	4,875		

	Pool £	Typewriter £	Allowances £
1989/90 **Year to 31.12.1988**			
Transfer to separate pool	(600)	600	
	4,275	600	
WDA	1,069	150	1,219
c/f	3,206	450	
	=====	===	
Less: Private use - ½			75
			1,144
			=====

Comprehensive Illustration

Kings and Lynne are partners in a manufacturing business, sharing profits and losses equally. After the capital allowances given in the 1988/89 assessment on the firm's profits, the brought-forward figures of assets at 5th April 1989 were:

	£
Plant	27,300
Volvo motor car used by Lynne partly for private purposes	1,125

In the year ended 31st December 1988, the following movements in assets took place:

Additions   £

i)   A new grinder was purchased for   4,000

ii) A second-hand weighing machine was purchased for   800

iii) A motor lorry was bought on hire purchase. The cash price was £13,000, hire purchase charges £1,500. A deposit of £1,800 was paid followed by 36 equal monthly instalments commencing on 15th July 1988.

iv) A Rolls Royce for Kings costing   22,000
     There was no private use.

v)   A second-hand hoist was acquired from Lynne's brother costing   3,000

vi) A new car was purchased for the use of the sales manager. The private use was agreed at 25%.   6,000

vii) A second-hand Ferrari was purchased for Lynne's use to replace the car sold - cost   9,000
     Private use was agreed at 30%

Disposals   £

i)   Plant acquired second-hand in 1973 was sold and
      realised   50

ii)   A lathe acquired in 1978 for £1,200 was sold and
      realised   1,500

iii) The car used by Lynne was sold for £1,400. It was
      acquired in 1985 for £2,666 and the personal usage
      element was agreed at:

                        1986/87   1/4

                        1987/88   1/3

                        1988/89   1/5

Calculate the capital allowances for 1989/90.

| | Pool | | Separate Pools | | King's | Total |
| | General | Cars | Lynne's Cars Volvo | Ferrari | Rolls-Royce | Allowances |
	£	£	£	£	£	£
Year ended 31.12.88 1989/90						
brought forward	27,300		1,125			
Non-Qualifying Additions:						
Rolls-Royce					22,000	
Hoist	3,000					
Sales Manager's Car		6,000				
Ferrari				9,000		
Lorry	13,000					
Grinder	4,000					
Weighting machiner	800					
	48,100	6,000	1,125	9,000	22,000	
Disposal Proceeds of Assets sold						
Plant £ 50						
Lathew (restricted to cost) 1,200	1,250					
Lynne's car			1,400			
	46,850		B/C 275			
WDA	11,713	1,500		(Rest) 2,000	(Rest) 2,000	17,213
	35,137	4,500		7,000	20,000	
Less: Private use - Lynne (30% x 2,000)						600
						16,613

The balancing charge will be assessed as under:

Lynne's Volvo

	£	£		£
Cost	2,666			
WDA 1986/87	666	- 1/4	166	500
	_____			
	2,000			
WDA 1987/88	500	- 1/3	166	334
	_____			
	1,500			
WDA 1988/89	375	- 1/5	75	300
	_____			_____
	1,125			1,134
	=====			=====

$$275 \times \frac{1.134}{666 + 500 + 375} = £202$$

2.7 Reduction of allowances

In certain cases a trader's profit may be very small and deduction of the full amount of capital allowances may result in a situation where he is unable to obtain full relief for his personal allowances. In such a situation he has the option of not claiming some or all of his WDA. If he does this, he cannot reclaim them in a subsequent year.

Illustration

C makes up accounts to 31st December 1988, and for that year has adjusted profits of £5,000. He has qualifying expenditure in the pool of £3,500, brought forward, and buys a lathe on 30th June 1988 for £2,400. He is married.

If he claims all his capital allowances the position will be:

1989/90	£	£
Schedule D Case I profits		5,000
Less: Capital allowances:		
Pool b/f	3,500	
Lathe	2,400	
	_____	
	5,900	
WDA 25%	1,475	
	_____	1,475
	4,425	_____
	=====	3,525
Less: Personal allowances		4,375
		_____
		NIL
		=====

Personal allowances lost £850
                        ====

As personal allowances cannot be carried forward, C should consider making a reduced claim.   The revised computation could appear as under:

	£	£
Schedule D Case I profits		5,000
Less: Capital allowances:		
Pool b/f	3,500	
Lathe	2,400	
	5,900	
WDA (restricted)	625	625
	5,275	
		4,375
Less: Personal allowances		4,375
		NIL

2.8 Election for treatment as a short-life asset

Short-life plant, i.e. that which the trader intends to sell or scrap within 5 years of acquisition, may be excluded from the pool where it is acquired after 31st March 1986. Certain types of plant will not qualify for this treatment; they include:

(a)   ships;

(b)   cars but not vans;

(c)   certain leased assets;

(d)   plant with an element of private use.

All short-life assets are deemed to be used in a separate trade and therefore will be in individual pools. If the asset is sold or scrapped the notional separate trade is deemed to have been discontinued and there will be a balancing charge or allowance. A similar treatment is applied when there is the commencement of part private use.

If at the end of 4 years after the end of the accounting period in which it was acquired, the asset has not been sold or scrapped it will be transferred to the general pool at its tax-written-down value at the beginning of the next accounting period. An election to 'depool' short life assets must be made within 2 years of the end of the accounting period in which the assets are acquired and is irrevocable.

Illustration

In the year to 31st December 1986 A bought the following items of plant:

		£
1.2.1986	Printing machine	20,000
1.6.1986	Computer	10,000
1.11.1986	Grinder	8,000

The balance in the pool at 5th April 1987 was £6,000. An election was made to treat the computer and grinder as short-life assets. The computer was sold for £4,000 in the year to 31st December 1989.

		Pool	Short-Life Pools		Allowances
1987/88			Computer	Grinder	
Year to 31.12.1986	£	£	£	£	£
b/f		6,000			
Additions:					
Printing machine	20,000				
Computer			10,000		
Grinder				8,000	
Allowances:					
WDA - 25%		1,500	2,500	2,000	6,000
		4,500	7,500	6,000	
FYA - 50%	10,000	10,000			10,000
		14,500			16,000
1988/89					
Year to 31.12.1987					
WDA - 25%		3,625	1,875	1,500	7,000
		10,875	5,625	4,500	
1989/90					
Year to 31.12.1988					
WDA - 25%		2,719	1,406	1,125	5,250
		8,156	4,219	3,375	
1990/91					
Year to 31.12.1989					
DP			4,000		
BA			219		219
WDA - 25%		2,039		844	2,883
C/Fwd		6,117		2,531	3,102

		Pool	Short-Life Pools		Allowances
			Computer	Grinder	
		£	£	£	£
	b/fwd	6,117		2,531	
1991/92 **Year to 31.12.1990**					
WDA - 25%		1,529		633	2,162
		4,588		1,898	=====
1992/93 **Year to 31.12.1991**					
Transfer to general pool		1,898		(1,898)	
		6,486		———	
WDA - 25%		1,622			1,622
c/f		4,864			=====
		=====			

Where a short-life asset is sold to a connected person it will normally be transferred at market value. Where they jointly elect, however, it can be transferred across at tax-written-down value with the person acquiring it stepping into the shoes of the vendor as far as the 5-year period is concerned.

2.9 Capital allowances for fixtures

In **Stokes v. Costain (1984)** the Court of Appeal held that fixtures in a building inserted by the lessee did not qualify for capital allowances as they became landlord's fixtures and thus did not 'belong' to the taxpayer lessee.   For expenditure incurred after 11th July 1984 it is now provided that where a person who has an interest in land incurs capital expenditure on plant or machinery and that subsequently becomes a landlord's fixture, then the fixture is deemed to belong to that person with the interest in the land (i.e. normally the tenant). Where expenditure has been incurred by the landlord, who subsequently grants a lease on the property, the lessor and lessee may elect to transfer the right to receive allowances to the lessee.

3.0   INDUSTRIAL BUILDINGS

3.1 Definition

An industrial building includes:

(a) a building used in a manufacturing trade, mining, oil exploration or fishing;

(b) warehouses for the storage of stock to be used in the manufacturing trade, deriving from the manufacturing trade or included as work in progress, and buildings used for the repair or maintenance of goods in such a trade;

(c) canteens or other buildings provided for the welfare of employees engaged in a trade in (a) and (b) above;

(d)   sports pavilions in any trade;

(e)   certain hotels.

Buildings overseas can qualify for relief if the trade carried on is assessable
in the UK under Schedule DI.

3.2   Case law

Bourne v Norwich Crematorium Ltd. (1967)
A crematorium was held not to be an industrial building as it did not subject
the human body to an industrial process.

Buckingham v Securitas Properties Ltd. (1980)
A building used for breaking down bulk cash into individual wage packets did not
qualify as an industrial building.

CIR v Lambhill Ironworks (1950)
An engineering drawing office qualified as an industrial building.

3.3   The quantum of relief

Relief is only available for the cost of construction, which does not include
the cost of the land, but includes the cost of foundations etc. Where a
building includes a non-qualifying part, such as offices or showrooms, that part
will not qualify for relief unless the cost of that part, exclusive of land,
does not exceed 25% of the cost of the whole of the structure, exclusive of
land. Prior to 16th March 1983 the relevant percentage was 10%. There is no
marginal relief; it is all or nothing.

Illustration

A erects an industrial building, the cost of which is as follows:

	£
Land	40,000
Factory block	35,000
Canteen	6,000
Digging foundations	4,000
Sales office	10,500
	95,500

The cost of the sales office will qualify for industrial buildings allowance
(IBA) as it does not exceed 25% of the cost of the total structure:

$$£10,500 > 25\% \text{ of } £55,500$$

If, however, the cost of the sales office were £16,000, it would not qualify for
IBA as the cost would exceed the 25% limit:

$$£16,000 > 25\% \text{ of } £61,000 \text{ (i.e. } £55,500 + £5,500)$$

Where a building is purchased **before** it has been used as an industrial building,
the purchaser will receive IBA on:

(a)   the full purchase price, if the building is purchased from a builder in the normal course of business;

(b)   the lower of the full purchase price or the vendor's original cost of construction, if the building is purchased other than from a builder.

The allowances available consist of:

(a)   initial allowances, and

(b)   writing-down allowances.

(a)   Initial allowances

These were given on the cost of the structure, less any government or local authority grants or sums received from a landlord, excluding regional development grants. It was given for the fiscal year for which the accounting period in which the expenditure was incurred forms the basis period. The building did not have to be in use to qualify for initial allowance. The rates were:

Expenditure incurred

8.4.59 to 16.1.66	5%
17.1.66 to 5.4.70	15%
6.4.70 to 21.3.72	30%
22.3.72 to 12.11.74	40%
13.11.74 to 10.3.81	50%
11.3.81 to 13.3.84	75%
14.3.84 to 31.3.85	50%
1.4.85 to 31.3.86	25%
From 1.4.86	NIL

An individual or a company could take a smaller amount of initial allowance other than the above maxima.

(b)   Writing-down allowances

WDA are available provided that:

i)   the building is in use at the end of the basis period, and
ii) the person claiming the allowances has the relevant interest.

The rates are:

Expenditure incurred:

6.4.1946 to 5.11.1962	2% on cost
6.11.1962 onwards	4% on cost.

WDA cannot be disclaimed.

Both of these allowances are **straight line** which means that the building has a definite life for tax purposes - 50 years for pre-6th November 1962 expenditure and 25 years for post-5th November 1962 expenditure. No writing-down allowance is available after the end of the 50th or 25th year of ownership of a building and the total allowances cannot exceed the total qualifying cost of the building, which means in practice that where initial allowances have been claimed, allowances often cease much earlier.

For the purpose of calculating allowances, each new building or addition to a building is treated as a separate item.   Alterations qualify for industrial buildings allowance if appropriate;   if, however, they are incidental to the installation of plant and machinery, they will qualify for plant and machinery allowances.

The relevant interest is the freehold or the leasehold interest that the person incurring the expenditure has in the property. For a subsequent purchaser to obtain capital allowances he must obtain the relevant interest. The term is interpreted strictly; in **Woods v Mallen Engineering Ltd. (1983)** the grant of a sublease for three days shorter than the term of the original lease was not treated as a transfer of the relevant interest as the new lease was not identical with that of the person originally incurring the expenditure. It can be seen therefore that if a person owning the freehold of a property incurs expenditure qualifying for IBA and subsequently grants a lease to another manufacturer, the purchaser will not be able to qualify for IBA even though he pays a premium to the vendor as he will not have the same relevant interest, (i.e. the freehold interest) as the person who erected the building had at the time he incurred the expenditure.

To alleviate this problem it is provided that where a person with the relevant interest in an industrial building grants a **long** lease to another then the vendor and the purchaser may jointly agree that this can be treated as the transfer of the relevant interest and thus the lessee will qualify for capital allowances in respect of the expenditure incurred by the landlord.   Expenditure incurred by a tenant will qualify for allowances in his lands.

Illustration

B acquired a factory new on 1st June 1962 at a cost of £50,000 including land costing £10,000 and offices which cost £4,500. On 1st September 1969 he had an extension built at a cost of £15,000. He sold the factory and extension on 1st June 1989 for £100,000 (exclusive of land) of which £90,000 was attributable to the original factory and included £6,000 for the office. B makes up his accounts to 31st December each year.

Original Factory	£	Extension	£
Cost	50,000	Cost	15,000
Less: Land	10,000		
	40,000		
Less: Office (being more than 10% of £40,000)	4,500		
	35,500		

1963/64	£	1970/71	£
IA - 5%	1,775	IA - 15%	2,250
WDA - 2%	710	WDA - 4%	600
c/f	2,485		2,850

	£	£		£	£
b/f	2,485	35,500		2,850	15,000
1964/65 - 1989/90			1971/72 - 1989/90		
WDA 26 x £710	18,460		19 x £600	11,400	
		20,945			14,250
Residue of expenditure		14,555			750

3.4 Sale of a building

On the disposal of an industrial building, there will be a balancing charge or
allowance. This is found by deducting the disposal proceeds of the structure
only, (or market value if the disposal is other than at open market value) from
the tax-written-down value, known in this case as the 'residue of expenditure'.
A balancing charge cannot exceed the allowances given and no balancing
adjustment will arise if the building is sold after the end of its 'tax life',
i.e. after 50 or 25 years from the date of first use. Any costs of demolition
are added to the residue of expenditure before calculating the balancing
adjustment.

	£	£
Residue of expenditure	14,555	750
Disposal proceeds £(90,000 - 6,000)	84,000	10,000
Balancing charge	69,445	9,250
Restricted to	20,945	

3.5 Allowances available to a subsequent purchaser

A subsequent purchaser of a used industrial building will, provided that he uses
it as an industrial building, be able to claim capital allowances. The only
capital allowance available is a writing-down allowance calculated by using the
formula:

Residue of expenditure plus any balancing charge or less any balancing allowance
        Tax life of building less period of previous ownership from first use

No initial allowance was available. In the illustration, the allowance available
to a subsequent purchaser would be:

	£	£
Original factory		
Residue of expenditure	14,555	
Add: Balancing charge	20,945	
	35,500	

$$\frac{£35,500}{50 - 27} \qquad = \qquad 1,543 \quad C/fwd$$

		£	£
	B/fwd		1,543
Extension			
Residue of expenditure		750	
Add: Balancing charge		9,250	
		───────	
		10,000	
		══════	

$$\frac{£10,000}{25 - 19\ 9/12} = \quad\quad 1,905$$

$$3,448$$

In most cases, the numerator will be equal to the lower of the sales proceeds or the original cost for capital allowance purposes.

3.6 Non-industrial use

If at the end of the basis period the building is not in industrial use or is being used for a non-industrial purpose no WDA will be available unless the period of non-use is merely temporary. Where there is a period of non-industrial use, notional WDAs, i.e. allowances calculated but not deducted from profits, will be deducted from cost in arriving at the residue of expenditure. In finding the balancing charge or allowance the calculations will differ depending upon whether the building is sold for more or less than the original cost.

(a)   Sale for more than cost

The balancing adjustment will be calculated as under:

	£	£
Cost		x
Less:IBA for periods of industrial use	x	
Notional WDA for periods of non-industrial use	x	
	─	x
		─
Residue of expenditure		x
Disposal proceeds		x
		─
Balancing charge		x
		═

The balancing charge will be restricted to the allowances actually given.

Illustration

Anton bought a factory on 15th December 1980 for £10,000 exclusive of land. He used it for non-industrial purposes throughout the period 7th November 1982 to 18th March 1984. He sold it on 15th December 1990 for £11,000 exclusive of land. Accounts are made up to 31st December throughout.

		£	£
1981/82	Year ended 31.12.80		
	Cost		10,000
	IA - 50%	5,000	
	WDA - 4%	400	
			5,400
			4,600
1982/83	Year ended 31.12.81		
	WDA 4%		400
			4,200
1983/84	Year ended 31.12.82		
	Notional WDA (buildings not in use at end of basis period)		400
			3,800
1984/85	Year ended 31.12.83		
	Notional WDA (buildings not in use at end of basis period)		400
			3,400
1985/86 to	Years ended 31.12.84 to 31.12.89		
1990/91	WDA - 4% x 6 years		2,400
	Residue of expenditure before sale		1,000
1991/92	Year ended 31.12.90		
	Sale of building - proceeds		11,000
			10,000

The balancing charge will be limited to the allowances given:

£5,400 + £400 + £2,400   £8,200

The allowances available to a subsequent purchaser would be:

	£
Residue of expenditure	1,000
Balancing charge	8,200
	9,200
divided by (25 - 10)	613 p.a.

(b) Sale for less than cost

The balancing adjustment would be:

	£	£
Cost		x
Less: IBA for periods of industrial use	x	
Notional WDA for periods of non-industrial use	x	
	—	x
		—
Residue of expenditure		x
		=
Cost		x
Less: Sales proceeds		x
		—
Net cost		x
Less: Proportion attributable to non-industrial use:		
Net cost x $\dfrac{\text{Period of non-industrial use}}{\text{Period of ownership from first use}}$		x
Adjusted net cost		x
Less: Allowances actually given		x
		—
Balancing charge (or Balancing allowance)		x
		=

Illustration

B makes up accounts to 31st December annually. On 30th June 1976 she acquired a factory from a builder at a cost of:

	£
Land	50,000
Building	150,000
	200,000

It was first brought into use on 31st December 1976. It was out of industrial use for the period from 1st August 1981 to 31st January 1983. On 31st December 1990 the factory was sold for £30,000 (excluding land). Only 40% of the cost was claimed as an initial allowance.

		£	£
1977/78	Year to 31.12.76 - Cost		150,000
	IA - 40%	60,000	
	WDA - 4%	6,000	
			66,000
			84,000
1978/79 to	Years 31.12.77 to 31.12.80		
1981/82	WDA - 4% x 4		24,000
			60,000
1982/83	Year to 31.12.81		
	Notional WDA - 4%		6,000
			54,000
1983/84	Year to 31.12.82		
	Notional WDA - 4%		6,000
			48,000
1984/85 to	Years 31.12.83 to 31.12.89		
1990/91	WDA - 4% x 7		42,000
	Residue of expenditure		6,000

	£
Cost	150,000
Disposal proceeds	30,000
	120,000
Less: Proportion attributable to non-industrial use - 1½/14	12,857
Adjusted net cost	107,143
Less: Allowances actually given	132,000
Balancing charge - 1991/92	24,857

Allowances available to subsequent purchaser:

	£
Residue of expenditure	6,000
Balancing charge	24,857
	30,857
But restricted to cost to subsequent purchaser	30,000
divided by 25 - 14	2,727 p.a.

3.7 Manner of making allowances

Where the industrial building is used by a trader, the allowances will be given against the Schedule D Case I assessments - i.e. in taxing the trade. If the building is leased, then the lessor will receive the allowances by discharge or repayment of tax against any rental income. In the case of leased industrial buildings any balancing charge will be assessed under Schedule D Case VI.

3.8 Hotels

IBA can be claimed in relation to a 'qualifying hotel' as if it were an industrial building or structure.

The allowances available are:

(a)   Initial Allowance:
           Expenditure incurred from 12.4.1978 to 31.3.1986   20%
                                     after 31.3.1986   NIL

(b)   Writing-down allowance:
           4% straight line.

A 'qualifying hotel' is an hotel the accommodation in which is in a building or buildings of a permanent nature and which complies with the following requirements:

(a)   that it is open for at least four months in the season (April to October);

(b)   that during the time when it is open in the season:

     i)   it has at least ten letting bedrooms;

     ii)   the sleeping accommodation offered at the hotel consists wholly or mainly of letting bedrooms; and

     iii) the services provided for guests normally include the provision of breakfast and an evening meal, the making of beds and the cleaning of rooms.

A letting bedroom is defined as a private bedroom available for letting to the public generally and not normally in the same occupation for more than one month.

In determining whether the hotel is qualifying, the various conditions must be satisfied for the twelve months prior to the end of the basis period for which allowances are claimed. Thus if C makes up accounts as under, the relevant periods will be:

                Year ended 31.12.1988   1.1.88 - 31.12.88
                18 months to 30.6.1990   1.7.89 - 30.6.90

Any building (whether or not on the same site as any other part of the hotel) which is provided by the person carrying on the hotel for the welfare of workers employed in the hotel and which is in use for that purpose, is treated as included in a 'qualifying hotel'. However, where a qualifying hotel is carried on by an individual, (whether alone or in partnership), any accommodation which, during the time when the hotel is open in the season, is normally used as a dwelling by that person or by any member of his family or household, must be excluded from relief, unless it falls uinder the 25% (10%) de minimis rule for non-qualifying parts of an industrial building.

On the sale of an hotel, the calculation of the balancing charge or allowance follows the normal rules except that a balancing adjustment will also be made if the hotel has ceased to be used for a qualifying purpose for a period of two years.

3.9 Assured tenancies

Capital allowances are available to a company which incurs expenditure on dwellings let at freely-negotiated rents that are not subject to the Rent Acts. The allowances are available for expenditure incurred between 10th March 1982 and 31st March 1992 as a result of a contract to acquire land or property made before 15th March 1988.

The allowances are:

(a)   Initial allowance
      Expenditure incurred from:
                     10.3.82 to 13.3.84   75%
                     14.3.84 to 31.3.85   50%
                     1.4.85 to 31.3.86   25%
                     From 1.4.86   NIL

(b)   WDA is 4% straight line.

Allowances may be claimed on expenditure on the buildings.   There is no provision for any disclaimer.

The expenditure that qualifies for relief is a maximum of £60,000 per dwelling in Greater London or £40,000 per dwelling elsewhere.   Expenditure incurred in erecting a block of flats is apportioned rateably.   Relief is given by discharge or repayment of tax against rental income.

Disposals will result in balancing adjustments with a purchaser entitled to claim WDA on the residue of expenditure using the normal industrial buildings formula.

3.10 Industrial and commercial buildings in enterprise zones

Expenditure on the construction of an industrial building or a qualifying hotel, or a commercial building or structure, will qualify for industrial building allowances if, at the time the expenditure was incurred, the site of the building is in an enterprise zone.   The expenditure must have been incurred within ten years of the site having been included in the zone.

A commercial building is one which does not already qualify for relief, which is used for the purposes of a trade, profession or vocation, or in any case is used as an office, excluding any building in use as or as part of a dwelling house.

The initial allowance available is up to 100% subject to the right of reducing the claim to a lesser amount; a straight-line writing-down allowance of 25% is available on the balance of expenditure (if any). The WDA cannot be disclaimed nor reduced.

The tax life of an enterprise zone building is 25 years from first use and on the disposal of a building in this period, there will be a balancing adjustment. A subsequent purchaser of a used enterprise zone building will qualify for WDA on a straight line basis over the remainder of the 25 year tax life.

4.0 AGRICULTURAL BUILDINGS AND WORKS

4.1 Expenditure incurred prior to 1st April 1986

4.1.1   General

This is an allowance given to the owner or tenant in respect of expenditure incurred on the following:

(a)   construction or extension of farmhouses and farm cottages;

(b)   construction of farm or forestry buildings including intensive rearing houses;

(c)   drainage, sewerage and land reclamation works, erection of fences and installation of gas and electricity services, etc.

Any grants received must be deducted from the cost of the works before claiming allowances. In respect of expenditure on the farmhouse, no more than one-third of the cost qualifies for relief.

4.1.2   Allowances available

(a)   Initial allowance of 20%. This allowance was available only in respect of expenditure incurred after 11th April 1978 - before that date only writing-down allowances were available.

(b)   WDA of 10%.   This was a straight-line allowance, calculated on the expenditure incurred, and given until the allowances equal the expenditure.

Unlike other types of allowances, these allowances were given in the fiscal year following the year to **31st March** in which the expenditure was incurred.

Illustration

J made up accounts for the year to 31st December 1985. In that year he incurred the following expenditure:

		£
(a)	Additions to barn on 31.1.85	8,000
	(a grant of £2,000 was received)	
(b)	New bathroom for farmhouse on 10.4.85	1,500

Capital allowances can be claimed as under:

	£	£	£	£
1985/86				
Expenditure to 31.3.1985				
Additions to barn	8,000			
Less: Grant	2,000			
		6,000		
Initial allowance - 20%	1,200			
WDA - 10%	600			
		1,800		1,800
		4,200		
1986/87				
Expenditure to 31.3.1986				
New bathroom (1/3 x £1,500)			500	
Initial allowance - 20%	100			
WDA - 10%	50			
			150	150
WDA on barn		600		600
Carried forward		3,600	350	750

Note the first WDA was available in the same year as the initial allowance.

To avoid the problems associated with allocating expenditure incurred in an accounting period to different fiscal years for the purpose of determining the allowances, an individual taxpayer could agree with the Inspector to substitute his own accounting year date for 31st March.

4.1.3   Manner of giving allowances

Agricultural buildings allowances were given against agricultural income, any excess being carried forward against the same income for future years. Alternatively the taxpayer could elect under CAA 1968,s.71 to have the excess offset against other income. The time limit for this claim was two years after the end of the year of assessment.

4.1.4   Sale of agricultural buildings

On the sale of an agricultural building there was no balancing adjustment. The transferee could obtain the allowance for the remaining part of the original writing-down period and in the fiscal year of transfer any allowance was apportioned on a time basis.

Illustration

Following the first illustration in section 4.1.2, if J sold his barn to S on 30th June 1989 for £9,000, for the fiscal year 1989/90 the allowance would be split between them by reference to the respective periods of ownership in the year to 31st March 1990.

```
                                            £
            J
            3/12 x £600                    150

            S
            9/12 x £600                    450
                                           ___
                                           600
                                           ===
```

S would continue to get capital allowances of £600 per annum for the next three
years.

Where the person incurring the expenditure on agricultural buildings etc., is the
tenant and the tenancy comes to an end, the remaining allowances passed as
under:

(a) if there was an incoming tenant and he made any payment to the outgoing
     tenant in respect of the relevant expenditure then the remaining allowances
     would go to the incoming tenant;

(b) in any other case, e.g. when no payment was made or another tenancy was not
     granted, the allowances would pass to the immediate landlord.

4.2 Expenditure incurred after 31st March 1986

4.2.1   General

For expenditure incurred after 31.3.1986 there were detailed changes to the
legislation many of which are similar to the procedures already applied to
industrial buildings. Broadly allowances will be given on capital expenditure
as in 4.1.1 above where the person incurring the expenditure has a major
interest in the property. A major interest is:

(a) a freehold interest, or

(b) a lease.

4.2.2   Allowances available

A writing-down allowance is given at 4% per annum straight line over a period of
25 years.   The allowance is first given for the fiscal year for which the
accounting period forms a basis period. As with the previous legislation,
allowances are only given on a maximum of 1/3rd of the cost of expenditure on
the farmhouse. For an investor ABA are given for the fiscal year in which the
expenditure is incurred.

Illustration

K, a farmer, makes up accounts to 31st December 1989. In that year she spends
£20,000 on a new barn.

		£
1990/91	Year to 31st December 1989	
	Cost	20,000
	WDA - 4%	800
	c/f	19,200

4.2.3   Manner of giving allowances

ABA on expenditure incurred after 31st March 1986 is normally given in taxing the trade and can thus qualify for S.380 relief unless the property is held as an investment when the allowances will continue to be given by discharge or repayment of tax primarily against agricultural or forestry income.

4.2.4   Sale of an agricultural building etc

If an asset on which ABA has been claimed is sold before having been brought into use, then there will be a clawback of any WDA previously claimed. The person acquiring the relevant interest in the property will be able to claim WDA on the lower of:

(a) cost to the original owner, or

(b) price paid by the subsequent purchaser.

Where a person disposes of his interest in the property to another during the tax life, it is possible to have two differing treatments:

(a) no balancing adjustment;

(b) a balancing adjustment.

If no claim is made for a balancing adjustment on disposal, the purchaser of the relevant interest steps into the shoes of the vendor and becomes entitled to receive the WDA for the remainder of the building's tax life. If the disposal occurs in the middle of a basis period then the allowances available for the relevant fiscal year will be restricted by the length of the period of ownership in the period.

Where it is desired to have a balancing adjustment, then a balancing charge or allowance is calculated in the normal way. The subsequent purchaser can obtain a writing-down allowance by using the formula:

$$\frac{\text{Residue of expenditure plus any balancing charge or less any balancing allowance}}{\text{Tax life of the asset less any previous period of ownership}}$$

Illustration

L makes up accounts to 31st December annually. On 1st December 1987 he acquires a barn for £10,000. On 1st December 1990 he sells it to M for £9,000. A claim is made to treat the sale as a balancing event.

		£
1988/89	Year to 31st December 1987	
	Cost of barn	10,000
	WDA	400
		9,600
1989/90	Year to 31st December 1988	
	WDA	400
		9,200
1990/91	Year to 31st December 1989	
	WDA	400
		8,800
1991/92	Year to 31st December 1990	
	Disposal proceeds	9,000
	Balancing charge	200

Allowances available to M:

$$\frac{£8,800 + £200}{25 - 3} \quad = \quad £409 \text{ p.a.}$$

An election to treat the disposal as a balancing event must be made within two years of the end of the year of assessment in the basis period of which the event occurs. A company must make the election within two years of the end of the relevant accounting period. When the event is a sale, the election must be made jointly by buyer and seller otherwise, e.g. in the case of destruction etc. of the asset, the election need only be made by the former owner.

5.0 PATENTS

5.1 Expenditure incurred before 1st April 1986

5.1.1   General

There are two basic types of expenditure on patents:

(a)   the cost of creating a patented process:
this is treated as a revenue expense and deducted from trading profit;

(b)   the cost of purchasing patent rights these attract capital allowances.

5.1.2   Allowances available

The allowance is a WDA given over 17 years if a new patent, or its life if that is a shorter period.

Illustration

Y acquires the rights to two patents:

(a)   a new one costing £34,000;
(b)   one with ten years to run also costing £34,000.

Allowances available:

(a)   £34,000/17   =   £2,000 per annum
(b)   £34,000/10   =   £3,400 per annum

Where the owner of the patent rights is a trader, the writing-down allowance can be given against trading profits. If he is not a trader, it can only be given against patent income, any excess being carried forward and relieved when such income is available.

Illustration

Z is a pensioner who receives a state retirement pension of £2,000 per year. To provide for his retirement, he acquires the rights to a revolutionary process on 30th June, 1985. The patent has ten years to run and cost £20,000. His income from the royalties is:

1985/86	£1,400
1986/87	£3,000

		£	£	£
1985/86	Patent royalties	1,400		
	WDA £20,000/10	2,000		
		_____		
	c/f	600		
		=====		
	Pension			2,000
	Total income			2,000
				=====
1986/87	Patent royalties			3,000
	WDA brought forward		600	
	for the year		2,000	
			_____	2,600
				_____
				400
	Pension			2,000
	Total income			2,400
				=====

5.1.3   Sale of a Patent

The sale of a patent can be either partial or total:

(a)   Partial sale

The sale proceeds of the part sold are deducted from the written down value brought forward. A new WDA is then calculated by dividing the remaining figure by the residual life of the patent.

Illustration

In 1987/88 Z sold part of his patent for £4,000.   £

WDV brought forward (£20,000 - £4,000)	16,000
Less: Partial sale proceeds	4,000
	12,000
WDA 1987/88 and subsequent years: £12,000/8	1,500
	10,500

(b)   Total sale

The sale of the whole of the patent will give rise to a balancing charge or allowance.   The balancing charge cannot exceed the allowances actually given. The balancing charge will be assessed as a trading profit where the owner is a trader.   If the patent is held as an investment the charge will be assessed under Schedule D Case VI.

Illustration

In 1989/90 Z sold the remainder of the patent for £15,000.

		£
1989/90	WDV brought forward	10,500
	Sales proceeds	15,000
	Balancing charge	4,500

Where the patent is sold for more than its original cost, the balancing charge will be restricted to the allowances given and there will be an additional charge to income tax on the excess of sales proceeds over original cost. This sum is assessable under Schedule D Case VI and provided the vendor is a UK resident, is spread equally over the year of receipt and the five successive years. Alternatively, the taxpayer may, by election within two years of the end of the year of receipt, be assessed on the whole amount in the year of receipt.

Illustration

If Z sold the remainder of the patent rights for £18,000 instead of £15,000, the calculation would be:

			£
1989/90	WDA brought forward		10,500
	Sales proceeds		18,000
			7,500

		£
Balancing charge (restricted to allowances given £2,000 + £2,000 + £1,500)		5,500
Capital profit		2,000

The capital profit will be divided by six and assessed in six equal sums for the years 1989/90 to 1994/95 inclusive.

Where patent royalties are received by the person who created the patent, they are classed as earned income.

5.2 Expenditure incurred after 31st March 1986

5.2.1   General

Expenditure on the acquisition of patent rights incurred after 31st March 1986 is dealt with in a similar way to expenditure on plant and machinery.

5.2.2   Allowances available

There is a writing-down allowance of 25% on the reducing balance in the pool of expenditure incurred after 31st March 1986.   The format of the computation is:

	£
Tax written-down value in pool b/f	x
Add: Expenditure on patent rights in the basis period	x
	x
Less: Disposal proceeds of patent rights disposed of in the period	(x)
	x
WDA at 25%	(x)
c/f	x

Illustration

A bought patent rights for £50,000 on 30th June 1988.   He makes up accounts to 31st December annually.   A is a trader.

		£
1989/90	Year to 31st December 1988	
	Cost of patent	50,000
	WDA - 25%	12,500
	c/f	37,500

In the year to 31st December 1989 A acquired rights to a further patent with 10 years to run, for £12,000.

		£
1990/91	Year to 31st December 1989	
	TWDV b/f	37,500
	Additions	12,000
		49,500
	WDA - 25%	12,375
	c/f	37,125

5.2.3   Sale of a Patent

Where patent rights are sold, the disposal proceeds will be deducted from the pool as in 5.2.2 above.   Under no circumstances can disposal proceeds exceed cost.   Any capital profit is dealt with as in 5.1.3 above.

In the year to 31st December 1990 A sold the rights to the first patent for £14,000 and acquired rights to a further patent with 2 years to run for £6,000.

		£
1991/92	Year to 31st December 1990	
	TWDV b/f	37,125
	Additions	6,000
		43,125
	Disposal proceeds	14,000
		29,125
	WDA - 25%	7,281
	c/f	21,844

A balancing charge will arise if the disposal proceeds of sales exceed the balance in the pool.

There will be a balancing allowance where:

(a)   the disposal proceeds of the remaining patent rights are less than the balance in the pool;

(b)   the life of the last patent remaining in the pool comes to an end and it is not renewed;

(c)   there is the cessation of the trade.

In the year to 31st December 1991 A sold the second patent for £20,000.   The third patent expired on 31st October 1992.

		£
1992/93	Year to 31st December 1991	
	TWDV b/f	21,844
	Disposal proceeds of patent 2 - £20,000, but restricted to	12,000
		9,844
	WDA - 25%	2,461
		7,383
1993/94	Year to 31st December 1992	
	As the last patent has expired there will be a balancing allowance of	7,383

There are restrictions on the cost of the patent qualifying for allowances where the patent has been acquired from a connected person or where it appears that the obtaining of capital allowances is the sole or main purpose of the acquisition.

6.0   SCIENTIFIC RESEARCH

6.1   General

Expenditure on scientific research can consist of capital and revenue expenditure on pure research or contributions to research establishments or universities. Scientific research is defined as activities in the fields of natural or applied science for the extension of knowledge. No allowance is normally given on land acquired after 31st March 1985.

6.2   Allowances available

The whole of the expenditure, whether capital or revenue, is treated as a deduction in the accounting period in which it is made.   Revenue expenditure is deductible as a trade expense; capital expenditure is given as a 100% capital allowance in taxing the trade.

6.3 Sale of an asset

Where the capital asset ceases to belong to the trader, the disposal proceeds, or open market value if more, up to the amount of the original expenditure, are treated as a trading receipt accruing at the time of sale.

7.0   KNOW-HOW

7.1 Expenditure incurred before 1st April 1986

7.1.1.   General

Know-how is defined as any industrial information and techniques of assistance in:

(a)   manufacturing or processing goods or materials;

(b)   working or searching for mineral deposits;

(c)   agricultural, forestry or fishing operations.

7.1.2   Allowances available

A WDA of 1/6th of the cost of the know-how was available. It was given first for the fiscal year for which the accounting period in which it was acquired forms the basis period and for the following five years.

7.2 Expenditure incurred after 31st March 1986

Expenditure incurred after 31st March 1986 is treated in a similar way to that of patent rights except that on a disposal the entire disposal proceeds (not just restricted to cost) are included in the capital allowance computation.

8.0   THE BASIS PERIODS FOR CAPITAL ALLOWANCES

8.1 Normal basis

The basis period determines when the capital allowances are given and against which profits they are available for set-off. It follows, therefore, that the capital allowances basis period is derived from the basis period for adjusted profits under Schedule D Cases I and II. In fact, with the exception of commencements, cessations and changes of accounting date, the basis periods are identical.

If a taxpayer has made his accounts to 31st December 1989, the profit shown by them will be assessed in 1990/91. The basis period for calculating capital allowances deductible in arriving at the net income for 1990/91 will be 1st January 1989 to 31st December 1989, the accounting period. Capital allowances will be calculated after including all new assets acquired during that year and after excluding all assets sold during it.

Where WDA are claimed they will be reduced proportionately if the basis period is less than twelve months in length.

8.2 Commencement

On a commencement there will be an overlap of basis periods. Where there is such an overlap, it will be allocated to the earliest basis period. This will ensure that expenditure will qualify for allowances as early as possible.
Illustration

X commenced trading on 1st January 1989 and made her first acounts to 31st December 1989 and thereafter annually.

The basis periods will be:

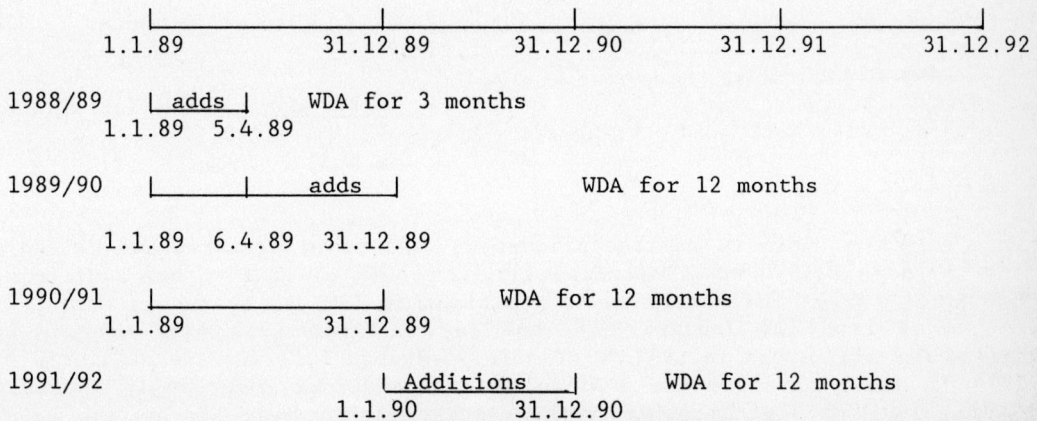

```
        |_____|_____|_____|_____|
      1.1.89          31.12.89         31.12.90         31.12.91         31.12.92

  1988/89   |_adds_|     WDA for 3 months
          1.1.89  5.4.89

  1989/90   |_____|___adds__|                WDA for 12 months

          1.1.89  6.4.89  31.12.89

  1990/91   |_____|                WDA for 12 months
          1.1.89          31.12.89

  1991/92                     |_Additions___|     WDA for 12 months
                            1.1.90       31.12.90
```

Thus in the fiscal year 1988/89, capital allowances will be due on all expenditure between 1st January 1989 and 5th April 1989 and WDA for three months only as the basis period is only three months.

In 1989/90 capital allowances are due on expenditure in the period from 6th April 1989 to 31st December 1989 and as the basis period (ignoring the overlap) is twelve months in length a full WDA will be available.

In 1990/91 a full WDA will be available.

If an election were made under TA 1988,s.62 the basis period would become:

```
 |_____|_____|_____|_____|
1.1.89          31.12.89        31.12.90        31.12.91        31.12.92

1988/89     |_adds_|      WDA for 3 months
          1.1.89  5.4.89

1989/90          |_Additions_|           WDA for 12 months
              6.4.89      5.4.90

1990/91               |_Additions___|            WDA for 12 months
                   6.4.90        5.4.91
                                   |
1991/92          |_____| |  WDA for 12 months
              1.1.90        31.12.90 |
                                   |
1992/93                    |_____| adds_|  WDA for 12 months
                        1.1.91   31.12.91
                              6.4.91
```

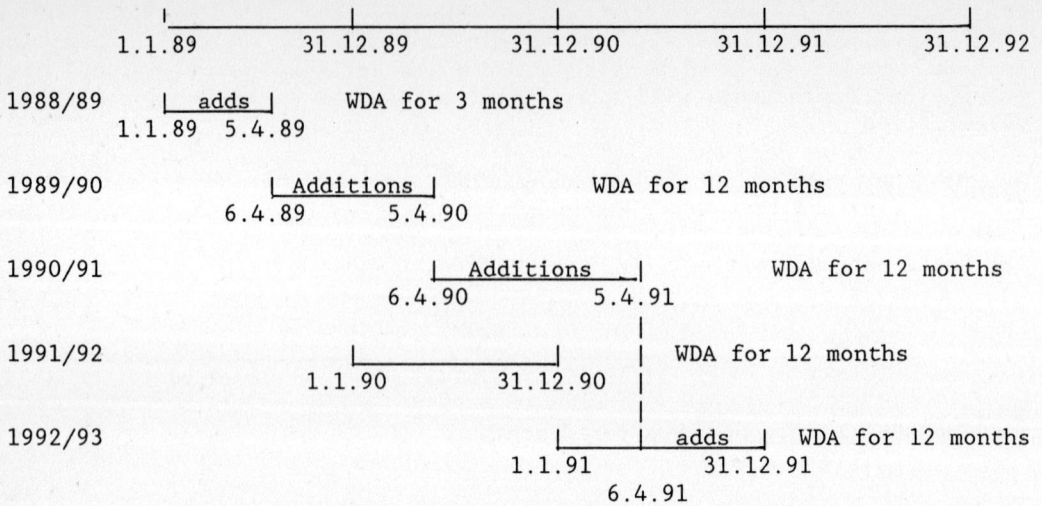

In this case the claim to capital allowances will be accelerated and by the end of the third year 1990/91 allowances will have been claimed on all additions up to 5th April 1991.   There will be no additions in 1991/92 as expenditure in the basis period from 1st January 1990 to 31st December 1990 will already have qualified for allowances in 1989/90 or 1990/91 though full WDA are available.   In 1992/93 capital allowances are available on expenditure incurred in the period 6th April 1991 to 31st December 1991 together with a full WDA on the balance brought forward.

Capital expenditure incurred before the commencement of trading is treated as having been incurred on the first day of trading.

Illustration

R commenced in business on 1st January 1988 and his profits, adjusted for income tax purposes, were:

1st January to 31st May 1988		£ 4,975
Year ended 31st May 1989		£ 7,416
Year ended 31st May 1990		£12,120

The following assets, on which capital allowances were claimed in full, were acquired as shown:

Item	Date of Purchase	Cost £
Plant and machinery	1st January 1988	1,825
Motor car (used 1/4 privately)	28th February 1988	1,200
Plant and machinery	15th June 1988	2,180
Motor car (used entirely for business purposes)	31st December 1988	640
Office furniture	1st June 1989	250
Motor van	31st July 1989	900

You are required to compute the Schedule D Case I assessments for the years 1987/88 to 1989/90 and the capital allowances for those years.

	Normal £	Revised £
The assessments are:		
1987/88 3/5 x £4,975	2,985	
	=====	
1988/89 1st 12 months	9,301	
Actual		8,170
1989/90 1st 12 months reassessed	9,301	
Actual		11,336
	18,602	19,506
	=====	=====

No revision to actual.
   The basis periods will be:

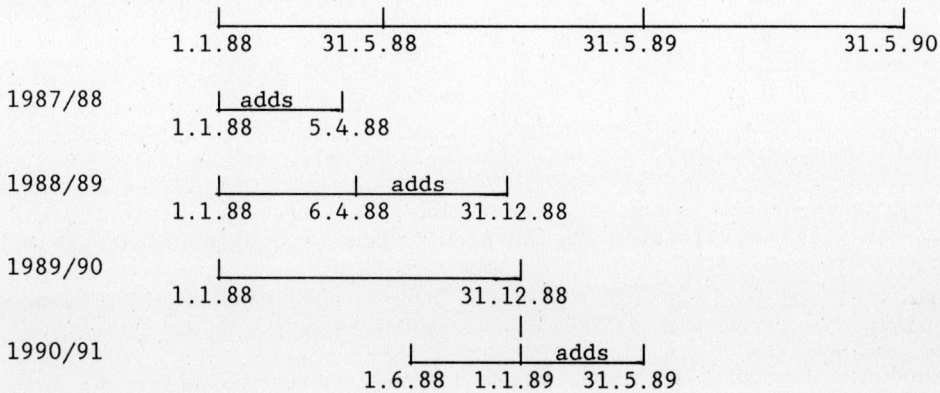

```
        |           |              |             |
      1.1.88     31.5.88        31.5.89       31.5.90
1987/88   |  adds   |
        1.1.88    5.4.88

1988/89   |        |  adds   |
        1.1.88  6.4.88    31.12.88

1989/90   |                 |
        1.1.88            31.12.88
                            |
1990/91              |       |  adds  |
                  1.6.88  1.1.89  31.5.89
```

Capital Allowances:

1987/88 **Additions**	**Pool** General	Cars	**Motor** Car		**Allowances**
	£	£	£		£
1.1.88	1,825				
28.2.88			1,200		
WDA				Private use	
25% x 3/12	114		75	- (1/4)19 = 56	170
	1,711		1,125		170
					====

1988/89   Additions

15.6.88	2,180			
31.12.88 (car)		640		
	3,891		Private use	
WDA 25%	973	160	281 - (1/4)70 = 211	1,344
	2,918	480	844	

1989/90

WDA 25%	729	120	211 - (1/4)53 = 158	1,007
	2,189	360	633	

1990/91

WDA 25%	547	90	158 - (1/4)39 = 119	756
	1,642	270	475	

8.3 Cessation

In the case of a taxpayer who ceases to trade, there will be a gap between basis periods. This gap will be allocated to the penultimate or prepenultimate years as appropriate.

Illustration

Y makes up accounts to 30th September annually and ceases to trade on 30th September 1989. Assuming a normal basis the basis periods would be:

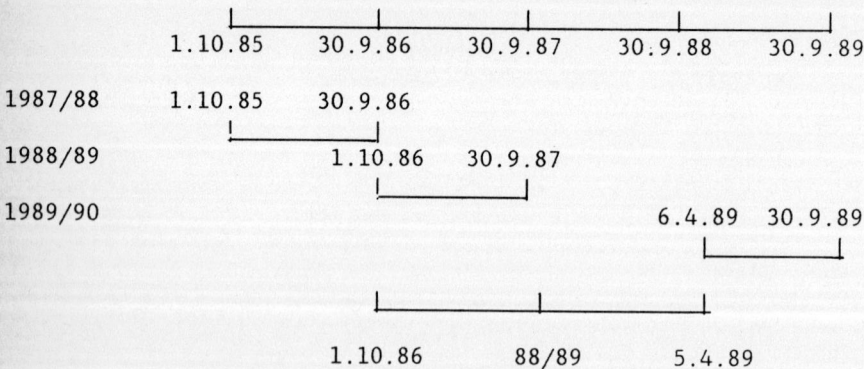

```
        |_____|_____|_____|_____|
      1.10.85    30.9.86    30.9.87    30.9.88    30.9.89

1987/88   1.10.85    30.9.86
          |_____|
1988/89              1.10.86    30.9.87
                     |_____|
1989/90                                   6.4.89   30.9.89
                                          |_____|

                     |_____|_____|
                   1.10.86      88/89      5.4.89
```

Applying this rule, the above basis periods become:

1987/88	1.10.85	to	30.9.86
1988/89	1.10.86	to	5.4.89
1989/90	6. 4.89	to	30.9.89

and any asset purchased between 1st October 1986 and 5th April 1989 will be included before calculating 1988/89 allowances. Although the basis period is two-and-a-half years, only twelve months WDA is given.

If adjustment under s.63 is made, the assessment basis periods are:

1986/87	1.10.84	to	30.9.85
1987/88	1.10.85	to	5.4.88
1988/89	6. 4.88	to	5.4.89
1989/90	6. 4.89	to	30.9.89

Expressed diagrammatically as follows:

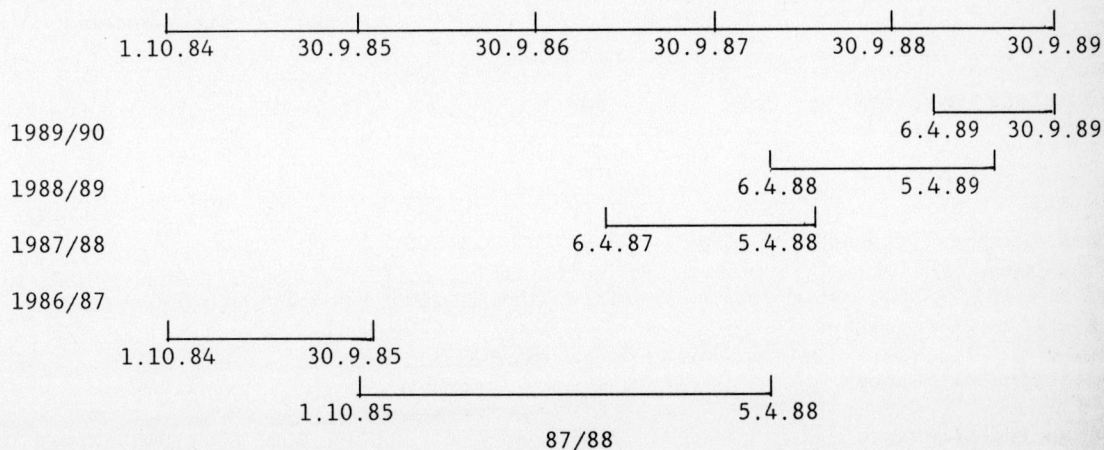

```
     |_____|_____|_____|_____|_____|
  1.10.84   30.9.85  30.9.86  30.9.87  30.9.88  30.9.89

1989/90                                      |_____|
                                           6.4.89  30.9.89

1988/89                               |_____|
                                    6.4.88           5.4.89

1987/88                        |_____|
                             6.4.87           5.4.88

1986/87
               |_____|
            1.10.84          30.9.85
               |_____|
            1.10.85                            5.4.88
                              87/88
```

Where the gap arises because of a cessation, the somewhat complicated position can be expressed as follows:

(a) if adjustment is **not** made under s.63 for actual, the gap forms the end of the basis period for the penultimate year of assessment;

(b) if adjustment is made under s.63 for actual, the gap forms the beginning of the prepenultimate year of assessment.

On a cessation the Revenue decide whether or not to revise the assessments without taking into account the effect of capital allowances.

When a trader ceases, there will normally be no WDA available for the last fiscal year. At the end of the last period of trading all plant and machinery not sold must be valued and an overall balancing charge or allowance calculated. If demolition costs are incurred in removing machinery, they are added to the balance in the pool and decrease the amount of the balancing charge or increase the balancing allowance. Items taken over by the trader will be included at their proper market value.

Illustration

D ceases trading. At the beginning of the final period she has:

Balance in pool b/f	£3,000
Motor car (no private use)	£2,000

In the final period she buys a machine, which she uses in her trade, for £500; she sells most of the plant for £1,500. At the end of the accounting period the value of the remaining plant is £600 and D takes over the car at £1. Its proper market value is £ 1,000. The cost of demolishing part of the plant was £100.

	£	Pool £	Motor Car £	Total Allowances £
WDV b/f		3,000	2,000	
Additions: Machine	500			
Demolition costs	100			
	___	600		
		_____		
		3,600		
Less: Disposal proceeds of plant		1,500		
		_____		
		2,100		
Valuation of remainder		600	1,000	
		_____		
Balancing allowance		1,500		1,500
		=====		
Balancing allowance			1,000	1,000
			=====	
Total allowances				2,500
				=====

8.4   Change of accounting date

On a change of accounting date the rules for ascertaining the basis periods are:

(a) if there is an overlap, the common period always falls into the earliest basis period;

(b) if there is a gap, the missing period always falls into the later basis period.

Illustration

O decided to change his accounting date; his accounting periods are:

Year ended	30.9.1988
Year ended	30.9.1989
9 months to	30.6.1990

This is similar to an earlier illustration.

The basis periods will be:

        1991/92   1. 7.1989 - 30.6.1990
        1990/91   1.10.1988 - 30.9.1989
        1989/90   1.10.1987 - 30.9.1988

Expressed diagrammatically as:

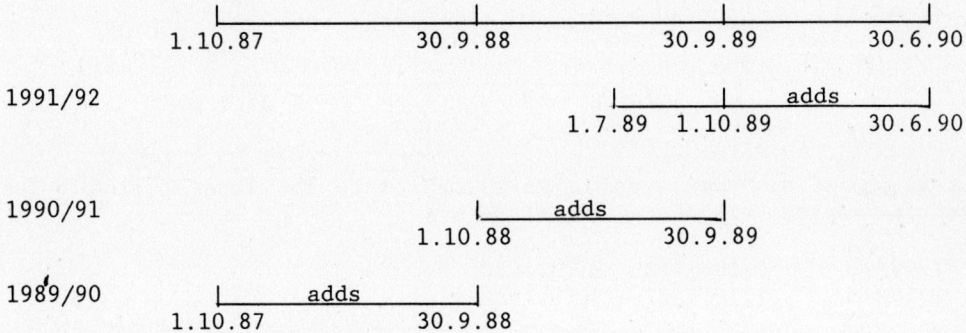

```
         |_____|_____|_____|
       1.10.87           30.9.88           30.9.89   30.6.90

1991/92                                  |_____|____adds____|
                                       1.7.89 1.10.89      30.6.90


1990/91                            |_____adds_____|
                                 1.10.88          30.9.89

1989/90      |_____adds_____|
           1.10.87           30.9.88
```

WDA for twelve months throughout.

As can be seen, the period 1st July 1989 to 30th September 1989 is common to the
years 1990/91 and 1991/92. It will therefore be allocated to the earliest basis
period. The basis periods for capital allowances will be:

        1991/92   1.10.1989 - 30.6.1990
        1990/91   1.10.1988 - 30.9.1989
        1989/90   1.10.1987 - 30.9.1988

Illustration

B makes up accounts as under:

        Year ended   30.9.1988
        Year ended   30.9.1989
        6 months ended   31.3.1990

Again this is similar to an earlier illustration.

The basis periods would be:

        1990/91   1. 4.1989 - 31.3.1990
        1989/90   1.10.1987 - 30.9.1988

Expressed diagrammatically as:

```
            |_____|_____|_____|
          1.10.87              30.9.88               30.9.89    31.3.90
```

```
1990/91                                          |_____|
                                              1.4.89                        31.3.90
```

```
1989/90            |_____|
                 1.10.87                  30.9.88
```

```
                                  |_____|
                                1.10.88                                  31.3.90
```

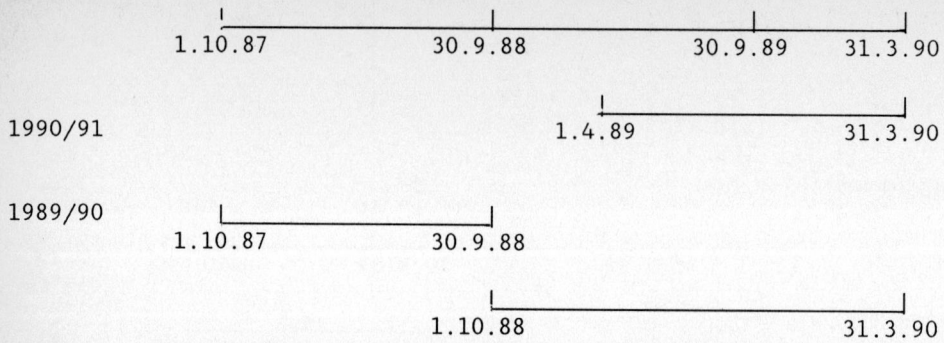

As there is a gap of six months, this is allocated to the later period.   The
basis periods for capital allowances are therefore:

        1990/91   1.10.1988 - 31.3.1990
        1989/90   1.10.1987 - 30.9.1988

WDA is for twelve months throughout.

CHAPTER SIX

Losses

1.0 GENERAL

A trading loss can be relieved in four main ways:

(a) by carry forward and offset against future trading profits - TA 1988,s.385;

(b) by offset against total income liable to income tax of the fiscal year in which the loss was incurred, and if claimed, the following year - TA 1988,s.380;

(c) by offset against income received from a limited company when the business producing the loss has been incorporated - TA 1988,s.386;

(d) by carry back where the loss arises on a commencement or on a cessation - TA 1988,s.381, TA 1988,s.388.

2.0 CARRY FORWARD (TA 1988,s.385)

A trading loss can be carried forward and offset against the first **available profits** of the same trade, profession or vocation carried on by the same owner without time limit. A formal claim to obtain relief under this section must be made within six years of the end of the year of assessment for which relief is claimed.

Illustration

A had the following results:

	Year ended 30.6.1988	Loss	£6,000
	Year ended 30.6.1989	Profit	£4,000
	Year ended 30.6.1990	Profit	£1,000

			£
1989/90	Year ended 30.6.88 (Loss c/f £6,000)	DI	Nil
1990/91	Year ended 30.6.89	DI	4,000
	Less: s.385 relief		(4,000)
			NIL

			£
	(Loss c/f £2,000)		
1991/92	Year ended 30.6.90	DI	1,000
	Less: s.385 relief		(1,000)
	(Loss c/f £1,000)		NIL

It is important to appreciate that once a claim is made under s.385 the loss
must be offset against the earliest available future trading profit, even if
this results in a possible loss of personal allowances.

3.0 OFFSET AGAINST OTHER INCOME - TA 1988,s.380

3.1 General - the concessional basis

Instead of carrying a loss forward, a taxpayer may elect to offset it against
other income of the fiscal year in which it was incurred and the next following
fiscal year. Normally, for s.380 the year 'in which the loss was incurred' will
be the fiscal year in which the accounting period producing the loss ends. Thus
if B makes a trading loss in the year ended 31st December 1989 it will be
incurred in 1989/90 and s.380 relief may be claimed in 1989/90 and 1990/91. A
s.380 claim is voluntary and can be made for the first year, the first and second
years, or the second year. The time limit for making the claim is two years from
the end of the year of assessment for which relief is claimed, thus in the above,
the time limits would be:

1989/90	-	5th April 1992
1990/91	-	5th April 1993

The claim against other income under s.380 is for **two years only**; any unrelieved
losses go forward under s.385.

Illustration

B makes up accounts to 30th June, each year. She provides you with the following
information; she has no other income.

Year ended 30.6.1988	Profit	£ 6,000
Year ended 30.6.1989	Loss	£10,000
Year ended 30.6.1990	Profit	£ 5,000

First year of s.380 claim - 1989/90

	£	£
1989/90		
Sch. D Case I		
Year ended 30.6.1988		6,000
Sch. D Loss		
Year ended 30.6.1989	(10,000)	
s.380 claim	6,000	(6,000)
	(4,000)	NIL

		£		£
1990/91				
Sch. D Case I				
Year ended 30.6.1989				NIL
(No s.380 claim)				======

		£		£
1991/92				
Sch. D Case I				
Year ended 30.6.1990				5,000
s.385		4,000		(4,000)
		-		1,000
		======		======

3.2 Order of set-off

Where a claim is made under s.380 to offset the trading loss against other
income, the offset is made in the following order:

(a)   against the loss-maker's earned income   )
)
(b)   against the loss-maker's unearned income   )

          then

(c)   against the spouse's earned income   )
)
(d)   against the spouse's unearned income   )

The claim is made against the whole of the loss-maker's earned and unearned
income then against the whole of the spouse's earned and unearned income.
However, a claim can be made which excludes the whole of the spouse's income.
This is to avoid the waste of personal allowances, which cannot be carried
forward, or transferred to another taxpayer.

Illustration

C advises you of the following income:

Trading profit (loss):

Year ended 31.3.1989	£ 6,000
31.3.1990	£(15,000)

Other income:

Self - unearned	£1,000 pa
Wife - earned	£1,600 pa
- unearned	£4,500 pa

Personal allowances are £6,200 per annum.

---

(1)   Assuming the claim does not exclude the wife's income:

	£	£
1989/90		
Mr C		
Schedule D Case I		
Year to 31.3.1989	6,000	
Unearned income	1,000	
	‾‾‾‾‾	7,000
Mrs C		
Earned income	1,600	
Unearned income	4,500	
	‾‾‾‾‾	6,100
		13,100
Loss - Year ended 31.3.1990	(15,000)	
s.380 relief	13,100	
	‾‾‾‾‾	(13,100)
		‾‾‾‾‾
		-
		═══════

Personal allowances lost

	£	£
1990/91		
Mr C		
Schedule D Case I		
Year to 31.3.1990	NIL	
Unearned income	1,000	
	‾‾‾‾‾	1,000
Mrs C		
Earned income	1,600	
Unearned income	4,500	
	‾‾‾‾‾	6,100
		‾‾‾‾‾
		7,100
s.380 relief - balance		(1,900)
		‾‾‾‾‾
		5,200
Less: Personal allowances		6,200
		‾‾‾‾‾
		-
		═════

(2)   Assuming wife's income excluded from claim:

	£	£
1989/90		
Mr C		
Schedule D Case I		
Year to 31.3.1989	6,000	
Unearned income	1,000	
	‾‾‾‾‾	7,000

	£	£
Loss - year ended 31.3.1990	(15,000)	
s.380 relief	7,000	
	———	(7,000)
	(8,000)	———
	=====	-
Mrs C		
Earned income	1,600	
Unearned income	4,500	
	———	6,100
		———
		6,100
Less: Personal allowances		6,200
		———
		-
		=====

	£	£
1990/91		
Mr C		
Schedule D Case I		
Year to 31.3.1990	Nil	
Unearned income	1,000	
	———	1,000
Less: s.380 relief		(1,000)
		———
		-
Mrs C		
Earned income	1,600	
Unearned income	4,500	
	———	6,100
		———
		6,100
Less: Personal allowances		6,200
		———
		-
		=====

Balance of loss carried forward to be relieved under s.385 of (£15,000 - £7,000 - £1,000) = £7,000.

Thus by excluding the spouse's income from the claim and making the maximum use of personal allowances the same result is obtained in both cases for the years 1989/90 and 1990/91 but there is still a balance of loss carried forward for future relief.

A working wife is entitled to a wife's earned income relief (WEIR) of the lower of:

(a) her earned income, or

(b) £2,785.

If the husband makes an s.380 claim and extends it to the wife's income it will
be offset against her earned income first and this may reduce the entitlement to
WEIR.

Illustration

D has the following income for 1989/90:

	£
Self:	
Trading Profits - year to 31.12.88	5,360
Wife:	
Salary	2,660
Rents	4,800

There is a loss of £6,700 for the year to 31st December 1989.

Personal allowances are:

Married	£4,375
WEIR	£2,785

If the loss claim is extended to the total income:

		D Earned Income	Mrs D Earned Income	Unearned Income
	£	£	£	£
Schedule DI -				
Year ended 31.12.88		5,360		
Salary			2,660	
Rents				4,800
Loss - Year ended 31.12.89	(6,700)			
s.380 relief	6,700	(5,360)	(1,340)	
		NIL	1,320	4,800

                                   |_____|

                                   6,120

Personal allowances:		
Married	4,375	
WEIR restricted to	1,320	
		5,695
Taxable		425

If the loss claim is restricted to the husband's income:

	£	£	£	£
Schedule DI		5,360		
Salary			2,660	
Rents				4,800
		5,360	2,660	4,800
Loss as before	(6,700)			
s.380 relief	5,360	(5,360)		
Loss c/f	(1,340)	Nil		7,460

Personal allowances:		
Married	4,375	
WEIR	2,660	
		7,035
Taxable		425

Thus by utilising the WEIR further losses are available for future relief.

It is vitally important to appreciate that the claim is against the **whole** of the loss-maker's earned **and** unearned income and then (if appropriate) the spouse's earned **and** unearned income. In particular it is **not** possible to claim just enough relief to utilise the whole of the personal allowances.

3.3 Successive losses

Where losses are sustained in successive years, the balance of any loss not relieved under s.380 in the first year will be relieved in the second year in priority to the loss of that second year. This will enable relief for the loss of the second year to qualify for s.380 relief in the subsequent year of assessment.

Illustration

E has the following income:

        Trading results - Year ended 31.12.88 - £ 2,000   profit
                                 31.12.89 - £(14,000)   loss
                                 31.12.90 - £ (3,000)   loss
                                 31.12.91 - £ 5,000   profit

She has investment income of £3,000 per annum.

Loss relief is to be claimed as early as possible.

	£	£
1989/90		
DI - Year to 31.12.88		2,000
Investment income		3,000
		5,000
Loss - Year to 31.12.89	(14,000)	
s.380 relief	5,000	(5,000)
	(9,000)	Nil
1990/91		
DI - Year to 31.12.89		Nil
Investment income		3,000
		3,000
s.380 relief	3,000	(3,000)
		Nil
c/f s.385	(6,000)	
1991/92		
DI - Year to 31.12.90		Nil
Investment income		3,000
		3,000
Loss - Year to 31.12.90	(3,000)	
s.380 relief	3,000	(3,000)
		Nil
1992/93		
DI - Year to 31.12.91		5,000
s.385 relief		(5,000)
		Nil
Investment Income		3,000
		3,000

In the year 1990/91 it was possible to claim s.380 relief for both losses:

	1989/90	1990/91	1991/92
Year to 31.12.89	1st year	2nd year	
Year to 31.12.90		1st year	2nd year

Priority has to be given for the second year claim of the 1989 loss.

If, however, the investment income of 1990/91 had been £15,000, relief for both losses would have been available:

1990/91	£	£
DI		Nil
Investment Income		15,000
		————
		15,000
s.380 relief:		
Loss - Year to 31.12.89	(9,000)	
Year to 31.12.90	(3,000)	
	————	(12,000)
		————
		3,000
		======

3.4 The deduction of charges

Charges on income are deducted before giving loss relief. TA 1988,s.835 gives the taxpayer almost complete freedom to deduct charges from income in the most beneficial way.

3.5 The utilisation of capital allowances

Capital Allowances - TA 1988,s.383

TA 1988,s.383 provides that capital allowances may be used to augment a loss or to convert a profit into a loss. The capital allowances used are those relating to the basis period which produced the loss. Thus, if a loss was incurred for the year ended 30th September 1989 it could be augmented by the capital allowances for 1990/91 - based on the assets owned at the end of the year to 30th September 1989.

Illustration

E had alternatively (a) a trading loss of £400 or (b) a trading profit of £400 for the year to 31st December 1989. The capital allowance computation for 1990/91 showed allowances of £1,000.

	(a)	(b)
	£	£
Trading loss - year ended 31.12.1989	400	
Schedule D Case I assessment 1990/91		400
Capital allowances	1,000	1,000
	————	————
Loss relief available on	(1,400)	(600)
	=====	=====

In both cases the first year for loss relief under s.380 will be 1989/90.

If the option to augment the loss or to turn a profit into a loss is not exercised, the capital allowances will be carried forward.

Illustration

F is a bachelor. He gives you the following details regarding his trading
income; he has no other income.

Year ended 31.12.1988	Profit	£4,000
Year ended 31.12.1989	Loss	£3,000
Year ended 31.12.1990	Profit	£6,000

Capital allowances:

1989/90	£1,900
1990/91	£1,500
1991/92	£1,000

He wishes to claim relief under s.380.

1989/90	£		£
Year ended 31.12.1988			
Schedule D Case I			4,000
Less: Capital allowances			1,900
			2,100
Trading loss - year ended 31.12.89	(3,000)		
Add: Capital allowances 1990/91	(1,500)		
	(4,500)		
s.380 relief	2,100		(2,100)
			NIL
	(2,400)		

1990/91			
Year ended 31.12.1989			
Schedule D Case I			NIL

1991/92			
Year ended 31.12.1990			
Schedule D Case I			6,000
Less: Capital allowances 1991/92			1,000
			5,000
Less: s.385 loss brought forward		2,400	(2,400)
			2,600

In certain cases, it may be beneficial to restrict a claim to capital allowances
to obtain maximum loss relief.

Illustration

G, a married man, has income in 1989/90 of £10,500. For the year ended 31st December 1989 he makes a trading loss of £4,200. The written-down value of plant and machinery at 5th April 1990 was £13,200 and in the year to 31st December 1989 he bought plant costing £12,000.

1989/90	£	£	£
Income			10,500
Loss - Year to 31.12.89		(4,200)	
Capital allowances 1990/91			
b/f	13,200		
Additions	12,000		
	25,200		
WDA - 25%	6,300	(6,300)	(10,500)
			-
c/f	18,900		

Personal allowances £4,375 lost.

To ensure no loss of personal allowances, the claim to capital allowances should be restricted to:

1989/90	£	£	£
Income			10,500
Loss - Year to 31.12.89		(4,200)	
Capital allowances 1990/91			
b/f	13,200		
Additions	12,000		
	25,200		
WDA restricted to	1,925	(1,925)	6,125
c/f	23,275		4,375
PA			4,375
			NIL

3.6 Restrictions on claiming relief

Relief under s.380 will not be given where:

(a)   the trade, profession or vocation was not being carried on on a commercial basis and with a view to the realisation of profit - TA 1988, s.384;

(b)   in the case of farmers and market gardeners, if in the five preceding years of assessment, trading losses were incurred. Section 380 relief may, however, be given in the sixth year, if the Revenue are satisfied that the farming etc. activities in that year are being carried on in a way which might reasonably be expected to produce profits in the future - TA 1988,s.397.

Relief for the loss will therefore be restricted to a carry-forward under s.385.

3.7 Section 380 relief - the strict basis

Up to this stage, the method of allocating losses for relief under s.380 has been on the concessional basis. This is commonly used as a simple effective way of allocating the loss. In strictness, however, the loss available for relief should be calculated by splitting the taxpayer's results to obtain the actual loss of the actual fiscal year. This will often involve the amalgamation of profits and losses.

Illustration

L made up accounts to 30th June annually; his results were:

Year ended 30th June 1988	Profit	£6,000
Year ended 30th June 1989	Profit	£5,000
Year ended 30th June 1990	Loss	£8,000
Year ended 30th June 1991	Profit	£2,000

The amount available for s.380 relief in the fiscal year 1989/90 will be:

		£	
6.4.1989 - 30.6.1989 - 3/12 x £5,000		1,250	P
1.7.1989 - 5.4.1990 - 9/12 x £8,000		(6,000)	L
		(4,750)	

This is then available for relief against the assessment for 1989/90

	£
1989/90 Schedule D Case I - Year to 30.6.88	6,000
s.380 relief	(4,750)
	1,250

For the year 1990/91 the amount available for relief will be:

		£	
6.4.1990 - 30.6.1990 - 3/12 x £8,000		(2,000)	L
1.7.1990 - 5.4.1991 - 9/12 x £2,000		1,500	P
		(500)	

This can then be relieved:

	£
1990/91 Schedule D Case I - Year to 30.6.89	5,000
s.380 relief	(500)
	4,500

It is important to appreciate that the amalgamation of profits and losses to find the net losses of the various fiscal years is a memorandum calculation only and does not mean that part of the loss is unrelieved. To the extent that loss relief is not available under s.380 it will be available under s.385. Thus:

	£	£
Loss - Year ended 30.6.90		(8,000)
Available - s.380 1989/90	4,750	
1990/91	500	
		5,250
Available for carry forward - s.385		(2,750)

The strict basis will be applied:

(a)   in the commencing three fiscal years of the business (and normally in following years until a profit is made);

(b)   in the ultimate year;

(c)   when the taxpayer wishes to use it. This will normally be so, where the taxpayer wishes to relieve the loss in an earlier fiscal year than would be available under the concessionary basis.

4.0   RELIEF FOR TAXED PAYMENTS (TA 1988, s.387)

When a taxpayer pays a charge under deduction of tax which is made wholly and exclusively for the purposes of a trade and, because of an insufficiency of income, becomes liable to an assessment under s.350 (see page 6.24), the amount of that assessment can be carried forward under s.387 and relieved against future trading profits in subsequent years.

Illustration

G advises you of the following results:

Trading results	£
Year to 31.12.1988	400
Year to 31.12.1989	200
Schedule A income assessable	
1989/90 and 1990/91	300

She pays patent royalties under deduction of tax of £1,000 (gross) for the fiscal year 1989/90.

```
            1989/90                                    £
            Schedule D Case I                         400
            Schedule A                                300
            s.350 assessment (Note 1)                 300   c/f s.387 £300
                                                    1,000


                                                    1,000
            Less: Patent royalties                 (1,000)

            Total income                              -
                                                    =====


            1990/91
            Schedule D Case I                         200
            s.387 relief                              200   c/f s.387 £100

                                                       -
            Schedule A                                300

            Total income                              300
                                                    =====
```

Note   -   As the patent royalties exceed income liable to tax by £300 (£400 +
               £300 - £1,000), the s.350 assessment will be in the sum of £300.

5.0   LOSSES ON A COMMENCEMENT

5.1   A loss in the first accounting period followed by a profit in the second - the rule in IRC v. SCOTT-ADAMSON (1932)

When this situation occurs and the first accounting period is less than twelve
months, it will be necessary to amalgamate together profits and losses to find
the assessments. When the profits exceed the losses the net profit will be
assessed. When the losses exceed the profits the assessment will be nil. Each
time that the loss is amalgamated with a profit, that part of the loss is deemed
to have been used.

Illustration

M commenced trading on 1st January 1989 and makes up accounts to 30th September
annually. His results adjusted for tax purposes were:

```
                                                           £          £
9 months to   30.9.1989       £1,800          Loss
Year ended    30.9.1990       £2,000          Profit

1988/89       1.1.1989 -  5.4.1989 :  3/9 x £1,800  Loss
                                                               NIL
1989/90       1.1.1989 - 31.12.1989:                        =====

              1. 1.1989 - 30. 9.1989          Loss      (1,800)
              1.10.1989 - 31.12.1989
                 Profit 3/12 x £2,000                      500      NIL
                                                        ------    =====
```

			£	£
1990/91	1.1.1989 - 31.12.1989 : as before			
	1. 1.1989 - 30. 9.1989	Loss	(1,800)	
	1.10.1989 - 31.12.1989			
	Profit 3/12 x £2,000		500	NIL
1991/92	Year to 30.9.1990		2,000	
	Less: Loss b/f not yet utilised			
	£(1,800 - 500 - 500)		(800)	
				1,200

5.2 A profit in the first accounting perid followed by a loss in the second

In this case it will again be necessary to amalgamate profits and losses if the first accounting period is less than twelve months. The difference between this and the **Scott-Adamson** principle is that, provided that the loss used in aggregation is that of the same period of time, then no matter how many times it is aggregated with a profit to find an assessment, it is only treated as having been used once.

Illustration

N commenced to trade on 1st January 1989; adjusted results are:

9 months to 30.9.1989	Profit	£2,400
12 months to 30 9.1990	Loss	£1,800
12 months to 30.9.1991	Profit	£1,600

			£	£
1988/89				
1.1.1989 -	5.4.1989		Profit	800
1989/90				
1.1.1989 -	**31.12.1989**			
1.1.1989 -	30.9.1989	Profit	2,400	
1.10.1989 -	31.12.1989			
Loss 3/12 x £1,800			(450)	
				1,950
1990/91				
1.1.1989 -	31.12.1989			
1.1.1989 -	30.9.1989	Profit	2,400	
1.10.1989 -	31.12.1989			
Loss 3/12 x £1,800			(450)	
				1,950
1991/92				
12 months to 30.9.1990				NIL

		£	£
1992/93			
12 months to 30.9.1991	Profit	1,600	
Loss brought forward		(1,350)	
		─────	250
			══════

The loss for the year to 30th September 1990 is divided into two periods:

$$
\begin{array}{llll}
1.10.1989 & - \quad 31.12.1989 & - \quad 3/12 \times £1,800 \ = & £ \ \ 450 \\
1.1.1990 & - \quad 30.9.1990 & - \quad 9/12 \times £1,800 \ = & £1,350
\end{array}
$$

The period 1st January 1990 - 30th September 1990 has not been used in aggregation and can therefore be carried forward intact. The fact that the period 1st October 1989 to 31st December 1989 has been used twice is immaterial.

As an alternative to the normal basis of assessment, revision to actual may be claimed.

		£	£	
1988/89				
as before			800	Profit
				══════
1989/90				
6.4.1989 - 30.9.1989				
6/9 x £2,400	Profit	1,600		
1.10.1989 - 5.4.1990				
6/12 x £1,800	Loss	(900)	700	Profit
				══════
1990/91				
6.4.1990 - 30.9.1990				
6/12 x £1,800	Loss	(900)		
1.10.1990 - 5.4.1991				
6/12 x £1,600	Profit	800		NIL
		─────		══════
1991/92				
Year to 30.9.1990				NIL
				══════
1992/93				
Year to 30.9.1991		1,600		
Loss not used in aggregation				
b/f £(1,800 - 900 - 800)		(100)		
		─────		1,500
				══════

The comparative position will therefore be:

	Normal basis £	Revised basis £
1988/89	800	800
1989/90	1,950	700
1990/91	1,950	-
1991/92	-	-
1992/93	250	1,500
	4,950	3,000

So far the loss has been relieved in aggregation, i.e. in finding the assessment, with any unused loss being carried forward under s.385 for offset against future trading profits. The taxpayer, if he wishes may also claim relief under TA 1988, s.380 or under TA 1988,s.381 for the loss. In both cases, the amount that will qualify for relief will be calculated on the strict basis. Where a claim has been made in this way then the amount of loss used will reduce the loss available for aggregation in later fiscal years.

Illustration

The results of M are:

| 9 months to 30.9.1989 | £1,800 | Loss |
| 12 months to 30.9.1990 | £2,000 | Profit |

M claims relief under s.380; he has abundant other income.

			£	£
1988/89	1.1.1989 - 5.4.1989 3/9 x £1,800 = £(600) available on a strict basis for s.380 relief			NIL

(£600 used against other income).

1989/90	1.1.1989 - 31.12.1989: 1.1.1989 - 30. 9.1989 Less: relieved under s.380	Loss	(1,800) 600	
			(1,200)	
	1.10.1989 - 31.12.1989 3/12 x £2,000		500	NIL

	s.380 claim on strict basis: 6.4.1989 - 5.4.1990 6.4.1989 - 30.9.1989 6/9 x £1,800	Loss	(1,200)	
	1.10.1989 - 5.4.1990 6/12 x £2,000	Profit	1,000	
	s.380 claim		(200)	

			£	£
1990/91	As before			
	1. 1.1989 - 31.12.1989:			
	1. 1.1989 - 30. 9.1989	Loss	(1,200)	
	1.10.1989 - 31.12.1989			
	3/12 x £2,000		500	
			‾‾‾‾‾	NIL
				═════

		£	
No s.380 relief available		£	
Loss carried forward			1,800
Less: 1988/89 s.380		600	
1989/90 aggregation		500	
1989/90 s.380		200	
1990/91 aggregation		500	
		‾‾‾	1,800
			‾‾‾‾‾
			NIL
			═════

1991/92	Year ended 30.9.1990	2,000
		‾‾‾‾‾
		2,000
		═════

In this last example, the amount of loss and the relief obtained were identical.
It may be possible to obtain more relief than the amount of loss.

Illustration

N commenced to trade on 1st May 1989 and made up accounts as follows:

8 months to 31.12.1989	£(2,000)	Loss
Year to 31.12.1990	£ 3,600	

		£	£
1989/90			
1.5.1989 to 5. 4.1990			
8 months to 31.12.1989		(2,000)	
3 months to 5. 4.1990			
3/12 x £3,600		900	
		‾‾‾‾‾	NIL
			═════

		£	£
1990/91			
1.5.1989 to 30. 4.1990			
8 months to 31.12.1989		(2,000)	
4 months to 30. 4.1990			
4/12 x £3,600		1,200	
		‾‾‾‾‾	NIL
			═════

1991/92
    Year to 31.12.1990   3,600
    Loss c/f   (2,000)
    Less: Used in aggregation: £
                1989/90   900
                1990/91   1,200
                               _____
                                                          2,100
                                                         _____   NIL
                                                                        _____
                                                                         3,600
                                                                        ======

The amount of loss claimed under s.380 can be augmented by capital allowances.

It can be seen that problems in aggregation have been caused by a combination of profits and losses and a first accounting period of less than twelve months in duration. It follows that there will be no difficulties:

(a) if the first accounting period is twelve months or more in length; or

(b) if both the first and second accounting periods produce losses.

6.0   FURTHER RELIEF FOR LOSSES IN EARLY YEARS OF TRADE (TA 1988, s.381)

An individual who incurs a loss in his trade, profession or vocation in the year of assessment in which the trade etc. commenced or in any of the three succeeding years of assessment, may claim to carry the loss backwards to set against his income for the three years of assessment prior to that in which the loss was incurred. The set off is on a FIFO basis, i.e. relieving the earliest year first. As the loss is for a year of assessment it is calculated in the same way as under s.380 strict. A claim under s.380 is a single claim so that:

(a) the loss must be offset against the available income of <u>all</u> the three preceding fiscal years; and

(b) the treatment of a spouse's income must be the same for each of those years.

Any relief available under s.380 or s.385 remains available, relief under s.381 being an alternative. It is not possible to have relief for the same loss more than once. The claim for relief under s.381 must be made within two years of the end of the year of assessment in which the loss arose. For a claim to be valid the trade must have been conducted on a commercial basis and with a reasonable expectation of profit.

To prevent loss relief being manufactured by transferring trades between spouses, it is provided that no relief can be given for any loss incurred later than the third year of assessment following that in which the first spouse started to trade.

As mentioned above s.381 is an alternative claim to s.380 or s.385. The taxpayer can claim whichever relief he wishes and if the loss exceeds relief under a given loss-relieving section, then the remainder is available for relief under another; partial claims however cannot be made - **Butt v. Haxby (1983)**.

Illustration

P, who was an employee of a company manufacturing breakfast cereals, resigned on 31st May 1990, to become a freelance cornflake salesman. His income has been as follows:

		£
Salary	1987/88	6,000
	1988/89	7,000
	1989/90	7,500
	2 months to 31.5.90	3,000

Adjusted Schedule D Case I Loss	
Year to 31.5.91	(6,000)
Year to 31.5.92	(12,000)

Assessment - normal basis

1990/91	1.6.90 - 5.4.91	NIL
1991/92	1.6.90 - 31.5.91	NIL
1992/93	Year to 31.5.91	NIL
1993/94	Year to 31.5.92	NIL

Loss available for relief calculated on the strict basis:

		£
1990/91	1.6.90 - 5.4.91	
	10/12 x £(6,000)	(5,000)
1991/92	6.4.91 - 5.4.92	
	2/12 x £(6,000)	(1,000)
	10/12 x £(12,000)	(10,000)
		(11,000)

There will presumably be no advantage in claiming s.380 relief in 1990/91 as personal allowances will cover the other income.

Assuming s.381 relief is claimed the position will become:

	Income	s.381 Relief 1990/91	s.381 Relief 1991/92	Taxable
	£	£	£	£
1987/88	6,000	5,000	-	1,000
1988/89	7,000	-	7,000	-
1989/90	7,500	-	4,000	3,500
1990/91	3,000	-	-	1,000
		5,000	11,000	

As with relief under s.380 it is possible to augment or create losses by deduction of capital allowances.

7.0 THE CARRY FORWARD OF A LOSS WHERE A BUSINESS IS TRANSFERRED TO A LIMITED COMPANY (TA 1988,s.386)

When a sole trader or partnership transfers a business to a limited company there will be a cessation. However, provided:

(a) the business was transferred mainly for shares in the company, and

(b) the business transferred continues to be carried on by the company,

any trading losses unrelieved may be carried forward and offset against income received from the company during any fiscal year throughout which the shares continue to be held by the individual. The losses are normally offset in the following order:

(a) against earned income i.e. directors' salaries and fees, then

(b) against other income received from the company such as dividends.

Revenue practice is to give relief when at least 80% of the shares allotted to the transferor are retained by the claimant.

Relief is expressed to be in accordance with s.385 which will mean offset against the first available income received from the company. Relief must be claimed within six years of the end of the relevant year of assessment.

Illustration

K decides to incorporate her business on 31st March 1990 and transfers her business on that day to K Ltd. At the time of transfer there were unrelieved losses of £2,400. Income received from the company in the year 1990-91 consisted of:

Director's fees	£1,800	
Dividends (net)	£ 750	
Relief will be given as under:	£	£
1990/91		
Schedule E - Director's fees	1,800	
s.386 relief	(1,800)	
	――――	-
Dividends received	750	
Tax credit 25/75	250	
	――――	
	1,000	
s.386 relief - balance	(600)	
		400
		――――
		400
		===

8.0 TERMINAL LOSSES (TA 1988,s.388)

8.1 General

On the permanent discontinuance of any trade, profession or vocation, any loss incurred in the twelve months preceding discontinuance, may (so far as it is unrelieved) be carried back and offset against adjusted trading profits of the three preceding years of assessment on a LIFO basis. It is not necessary to take terminal loss relief if another form of relief can be claimed such as s.380. If part is claimed under s.380, the balance can be dealt with in a terminal loss claim.

8.2 Calculation of terminal loss

A terminal loss normally consists of four main elements:

(a)   the loss arising in the last fiscal year;

(b)   the capital allowances of the last fiscal year, if any;

(c)   the balance of the loss (if any) arising in the remainder of the twelve months preceding discontinuance;

(d)   the lower of:

   i)   a proportion of the capital allowances of the fiscal year preceding discontinuance, or

   ii)   the amount of the capital allowances for that year unrelieved.

In finding items (a) and (c) it may be necessary to amalgamate profits and losses. If the net result is a profit then it is included as 'Nil'; it does not reduce the loss claim.

Illustration

H made up accounts to 31st December each year until 31st December 1990, when he ceased to trade. His adjusted results and capital allowances were:

Years ended:			£
31.12.1986	Profit		1,900
31.12.1987	Profit		1,200
31.12.1988	Profit		600
31.12.1989	Profit		400
31.12.1990	Loss		1,800

Capital allowances:
1987/88   £100;   1988/89   £300;
1989/90   £200;   1990/91   £600.

In this case, there will be no revision to actual by the Revenue as profits are on a declining trend.

Calculation of Terminal Loss: £

(a) The loss of the last fiscal year 1990/91: 6.4.1990 - 31.12.1990

                          9/12 x £1,800   1,350

(b) Capital allowances of the last fiscal year - 1990/91   600

(c) The balance of the loss arising in the remainder of the 12 months
preceding discontinuance - 1.1.1990 - 5.4.1990

                          3/12 x £1,800   450
                                                              2,400

(d) The lower of:

   i)   a proportion of the previous year's capital allowances:
          1.1.1990 - 5.4.1990 = 3/12 x £200 =   £50

   ii)   capital allowances unrelieved   £Nil

       (all offset against 1989/90 assessment)   Nil
                                                          2,400

Loss relieved:

	1987/88 £	1988/89 £	1989/90 £
DI	1,900	1,200	600
Less: Capital Allowances	100	300	200
	1,800	900	400
Terminal Loss Relief	1,100 (3)	900 (2)	400 (1)
	700	NIL	NIL

A repayment of tax will occur where the tax due on the revised assessment
differs from that originally.

If instead of H's last accounting period being to 31st December 1990 it was to
30th September 1990, the calculation of the terminal loss would be as under:

	£	£
(a) Loss 6.4.1990 - 30.9.1990		
6/9 x £1,800		1,200
(b) Capital allowances 1990/91		600
(c) Balance of loss 1.10.1989 - 5.4.1990		
3/12 x £400	100 P	
3/9 x £1,800	600 L	
	___	500
(d) Capital allowances 1989/90		Nil
		2,300

In (c) profits and losses are aggregated to give a smaller loss. Had the figures been reversed, i.e.   100 L

600 P

the amount included in the computation would have been NIL.

8.3 The inclusion of s.350 assessments

Where there are s.350 assessments in respect of trade charges which cannot be relieved because of the cessation of trade, they may, to the extent that they are paid in the year of assessment falling into the last twelve months trading, be included in the terminal loss computation. Thus two additional elements may appear in the terminal loss computation:

(a)   the s.350 assessment on unrelieved retainable trade charges of the ultimate fiscal year;

(b)   a proportion of any similar assessment of the penultimate fiscal year.

Illustration

J ceased trading on 30th June 1990 having previously made up accounts to 31st December.   His trading results, adjusted for tax purposes, were:

Year ended 31.12.1986	Profit	£3,600
Year ended 31.12.1987	Profit	£2,400
Year ended 31.12.1988	Profit	£ 600
Year ended 31.12.1989	Loss	£ 720
1.1.1990 to 30.6.1990	Loss	£3,000

Capital allowances:

1987/88	£1,000
1988/89	£ 400
1989/90	£ 350
1990/91	£ 700

J paid £400 (gross) per annum under deed of covenant to a trade association on 1st May each year. He has no other income; s.380 relief is not claimed.

Calculation of Terminal Loss: £   £

(a) 1990/91 - loss 6.4.1990 - 30.6.1990
         3/6 x £3,000   1,500

(b) 1990/91 - Capital allowances   700

(c) 1990/91 - s.350 assessment Covenant paid 1.5.1990   400

(d) 1989/90 - loss 1.7.1989 - 5.4.1990
         6/12 x £720   360
         3/6 x £3,000   1,500
                                                                          _____
                                                                                       1,860
                                                                                       _____
                                                                                       4,460

(e) 1989/90 - Capital allowances lower of 9/12 x 350   262
                                                                          ======

                     or

         unrelieved allowances of 1989/90   NIL
                                                                          ======   NIL

(f) 1989/90 - Proportion of s.350
         Assessment:
         Schedule D Case I   600
         Less: Capital allowances   350
                                                       c/f   250

         s.350 Assessment   150
                                                                          _____
                                                                            400
         Less: Charge   400

                                                                              -
                                                                          ======

         9/12 x £150   112
                                                                                       _____
                                                                                       4,572
                                                                                       ======

When the terminal loss is carried back for relief any charges must be deducted in priority to terminal loss relief.

	1987/88	1988/89	1989/90
	£	£	£
Schedule DI	3,600	2,400	600
Capital Allowances	1,000	400	350
	2,600	2,000	250
Charges	400	400	400
	2,200	1,600	NIL
Terminal Loss Relief	(2,200)(2)	(1,600) (1)	
	NIL	NIL	

The balance of the terminal loss relief will be lost.

As already mentioned, it is possible to claim s.380 relief instead of terminal loss relief if the taxpayer wishes. If in 1990/91 J had other income of £1,000 he could claim s.380 relief against that income. The amount of the loss to be included in the terminal loss computation would then be:

		£
Loss	1990/91	(1,500)
Less:	Relieved s.380	1,000
		(500)

If there are non-trade charges in the carry-back period, they will reduce the amount of the terminal loss to be carried back into an earlier period. If it is possible both trade and non-trade charges may be offset against other income rather then trading income (TA 1988,s.835). This will increase the trading income available to cover terminal loss relief.

Illustration

P has a terminal loss of £(20,000). It can be carried back into the fiscal years 1988/89, 1989/90 and 1990/91. Details for those years are as under:

Assessable trading profits:

1988/89	£14,000
1989/90	£ 6,000
1990/91	£ 3,000

Other income:

1988/89	£ 2,000
1989/90	£ 520

Patent royalties and deeds of covenant to charity of £500 and £30 respectively are paid annually:

	1988/89 £	1989/90 £	1990/91 £
Schedule DI	14,000	6,000	3,000
Less: charges	-	10	530
	14,000	5,990	2,470
Terminal loss relief	(11,510)	(5,990)	(2,470)
	2,490	NIL	NIL
Other income	2,000	520	
Less: charges	530	520	
	1,470	NIL	
TOTAL INCOME	3,960	NIL	NIL
Terminal loss			(20,000)
Less: Relieved			2,470
			(17,530)
Less: Reduction for non-trade charges deducted			30
Relieved	(11,510)	(5,990)	(17,500)

Note: In 1989/90 the non-trade charges have been deducted from the other income first, to prevent any restrictions of the terminal loss available for carry back into 1988/89.

9.0   RELIEF FOR LOSSES ON SHARES IN UNQUOTED TRADING COMPANIES

TA 1988,s.574 to 576 provides that where a person **subscribes** for shares in an unquoted trading company and makes a capital loss on a disposal at arm's length it is possible to offset that loss against income.

The loss is calculated as for CGT purposes and may be offset against income in:

(a)   the fiscal year in which disposal takes place; and if desired,

(b)   the next fiscal year.

The order of offset is as for s.380; however, s.574 takes priority over s.380. Like s.380, the spouse's income may be excluded from the claim.

A qualifying trading company is an unquoted company which:

(a)   is a trading company at disposal or which ceased to be such a company not more than three years before such a disposal;

(b)   is resident in the UK;

(c)   has traded for at least six years prior to the date of disposal, subject to certain conditions.

Companies which trade in stocks and shares, land or commodity futures or have not traded with a reasonable expectation of profits are not eligible for relief. The disposal must be at arm's length or by way of a distribution in a winding up.

If the subscriber for shares is an investment company, then it may offset the loss against the other income in the same way as a loss under s.393.

If relief is not claimed under s.574 then normal CGT relief is available. Detailed computations appear in the Capital Gains Tax section of the manual.

CHAPTER SEVEN

Partnerships

1.0 DEFINITION

Partnership is the relationship which subsists between two or more persons carrying on business in common with a view to profits. To be taxable a partnership must exist in fact; the existence of a partnership agreement will not be conclusive if the facts clearly show that the partnership is non-operative in practice. In **IRC v. Williamson (1928)** Lord President Clyde said:

> '...you do not constitute or create or prove a partnership by saying that there is one'.

In **Fenstone v. Johnson (1940)** the taxpayer wished to acquire some property but lacked the necessary finance. He agreed with another person that the other would provide finance and assist in the development. The agreement stated that there was to be no partnership and described the other's share as a fee. Held there was a partnership.

A partnership agreement is not effective for tax purposes prior to the date of execution unless a partnership de facto existed prior to that date.

In **Waddington v. O'Callaghan (1931)**, W, a solicitor, told his son on 31st December 1928 that he intended taking him into partnership as from that date. On 11th May 1929 the agreement was executed expressing to have effect from 1st January 1929. Held that the facts showed that no partnership was contemplated until the deed was executed.

2.0 ASSESSMENT

Although the partnership is assessed in the partnership name, the liability to tax of the partners is joint **(Harrison v. Willis Bros (1966))**. Thus if one partner is unable to pay the tax on his apportioned share of the profits, the Revenue can proceed against the other partners. The precedent acting partner is responsible for returning to the Inland Revenue the total profits of the partnership and in addition each individual partner must return his share on his own tax return.

3.0 THE APPORTIONMENT OF THE ASSESSMENT

As already mentioned the business is the unit of assessment and it is therefore the adjusted profits of the partnership that will need to be apportioned between the partners. Like any trader, the profits available for division can take one of three main forms:

(a) interest on capital;

(b) salaries;

(c) residual profits.

The first two items will have already been added back in arriving at the adjusted profit. The basic rule for the allocation of profits between the partners is that they will be divided between them in accordance with the **profit-sharing arrangements of the fiscal year for which the accounting period forms the basis period.** Thus the adjusted profits of the year ended 31st December 1989 will be divided between the partners in accordance with the profit sharing arrangements of the period 6th April 1990 to 5th April 1991 - the fiscal year for which those profits are assessed. As can be appreciated, a change in the profit sharing arrangements can mean a different allocation of profits for accounts purposes from that applying for tax. When this occurs one partner will compensate the other for any increase or reduction in his liability.

Illustration

A, B and C are in partnership sharing profits equally; as from 6th April 1989 they decide to share profits 3:2:1.

The adjusted profits for the year to 31st December 1988 are £9,000.

For tax purposes the profit of £9,000 will be divided between the partners in accordance with the profit sharing arrangements of the fiscal year for which it will be assessed i.e. 1989/90.

	Total	A	B	C
1989/90	£	£	£	£
Profits	9,000	4,500	3,000	1,500

Assuming a basic rate of tax of 25% and no personal allowances the appropriate adjustment between partners would be:

	A	B	C
	£	£	£
Per accounts	3,000	3,000	3,000
For taxation	4,500	3,000	1,500
	(1,500)	-	1,500
@ 25%	(375)		375
In current accounts	Cr		Dr

Where it is necessary to apportion the adjusted profits, a strict time basis is applied.

Illustration

The facts are as in the above Illustration except that the partners changed their profit sharing arrangements on 30th June 1989.

	Total £	A £	B £	C £
1989/90				
6.4.89-30.6.89				
3/12 x £9,000	2,250	750	750	750
1.7.89-5.4.90				
9/12 x £9,000	6,750	3,375	2,250	1,125
	9,000	4,125	3,000	1,875

Where the partners receive interest on capital and salaries, these receive priority in the apportionment of the profits.

Illustration

A and B had the following annual profit sharing arrangements up to 30th September 1989:

	Salaries £	Interest on Capital £
A	1,000	500
B	500	400

Until this date they shared residual profits and losses equally. From 1st October 1989 they divided profits as under:

	Salaries £	Interest on Capital £
A	2,000	300
B	1,000	300

As from this date, residual profits are to be shared 2:1. The adjusted profits for the year to 30th June 1988 were £6,000.

	Total £	A £	B £
1989/90			
6.4.89-30.9.89			
6/12 x £6,000 = £3,000			
Salaries	750	500	250
Interest	450	250	200
Balance	1,800	900	900
	3,000	1,650	1,350

		Total £	A £	B £
1.10.89-5.4.90				
6/12 x £6,000	= £3,000			
Salaries		1,500	1,000	500
Interest		300	150	150
Balance		1,200	800	400
		3,000	1,950	1,050
TOTAL		6,000	3,600	2,400

Where salaries and interest on capital exceed the adjusted profits, they are nevertheless given in full, even though this will have the effect of creating a negative balance. This negative balance is divided between the partners in the same way as a positive balance would have been.

Illustration

A, B and C have the following profit sharing arrangements:

	Salaries £	Interest on Capital £	Balance
A	2,000	500	3
B	2,000	300	2
C	1,000	200	1

The adjusted profit for the year ended 30th June 1989 was £4,500.

	Total £	A £	B £	C £
1990/91				
Salaries	5,000	2,000	2,000	1,000
Interest	1,000	500	300	200
	6,000	2,500	2,300	1,200
Balance	(1,500)	(750)	(500)	(250)
	4,500	1,750	1,800	950

Although the profits may be said to consist of salary, interest on capital, etc., they are all assessed under Schedule D Case I or II. There is no assessment of the salary under Schedule E, or the interest under Schedule D Case III.

In certain cases the allocation of a negative balance to one partner may result in his share of profit being turned into a loss. The Inland Revenue will not allow one partner loss relief when the overall result of the partnership is a profit. The notional loss must be apportioned to the remaining partners in proportion to their respective shares of profit as determined before making any adjustment for the loss.

Illustration

X, Y and Z have the following profit sharing arrangements:

	Salaries £	Balance
X	2,000	3
Y	2,000	2
Z	500	3

The adjusted profit for the year ended 30th April 1989 was £2,500.

	Total £	X £	Y £	Z £
1990/91				
Salaries	4,500	2,000	2,000	500
Balance	(2,000)	(750)	(500)	(750)
	2,500	1,250	1,500	(250)
Z's 'loss' divided £1,250:£1,500		(114)	(136)	250
	2,500	1,136	1,364	-

A similar procedure would apply when one partner has a profit and the others losses.

Where a partner is entitled to a guaranteed share of profits, any deficiency in his allocation of profits will be given to him and divided between the remaining partners in the proportion in which they share the residual profits.

Illustration

A, B and C share profits 3, 2 and 1 after salaries of £3,000, £2,000 and £2,000 respectively. As from 1st January 1990, C is to have a minimum share of partnership income of £4,000. The adjusted profits for the year ended 31st December 1989 are £ 10,000.

	Total £	A £	B £	C £
1990/91				
Salaries	7,000	3,000	2,000	2,000
Balance	3,000	1,500	1,000	500
	10,000	4,500	3,000	2,500
Adjustment to bring C up to minimum share divided 3:2		(900)	(600)	1,500
	10,000	3,600	2,400	4,000

It will be noted that the new arrangement covers the fiscal year 1990/91, and therefore C will be assessed on his share of profits under the new arrangements. For accounts purposes, however, there was no guaranteed share for the year ended 31st December 1989.

4.0 CAPITAL ALLOWANCES

When capital allowances are due to the partnership, they will be deducted from the assessment before division between the partners. Where a partner has capital allowances due to him personally - for example, for the business use of his private car - they are deducted from his individual share of profits.

5.0 OTHER PARTNERSHIP INCOME

If the partnership receives other income such as dividends, rent, interest, etc. then this must be treated entirely separately from the trading or professional income of the partnership.   Each partner will be assessed as an individual and his share of that income split in the ultimate profit-sharing arrangements of the fiscal year for which it is assessed.

Illustration

C and D are in partnership sharing profits 3:2.   They receive the following income apart from trading income:

	£
Rents received annually in advance on 1st January each year	
Received 1.1.1989	10,000
Received 1.1.1990	12,000
National Savings Account interest, credited as under:	
30.6.1988	400
31.12.1988	500
30.6.1989	480
31.12.1989	590

For the fiscal year 1989/90, the partners will be assessed on:

	£	£
Schedule A - Rents (actual basis)		12,000
Schedule DIII - NSB interest (preceding year basis)		
30.6.1988	400	
31.12.1988	500	
		900
		£12,900

	C	D
Split: 3:2	£7,740	£5,160

If there is a change in profit sharing ratio etc., the assessible income will be apportioned in the same way as profits.

If taxed income such as dividends etc. is received it will normally be split in the same way.   If, however, there is a change in profit sharing ratios or a partner joins or leaves the partnership, then the taxed income is split into the relevant periods on the basis of when it is received.

Illustration

E and F are in partnership as solicitors sharing profits equally to 31st October 1989 and thereafter 2:1.   In the year to 5th April 1990 they received the following additional income:

	£
Rents received on the usual quarter days	500 per quarter

Dividends received (including tax credit)

30.6.1989	600
31.12.1989	700

		E £	F £
Rents 4 x £500	£2,000		
$^7/12$ x £2,00 split equally		583	583
$^5/12$ x £2,000 split 2:1		556	278
		1,139	861

Dividends

Received 30.6.1989 split equally	300	300
31.12.1989 split 2:1	467	233
	1,906	1,394

6.0 PERSONAL ALLOWANCES

Once the partnership assessment has been divided between the partners, each partner may deduct from his share the personal allowances etc. to which he is entitled.   If one partner has an excess of personal allowances they may not be transferred to another partner.

Illustration

A and B are trading in partnership as nurserymen sharing profits and losses in the ratio of 2:1 after paying B a salary of £6,000.   For the year ended 31st December 1988 the partnership had an adjusted profit of £45,000.

Neither partner has any other income and their entitlements to personal allowances are as follows:

A - Married
B - Unmarried, supporting his widowed mother who has no income apart from her state retirement pension.   In 1989/90 he paid a mortgage interest of £900 gross. MIRAS does not apply.

	Total £	A £	B £
1989/90			
Year to			
31.12.88			
Salary	6,000		6,000
Balance	39,000	26,000	13,000
	45,000	26,000	19,000
Charges	900		900
	44,100		18,100

Personal allowances

	£			
MA	4,375		4,375	
SA	2,785			2,785
		7,160		
		36,940	21,625	15,315

Tax

		Total	A		B	
36,015 @ 25%		9,004	20,700 @ 25%	5,175	15,315 @25%	3,829
925 @ 40%		370	925 @ 40%	370		
		9,374		5,545		3,874

7.0   PARTNERSHIP CHARGES

Where a partnership pays annual charges, they are divided between the partners on the same basis as they agree to share residual profits. For tax purposes the charges are taken into account in the fiscal year in which they are paid and the basis for division is the profit sharing arrangement of that fiscal year.

Illustration

A and B are in partnership sharing profits and losses equally to 31st December 1988 and thereafter 2:1. Their profit and loss account for the year ended 31st December 1988 was as under:

	£	£		£
Office expenses		6,000	Trading profit	12,000
Annuity to wife of				
retired partner		600		
Balance: A	2,700			
B	2,700	5,400		
		12,000		12,000

The annuity was an amount of £100 per month and commenced on 1st July 1988.

		£
Adjusted profit Per Accounts		5,400
Add: annuity		600
		6,000
		=====

Divided:	Total	A	B
1989/90	£	£	£
Profit	6,000	4,000	2,000
Less: Charges 1989/90	1,200	800	400
	4,800	3,200	1,600
	=====	=====	=====

If during a fiscal year, there is a change in profit-sharing arrangements or a
partner joins or leaves the partnership, the charges are apportioned to the parts
of the fiscal year before and after the change by reference to the amounts paid
in those periods.

8.0 CHANGES IN THE PARTNERSHIP

8.1 Assessments

Whenever there is a change in the partnership, either by one partner being
admitted or another leaving, retiring or dying, there is a deemed cessation and
recommencement for tax purposes even though there is no physical break in the
trade. As a result it is necessary to treat the old partnership as having ceased
on the date of the change and a new partnership as having immediately commenced
(TA 1988, s.113(1)). This will necessitate the application of the cessation and
commencement provisions of the Taxes Acts.

Illustration

X and Y make up accounts to 31st December annually. On 1st October 1989 Z was
admitted as a partner. The adjusted profits of the firm were:

	£
31st December 1986	8,000
31st December 1987	10,000
31st December 1988	12,000
31st December 1989	9,000
31st December 1990	11,000
31st December 1991	14,000
31st December 1992	16,000
31st December 1993	20,000
31st December 1994	15,000

The old partnership is deemed to have ceased on 30th September 1989 and a new
partnership commenced on 1st October 1989.

Old Partnership (X and Y)
1989/90
6.4.89-30.9.89
6/12 x £9,000   £4,500
                                                                    ======

1988/89
P.Y. (year to 31.12.1987)   £10,000
                                               =======

                                                                    £18,000
1987/88   =======
P.Y. (year to 31.12.1986)   £8,000
                                               ======

Revised s.63   £
1988/89
9/12 x £12,000   =   9,000
3/12 x £ 9,000   =   2,250   £11,250
                                               =======

                                                                    £21,750
                                                                    =======

1987/88
9/12 x £10,000   =   7,500
3/12 x £12,000   =   3,000   £10,500
                                               =======

FA 1985 introduced amendments to the legislation dealing with partnership
changes whenever there is an admission or retirement of a partner to or from an
existing partnership on or after 20th March 1985. Whilst the normal cessation
rules will apply to the old partnership, the assessments for the first four
fiscal years of the new partnership will be calculated on an actual basis. The
assessments for the fifth and sixth years will be on the preceding year basis
unless the partnership elects to have those assessed on an actual year basis
also. Thereafter the preceding year basis applies.

In the preceding example the assessments on the new partnership would be:

		£	£
1989/90	1.10.89-5.4.90		
	3/12 x £9,000	2,250	
	3/12 x £11,000	2,750	
			5,000
1990/91	6.4.90-5.4.91		
	9/12 x £11,000	8,250	
	3/12 x £14,000	3,500	11,750
1991/92	6.4.91-5.4.92		
	9/12 x £14,000	10,500	
	3/12 x £16,000	4,000	14,500
1992/93	6.4.92-5.4.93		
	9/12 x £16,000	12,000	
	3/12 x £20,000	5,000	17,000

		£
1993/94	Year to 31.12.1992	16,000
1994/95	Year to 31.12.1993	20,000

or actual for 1993/94 and 1994/95 if appropriate.

If the partners wish, they may avoid the s.113(1) treatment of cessation and recommencement by making an election under TA1988, s.113(2). If such an election is made, there is no deemed cessation and the assessments continue on the normal preceding year basis throughout. The conditions for a valid election are:

(a) it must be made in writing to the Inspector of Taxes within two years of the change;

(b) it must be signed by all the partners of both the old and the new firm (if one is dead, his personal representative will sign);

(c) there must be at least one partner common to both old and new partnerships.

Revenue Practice is to allow an election if made, to be revoked within the time limit.

A comparison of the assessments will be:

	s.113(1)	s.113(2)
	£	£
1987/88	10,500	8,000
1988/89	11,250	10,000
	{ 4,500	12,000
1989/90	{ 5,000	
1990/91	11,750	9,000
1991/92	14,500	11,000
1992/93	17,000	14,000
1993/94	16,000	16,000
1994/95	20,000	20,000
	110,500	100,000

The basis of assessment for the first six years of the new partnership will not apply where:

(a) a sole trader takes in one or more partners, or

(b) a partnership of not more than two loses a partner.

In these cases the normal rules of cessation and commencement apply. Thus if in the above illustration Y had left the partnership rather than Z joining it, the position would be:

1989/90	1.10.89-5.4.90	£	
	3/12 x £ 9,000	2,250	
	3/12 x £11,000	2,750	
			£5,000

1990/91	First 12 months		
	3/12 x £ 9,000	2,250	
	9/12 x £11,000	8,250	
			£10,500

1991/92	PY (year to 31.12.1990)	£11,000

or s.62 if appropriate, for 1990/91 and 1991/92.

Where there are successive changes in the partnership it is possible that a later change may have an effect on a partner who has left the partnership at an earlier date.

Illustration

X, Y and Z have been in partnership for many years sharing profits one-half, one-third and one-sixth after allowing Z a salary of £1,500. They made their accounts up to 30th November each year and the results, adjusted for tax purposes, of recent years, have been:

		£
Year ended:	30.11.87	6,360
	30.11.88	7,740
	30.11.89	8,400
	30.11.90	7,200
	30.11.91	6,300

X retired on 30th November 1989 and Y and Z continued in business sharing profits equally, without either partner drawing a salary, until 1st December 1990 when M was admitted to the partnership receiving a salary of £1,000 and one-sixth of the profit while Y and Z continued to share the balance equally. On the retirement of X an election was made for continuation, but no such election was made on the admission of M.

Assessment up to X's retirement	Total	X	Y	Z
	£	£	£	£
1988/89 (y/e 30.11.87)				
Salaries	1,500			1,500
Balance (3:2:1)	4,860	2,430	1,620	810
	6,360	2,430	1,620	2,310

	Total	X	Y	Z
	£	£	£	£
1989/90 (y/e 30.11.88)				
To X's retirement				

6.4.89 to 30.11.89
8/12 x £7,740   =   £5,160

	Total	X	Y	Z
Salary	1,000			1,000
Balance (3:2:1)	4,160	2,080	1,387	693
	5,160	2,080	1,387	1,693

Assessment on Y and Z only:
1989/90 from X's retirement
1.12.89 to 5.4.90

	Total	X	Y	Z
4/12 x £7,740	2,580		1,290	1,290

Because no election was made when M was admitted to the partnership and 1st December 1990 falls in the tax year 1990/91 the partnership will be deemed to be discontinued on that date and the Schedule D Case I assessments then become:

Original Assessment		**Final Assessment**	
	£		£
1988/89 y/e 30.11.87	6,360	6.4.88 to 5.4.89	
		8/12 x £7,740 + 4/12 x £8,400	7,960
1989/90 y/e 30.11.88	7,740	6.4.89 to 5.4.90	
		8/12 x £8,400 +4/12 x £7,200	8,000
	14,100		15,960

1990/91 6.4.90 to 30.11.90   8/12 x £7,200   £4,800

The Revenue will revise the penultimate and prepenultimate years onto an actual basis.

As a result of the revision of the penultimate and prepenultimate years onto actual it will be necessary to revise the division of assessments for 1988/89 and 1989/90 between the partners and raise additional assessments on all individuals who were partners during those years, including X.

	Total	X	Y	Z
1988/89	£	£	£	£
(6.4.88-5.4.89)				
Salaries	1,500			1,500
Balance (3:2:1)	6,460	3,230	2,154	1,076
	7,960	3,230	2,154	2,576

1989/90
(6.4.89-30.11.89)
8/12 x £8,000

Salaries	1,000			1,000
Balance (3:2:1)	4,333	2,167	1,444	722
	5,333	2,167	1,444	1,722
	=====	=====	=====	=====

(1.12.89-5.4.90)
4/12 x £8,000

	2,667	-	1,333	1,334
	=====	=====	=====	=====

8.2 Effects of a change in partnership

(a) Capital Allowances

On a s.113(1) cessation, all assets on which capital allowances have been claimed will be treated as though they were transferred to the new partnership at market value. Alternatively, an election may be made by the successor and predecessor (if they are connected persons) to transfer the assets at tax-written-down values.

If a s.113(2) election is made the capital allowances computation continues on the normal basis throughout.

(b) Losses

Where there is a s.113(1) cessation, a retiring partner may claim terminal loss relief, but this is not available to the continuing partners. If there have been losses before the cesssation, then the continuing partners may carry forward their shares of loss against future profits. This will also apply to their shares of unused capital allowances. A new partner may claim s.381 relief in respect of losses in the first four fiscal years. This is not available to continuing partners.

9.0 PARTNER'S LOANS TO THE PARTNERSHIP

Interest paid by the firm on a loan by a partner, as distinct from interest paid on capital, is treated as unearned income.

10.0 PARTNERSHIP LOSSES

Where a partnership makes a loss it will be necesary to divide the adjusted loss between the partners. As a partnership is a collection of individuals, each may choose the relief that he requires for his share of the loss. There are two basic methods of apportioning the loss:

(a) Relief under s.380 (concessional basis)

The adjusted loss is divided between the partners in accordance with their profit-sharing arrangements of the fiscal year in which the accounting period producing the loss ends.

(b) Relief under s.385

The adjusted loss is divided between the partners **in accordance with their
profit-sharing arrangements of the acounting period producing the loss.**

The results of (a) and (b) will only differ if the profit sharing between
partners alters during the basis periods.

Each partner may claim the loss relief that he requires and the total relief
granted to any partner may not be less than is available under s.385.

Illustration

A and B make up accounts to 31st December 1989. Their profit and loss account
for that year is as below:

	£	£		£	£
Trade Expenses		6,000	Trading profit		1,000
Salaries: A	2,000		Loss: A - 2/3	6,000	
B	2,000		B - 1/3	3,000	
	─────	4,000		─────	9,000
		10,000			10,000
		══════			══════

As from 1st January 1990 they decided to share profits equally, salaries as
before. Both claim relief under s.380.
    The adjusted loss is:

	£
Loss for the year	(9,000)
Less: Salaries	4,000
	─────
	(5,000)
	═════

Its apportionment under s.380 would be:

	Total £	A £	B £
6.4.89-31.12.89			
9/12 x £(5,000) = (£3,750)			
Salaries	3,000	1,500	1,500
Balance	(6,750)	(4,500)	(2,250)
	(3,750)	(3,000)	(750)
	═════	═════	═════
1.1.90-5.4.90			
3/12 x (£5,000) = (£1,250)			
Salaries	1,000	500	500
Balance	(2,250)	(1,125)	(1,125)
	(1,250)	(625)	(625)
	═════	═════	═════
	(5,000)	(3,625)	(1,375)
	═════	═════	═════

and under s.385 it would be:

	Total £	A £	B £
Salaries	4,000	2,000	2,000
Balance	(9,000)	(6,000)	(3,000)
	(5,000)	(4,000)	(1,000)

As A cannot get less relief than he would have been entitled to receive under s.385 he will receive loss relief of £4,000 in total. Only £3,625 of this relief, however, will be available under s.380, the balance will be given under s.385. Thus the total loss relief that could be given is £5,375.

If the s.380 claim is computed on a strict basis, it will still be divided as in (a) but the loss will be that of the tax year (or years) of loss found by aggregating parts of accounting periods.

Illustration

A,B and C are in partnership sharing profits and losses 4:3:3 respectively. Results for recent years have been:

	£
Year ended 30.11.1988	19,500
30.11.1989	(48,000)
30.11.1990	36,000

A retires on 30th November 1989 and D is admitted with a profit share of 40%, the other partners remaining as before. An election is made under s.113(2); loss relief under s.380 is claimed on a strict basis.

1988/89	Total £	A £	B £	C £	D £
6.4.88-30.11.88					
8/12 x £19,500	13,000	5,200	3,900	3,900	
1.12.88-5.4.89					
4/12 x £(48,000)	(16,000)	(6,400)	(4,800)	(4,800)	
	(3,000)	(1,200)	(900)	(900)	
1989/90					
6.4.89-30.11.89					
8/12 x £(48,000)	(32,000)	(12,800)	(9,600)	(9,600)	
1.12.89-5.4.90					
4/12 x £36,000	12,000		3,600	3,600	4,800
	(20,000)	(12,800)	(6,000)	(6,000)	4,800
Eliminate D		2,478	1,161	1,161	(4,800)
	(20,000)	(10,322)	(4,839)	(4,839)	NIL

For chargeable periods beginning after 19th March 1985 any loss allocated to a limited partner will be restricted as far as the offset under s.380 TA 1988 is concerned, for any year of assessment, to the amount of the partner's contribution to the partnership trade at the end of that year.

The amount of the partner's contribution is the aggregate of the amount he has contributed as capital and which he has not withdrawn, together with the amount of that partner's share of the profits or gains of the trade, which he has not received in money or money's worth.

11.0 PARTNERSHIP TERMINAL LOSSES

Where there is a cessation or deemed cessation (as in s.113(1)) of a partnership, terminal loss relief is available.

12.0 PARTNERSHIP RETIREMENT ANNUITIES

12.1 General rules

Where annual payments are made under the terms of a partnership agreement for the benefit of a former partner, who has retired because of old age or ill-health, or to his widow on his death, they may be treated as earned income in the hands of the recipient. To qualify in full they must not exceed 50% of the average of the former partner's profit share in the best three out of the last seven complete years of assessment in which he was required to devote substantially the whole of his time to the partnership.

Where the annuity exceeds the limit the excess will be treated as unearned income.

For the remaining partners who pay the annuity, relief will be available as a charge on income in their total income computation, thereby reducing their liability to higher rate tax where applicable. It should be noted that the charge will not reduce their income liable to investment income surcharge, except and to the extent that it is treated as unearned income in the hands of the former partner.

FA 1982 provided with retroactive effect that the profit shares used in the computation may be indexed upwards by increases in the Retail Price Index between December in the relevant fiscal year and December in the final year.

12.2 Index-linked annuities

Traditionally, annuities were fixed sums of money paid annually, but with the recent emphasis on the effects of inflation many annuities are now inflation adjusted, allowing for predetermined increases in the annuity or index-linking them.

As from the fiscal year 1980/81 it is possible to increase the amount of a retired partner's annuity that qualifies as earned income, by reference to the Retail Prices Index. If the index for the month of December immediately preceding the year of assessment shows an increase over the index for the month of December in the year of assessment in which the partner retired, the limit that qualifies as earned income can be increased by the same percentage increase in the index.

13.0 PARTNERSHIP SERVICE COMPANIES

A partnership may set up a service company to own assets of the partnership and to provide services to the partnership. In return, the company charges fees to the partnership which will be deducted as an expense in the partnership accounts. By doing this profits can be removed from the partnership and sheltered within the company. If the company is small within the terms of s.13 TA 1988, profits not exceeding £100,000 will only be charged at 25%. The retained profits may be taken out by means of dividend or salary in years in which other income is low. Doing this effectively will depend on the profit uplift applied to the charge from the company to the partnership. If this exceeds 5-15% then the Revenue may seek to disallow some of the charge in the partnership's computation as not having been incurred wholly and exclusively for the purposes of the trade, **(Stephenson v Payne, Stone, Frazer & Co 1967)**.

In the opening years of a partnership this can be very advantageous as whilst the expense will be allowed several times in the case of the partnership it will only be taxed once in the company. Whilst the service company will normally be close there will be no apportionment problems unless it receives property or investment income. A point that must be borne in mind, however, is that the excess profits removed into the company will be liable to corporation tax nine months after the end of the company's accounting period. This is disadvantageous compared to the much longer period that might be available within the partnership before the payment of income tax.

14.0 SLEEPING PARTNERS

When a partner acts in a 'sleeping' role, his share of the partnership profits is classed as unearned income.

15.0 AVERAGING CLAIMS FOR FARMING PARTNERSHIPS

The averaging rules for individuals apply to trades carried on by partnerships in much the same way, subject to the following modifications:

(a)   the averaging calculation is applied to the partnership assessment, not to the individual partner's share of that assessment,

(b)   any claims must be made jointly by all the partners,

(c)   if on a partnership change an election under TA 1988, s.113(2) is made (continuing basis), any claim for averaging must be made jointly by all parties who were engaged in the trade at any time during the two year-period.

CHAPTER EIGHT

Investments

1.0 GENERAL

Most taxpayers have some investments. The income from investments is classified as unearned income and for many years was liable to an additional tax if it exceeded given limits. This additional charge has now been abolished.

Certain investments, e.g. in land, have already been considered but there are many others some of which offer particular tax advantages in terms of tax free income or which are designed to encourage investment in growing companies.

2.0 TAX EFFICIENT INVESTMENTS

Certain investments are tax efficient because income or capital gains arising from them is wholly or partly tax free. These investments include:

2.1 National Savings Certificates

These can be purchased in various denominations and are redeemable at a premium over cost price. After the end of a fixed period of time, often 5 years, the certificate can be redeemed and the premium will be exempt from all taxes. This can be very advantageous to higher rate tax payers; a tax free yield of 10% grossing up at 40% to the equivalent of 17%. If the certificate is held for a shorter period of time a reduced premium will be paid. Each issue of savings certificates is subject to a maximum holding; the premium on certificates held in excess of the maximum is fully taxable.

Indexed linked savings certificates provide an alternative option. They will rise in value in line with the retail price index and again the increase in value is free of all taxes. There are limits on the amount of each issue that can be held.

2.2 National Savings Bank Ordinary accounts

The first £70 of annual interest in an NSB ordinary account is free from income tax.

2.3 Premium bonds

Whilst no interest is paid on these bonds, they qualify for prizes in a monthly draw. The prizes are exempt from all tax and if desired, the bonds can be repaid at par.

2.4 Save As You Earn

SAYE schemes are offered by the national savings movement and building societies. The national savings movement requires monthly savings which accumulate towards the purchase of an annual certificate which if held for a fixed period of time gives a tax free yield. The building societies operate a similar monthly savings plan. Whilst both types of investment produce tax free yields, the yields are maximised if the investment is held for a fixed period of time.

2.5 Gilt Edged securities and corporate bonds

Capital gains, often representing an element of accrued income, are exempt.

2.6 Personal Equity Plans

With effect from 1st January 1987, individuals may make investments in personal equity plans [PEP]. These are intended, through certain tax concessions, to encourage wider share ownership.

The schemes are open to individuals aged 18 or more who are resident and ordinarily resident in the UK. They may invest up to £4,800 per fiscal year with an authorised PEP manager who will invest the money in equities dealt in on a recognised stock exchange or on the USM. Provided that the investment is retained for a minimum period, any reinvested income will be free of tax (the PEP manager recovering the tax credit on income from the Inland Revenue) and there will be no liability to capital gains tax on any capital gains. Capital losses on a PEP investment will similarly not be allowable.

The managers of the PEP will act on the instructions of the individual investor as to the choice of investments, which must be ordinary shares quoted on the stock exchange or on the Unlisted Securities Market. A maximum of £2,400 per year can be invested in unit or investment trusts. The managers can deal in the plan investments normally without any tax charge provided the proceeds are reinvested within 31 days.

Once the minimum period has been satisfied the shares can be sold or transferred to the owner of the PEP. For CGT purposes the cost of the shares to the owner in the case of a withdrawal, is market value at that date.

Whilst there are tax advantages such as exemption from tax of any accumulated income and capital gains, there is no tax relief for the payments made into the PEP

3.0   SCHEDULE D CASE III - INCOME ASSESSABLE

(a) Under Schedule D Case III there is assessed any interest, annuity or other
annual payment. In particular there is assessed: interest not already taxed
at source, including certain bank interest, interest on certain Government
securities such as three and half per cent War Loan and interest received on
deposits in the National Savings Bank.

In respect of interest on deposits in the NSB the first £70 interest
received on deposits in the Ordinary Department is exempt from tax. Where
husband and wife have a joint account the first £140 interest is exempt.

Illustration

A husband and wife receive the following interest on their deposits in the
Ordinary Account of the NSB:

Husband	£80
Wife	£60

The amount assessable will be:

	Husband	Wife
	£	£
Interest	80	60
Exempt	70	70
	10	-

There is no transfer of the balance of the wife's exemption to the husband.
If, however, they had a joint account all the interest would have been
exempt.

Interest paid by banks and similar institutions on relevant deposits will be
paid net of basic rate tax under the composite rate scheme. The recipient
of the interest will be liable to tax on the gross amount and will be able
to deduct the tax credit against a tax liability. He will not be able to
recover the tax credits by repayment.

A relevant deposit is basically one made with a bank by an individual, a
partnership being a collection of individuals. A person not ordinarily
resident in the UK may make a declaration to that effect to the bank and the
interest will continue to be paid gross. The person concerned must undertake
to notify the bank of any changes in his circumstances. Interest paid to
charities, clubs, companies and other persons not being individuals will
remain gross. Interest paid on deposits made by trustees will be within the
scheme unless the trust is discretionary or interest in possession.

The following are excluded from being relevant deposits:

i)   deposits held by a UK resident bank at an overseas branch;
ii) interbank loans;

---

iii) time deposits of at least £50,000 (or the foreign currency equivalent) the terms of which prevent part withdrawals and prohibit repayment within 7 days;

iv) bank certificates of deposit of at least £50,000 with a term of at least 7 days.

Interest paid by the National Savings Bank is paid gross.

(b) Discounts on Treasury Bills;

(c) Sickness and disablement benefits received from insurance companies and friendly societies for periods in excess of one year;

(d) Income from deep discount securities. This will be taxable under Schedule D Case IV if they are deep discount foreign securities.

3.1 Schedule D Case III basis of assessment

3.1.1   Normal basis

The normal basis of assessment is the income arising in the preceding year of assessment. Income arises when it becomes under the control of the recipient such as being credited to a bank deposit account. Accrued interest is not assessable and each individual investment is regarded as a separate source of income.

Illustration

In the years to 5th April 1989 and 1990 X received the following:

	£	£
£1,000 3½% War Loan:		
Interest payable 1st May and 1st November		
National Savings Bank Ordinary Account interest:		
30th June 1988		44
31st December 1988		39
		===
Assessable: 1989/90		
War Loan Interest		35
NSB Interest	83	
Less:	70	
	—	13
		48
		===

Income received from small maintenance payments is always assessed on actual basis; the person making such payments may treat them as a charge on income.

3.1.2   Commencement

On the commencement of a new source of interest the following rules apply:

First year   -   the actual income arising in that year.
Second year   -   the actual income of the second year.
Third and
subsequent years -   the income arising in the preceding year of assessment.

In the third year the taxpayer may elect to substitute the actual income of that year if it is advantageous to him. The election must be made within six years of the end of the third year of assessment.

Illustration

A, made a loan to his friend B, on 1st July 1987 and the following interest was paid to him:

	£		£
December 1987	70	June 1989	170
June 1988	145	December 1989	120
December 1988	160		

Schedule D Case III Assessments

Original		£	Revised	£
1987/88	Actual	70		
1988/89	Actual £(145+160)	305		
1989/90	Preceding year	305	Revised to actual at taxpayer's option	290
1990/91	Preceding year	290		

Therefore, the taxpayer will revise the assessment of 1989/90 on to an actual basis.

Where income first arose on 6th April in the first year of assessment, the preceding year basis will first apply to the second year of assessment as will the taxpayer's right to revise the actual.

3.1.3   Cessation

On the cessation of a source, the assessment will be adjusted as under:

Ultimate year   -   the actual income arising from 6th April to cessation.
Penultimate year -   the income arising in the preceding year of assessment.

The Revenue must adjust the assessment of the penultimate year on to an actual basis if it is to their advantage.

Illustration

B, had a special investment account with the National Savings Bank for many years. On 31st December 1989 he decided to close the account. The interest credited was as follows:

	1986	1987	1988	1989
	£	£	£	£
June	500	580	690	835
December	520	630	760	620

Schedule D Case III Assessments

Original		£	Revised	£
1987/88	Preceding year £(500 + 520)	1,020		
		=====		
1988/89	Preceding year £(580 + 630)	1,210	Revised to actual by Revenue	1,450
		=====		=====
1989/90	Actual	1,455		
		=====		

Therefore the Revenue will revise the 1988/89 assessment on to an actual basis.

Where a source fails to produce income for six separate years of assessment the taxpayer may, by election made within two years from the end of the six-year period, treat the source as if it had ceased at the date on which it last produced income. When it again produces income it will be assessed as if it were a new source.

4.0   THE RULE IN HART v. SANGSTER (1957)

It was held in **Hart v. Sangster** that each deposit in a bank deposit account represented a separate source of income and that each withdrawal represented the cessation of a source. To prevent the difficult situation that could arise if this was applied strictly, the Revenue only apply the rule to large deposits and withdrawals. To prepare a computation it is essential to divide the deposits and withdrawals into separate columns and to deal with each deposit or withdrawal individually, on a first in, first out basis.

Illustration

A paid £10,000 into a National Savings Bank special investment account in 1963 and the interest was credited to his current account each half year. On 31st December 1988 he withdrew £5,000 and on 30th June 1990, he closed the account. Interest paid to A in recent years was:

	£		£
31st December 1985	370	30th June 1988	370
30th June 1986	380	31st December 1988	350
31st December 1986	400	30th June 1989	180
30th June 1987	420	31st December 1989	190
31st December 1987	400	30th June 1990	170

	£5,000 Withdrawn 1988			£5,000 Withdrawn 1990	Total
	£	£		£	£
1987/88					
P/y ½ x £(380 + 400)	390				
Revised ½ x £(420 + 400)	410				
I.R. to actual		410	P/y ½ x £(380 + 400)	390	800
	£	£			
1988/89 Actual ½ x £(370 + 350)		360	P/y ½ x £(420 + 400)	410	770
1989/90			P/y ½ x £(370 + 350)	360	
			Actual £(180+190)	370	
			I.R. to actual		370
1990/91			Actual		170

5.0   THE DEDUCTION OF INCOME TAX AT SOURCE (TA 1988,ss.348 and 349)

Income tax at the basic rate is normally deducted from certain annual payments. These are:

(a)   any annuity or annual payment other than interest - mostly from deeds of covenant (mortgage interest on a qualifying loan is paid net under the MIRAS Scheme);

(b)   patent royalties;

(c)   certain mining rents and royalties.

Where the payment is made out of income liable to tax the payer may deduct tax from it at the basic rate in force at the due date of payment irrespective of when it was paid (TA 1988,s.348). The payment when grossed-up is treated as a charge on the income of the payer and reduces his total statutory income. To avoid obtaining double relief for the charge, the tax deducted is added to the individual's tax liability.

Illustration

X, a single man, has Schedule D Case I assessable income of £4,000 for 1989/90. He makes an annual payment of £400 from which he deducts income tax at 25% - £100.

	£	£	£
DI			4,000
Less: Annual payment:			
net paid to recipient		300	
+ tax deducted		100	
			400
			3,600
Less: Personal allowances			2,785
			815

Income tax: £815 @ 25%	204
Add: tax deducted from deed of covenant	100
1989/90 liability	304

Where the annual payments made under deduction of tax exceed the taxpayer's
income brought into charge to tax, the payer must deduct tax at the basic rate
in force at the date the payment was made and must inform the Revenue which will
raise an assessment under TA 1988,s.349 to recover the tax. The procedure of
raising the assessment under s.349 is to give the taxpayer the opportunity of
appealing against it. As, however the normal rule is that income tax is only
payable on income it means that the s.349 assessment is treated as notional
income.

Illustration

The facts are as in the previous illustration except that Mr X has no income for
1989/90.

As he has no income the income tax deducted from the annual payment will be paid
over to the Revenue by means of the s.349 assessment.

	Income £	Tax due £
Schedule D I	NIL	NIL
s.349 assessment	400	100
	400	100
From this can be deducted the annual payment of	400	
To give total statutory income of	NIL	

and the £100 tax due on s.349 assessment is satisfied by paying to the Revenue the tax deducted from the annual payment	100
	NIL

Where there is some income then the s.349 assessment can be reduced.

Illustration

The facts are as in the first Illustration in this section, except that Mr X has Schedule D Case I assessable income of £160.

Of the annual payment of £400, £160 is paid out of income and the rest out of capital. There will therefore be a s.349 assessment on £400 - £160 = £240.

6.0 SCHEDULE D CASE VI

This is charged on a wide variety of miscellaneous receipts including:

(a)   furnished lettings;

(b)   certain balancing charges;

(c)   capital profits on patent rights;

(d)   sub-underwriting commissions;

(e)   isolated commissions;

(f)   casual authorship;

(g)   certain introduction fees;

(h)   certain post-cessation receipts.

The income assessable is that arising in the year of assessment.

If losses are made on Schedule D Case VI transactions they may be deducted from other Schedule D Case VI income of the year of assessment and the balance may be carried forward against future Schedule D Case VI income from any source. They may not be offset against general income.

7.0 TRUSTS AND SETTLEMENTS

7.1. Income settlements

(a)   Deeds of Covenant

Deeds of covenant are a means of settling income on an individual or organisation for a specified period without having to lose control of the capital.

In order to be allowed for tax purposes the deed of covenant must satisfy the following conditions:

i)   it must be capable of exceeding six years or three years for convenants to charities;

ii)   it must be irrevocable.

Most deeds of covenant are only eligible for relief from income tax at the basic rate, which is given by retention of the tax deducted at source. There is normally no benefit in entering into a deed of covenant unless the beneficiary is able to reclaim the tax deducted and retained by the covenantor.

The deeds of covenant which are allowable for higher rate taxes are:

i)   all deeds entered into before 7th April 1965 provided they are payable to a named individual who is not, at the time of payment, either a servant, employee or agent of the covenantor;

ii)   deeds entered into after 6th April 1965 only if they are:

     (1)   entered into under a partnership deed for the benefit of a former partner or his widow;

     (2)   entered into in connection with the payer's business;

     (3)   entered into in accordance with a settlement arising from divorce or separation.

iii) deeds of covenant payable to charities.

For payments made after 14th March 1988 annual payments will not be treated as an allowable charge to the payer nor be assessable on the recipient unless they are:

i)   Payments made under an existing obligation - payments made under a deed executed before 15th March 1988 and received by an Inspector of Taxes before 30th June 1988; or

ii)   Payments made under (ii) 1 and 2 above.

To decide whether a covenant is capable of exceeding six years (or three years if appropriate) the relevant date is that on which the deed is signed and not that of the first payment. Thus if the deed contains a provision for seven annual payments but is signed after the first payment is made it may be invalidated. **(IRC v. Trustees of the Hostel of St.Luke).**

(b)   Life Interests and Life Tenants

Another form of income settlement is obtained where a person settles property for life or a period of time determined by reference to the life or lives of identifiable persons, so that those persons can enjoy that property or the income therefrom during the period specified. The person able to enjoy the income is known as the life tenant and his right to the income is known as a life interest.

The life tenant is deemed to have received the income arising from the trust property the moment it is received by the trustees, irrespective of when and how much of it they release to the life tenant. The extent of the life tenant's liability to income tax is determined by the income of the trust, or his share of the income if there is more than one life tenant, after payment of the trustees' expenses properly attributable to income.

7.2 Settlements of capital

A settlement of capital may be:

(a) Absolute - where the capital becomes the property of the beneficiary as soon as the trust is created and the trustees' actions are treated as those of the beneficiary. Any income arising under the trust is taxed as the income of the beneficiary immediately, even if it is not distributed to him.

(b) Contingent - here the capital will not vest in the beneficiary unless a specified event happens, e.g. when he attains the age of 25 years or earlier marriage. In such circumstances only income actually distributed to the beneficiary is considered as his.

(c) Discretionary - in this case the treatment is somewhat similar to the contingent settlement except that the distribution of income and capital is totally at the discretion of the trustees and the trust terms are such that the settlement is likely to continue for many years.

Where a distribution is made out of a trust it will be considered as being made net of tax and must be grossed-up for inclusion in the recipient's taxable income. The rate at which the grossing-up takes place is dependent upon the type of settlement involved. Any income arising to trustees under a discretionary or accumulation trust is liable to additional rate tax at 10% as well as the basic rate of tax. In such circumstances the grossing-up rate will be 35% for 1989/90 - 25% basic rate tax and 10% additional rate; in all other cases the rate will be 25% basic rate only.

As regards the trust, all income received is liable to tax in the normal way either by deduction at source or by direct payments by the trustees. As indicated above, there is a liability to additional rate tax in the case of discretionary etc. trusts.

The trustees are required to make a return annually to the Revenue of the income and charges of the trust and from this will be calculated the liability of the trust to tax.

Illustration

The AB Will Trust consists of the following assets:

House let since 1965 at £900 per annum, the tenant paying the rates and being responsible for internal repairs. During 1989/90 the landlord paid £90 for external decorations and £30 management expenses.

£6,000 9% Treasury Stock 1999 (bought 6th May 1973, interest payable 17th May and 17th November).

8,000 shares in C Ltd of 25p each, fully paid, on which a dividend of 2.5p per share was paid on 3rd June 1989.

Lloyds Bank deposit (opened 1st January 1975) on which the interest received has been:

    1987/88 - £35;   1988/89 - £38;   1989/90 - £31

The trust expenses, other than those in respect of the house, payable out of income, amount to £50 per annum.

The net income of the trust for the year ended 5th April 1990 was fully distributed to the two beneficiaries, who are joint life tenants. (The trust is not discretionary.)

THE AB WILL TRUST
Statement of Trust Income

	£	£	Income Tax Due £
House - rent		900.00	
Less: repairs	90.00		
management expenses	30.00	120.00	
	—		
		780.00	195.00
£6,000 9% Treasury Stock 1999		540.00	135.00
Dividend from C Ltd	200.00		
Tax credit at 25/75	66.67	266.67	66.67
Lloyds Bank deposit interest		41.33	10.33
		1,628.00	407.00
Less: Income tax		407.00	======
		1,221.00	
Less: Trustees' expenses		50.00	
Net income available for division		1,171.00	

The certificate issued by the trustees to each of the beneficiaries will be as follows:

Certificate of Deduction of Tax - R 185 E

Gross amount of beneficiaries' share of trust income	Amount of income tax suffered thereon by the trust	Amount of net payment actually made to beneficiaries
(1) £	(2) £	(3) £
780.66	195.16	585.50

Notes: (1) The income tax column includes all the liability of the trust, not just the tax suffered by deduction.

      (2) If a statement of trust income is not required the beneficiaries' gross share can be calculated as follows:

	£
Net income from house	780.00
9% Treasury Stock	540.00
Dividend from C Ltd	266.67
Deposit interest	41.33
	1,628.00

Less: Trustees' expenses:
    £50 x $\dfrac{100}{75}$ 66.67

1,561.33 divided by 2 = £780.66

The trustees' expenses must be grossed-up as they are paid out of net income.

7.3 Settlements on children

Where a settlement is created by a parent in favour of the infant, unmarried child of the settlor then the distributed income is for tax purposes treated as the income of the parent. An infant child is one aged under 18 and includes the adopted, illegitimate or stepchild of the settlor. To avoid this, an accumulation and maintenance settlement may be created. In this type of settlement, income is accumulated and distributed only on the occurrence of a certain event, often when the child marries after reaching the age of 18 or attains a certain age. Whilst retained income is liable to basic and additional rate tax in the hands of the trustees it will not be assessable on the parent unless the income is distributed.

8.0 LIFE ASSURANCE

Prior to FA 1984 life assurance policies were extremely attractive investments. Not only did the premiums payable attract tax relief, up to certain limits, but income and gains received by the insurance company on the policy investments also attracted a favourable rate of tax. Insurance policies taken out after 13th March 1984 will not qualify for relief on the premiums paid though the favourable tax rates applying to income and capital gains still remain.

8.1 Relief for policies taken out pre - 14.3.1984

A deduction of 12½% is made from the qualifying premiums. The taxpayer pays the net premium to the life assurance company which then recovers the deduction from the Inland Revenue.

Illustration

C took out a qualifying life assurance policy in 1980; he pays a premium of £100 per year before relief.

	£
Gross premium	100.00
Tax relief	12.50
Paid to assurance company	87.50

The tax relief must not exceed 12½% of the greater of 1/6 of total statutory income, or £1,500.

Illustration

D has the following income for 1989/90

		£
Salary		10,000
Dividends gross		6,000

He pays mortgage interest of £1,600 gross and life assurance premiums of £2,250 after tax relief.

	£
Salary	10,000
Dividends	6,000
	16,000
Mortgage interest	1,600
Total statutory income	14,400

Life assurance relief available on the greater of

			£
(a)	1/6 x £14,400	=	2,400
	or		
(b)	£1,500		

As the gross premiums are £2,250 x 100/87.50 = £2,571

relief has been overclaimed on £2,571 - £2,400 = £171 and relief of £171 x 12½% = £21 will be clawed back.

To obtain relief for pre-14.3.1984 policies it was necessary for them to be qualifying policies; broadly the conditions were:

(a) the policy should be on the lives of the taxpayer or his spouse;

(b) the maturity date should be at least 10 years from the date the policy was taken out;

(c) the premiums have to be paid at annual or shorter intervals and not vary excessively from year to year.

Where a qualifying policy is varied after 13th March 1984 it will cease to qualify for relief.

8.2 Relief for later policies

No tax relief is given on policies taken out after 13.3.1984 but the income of the life assurance company still qualifies for tax exemptions.

8.3 Surrenders of policies

The surrender of a life assurance policy within 10 years can give rise to a liability to higher rate tax on any excess of surrender proceeds over premiums paid. Any excess is subject to top-slicing relief as under:

(a) find the profit;

(b) divide it by the life of the policy (complete years only);

(c) find the tax on the annual equivalent in (b) above treating it as the top slice of taxable income of the fiscal year in which surrender occurs;

(d) multiply the tax so found by the number of complete years.

Illustration

E has an income for 1989/90 of £21,400 after all deductions and personal allowances. In that year he surrenders a qualifying life assurance policy on its 6th anniversary. The surrender value was £9,200 and the premiums paid £6,200.

Gain on policy surrendered:

			£
Surrender value			9,200
Premiums paid			6,200
			3,000
Annual equivalent £3,000 6 =			500
Taxable income			21,400

		£	
Tax - £20,700 @ 25%			5,175
£ 700 @ 40%			280
			5,455
- On annual equivalent			
£500 @ 40%		200	
Less: Basic rate tax			
£500 @ 25%		125	
		75 x 6	450
			5,905

A similar treatment applies to non-qualifying policies and investment and property bonds. The latter are single premium policies which aim to give a substantial capital profit over a fixed term. They often include the right of a policyholder to make partial surrenders. These will be tax free if they do not exceed 5% of the original investment per year. This is calculated on a cumulative basis and if they do, the excess is charged to tax in the year the event occurs. At the end of the fixed term of the policy, partial withdrawals are included in finding the overall profit.

9.0 PURCHASED ANNUITIES

A person can make a lump sum purchase of an annuity. This will guarantee a payment on a regular basis for a fixed period of time, often for the recipient's life. The payment received from the assurance company will consist of a repayment of capital and an interest payment on the remainder of the investment. The amount of the capital element is fixed by the Inland Revenue, subject to appeal, and is tax free. The income element will be subject to basic rate tax prior to receipt by the annuitant.

10.0 ENTERPRISE FUNDING

10.1 General

In recent years, a number of incentives have been given to encourage investment in new or existing enterprises. They can be loosely classified as:

(a) Reactive incentives
(b) Pro-active incentives.

Reactive incentives take the form of relief given for a loss. They include relief for losses on shares subscribed for in a qualifying trading company s.574, TA 1988, relief for losses incurred by an individual in the first 4 years of trading s.381, TA 1988, and relief for losses made on loans and guarantees to traders.

Proactive incentives are relief given at the time of the investment irrespective of the outcome. They can include regional development grants, the enterprise allowance, personal equity plans and the business expansion scheme.

10.2 Relief for investment in corporate trades - the business expansion scheme

10.2.1   General

This relief is designed to encourage investment in unquoted companies. It is unusual inasmuch as it allows a deduction from income in order to acquire a capital investment. The relief is available to qualifying individuals who subscribe for eligible shares in a qualifying company which carries on a qualifying activity.

10.2.2   Definitions

(a) Qualifying individuals

An individual will qualify if he is resident and ordinarily resident in the UK at the time the shares were issued and he is not connected with the

company at any time during the qualifying period which and ends five years
after the share issue. Crown employees working abroad are treated as
resident and ordinarily resident in the UK for BES relief.

He will be connected with the company if he or an associate is:

(1) an employee of the company;

(2) a partner of the company;

(3) a director of the company, unless no payment is received from the
     company other than reasonable expenses or normal dividends on the
     shares issued;

(4) entitled, with associates, to possess either directly or indirectly
     more than 30% of the share capital or voting rights.

(b)   Eligible shares

These are new ordinary shares which carry no preferential rights to
dividends etc. for the period of five years from the date of issue.

(c)   Qualifying company

This is a company which, during the relevant period:

(1) is incorporated and resident in the UK;

(2) exists wholly or substantially for the purpose of carrying on a
     qualifying trade wholly or mainly in the UK;

(3) is not the subsidiary of another or which has its own subsidiary,
     unless the subsidiary would itself qualify for relief;

(4) is unquoted (this excludes USM companies);

(5) has all its shares fully paid up.

(d)   Qualifying trades

These must be bona fide trades carried on commercially and with a view to
profit. It will not qualify if it is a trade consisting of:

(1) dealing in land, commodities or shares;

(2) dealing in goods other than in the course of wholesale or retail
     distribution, dealing in collectible items normally held as
     investments; are excluded where the company holds stocks for excessive
     periods of time;

(3) banking, insurance or money lending;

(4) providing legal or accountancy services.

The trade must be carried on commercially through the relevant period which commences at the date on which the shares are issued and ends normally three years after the date of issue or three years from the start of trading if later. Relief is not available for shares issued after 18th March 1986 in companies which are substantially 'land backed'. These are companies which in the relevant period have more than 50% of their net assets in land. As an exception, for shares issued after 28th July 1988 and before 1st January 1994 BES relief will be available for shares in companies investing in the qualifying activity of letting dwelling houses on assured tenancies. The dwelling houses must not have a market value of more than £125,000 (in greater London) or £85,000 elsewhere.

(e)   Maximum investment

From 15th March 1988, a maximum is imposed on the amount that a company can raise in a given period. The maximum is normally:

i)   £500,000
ii)   £5,000,000   for companies letting dwelling houses on assured
                      tenancies, and for ship chartering companies.

The given period is the longer of:

i)   6 months preceding the issue, or
ii)   the period from the previous 6th April to the date of the issue.

No BES relief is given for any excess investment which is apportioned between the persons subscribing for shares pro rata to their qualifying subscriptions.

10.2.3   Relief available

The maximum relief available to an individual is £40,000 in any one year of assessment. The minimum investment in a company qualifying for relief is normally £ 500. Husband and wife are treated as one person. There is no restriction on the number of shares issued which qualify for relief though no individual must hold more than 30% (see above).

Illustration

X, Y and Z make the following investments in qualifying companies in 1989/90:

	Alpha Ltd	Beta Ltd
	£	£
X	200	400

No relief is available as the investment in either company is not at least £500.

	£	£
Y	400	11,000

Relief is available in respect of the investment in Beta Ltd. The investment in Alpha Ltd is under the £500 limit.

	£	£
Z	15,000	30,000
	======	======

Overall relief will be restricted to a maximum of £40,000.
The relief is given in the same way as a personal allowance after all other
reliefs; this gives a potential 40% maximum rate of relief.

Illustration

X has the following income for 1989/90:

Earned	£25,000
Unearned	£24,000

He is married and pays mortgage interest of £2,000 (not under MIRAS).   He makes
a qualifying investment of £12,000.

1989/90

	£	£
Earned income		25,000
Unearned income	24,000	
Less: Mortgage interest	2,000	
	_____	22,000
		_____
		47,000
Less: Personal allowances:		
MA	4,375	
Business Expansion Relief	12,000	
	_____	16,375
		_____
		30,625
		======

Tax:

£		£
20,700 @ 25%		5,175
9,925 @ 40%		3,970
_____		_____
30,625		9,145
_____		_____

From 6th April 1987 an element of carry back has been introduced into the
relief. Up to one-half of the amount subscribed before 6th October in a fiscal
year up to a maximum of £5,000 can be related back into the preceding fiscal
year and deducted there. The total of the amount paid in the earlier year and
the amount carried back cannot exceed the maximum £40,000 offset.

10.2.4   Withdrawal of relief

Relief will be withdrawn if during the relevant period - five years from the
date of issue of the shares - either:

(a)   the shares are disposed of; or
(b)   value is withdrawn from the company.

10.2.5   Disposal of shares

On a sale of shares the relief given will be clawed back via a Schedule D Case VI assessment for the fiscal year for which relief was originally given. For disposals by way of gift the relief is totally withdrawn. For all other disposals the relief is reduced by the amount of the consideration received. Where there has been more than one qualifying subscription for shares of the same class, disposals will be matched on a FIFO basis. Where the shares have been sold after five years, there will be no withdrawal of relief.

For CGT purposes, any excess of disposal proceeds over cost will be assessed as a capital gain. If the shares are sold at a loss, the amount of the loss will be reduced by any amount on which relief has been obtained under the Business Expansion Scheme.

Illustration

Y subscribed £10,000 for qualifying shares in 1984 obtaining relief at 60%. After 5 years they were sold for:

(a)   £14,000

(b)   £7,000

As the disposal took place after five years there will be no clawback of Business Expansion Relief. The CGT position (ignoring indexation) would be:

	(a) £	(b) £
Disposal proceeds	14,000	7,000
Cost	10,000	10,000
Chargeable gain	4,000	
Loss		(3,000)
Less: Amount on which relief obtained under Business Expansion Scheme		10,000
Allowable loss		NIL

If the disposal had taken place within five years, Business Expansion Relief would have been withdrawn on:

        (a)   £10,000 @ 60%   =   £6,000

        (b)   £ 7,000 @ 60%   =   £4,200

Where shares subscribed for after 18th March 1986 are sold they will not be liable to CGT provided that BES relief has not been withdrawn.

10.2.6   Value withdrawn

If the investor receives value from the company within five years of the issue
of the shares, relief will be withdrawn to the extent of the amount received.
Value received can include:

(a)   repayment of loans;

(b)   redemption of share capital;

(c)   payments for forgiveness of debts;

(d)   provision of benefits;

(e)   transfers at an undervalue.

CHAPTER NINE

Schedule E

1.0 SCOPE

Tax is charged under Schedule E on the 'emoluments of an office or employment'.

1.1 Definitions

'Emoluments'

These include all salaries, wages, fees, benefits, perquisites and profits whatsoever.

'Office'

An office is a position existing independently of the incumbent. The Archbishop of York holds an office.

'Employment'

Employment exists where there is a legal relationship of master and servant. This may be evidenced by a contract of employment or may be implied by conduct.

Whether the taxpayer is employed or self-employed is sometimes a matter of some difficulty to decide.

In **Stevenson Jordan and Harrison Ltd v. Macdonald & Evans Ltd (1952)**, Lord Denning looked to the place of the person in the organisation of the 'employer' and implied that if he occupied an integral part of that organisation then his relationship was more likely to be that of an employee and not that of an independent self-employed contractor.

In **Fall v. Hitchen (1973)** a professional ballet dancer worked under contract at Sadlers Wells. His contract was a full-time one and prohibited him from undertaking other duties without the consent of his employer. Held that the contract was one of service rather than one of services.

In deciding whether a person is employed or self-employed the following may be taken into account:

(a)   whether the person provides own equipment;

(b)   whether he can delegate his work to a third party;

(c)   the degree of freedom that he possesses in deciding where and when the work is performed;

(d)   what financial risk he undertakes;

(e)   whether he can profit by sound management.

2.0   INCOME ASSESSABLE

2.1   General

The income assessable under Schedule E is that received in the year of assessment.   Up to 1988/89 it was the income earned for the year.   In general emoluments will be treated as received at the earlier of:

(a)   when an actual payment is made of those emoluments, or a payment is made on account of them;

(b)   when a person becomes entitled to the payment of those emoluments.

For directors, they will be treated as received at the earlier of (a) or (b) above, or if earlier:

(c)   when an amount representing the emoluments is credited in the company's accounts, irrespective of any impediment imposed on withdrawal;

(d)   the end of the company's accounting period, if the accounts due have been finalised before then;

(e)   the date the final emoluments are determined if that is after the end of the accounting period.

If directors' remuneration is approved in annual general meeting, the date of the AGM on which the accounts are approved will be treated as the date of entitlement.

The change of the basis of assessment from the earnings to the receipts basis gives the possibility of a double charge to tax where, say, emoluments were earned in 1988/89 but received in 1989/90 or later years.,   Emoluments earned before 5th April, 1989 may, however, be assessed on the earnings basis provided that payment is received by 5th April, 1991 and written notice is given to the Inland Revenue by that date.

Benefits are not dealt with under the receipts basis and continue to be assessed when they are provided.

(a) wages and salaries;

(b) pensions from approved superannuation schemes, the State or any other source including a voluntary pension;

(c) other social security benefits, including retirement pensions, unemployment benefits and widows' pensions. Sickness, maternity benefits, attendance allowance and child benefit are **not** taxable.

Pensions and social security benefits are assessible in the fiscal year to which they relate.

To be liable to tax, the emoluments must **derive** from the office of employment. In **Hochstrasser v. Mayes (1959)** Upjohn J said:

> '... the payment must be made in reference to the services the employee renders by virtue of his office and it must be something in the nature of a reward for services past, present or future.'

The payments taxable are not merely those such as salaries and wages but can also include payments by way of bonus or appreciation for services.

In **Moorhouse v. Dooland (1955)** the taxpayer was a professional cricketer. Under the club rules, he was entitled to talent money and a public collection whenever he produced a particularly meritorious performance. In the 1951/52 season he so qualified on eleven occasions. Held the proceeds of the public collections were taxable. They were a contractual right and therefore an emolument of the employment.

In **Seymour v. Reed (1927)** the taxpayer was again a professional cricketer and in 1920 was awarded a benefit which meant he was entitled to a public collection and the proceeds of one of the home matches. Held not taxable. The awards were not contractual and were in the form of an appreciation.

Certain principles can be drawn from these and similar cases:

(a) if the entitlement to a payment is contractual it is strong grounds for considering it to be an emolument **(Moorhouse v. Dooland)**;

(b) recurrence may be an important factor **(Seymour v. Reed)**.

In **Moore v. Griffiths (1972)**, Bobby Moore received a payment from the Football Association in recognition of England's victory in the 1966 World Cup. Held not taxable. The payment was intended to mark a great sporting achievement. It was 'one-off' and unlikely to be repeated;

(c) if the payment is made as a result of the office or employment the identity of the payer is irrelevant.

In **Blakiston v. Cooper (1909)** a vicar of a parish received the customary Easter offering from the parishioners. Held taxable. The payment was made in respect of the services performed as incumbent of a parish; the fact that the payment was voluntary and not made by the employer was irrelevant.

However, payments made as a mark of personal esteem may not be taxable even
if made by the employer.   In **Ball v. Johnson (1971)** an award made to a bank
clerk for passing the Institute of Bankers' examinations was held not to be
taxable.

2.2 Benefits

As already mentioned the emoluments assessable under Schedule E include benefits
in kind.   This term includes many items such as free holidays, housing and the
private use of a firm's car.   For the assessment of benefits, employees fall into
two classes:

(a)   Non-P11D Personnel

These are:

i)   employees earning less than £8,500 per annum;

ii)   directors who are full-time working directors, do not have a material
interest in the company, and who earn less than £8,500 per annum.

(b)   P11D Personnel

These are:

i)   directors, other than those in (ii) above;

ii)   employees earning £8,500 or more per annum.

A full-time working director is one required to devote substantially the
whole of his time to the service of the company in a managerial or technical
capacity.

A person will have a material interest if together with his associates he
can control more than 5% of the ordinary share capital of the company.   The
meanings of 'associates' and 'ordinary share capital' are as for Corporation
Tax.

Where a person is employed by more than one employer each employment will be
considered separately.   However, where there are two or more employments
with the same employer, including the situation where there are employments
with several companies within the same group, they will be considered as one
in deciding whether the individual has reached the £8,500 limit.

2.3 Treatment of benefits for lower paid (non-P11D) employees

The basic rule for the taxability of benefits for this group of employees is
that the benefit must be capable of cash convertibility.

In **Tennant v. Smith (1892)** the taxpayer was a senior employee of the Bank of
Scotland in Montrose.   He was required to live over the bank and could not leave
his accommodation for substantial periods without the consent of his employers.
He was not allowed to sublet the accommodation or use it other than for his
employer's business.   Held he was not assessable in respect of the benefit of his
occupation of the premises.   Per the Earl of Halsbury LC the benefit is,

' ... not income unless it can be turned into money.'

If the benefit is capable of cash conversion then the quantum will be the cash into which it could be converted.

In **Wilkins v. Rogerson (1961)** an employer arranged for all the employees to purchase at his expense a suit, overcoat or sports jacket up to a maximum cost of £15. Held to be taxable. The item of clothing was the employee's property and therefore capable of cash conversion. The quantum of the benefit was, however, only the second-hand value of the suit, £5.

Certain benefits may be received which are not capable of cash conversion, for example, if an employer pays a fine of an employee. Where the employer pays for an item which is the legal liability of the employee it is taxable irrespective of any cash convertibility.

In **Nichol v Austin (1935)** the taxpayer's contract of service provided that he should reside in his own house but that his employers should pay all expenses including rates, insurance, heating and maintenance of the house and gardens. Held that the payments constituted money's worth and were therefore taxable.

2.4 Benefits - directors and those employees earning over the income limit (P11D employees)

Members of this class of taxpayer are liable to tax in respect of any benefit provided by the employer. The value of the benefit is the cost to the employer. In deciding to which class of taxpayers the person belongs, all emoluments received by the employee are aggregated with the benefits valued as if they were received by a P11D employee. No expenses are deducted.

Benefits received by this class of employee must be returned on form P11D. Dispensations from the completion of all or part of the return may be given by the Revenue. If the dispensation is given the expenses and benefits will be disregarded in determining whether the £8,500 limit has been reached.

It is not necessary for the benefit to be provided to the employee direct, it will be taxable upon him if it is provided to a member of his family or household. The family includes a spouse, parents, sons or daughters and their spouses. Neither is it necessary that the employee should be the exclusive recipient of the benefit. It is enough if it is made available to him and he does not disclaim it. Also, the fact that he would have spent less on the benefit had he provided it himself is irrelevant.

In **Rendell v. Went (1964)**, a company director was charged with dangerous driving. The potential penalty, if he were convicted, was a term of imprisonment. The company did not wish to lose his services and employed legal representatives to defend him. Held he was liable to tax on the amount of the services provided. The fact that they also benefited his employers was immaterial.

Entertainment provided to an employee which:

(a) is by a person other than his employer, and

(b) is not provided as a reward for services performed or likely to be perfomed;

is not treated as a benefit.

2.5   Special classes of benefits

(a)   Motor Cars:

The benefit of the use of a car depends upon the nature of its use:

i)   The 'Perk' Car

This is a car provided for the use of an employee or director where the business use is insubstantial. This is where the business mileage is not more than 2,500 per annum. Also, where any second cars are provided, the 'perk car' rules apply to such cars irrespective of business use.

The benefit of a perk car is one and a half times cost price calculated in the same way as for a business car together with any appropriate petrol and other benefits.

ii)   The Business Car

Where the use of the car for business purposes is not insubstantial (i.e. the car is not regarded as a 'perk' car) the value of the benefit is established by reference to Tables which are updated periodically, and which are indicated below. If the business mileage is 18,000 or more annually, the benefit is reduced by one-half.

1989/90

Table 1
Cars with original market value of up to £19,250

Cylinder in cubic centimetres	Age at end of year of assessment	
	Under 4 years	4 years or more
	£	£
1,400 or less	1,400	950
1,401 - 2,000	1,850	1,250
2,001 or more	2,950	1,950

Table 2
Cars with original market value up to £19,250 but with no cylinder capacity

Original market value	Age at end of year of assessment	
	Under 4 years	4 years or more
	£	£
Less than £ 6,000	1,400	950
£6,000 - £8,499	1,850	1,250
£8,500 - £19,250	2,950	1,950

Table 3
Cars with original market value more than £19,250

Original market value	Age at end of year of assessment	
	Under 4 years	4 years or more
	£	£
£19,251 - £29,000	3,850	2,600
more than £29,000	6,150	4,100

The calculation of the benefit is as under: £   £

                    Benefit per table   x

          Less: Period of unavailability (see below)   x

                Private contribution for use of car   x

                                                              _   x
                                                                   _

          Assessable benefit   x
                                                                   =

The car will not be available on a day when it was not available for the employee to use or was incapable of being used provided in the last case that the period in which it was incapable of being used exceeded 30 consecutive days. This restriction also applies to fuel benefits (see below).

There will be a fuel benefit if **any** fuel is made available for the employee's private use. It will be made available if:

(a) any liability for the supply of fuel is discharged;

(b) a voucher or credit token is used to obtain fuel;

(c) a sum is paid for expenses in providing fuel.

If the car has travelled 18,000 or more business miles per annum the scale is reduced by one-half. The scale charge will be reduced to nil where:

(a) the fuel is only provided for business use, or

(b) the employee makes good the **whole** of any private fuel used.

Partial contribution towards private usage of fuel cannot be deduced. The amount of the benefit for 1989/90 is listed below:

Table 1
Cars with cylinder capacity

Cylinder capacity in cubic centimetres	Cash equivalent
1,400 or less	£480
1,401 - 2,000	£600
2,001 or more	£900

Table 2
Cars with no cylinder capacity

Original market value	Cash equivalent
Less than £6,000	£480
£6,000 - £8,499	£600
Over £8,499	£900

Where other expenses are reimbursed to the employee, there may be an additional benefit in respect of these expenses. These will only be treated as an additional benefit if they are round sum allowances.

Illustration

B has the use of a Silver Shadow Rolls Royce which cost £20,000 in 1972 and has a cylinder capacity of 7,941 cc. It was acquired by his present employers in 1975 for £ 10,000. In the year ended 5th April 1990 the running costs of the car were:

Paid directly by employer:

Tax	£100
Repairs	£950
Petrol (business use)	£2,300

Reimbursed to employee:

Insurance	£900
Private petrol	£700

It is estimated that of the total mileage of 20,000, 5,000 relates to business. B contributes £100 towards private use of the car. In the year, the car was involved in a serious accident and as a result was incapable of use for 49 consecutive days.

	£	£
Benefit per table	2,600	
Less: Period of inactivity $\frac{49}{365}$	349	2,251
Petrol benefit per table	900	
Less: Period of inactivity $\frac{49}{365}$	121	779
		3,030
Less: Private contribution towards use of car		100
		2,930

Private contributions towards petrol could not be deducted. The provision of a chauffeur would be an additional assessable benefit.

The cost of providing car parking facilities is not treated as a benefit.

    iii) The Pool Car

        Where the car is a 'pool' car there will be no assessable benefit. To qualify, the following conditions must be satisfied:

        (1) it must be available to two or more persons;

        (2) it must not normally be kept overnight at or near the residence of the employee concerned;

(3)   private use must be incidental.
      Regular travel between home and work would not be considered
      incidental.

(b)   Accommodation

Where accommodation is provided for any category of employee there is an
assessable benefit. This is equal to the higher of either the gross annual
value for rateable purposes, or the rent paid by the employer.

There is an additional charge levied where an employee is taxable in respect
of an occupation benefit and the cost of the accommodation (including
improvements) exceeds £75,000. This charge is calculated as:

(Cost of providing the accommodation - £75,000) x appropriate percentage

The appropriate percentage is the official rate of interest as applied to
beneficial loans at the beginning of the fiscal year - presently 14.5%.

The benefit can be reduced by any private contribution.

Illustration

A had the use of a company flat in 1989/90 which had a rateable value of
£800. It cost £240,000 to his employers. He contributes £2,000 per annum
for the use of the flat. Assume a beneficial interest rate of 14.5%.

	£
Annual value	800
Additional charge	
£240,000 - £75,000 = £165,000	
14.5% thereof	23,925
	24,725
Less: Contribution	2,000
	22,725

There is no assessable benefit either, on the annual value, rent or
additional charge when the employee's (whether higher or lower paid)
occupation is job-related. This is:

i)   where it is necessary that the employee should reside in the
      accommodation to properly perform his duties, or

ii)   where it is customary to provide employees of a particular class with
      accommodation to enable them to more effectively perform their duties,
      or

iii) where the premises are provided to counter a threat to the personal
      security of the employee.

The concept of job-related occupation under (i) and (ii) above will also apply to full-time working directors who do not have a material interest. Other directors are generally liable in full. Relief under (iii) is available to all employees and directors.

Where the services are provided in connection with the accommodation there is an assessable benefit on the recipient. This applies whether or not the occupation is job-related though if it is, no charge will be made for rates. A charge can therefore arise to higher-paid employees in respect of the following:

i)   lighting, heating and cleaning;
ii) repairs, other than structural repairs, maintenance and decoration;
iii) the provision of furniture, calculated as 20% of cost.

However, where the occupation is representative, the charge in respect of these services must not exceed a limit. This limit is 10% of the employee's total emoluments (excluding the above, and as reduced by other allowable expenses, capital allowances and pension, personal pensions or retirement annuity contributions), less any sum made good by the employee.

Illustration
C receives a salary of £20,000 from his employer together with a company car the assessable benefit of which is £700. He pays 10% of his basic salary to an approved pension scheme. He also occupies a company house and it is agreed that the accommodation is representative. In 1989/90 his employers pay the following expenses:

	£
Rates	1,200
Light and heat	1,350
Redecoration	220
Wages of cleaner	600
Benefits assessable:	
Light and heat	1,350
Redecoration	220
Wages	600
	_____
	2,170
	======

	£
Salary	20,000
Car benefit	700
	_____
	20,700
Less: Pension scheme contributions	2,000
	_____
	18,700
Accommodation benefit as above £2,170	
======	
restricted to 10% x £18,700	1,870
	_____
	20,570
	======

Where employees receive bed and board accommodation as part of their overall job package there will generally be no benefit in respect of lower-paid employees as the benefit will not be capable of cash conversion. For higher paid employees, the benefit will be the cost to the employer of providing such accommodation.

(c)   Loans (P11D employees only)

Where a director or employee (or his relative) has a loan from the employer and it is wholly or partly written off, the amount written off is a taxable benefit. There will be no benefit where the taxpayer can show that he is charged to tax elsewhere, e.g. as a participator in a close company, or where the loan was made to a relative and he can show that he received no benefit through it being written off. There will still be a benefit if the loan is written off after the employee has ceased employment unless the loan was written off as the result of the employee's death.

When a loan is made to an employee at a favourable rate of interest, the difference between the interest charged and that calculated by using an official rate is a taxable benefit but only if the difference exceeds £200. There is no liability where the interest would, if paid, have been allowed as a deduction for income tax purposes, e.g. to purchase a main residence.

The benefit will be either calculated on an informal or a formal basis:

i)   **Informal**:

$$\frac{\text{Balance of loan at beginning of fiscal year} + \text{Balance of loan at end of fiscal year}}{2} = \text{Average Loan}$$

	£
Average Loan x official rate of interest	x
Less: Payment made	x
	—
Benefit	x
	=

ii)   **Formal**:

Interest is calculated on a day to day basis.

The official rates of interest are:

        11.5% between 6.4.1987 to 5.6.1987
        10.5% between 6.6.1987 to 5.9.1987
        11.5% between 6.9.1987 to 5.12.1987
        10.5% between 6.12.1987 to 5.5.1988
         9.5% between 6.5.1987 to 5.8.1988
        12.0% between 6.8.1988 to 5.10.1988
        13.5% between 6.10.1988 to 5.1.1989
        14.5% between 6.1.1989 to 5.7.1989
        15.5% from 6.7.1989

Either the taxpayer or the Revenue can elect for the interest calculation to be on the formal basis.

Illustration

B had a balance on his loan account from his employer of £20,000 at 6th April 1989. He repaid £8,000 on 1st December 1989. The loan agreement with his employer provides that he is to be charged interest at 2% on the balance at the beginning of the fiscal year.

	£
Informal basis:	
$\frac{£20,000 + 12,000}{2}$ = £16,000	
£16,000 x 14.5% x 91/365	578
£16,000 x 15.5% x 274/365	1,861
	2,439
Less: Interest paid	400
	2,039
	=====

	£
Formal basis:	
£20,000 x 91/365 x 14.5%	723
£20,000 x 148/365 x 15.5%	1,257
£12,000 x 126/365 x 15.5%	642
	2,622
Less: Interest paid	400
Benefit	2,222
	=====

If the loan was for a qualifying purpose no charge would be made.

(d)   Other assets provided

Where other assets which remain the property of the employer are provided for the use of the employees or directors there is a benefit equal to the greater of:

i)   20% of the market value when they were made available as a benefit; and

ii)   the cost of hiring or leasing the asset.

In both cases the amount of the benefit is reduced by the contribution made by the employee.

Illustration

C, a higher-paid employee, has the use of a suit of clothes provided by his employer. It cost his employer £250.

Benefit - 20% x £250 = £50.

If it had been hired by his employers for £80 per year, the benefit would be the greater of:

£50   or   £80 = £80

Where the asset is given or sold to the employee then the benefit is the greater of:

	£
Market value at date of disposal	x
Less: Price paid by employee	x
	—
	x
	=

OR

Original market value		x
Less: Already assessed on employee		x
		—
		x
Less: Price paid		x
		—
		x
		=

Illustration

If after two years' use the suit was sold to C for £15 when its market value was £25, the benefit would be:

	£
Market value at disposal	25
Less: Price paid	15
	—
	10
	==
Original market value	250
Less: Assessed 2 x £50	100
	—
	150
Less: Price paid	15
	—
	135
	===
The greater is	135
	===

(e) **Vouchers etc.**

The provision of cash or non-cash vouchers is treated as an assessable emolument to both higher and lower paid employees. For cash vouchers the amount assessable is the cash into which it is convertible and for non-cash vouchers the benefit is the cost to the employer, less any amount made good by the employee.

Non-cash vouchers can include cheque vouchers and transport vouchers but exclude luncheon vouchers of a value of not more than 15p per day.

The provision of a credit token and any goods received by using the token are an emolument. A credit token is defined as any card, token, document etc. given to a person, which agrees to provide money, goods or services on credit.

A claim may be made to reduce the amount of the benefit by any genuine business expense.

Vouchers provided for entertainment by a person other than the employer will not represent a benefit unless they are intended to be a reward for services.

(f) Scholarships

A scholarship awarded as a result of a directorship or higher paid employment, will be subjected to income tax as a benefit in kind under Schedule E.

If the scholarship is not awarded as a result of such employment, no taxable benefit would arise if not more than 25% of such scholarship payments are made by reason of the employment. The 25% limit would include lower paid employees in receipt of such benefits but who are not taxed thereon as a benefit in kind.

(g) A summary of benefits is shown overleaf.

2.5 (g)   Benefit Summary

Type	Non-P11D Personnel	P11D Personnel
Luncheon vouchers	No benefit up to 15p per day	No benefit up to 15p per day
Meals in subsidised canteen	No benefit	No benefit where meals available to all members of staff
Use of car:		
(1) Insubstantial use	(No benefit in respect of capital value	(i) Charge at 150% of scale
(2) Substantial use	(possible benefit for private running (costs reimbursed, e.g. private petrol)	(ii) Charge as scale
(3) Pool cars	No benefit	(iii) No benefit
Accommodation	Annual value assessable Excluding representative accommodation	Annual value assessable Excluding representative accommodation (Directors with material interest may be taxed in full)
Running costs of accommodation	Normally not taxable	Taxable benefit as above
Private medical insurance	Not taxable	Taxable benefit equal to cost to employer
Private use of company assets	No benefit	Taxable benefit
Removal expenses	No benefit where required by employer to move elsewhere	No benefit where required by employer to move elsewhere
Beneficial loans	No benefit	Taxable benefit
Loans written-off	Amount written-off is benefit	Taxable benefit
Cash vouchers	Taxable benefit equal to cash benefit of voucher	Taxable benefit as before
Non-cash vouchers including travel and cheque vouchers	Taxable benefit equal to expense incurred in providing voucher	Taxable benefit as before
Scholarships for children of employee	Not assessable	Taxable benefit

Expenses reimbursed by an employer will in general be an allowable deduction for the employee and any question of disallowance will be dealt with in the employer's accounts. If the employee receives a "round sum" allowance this will be normally be considered as part of the emoluments of the employee and he will be responsible for claiming the amount spent which is allowable under the Schedule E expense rule. The employer will obtain full deduction for the whole of the lump sum.

3.0 EXPENSES

Where the director or employee incurs expenses in connection with his employment he can claim a deduction from his Schedule E assessable emoluments. The conditions that must be satisfied are laid down by TA 1988,s.198.

> 'If the holder of an office or employment is necessarily obliged to incur and defray out of the emoluments thereof the expenses of travelling in the performance of the duties of the office or employment or of keeping and maintaining a horse to enable him to perform the same, or otherwise to expend money wholly, exclusively and necessarily in the performance of the said duties, there may be deducted from the emoluments to be assessed the expenses so necessarily incurred and defrayed.'

As can be seen the Schedule E expenses rule is extremely strict: it divides expenses into two broad categories:

(a) travelling expenses;

(b) other expenses.

3.1 Travelling expenses

These will only be allowed as a deduction if they are incurred 'in the performance of the duties of the office or employment'.

In general the costs of travelling from home to work are not allowable. In **Ricketts v. Colquhoun (1926)** the taxpayer was Recorder of Portsmouth and regularly travelled from his home in London to hold Quarter Sessions. He was assessable under Schedule D Case II in respect of his London practice and under Schedule E in respect of his office of Recorder. Held the costs of travelling to Portsmouth were not allowed:

(a) they were not incurred in the performance of his duties which did not start until he arrived at Portsmouth;

(b) they were not incurred necessarily - a Recorder **could** have lived at Portsmouth.

In **Owen v. Pook (1969)** it was held that travel expenses from one place of work to another are generally deductible, and that in certain circumstances one place of work may be the taxpayer's home. Dr. Owen was a medical practitioner in Fishguard who held a part-time medical appointment at a hospital in Haverfordwest. At certain times he would be on standby duty and was required to be available by telephone. If called he would give advice and instructions and if necessary come out to the hospital. He was responsible for the patient immediately he received the telephone call. He claimed a deduction for travelling expenses between his home and the hospital. Held the expenses were allowable: he started work when he received the telephone call and travelling to the hospital was in the performance of his duties.

3.2 Other expenses

These will only be allowed if they are incurred 'wholly, exclusively and necessarily in the performance of the duties'.

The test is strict and disallows many expenses.

In **Brown v Bullock (1961)** a bank manager employed in the West End of London sought to deduct the subscription to a London club where he met clients rather than seeing them in his office. Held that the expenses were not allowable; they were not necessary - he could have seen his clients at the bank.

The requirement of an employer that the employee incurs expenditure is not necessarily a criterion of deductibility. In **Brown v Bullock** the requirement to join the club was 'virtually a condition of the bank manager's appointment' yet it was not enough. Per Donovan LJ

> ' ... the test is not whether the employer imposes the expense but whether the duties do'.

Thus in **Griffiths v. Mockler (1953)**, a major in the army was obliged to join the officers' mess and would have been subject to disciplinary action if he had not joined. Held that the expenses were not in the performance of his duties.

In **Humbles v. Brooks (1962)** a history teacher attended part-time lectures in order to improve his background knowledge. Held that the expense was not allowable; it was not incurred in the performance of the duties.

In **Newlin v. Woods (1966)** an employee was frequently obliged to work unsocial hours and bought a record player and records in order to stimulate his performance whilst working late at night. Held not allowed; it was not necessarily incurred in the performance of the duties. Per Cross J:

> '... it may well be that he was stimulated to work better by hearing good music, just as others may be stimulated to work better by drink...'!

Other cases of interest are:

Blackwell v. Mills (1945) A student employee required to attend part-time classes for a degree was not allowed to deduct expenses;

Sanderson v. Durbridge (1955) A clerk obliged to work in the evenings could not deduct the excess cost of a meal.

In certain cases clothing and food allowances may be negotiated by trade unions; fees paid to professional bodies may be allowed.

For 1989/90, donations to charities up to £480 per year will be allowed as a Schedule E deduction. The deduction will be made by employers from pre-tax earnings and will be passed over by them to designated charities through approved agents appointed for this purpose.

3.3 The expenses claim

To comply with the strict requirements of the law it is necessary to add all the assessable emoluments together and deduct from them the expenses incurred. An example appears in the personal computation section of this manual.

4.0 WAGES IN LIEU OF NOTICE

These are generally not taxable, but see section 6.0 below.

5.0 WORKERS SUPPLIED BY AGENCIES

When a worker is employed through an agency and renders services to a client, which are subject to supervision, direction or control by the client or the agency, he will be treated as assessable under Schedule E. This will not apply to:

(a) entertainers or fashion models,

(b) home workers, or

(c) construction sub-contractors.

The person paying the remuneration, normally the agency, must deduct tax under PAYE and account for it to the Revenue.

6.0 PAYMENTS ON REMOVAL OR RETIREMENT FROM OFFICE

Where an employee receives a lump sum on removal or retirement from his office or employment it is liable to tax under Schedule E. It is treated as earned income received at the date of removal or retirement and must be notified by the payer to the Revenue within 30 days of the year of assessment in which the payment is made.

6.1 Deductions

Although such a lump sum is liable to tax under Schedule E, there are several exemptions and reliefs which remove many payments from liability to tax, or otherwise reduce the tax payable. For payments received after 5th April 1988 the basic exemption is £30,000.

Illustration

D retired on 31st December 1989, having been employed by Global Company for the past 40 years. On retirement he received a lump sum payment of £60,000.

The amount that will be taxable is:

	£
Lump sum received	60,000
Less: exemption	30,000
Chargeable lump sum	30,000

Where any of the duties constitute 'foreign service', i.e. where such service would not have been liable to tax under Schedule E Case I, any sums chargeable can be reduced, or further reduced, by the fraction:

$$\frac{\text{foreign service}}{\text{total service}}$$

If in the above Illustration, D spent eight years abroad of the total period of service, the amount assessable would be further reduced:

	£
After exemption	30,000
Less: 8/40 x £30,000	6,000
	24,000

If the foreign service proportion is sufficiently high, the whole of the lump sum will be exempt. For this exemption, it must be shown that the foreign service comprised either:

(a)   three-quarters of the entire service; or

(b)   where total service exceeds 10 years, the whole of the last 10 years; or

(c)   where total service exceeds 20 years, one-half thereof, including any 10 of the final 20 years.

When a redundancy payment is received under the Redundancy Payments Act 1965, it is exempt from tax in the hands of the recipient. However, the maximum available exemption of £30,000 is reduced by such a payment.

Where the compensation payment is contractual and not ex gratia it will be fully taxable as a payment for services under TA 1988,s.19 and no deduction can be claimed therefrom.

In **Dale v. de Soissons (1950)** the contract of employment specified payments to be made in the case of the contract terminating before the end of its full term. The payment was held to be fully taxable, as an emolument.

6.2   Top slicing

To avoid the high effective rate of tax that would be payable if the chargeable amount of the lump sum was assessed in one year, 'top-slicing' relief could be claimed.

This relief has been abolished as from 6th April 1988.

7.0   THE BASIS OF ASSESSMENT

7.1   The cases

Liability to tax under Schedule E is under one of three cases:

(a)   Case I

This applies where the employee is resident <u>and</u> ordinarily resident in the UK.

The total emoluments earned by such a person will be liable to tax unless the duties are performed wholly or partly outside the UK when certain deductions may be allowed.

(b)   Case II

This applies where the employee is not resident in the UK or, if resident,
not ordinarily resident in the UK. The emoluments for duties performed in
the UK are taxable under this Case, subject to any deduction for 'foreign
emoluments'.

(c)   Case III

This applies to the emoluments of employees resident in the UK which are not
already liable under Cases I or II. This Case covers income earned abroad
from a non-resident employer and which is remitted to the UK. A charge
under Case I or II supersedes one under Case III.

7.2   Foreign emoluments

'Foreign emoluments' mean earnings of an employee not domiciled in the UK, from a
non-resident employer. Deductions were available up to 1988/89 but have been
abolished after that date.

**7.3   Deductions from the emoluments of an employee resident and ordinarily
          resident in the UK**

When the taxpayer is resident and ordinarily resident in the UK certain
deductions can be made from his assessable emoluments where the duties of the
employment are performed wholly or partly outside the UK.

If they are performed wholly or partly outside the UK and the employee has a
qualifying period of 365 days a deduction of 100% is made from the emoluments
assessable. Visits to the UK will not break the continuity of the qualifying
period of absence provided they do not exceed 62 consecutive days or more than
one-sixth of the total period, whether continuous or not. Days of arrival are
treated as days in the UK but not days of departure.

7.4   Calculation of the deduction

Where a taxpayer is absent for 365 days the period of return to the UK must be
not more than 60 days (1/6 x 365) and as they do not exceed 62 days they may be
continuous.

Where the taxpayer has regular visits back to the UK it is not possible to
consider the period as a whole. It must be divided into qualifying periods of:

(a)   period overseas;

(b)   period in UK;

(c)   period overseas.

At the end of each period the conditions must be satisfied if the taxpayer
wishes to qualify for the 100% deduction, i.e:

(a)   the period in the UK must not exceed 62 continuous days, and

(b)   must not exceed one-sixth of the total period.

Illustration

D goes abroad for 100 days, returns to the UK for 20 days and then goes abroad for a further 60 days.

Overseas	100 days
UK	20 days
Overseas	60 days

180 days x 1/6 = 30

The period qualifies as the days in the UK do not exceed one-sixth of the total. Although it is not yet possible to claim the 100% deduction it is possible to extend the qualifying period.

After the 60 days abroad he returns to the UK for a further 40 days and then goes abroad for a further 150 days.

Overseas	100 days
UK	20 days
Overseas	60 days
UK	40 days
Overseas	150 days

370 days x 1/6 = 61

It is now possible to qualify for the 100% deduction. All the conditions are satisfied - there is no continuous period of 62 days and the days back in the UK do not exceed one-sixth of the total period.

If the second period in the UK was one of 45 days, then the 100% deduction would not have been available:

Overseas	100 days
UK	20 days
Overseas	60 days
UK	45 days
Overseas	150 days

375 days x 1/6 = 62

The period in the UK is 65 days which exceeds one-sixth of the total period. The 100% deduction will now be lost.

It is important to appreciate that the period cannot be looked at as a whole but will be divided up into qualifying periods.

Thus if in the above example the structure of UK visits was:

Overseas	100 days
UK	40 days
Overseas	60 days
UK	20 days
Overseas	150 days

370 days

___

although the total visits to the UK do not exceed one-sixth of the total period
it will not be possible to qualify for the 100% deduction.

Overseas	100 days
UK	40 days
Overseas	60 days
	200 days x 1/6 = 33 days

The first period will not qualify, as the period of return to the UK exceeds the
maximum available.

It is possible at that stage to abandon the first period abroad and attempt to
build up another qualifying period commencing with the second trip:

Overseas	60 days
UK	20 days
Overseas	150 days
	230 days x 1/6 = 38 days

This does qualify but as it is not 365 days then no deductions are available.

The various percentage reductions are made to the emoluments of a qualifying
period, which need not necessarily be co-terminous with a year of assessment.
Thus if A who receives a salary of £12,000 per annum goes to work abroad on 1st
July 1988 returns on 1st August 1989 and then works abroad again for the month of
January 1990, his assessable emoluments will be:

1988/89 £ £

UK duties - 6.4.88 to 30.6.88
      86/365 x £12,000   2,827
Overseas duties - 1.7.88 to 5.4.89
      279/365 x £12,000   9,173
      Less: 100%   9,173
                                                      _____   NIL
                                                                          _____
                                                                          2,827
                                                                          ======

1989/90

Overseas duties - 6.4.89 to 31.7.89
      117/365 x £12,000   3,847
      Less: 100%   3,847
                                                      _____   NIL
UK duties - 1.8.89 to 31.12.89
      153/365 x £12,000   5,030

Overseas duties - 1.1.90 to 31.1.90
      31/365 x £12,000   1,019
No deduction as less than 365 days.

UK duties - 1.2.90 to 5.4.90
      64/365 x £12,000   2,104
                                                                          _____
                                                                          8,153
                                                                          ======

The deduction is applied to the average emoluments of the fiscal year. It may
be possible to establish with the Inland Revenue a higher figure to which the
deduction is to be applied where clearly a higher salary is paid for the
overseas duties.   The deduction is also applied to benefits etc. Where the
benefits clearly relate wholly to the overseas period they will qualify for a
full 100% deduction.   Where they clearly relate to the period of UK duties then
they will not normally qualify for any deduction.

The rules for expenses for employees working abroad are:

(a)   the expenses of travelling to and from the overseas employment are
          allowable. The expense must be borne by the employer or by the employee and
          be reimbursed. Where the employee performs part of his duties in the UK and
          part abroad, there is no limit to the number of trips abroad, the travel
          expenses of which are allowed, provided that the duties can only be
          performed abroad and that the journey is made solely for that purpose;

(b)   expenses of board and lodging are allowed if:

          i)   borne by the employer, or

          ii)   borne by the employee and reimbursed by the employer.

          No allowance is available if the costs were borne by the employee with no
          reimbursement;

(c)   family travel for the spouse or children is allowed if they are paid or
          reimbursed as in (b) above. Relief is, however, only available if the
          taxpayer is absent for a continuous period of at least 60 days and is
          restricted to two return journeys by the same persons in a fiscal year.
          Accommodation provided by the employer is assessable.

Similar relief is also available for non-UK domiciles working in the UK provided
that they were not:

(a)   resident in the UK in either of the two fiscal years immediately preceding
          their arrival in the UK, or

(b)   were not in the UK for any purpose at any time during the two years
          preceding the date of arrival.

Provided that the expense is borne by the employer or borne by the employee and
then reimbursed by the employer, travelling expenses will not be assessed where
they relate to:

(a)   journeys between the country of his normal residence and the UK and back, in
          order to perform his UK duties;

(b)   where he has been in the UK for a continuous period of 60 days or more
          family visits as in (c) above.

The reliefs are limited to a period of five years from the date of the
employee's arrival in the UK.

8.0 PAYE

8.1 General

Most of the tax levied under Schedule E is collected by the Pay As You Earn (PAYE) system which is operated by employers. Tax on the cash equivalent or car benefits, and petrol, etc., are also collected under the PAYE system. The main documentation and tables are as under:

8.2 Tax tables

There are two sets of tax tables used:

(a) Free Pay which by use of a code number allocates the employee's entitlement to personal allowances over the year. Thus an employee paid weekly will receive 1/52nd of his total allowances for that tax year (known as free pay). If he is paid monthly 1/12 of the total allowances will be deducted from his monthly salary before computing the tax payable. In finding the code number the last digit of the total allowances is omitted, so that a person with allowances of £ 2,785 will have a code number of 278. Each code number is followed by a letter L, H or T. 'L' shows that the recipient receives the lower rate of personal allowance and 'H' the higher rate. This enables alterations in personal allowances to be effected speedily. Where a taxpayer does not wish his or her marital status to be known, the code 'T' is given. When an employee commences work and has no code number he is taxed using an emergency code number. This gives him the basic single person's personal allowance. This will be amended once he has completed a return form and submitted it to the Revenue.

(b) Taxable Pay which gives the total tax due on the total remuneration to date less the appropriate proportion of the personal allowances.

Table B shows the tax payable on pay falling into the basic rate band; the table D shows the tax chargeable on pay falling into the higher rate bands.

8.3 Tax record sheets

These record the details of gross pay, free pay, taxable pay and tax due, week by week throughout the year. They also record additional information such as the employee's code number and national insurance number.

8.4 Form P45

This form is used when an employee leaves, and shows his total gross pay, taxable

pay, tax deducted and code numbers in accordance with the tax record sheet which is retained by the former employer. It also shows the week or month up to which entries have been made on the tax record sheet and enables the new employer to continue deducting tax in the correct manner.

8.5 Year-end procedures

At the end of the tax year the employer must provide each employee with a form P60 setting out his gross pay during the year and the total tax deducted therefrom. If the employee considers he has been overtaxed he can apply to his

Income Tax District for a formal assessment under Schedule E using the form P60 as evidence of the tax suffered during the year.

The employer must also send to the Inland Revenue a form P35 showing details of the total tax due to the Inland Revenue no later than 14 days after the end of the relevant fiscal year. This will be accompanied by a year-end return for each employee on form P14 (this is normally a copy of the P60) together with forms P9D (a return of taxable benefits received by non-PIID [lower paid] employees) and PIID where appropriate.

9.0 SHARE OPTION AND INCENTIVE SCHEMES

9.1 General

Share option and incentive schemes have been operated by companies for many years. Legislation introduced in the early 1970s made them unfashionable by subjecting profits to income tax. More recently the trend has been to provide relief for 'approved' schemes.

9.2 Unapproved schemes

Schemes designed purely for one sector or group of employees in general fall outside the approved schemes.

Share options TA 1988,s.186
An employee is liable to income tax under Schedule E on any benefit derived from a share option scheme in the tax year in which the option is exercised. The benefit is calculated by deducting the market value of the shares at the time the option is exercised, from the price paid for the shares by the employee and the price paid for the option (if any). If the right to exercise the option is capable of being exercised more than seven years after grant, there may be a charge to tax on the grant of the rights. Where bonus or rights issues are received, they are deemed to be acquired at the date of the original acquisition. In addition to the above a liability will arise on the final sale of the share-holding. The amount assessed under Schedule E is treated as an addition to the cost of acquiring the shares.

Where, under an option scheme, the employee has acquired shares which have subsequently fallen in value, he may have an agreement with his employer to sell his shares back at not less than that which he paid for them. This is termed a 'Stop Loss' agreement. Where such an arrangement applies it will be considered as being equal to the making of a loan which is then written off and a liability will result under Schedule E.

9.3 Approved Schemes

There are three main schemes. The first was introduced under the provisions of FA 1978 and the initial scheme was followed by variants firstly under the SAYE provisions and then in FA 1984 by a scheme which, though approved, is not entirely open to all employees.

Approved profit-sharing schemes - TA 1988,ss.186, 187 and Sch 9

Provided approval is obtained from the Inland Revenue, employees may acquire shares in their employing companies without any charge arising under Schedule E.

An approved scheme is one where the company provides trustees with cash to acquire shares in the company which they then appropriate to employees. The scheme must be open to all employees, and the shares must be fully paid, irredeemable and not subject to special restrictions. The shares may be quoted or unquoted.

The maximum annual value of shares appropriated to an employee must not exceed the greater of:

(a)   £2,000, or

(b)   10% of salary, exclusive of benefits, but after superannuation contributions, of the current or preceding year (if greater) up to a maximum of £6,000.

The participant must be bound by contract to allow the trustees to retain the shares for a period of retention. This will end at the earlier of:

(a)   the second anniversary of appropriation of the shares to the trustees;

(b)   the date of the participant's death;

(c)   the date on which the participant reaches pensionable age.

If the shares are sold either during the period of retention or within the next three years, tax will be charged under Schedule E on a percentage of the share valuation at the date of appropriation:

Period held	Percentage
During period of retention	100%
2 but less than 4 years	100%
4 but less than 5 years	75%

The 100% or 75% charge will be reduced to 50% if the employee ceases to be employed because of retirement, redundancy or injury.

If the disposal proceeds are less than the value on appropriation, the percentage charge will be applied to the disposal proceeds.

There will be a liability to CGT on the difference between the value on appropriation and the disposal proceeds.

Illustration

X had appropriated to him shares worth £1,000 under an approved profit-sharing scheme. He sold them after 4½ years for:

(a)   £1,800;

(b)   £800.

Sale for £1,800   £

    Schedule E charged on 75% x £1,000   =   £750
                                                                        ====

    CGT liability on £1,800 - £1,000   =   £800
    (subject to indexation)   ====

Sale for £800

    Schedule E charged on 75% x £800   =   £600
                                                                        ====

    Capital loss of £1,000 - £800   =   £200
                                                                        ====

Where the shares sold have been acquired on various dates, they will be identified on a FIFO basis for the purpose of ascertaining the Schedule E charge. For capital gains tax purposes, the normal rules will apply.

To avoid difficulties with private companies whose Articles of Association have required members of the company who are employees to sell their shares on leaving employment, provisions allow for approval for profit-sharing schemes operating this restriction, provided that:

(a)   the disposal consideration must be in cash;
(b)   the formula for calculating it must be specified in the Articles;
(c)   the formula must not discriminate between employee and non-employee shareholders.

FA 1986 has also allowed Workers Co-operatives to set up approved profit-sharing schemes using redeemable shares, broadly under the same conditions as normal approved schemes.

Employees may also participate in approved share option schemes conducted through the medium of an SAYE contract. Broadly, ordinary shares may be acquired from the proceeds of SAYE savings contracts up to a maximum monthly contribution of £150. The price of the shares must be fixed at the time that the employee obtains the option and must represent no less than 90% of the value of the shares at that time. The option will be exercised when the SAYE contract matures and the employee will not be liable to income tax on any profit made on the grant or exercise of the option. To be approved the scheme must be open to all employees and provide that the option cannot normally be exercised within three years of the date of the grant.

Approved Share Option Schemes - TA 1988 s.185 and Sch 9

In general, the existing rules for share option schemes provide that there will be a liability to Schedule E tax on the difference between the market value of the shares at the time the option was exercised and the amount paid for them. Provisions in TA 1988 avoid this charge in respect of approved schemes.

Obtaining approval

Application may be made to the Board of Inland Revenue to approve a share option scheme under the new rules. The Board may withdraw approval where it appears that the conditions are no longer satisfied. Appeals against the Board's decisions may be made to the Special Commissioners.

Conditions

In general, the scheme must provide that options can only be granted to full-time directors or qualifying employees of a participating company. They must be required to work for the company for at least 25 or 20 hours per week respectively. A person who leaves employment may exercise it subsequently and the personal representatives of a deceased employee may exercise it within 12 months of his death.

No options may be granted to an employee or director if he has, or had within the preceding 12 months, a material interest (more than 10% of the ordinary share capital) in a close-company whose shares might be acquired under an approved scheme.

The shares to be acquired under an approved scheme may be those in:

(a)   the company granting the option, or

(b)   its holding company.

The shares must be quoted or unquoted or be in a company controlled by a quoted company, fully paid up and not redeemable. The price to be paid for the shares must be stated when the option is granted and must not be manifestly less than their market value at the date the option was granted. The scheme must limit the value of the shares available to the employee under unexercised options to the greater of:

(a)   £100,000, or

(b)   four times the remuneration (excluding benefits, etc.) of the fiscal year for which the limit needs to be ascertained, e.g. because new options are to be issued, or

(c)   four times the remuneration of the preceding fiscal year.

Share options granted under the scheme must not be transferable. The option must be exercised not less than three, or more than ten, years after granting and not less than three years after the owner last exercised an option under the scheme.

Tax treatment

When the options are granted, there will be no liability under Schedule E except in the unusual circumstances where the price paid for the shares is less than their market value at the time the option was granted. When the option is exercised there will again be no liability provided that the scheme remains approved at that time. On disposal of the shares there will be a liability to CGT on the difference between the amount paid for the shares and the disposal proceeds.

Where a company offers shares to the public at a fixed price, a priority allocation may be made to employees or directors of the company. This allocation may mean that an individual employee etc. may receive more shares than an outside member of the public. In this case no benefit will arise:

(a) where the priority allocation of shares does not exceed 10% of the total;

(b) all employees and directors are treated on similar terms.

Employee Share Ownership Plans (ESOPs)

The FA 1989 has introduced a special relief to encourage the establishment of plans to encourage wider share ownership amongst employees.

Payments to an ESOP Trust by a company will allow the trust to acquire and distribute shares to the company's employees. The payments will qualify for corporation tax relief.

To qualify for relief, the trustees must use the funds provided, to acquire shares in the company which must be distributed to employees within seven years. The fund must include as beneficiaries all employees who have satisfied a minimum employment period and who have worked for 20 hours per week throughout this period. Only employees can be beneficiaries.

Employees can purchase shares from the trust at normal market value.

10.0 PROFIT RELATED PAY

This part of the Taxes Act 1988 allows part of an employee's pay to be free of income tax. The aim is to:

(a) give a personal incentive to employees;

(b) improve pay flexibility;

(c) reverse the trend towards the provision of benefits.

Any scheme to be set up requires registration by the Inland Revenue either by the employer or, in the case of a group scheme, by a holding company. Application for registration must be made at least 6 months before the first profit period to be covered by the scheme. The application must be accompanied by a certificate from an independent accountant certifying that:

(a) the scheme satisfies the statutory requirements, and

(b) the employer's records are adequate to provide the documentation and certification required by statute.

Employees of the Crown or a local authority or of a company controlled by them do not qualify for membership of such a scheme neither can employees, who with associates, control more than 25% of the ordinary share capital of the employer.

The rules of the scheme may:

(a)   exclude employees with less than 3 years service;
(b)   impose a minimum working period per week of at least 20 hours.

Apart from these restrictions at least 80% of the employees at the beginning of any profit period must be included in the scheme and broadly similar conditions must be applied to all employees.

The amount of tax-free pay available to an employee under a registered scheme must not exceed the lower of:

(a)   one-half of the profit-related pay of the relevant profit period;

(b)   10% of the total of normal pay and profit-related pay of the profit period excluding benefits;

(c)   £2,000 (reduced proportionately where the profit period is less than 12 months).

Illustration

A is an employee of Alpha plc. For a 12-month profit period he received:

	£
Salary	25,000
Car benefit	700
Profit related pay	4,200

The amount that will be exempt from income tax is the lower of:

(a)   50% x £4,200   £2,100

(b)   10% x (£25,000 + £4,200)   £2,920

(c)   £2,000

i.e.   £2,000

The amount of the profit-related pay that is exempt from income tax is still liable to National Insurance Contributions.

11.0 SUB-CONTRACTORS IN THE CONSTRUCTION INDUSTRY

Where a sub-contractor is providing labour on hire for use in the construction industry he must receive his payments from the main contractor after deduction of tax at 25% unless he holds an exemption certificate (form 714). An exemption certificate will only be issued by the Revenue if the sub-contractor can show that he had paid his past tax liabilities when they fell due and completed all the Income Tax Returns etc. which were required. If he had not been asked to complete any tax returns the Revenue must be satisfied that he would have completed them had he been required to do so.

Where the sub-contractor has been given an exemption certificate he must provide the main contractor with a receipt for payments received on a specially provided form (form 715) and he will receive these payments gross. The main contractor must forward all the forms 715 received by him together with a return showing the name and exemption certificate number of each sub-contractor; this must be done quarterly.

If the sub-contractor does not have an exemption certificate and thus suffers deduction at source he must obtain a certificate of deduction of tax (form SC 60) whenever he stops working for a specific main contractor. The main contractor is required to account for the tax deducted on a monthly basis in much the same way as for PAYE.

To obtain a certificate, applicants must:

(a) have been employed or self-employed for the previous three years;

(b) have complied with obligations under the Taxes Acts for the previous three years and the relevant National Insurance Acts for the same period.

In addition:

(a) the business must be carried on mainly through a separate business bank account;

(b) proper records must be kept;

(c) the business must be carried on from the proper premises with proper equipment, stock and other facilities;

The provisions regarding exemption certificates also apply to limited companies and agencies which supply construction workers.

Special regulations are in force for school and college leavers and others offering a guarantee. Broadly, a special certificate is available which will allow payments of up to £150 per week to be made gross.

12.0 NATIONAL INSURANCE

Employees and their employers pay class 1 national insurance contributions. Those paid by the employee are designated primary contributions and those by the employer secondary contributions.

Class 1 contributions are paid by all employees holding an office or employment and certain deemed employees, this latter class including agency and temporary workers. Certain employees and their employers are exempted from class 1 contributions, these include:

(a) persons earning less than the lower earnings limit (1989/90 - £43.00 per week);

(b) overseas employees;

(c) employees under 16 years of age;

(d) persons over pensionable age - 65 for a man, 60 for a woman.

The rates of contributions to 4.10.1989 are:

	Employee	Employer
Weekly Earnings		
0 - £42.99	NIL	NIL
£43.00 - £74.99	5%	5%
£75.00 - £114.99	7%	7%
£115.00 - £164.99	9%	9%
£165.00 - £325.00	9%	10.45%
over £325.00	Maximum of £29.25 per week	10.45%

from 5.10.1989:

	Employee	Employer
Weekly Earnings		
0 - £42.99	NIL	NIL
Then first £43.00	2%	No change
Remainder up to £325.00	9%	from above
Over £325.00	Maximum of £26.24 per week	

Employees who are members of approved occupational pension schemes or contribute towards a personal pension plan can be contracted out of the State Earnings Related Pension Scheme (SERPS) whilst retaining their right to the basic state pension. If contracting out occurs, the weekly contributions are reduced by:

(a) 2.0% for the employee
(b) 3.8% for the employer.

Where a person has more than one job he will be liable to pay contributions in respect of each employment. If his total contributions exceed £1,468.98 (contracted in) for 1989/90 his excess contributions will be refunded. No refund can be made of employers contributions. To prevent manipulation of the national insurance rules, if a person has several jobs with one employer or with associated employers, his earnings will be aggregated to find the correct levels. To prevent a possible overpayment of contributions by an employee, deferral can be sought for contributions on one or more employments.

Employees aged over 65 (male) 60 (female) will not be liable for primary contributions but an employer will still be liable for secondary contributions if earnings exceed the lower limit.

CHAPTER TEN

Pensions

1.0 GENERAL

For many years a major plank of social policy has been to encourage individuals, whether employed or self employed, to make adequate provision for retirement. Whilst the State provides a basic pension augmented partly by the state earnings related pension (SERPS) it is recognised that it does not provide adequately for an individuals retirement and, as it is effectively a 'pay as you go' system difficulties are likely to be faced in future in providing for a rapidly ageing population.

2.0 OCCUPATIONAL PENSION SCHEMES

These are schemes set up by an employer. They can be either approved or unapproved. If approval is obtained from the Superannuation Funds Office (SFO), the following benefits are available:

(a) the employer's contributions are an allowable trade expense and are not a benefit in kind to the employee;

(b) the employee's own contributions are tax deductible;

(c) the pension, when received, is taxed as earned income;

(d) the income and capital gains of the pension fund are not liable to tax.

If the scheme is not approved, such as an employer's top-up scheme, the employee's contributions will not be tax deductible and those of the employer will be taxed on the employee as a benefit. In addition the income and gains of the fund itself will be liable to tax.

Detailed rules are laid down by the SFO and although schemes must satisfy the basic conditions, there is considerable latitude allowed to approve schemes which vary the basic rules. These include:

(a) the scheme must be set up to provide benefits to the employee, his widow, children or dependants;

(b) it is recognised by employer and employee;

(c) there must be a UK resident administrator;

(d) the employer must contribute to the scheme.

The maximum contributions to a scheme made by an employee must not exceed 15% of remuneration. There is no ceiling on an employer's contributions so long as the overall benefits provided by the scheme do not exceed the permitted amounts. Thus the employer's contributions may be much more than those of an employee and can build up a maximum pension for a late entrant after 20 years service (10 years for members of existing schemes at 16th March 1987). It is possible for pension schemes to be financed wholly by an employer's contributions.

If the employee contributes less than the 15% maximum he may make additional voluntary contributions (AVC) up to the 15% maximum to increase the level of pension he may obtain. These contributions can be made to the employer's scheme or to a separate free-standing scheme of the employee's own choice. The AVCs can only be used to provide a pension; it is not possible to commute part into a tax-free lump sum.

Pensions may commence at age 60 for man and 55 for woman. Early retirement may be possible and if this is taken pensions may commence at age 50 or 45 respectively. The maximum benefit under a scheme must not exceed 1/60th final remuneration for each year of service up to a maximum of 40 years. Remuneration includes benefits in kind, but not taxable amounts under share options or incentive schemes. Part of the pension may be commuted into a tax-free lump sum. This must not exceed 3/80th final remuneration for each year's service up to a maximum of 40 and in any case must not exceed £ 150,000. Existing members of pension schemes at 16th March 1987 may have a higher amount.

FA 1989 has made important changes to the maximum pension benefits that can be obtained.   For new schemes set up after 13th March, 1989 or for those joining existing schemes on or after 1st June, 1989, the maximum figure of earnings on which a pension or lump sum can be calculated is £60,000.   This will be linked to the retail price index.

Provision can be made in a scheme for death in service and death after retirement benefits. There are provisions to deal with transferability between one pension scheme and another.

3.0 PERSONAL PENSION SCHEMES

These are available to persons who are self employed or who are in non-pensionable employment. In addition employees may from 6th April 1988 contract out of an employer's scheme and set up his own personal pension to which his employer may contribute. The maximum limits for relief for joint contributions are, however, as below and thus for many employees it might be better to remain in an employer's scheme. Originally the scheme was due to commence from 4th January 1988 but the new starting date was 1st July 1988.

Those in existing relevant annuity schemes at 30th June 1988 may continue with these schemes or make payments into a new personal pension plan.

The new legislation is a follow-on from the old retirement annuity schemes and most of the new legislation is very similar to that of the old law.

The retirement annuity/personal pension can be made with a life assurance company, bank, unit trust or building society. It must not normally start before the recipient reaches the age of 50 (60 for retirement annuity plans) nor after the age of 75. On retirement up to one-quarter of the value of the accumulated fund can be commuted into a tax-free lump sum.

These conditions may be varied with the agreement of the Revenue. Once the premium is paid, it is effectively lost until the date of payment of the pension as the contract once made is incapable of commutation, surrender or assignment. It is possible to use the policy as 'security' for loans to be repaid out of part of the proceeds of the policy.

Personal pension and retirement annuity contracts can be very tax efficient, in particular:

(a)   within the limits described, the premiums attract relief at the individual's highest rates of tax;

(b)   the pension when received is classed as earned income;

(c)   part of the capital fund provided under the policy can be commuted into a tax-free lump sum and can be used to repay a mortgage etc;

(d)   the income earned on the invested fund up to retirement is normally exempt from tax.

4.0 NET RELEVANT EARNINGS (NRE)

For 1989/90 the maximum allowable premiums expressed as a percentage of net relevant earnings are:

Age at beginning of fiscal year	Retirement Annuities (RAP)	Personal Pensions (PPS)
35 and under	$17\frac{1}{2}$%	$17\frac{1}{2}$%
36 to 45	$17\frac{1}{2}$%	20%
46 to 50	$17\frac{1}{2}$%	25%
51 to 55	20%	30%
56 to 60	$22\frac{1}{2}$%	35%
61 or more	$27\frac{1}{2}$%	40%

If a person has both a personal pension plan and a retirement annuity plan, the maximum personal pension payment is:

		£
Available relief under PPS		x
Less: RAP premiums restricted to RAP limits		(x)
Available for relief under PPS		x

5.0 UNUSED RELIEF

Any relief not used during the last six years may be carried forward and used to cover any qualifying premiums paid in excess of the limit for a future year, unused relief for earlier years being taken before that for later years.
This means that where in past years the premiums are less than 17½% of relevant earnings, the difference - called the unused relief - may be carried forward and used to justify the deduction of a premium greater than the 17½% limit.

Thus, if in the year 1989/90 the maximum possible premium was £3,000 but A only paid £1,900, there is unused relief of £1,100 which may be carried forward for the next six years - up to 1995/96 and used to cover a larger premium. If in 1991/92, A had NRE of £10,000 and paid a premium of £2,500:

	£	£
NRE		10,000
17½% thereof	1,750	
	=====	
Premium paid	2,500	

Normally ofset would be restricted to £1,750, however, as A has unused relief of £1,100 brought forward from 1989/90 he may use £750 of it to cover the excess premiums and therefore offset the whole

		2,500

		7,500
		=====

The following is a pro forma of an unused relief calculation for a taxpayer now aged 30:

Year	NRE £	17½% thereof £	RAP/PP paid £	Unused relief £	Total Unused relief £
1984/85	6,000	1,050	750	300	300
1985/86	8,000	1,400	1,400	-	300
1986/87	10,000	1,750	1,350	400	700
1987/88	9,000	1,575	1,275	300	1,000
1988/89	12,000	2,100	1,500	600	1,600
1989/90	21,000	3,675	2,675	1,000	2,600

If in 1990/91, the NRE are £12,000 and the premium paid is £3,000, the position is:

		£	£
NRE			12,000
17½% thereof		2,100	
		=====	
Premium paid		£3,000	

All these may be offset using firstly the
£2,100 allowance of the year and then the
unused relief from past years on a FIFO basis.
Thus £900 of unused relief will be taken,
identified as under:

  1 £300 from 1984/85
  2 £400 from 1986/87
  3 £200 from 1987/88   3,000

                       9,000

There is an element of carry-back in the system. Where a taxpayer pays a
premium in a year of assessment, he may elect to carry all or part of it back
into the immediately earlier year of assessment. If there are no relevant
earnings in that year, the premiums may be treated as being paid in the year
before that.

Illustration

X pays a personal pension premium of £4,000 per annum by four quarterly payments
of £ 1,000. His net relevant earnings are:

  1988/89   £30,000
  1989/90   £20,000

	1988/89	1989/90
	£	£
17½% NRE	5,250	3,500
Premiums paid	4,000	4,000
Unused relief	1,250	500
	=====	=====

X may elect before the end of the year of assessment in which the payment is
made to relate back up to £1,250 of the amount paid in 1989/90 into 1988/89 thus
maximising the offset in that year. It is possible to relate back part of a
premium.

It is appreciated that it would be possible to bring forward the 1988/89 unused
relief into 1989/90 and so obtain a full deduction of 1989/90 premium. In this
case, however, relating a premium back should obtain relief at a higher marginal
rate of tax.

Where an assessment is finalised more than six years after the end of the
relevant year of assessment, qualifying premiums which are paid within six
months of finalisation may be offset against the relevant earnings of the year in
which they are paid. This would prevent the loss of any unused relief which is
normally lost after six years.

Employees who set up their own pension plans can contract out of the earnings-related part of SERPS. They will still pay full contributions but the Department of Health will pay to the personal pension scheme the contracted-out rebate together with a bonus equal to 2% of earnings between the upper and lower earnings limits. This will not reduce the normal percentage limits. The bonus addition will apply until 5th April 1993.

Contributions to a personal pension plan are paid net of basic rate tax with higher rate tax relief being given in the assessment on relevant earnings.

CHAPTER ELEVEN

Personal Computations

1.0 GENERAL

Once the income of an individual has been ascertained it can be accumulated into a personal computation and the final amount of tax payable calculated. The personal computation basically divides into four main stages:

(a) the amalgamation of income to arrive at statutory income;

(b) the deduction of charges from statutory income;

(c) the granting of personal reliefs;

(d) the calculation of tax payable.

2.0 THE AMALGAMATION OF INCOME

Total income will include not only income which has not suffered tax at source but also that which has already had basic rate tax deducted. This income can include:

(a) building society interest and certain bank interest;

(b) dividends; and

(c) certain interest payments received from companies, national and local government.

This 'taxed' income must be 'grossed up' before being brought into the tax computation. The amount of the basic rate tax already deducted is allowed as a credit against the final tax liability. If the final tax liability is less than the tax deducted at source the excess will be repaid, but not to the extent that the tax deducted represents the tax credit on building society or certain bank interest received. The tax credit in respect of this income can only be offset against a tax liability, it can **never** be repaid in cash.

In setting out a computation it is advisable to group the income under four heads:

(a) Earned Income
Husband
Wife

(b) Unearned Income
Husband
Wife

Subject to the rules discussed below, husband and wife are treated as one taxable person. From 6th April 1990 however, husband and wife will be treated as independent taxpayers.

3.0 THE DEDUCTION FROM INCOME OF CHARGES AND EXPENSES

3.1 General

Certain payments can be deducted from an individual's total statutory income before charging it to tax. Other payments can only be deducted from specific types of income.

3.2 Charges deductible from specific types of income only

(a) Schedule E expenses - from Schedule E income.

(b) Personal pension scheme contributions, superannuation contributions and retirement annuity payments - from the income to which they relate.

(c) Section 380 losses - from trading profits of the same trade.

(d) Certain interest on loans to acquire land - from the income from that land only (see below).

3.3 Charges deductible from statutory income (SI)

These can consist of two broad types:

(a) interest payable;
(b) charges paid under deduction of tax.

3.4 Interest payable

In order to qualify for relief from income tax on the loan interest paid, the loan must have been used for one of the following purposes, within a reasonable time (twelve months) of the loan being raised:

(a) To purchase the taxpayer's main residence or that of his separated or former spouse or that occupied rent free by a dependent relative of himself or his spouse but only to the extent that the loan or loans do not exceed £30,000.

Ephraidge A. T. Rinomhota

The house must be in the UK or Eire and occupied by the taxpayer within one year of acquisition to qualify, though this period may be extended by the Revenue. The taxpayer's main residence is ascertained by fact and not by election. Relief for improvement loans and loans to acquire property to be occupied by a dependent relative has been withdrawn for new loans entered into after 5th April 1988.

If the taxpayer is moving he may during a bridging period have two loans running - one on the old property and one on the new. The taxpayer will continue to obtain interest relief on the old property for up to 12 months often extended to 24 months as long as the total of each of the old and new loans does not exceed £30,000. The MIRAS scheme (Mortgage Interest Relief at Source) applies to loans of up to £30,000.

(b) To purchase or improve property acquired for letting at a commercial rent. The property must be let for more than 26 weeks in any year and must be available for letting during the remainder of the time unless it is occupied as the taxpayer's main house or is uninhabitable due to repairs. The interest can only be set against letting income from property, any excess being carried forward for future relief.

(c) To purchase a life annuity, provided the taxpayer is over 65 and the loan is secured on his own home. No relief is available for interest paid on a loan in excess of £30,000.

(d) To introduce capital into a partnership. For interest paid prior to 11th March 1981 on such loans, it was a requirement that the partner should be an active member of the partnership.

(e) To pay inheritance tax before the grant of representation; the loan must be made to the personal representatives of the deceased.

(f) To purchase plant and machinery for use in an employment or partnership. The item must qualify for capital allowances and the interest is only allowable for three years from the end of the fiscal year in which the loan was received.

(g) To contribute capital to industrial co-operatives.

(h) To invest in an employee-controlled company. This is one where more than 50% of both:

i)   the issued ordinary share capital, and

ii) the voting power,

are owned by full-time employees of the company or their spouses. An employee together with his spouse cannot hold more than ten per cent of the ordinary share capital or the voting rights of the company. If the employee's spouse is also an employee of the company, no account will be taken of the spouse's shareholding in the company in determining the ten per cent limit. Each of them will have a separate ten per cent limit.

(i)   Persons taxable under Schedule D Cases I or II or Schedule E may obtain relief on the interest paid on a loan to purchase property whilst living in job-related accommodation. The property must have been used by the borrower as a residence at the time the interest is paid. Where interest is paid within twelve months of the loan, then the accommodation must be used by the borrower at some time within the twelve-month period.

This relief is also given where the borrower intends to occupy the accommodation as his **only or main** residence in due course.

The limit on the amount borrowed for which this relief is available is £30,000.

Accommodation is job-related where the borrower or his spouse is required under contract to carry on a trade, profession, vocation or employment in premises provided by another person. They must also live on those premises. The contract must have been entered into at arm's length.

Accommodation is not job-related where the borrower or his spouse live in accommodation where the agreement is entered into with a company in which the borrower, his spouse or his business partner have a material interest.

(j)   To purchase ordinary shares in, or to make a loan to, a close company provided that when the interest is paid the person concerned has either:

i)   a material interest (more than five per cent of the ordinary share capital) in the company; or

ii)   works full time as a manager or director of the company and also is a shareholder in the company.

No interest relief is available if the shares were issued after 13th March, 1989 and BES relief was given on the purchase price.

If interest is paid by a trader on an overdraft or loan for use in his business that interest will be allowed as a trading expense.

All these charges are allowable as a deduction for both basic and higher rates of tax. Subject to the previous paragraph no relief is available for bank overdraft interest.

3.5 Charges paid under deduction of tax

There are a number of types of payment which fall into this category such as payments under deed of covenant, maintenance payments, patent royalties, etc. These are all paid under deduction of tax and are known as retainable charges.

Before they are deducted in the personal computation it is necessary to gross the payment. Most of these charges are allowed for basic and higher rates of tax.

Special rules apply to deeds of covenant entered into before 15th March 1988. These will be allowed as a deduction for basic and higher rate tax so long as they are to continue in force and are made:

(a)   in connection with the acquisition of a business;

(b)   to a former partner or the widow of a former partner;

(c)   between husband and wife after their divorce or permanent separation;

(d)   before 7th April 1965 and are not, at the time of payment, for the benefit of:

    i)   an employee or agent;

    ii)   an infant unmarried child of the covenantor.

    The payment under this exception must be to a named individual.

(e)   to a charity; deeds to a charity are exempt up to any amount.

Deeds of covenant are only effective for tax purposes where they are for a period which is capable of exceeding six years, or three years where they are made to a charity.

As from 15th March 1988 new deeds will only be allowed if they are in favour of a charity or for the purposes of the payer's business.

MIRAS (Mortgage Interest Relief at Source) was introduced as from 1983/84. If a qualifying borrower pays relevant loan interest to a qualifying lender then he may deduct basic rate tax before paying the interest. Where relief is due at the higher rates, this will still be given by adjusting the code number. A qualifying lender can recover from the government any tax deducted by the borrowers. The system applies to loans of up to £30,000, and if the loan exceeds this figure interest will still be gross unless the lender agrees that interest on the first £30,000 of a loan can be paid net and the rest gross. As from 6th April 1987 this treatment will be applied to all new loans.

A qualifying borrower is basically an individual who pays relevant loan interest apart from an individual whose income from employment is exempt from tax in the UK e.g. a diplomat.

A qualifying lender includes banks, building societies, local authorities and others designated by the Treasury.

Relevant loan interest is interest to purchase or, for loans made before 5th April 1988, improve the taxpayer's only or main residence in the UK or to purchase an annuity by a taxpayer aged 65 or more secured on his house; 3.4 (a) and (b) above.

Where the borrower or lender considers they are no longer qualifying, or where the interest no longer is relevant loan interest, the Inland Revenue must be informed.

3.6 The deductibility of retainable charges

It has already been mentioned that:

(a) all retainable charges are paid after deducting basic rate tax; and

(b) they are allowable as a deduction from basic or basic and higher rates of
     tax at the **gross** figure.

Clearly, unless measures were taken to prevent it, the taxpayer could possibly
get substantial tax savings out of paying a retainable charge. By, for example,
paying patent royalties of £75 net in the fiscal year 1989/90 he could:

		£
(a)	Get relief for tax at up to 40% on the gross amount of £100	40
(b)	Retain the basic rate tax of 25%	25
		65

To make certain that this situation does not apply it is necessary to ensure that
credit is given to the Revenue for the £25 basic rate tax deducted and retained.
This is normally done by increasing the tax liability by the amount of the basic
rate tax retained.

Illustration

A, a bachelor, has an earned income in 1989/90 of £4,000 and pays a charge of
£300 from which he deducts tax at source of £75. His liability to income tax is:

	£
Earned Income	4,000
Less: Charge	300
Total Income	3,700
Less: Personal allowance	2,785
	915
Income tax @ 25% on £915	229
Add: Income tax retained	75
	304

An alternative way of dealing with it is to ignore the charge altogether.

Illustration

	£
Facts as before:	
Earned Income	4,000
Less: Personal allowance	2,785
	1,215

	£
Income tax @ 25% on £1,215	304
Add: Income tax retained	-
	304

It can thus be seen that no tax saving is achieved by paying a retainable charge and obtaining relief at the basic rate only.

Of the two methods, that shown in the first illustration should be used as it gives the correct figure of total income.
Where the charge is allowable at the higher rates of tax, the calculation would appear as under:

Illustration

B, a married man with no children or other dependants, is in receipt of the following income in 1989/90:

	£
Earned	22,700
Unearned (gross)	11,000

He pays a charge, which is allowable as a deduction when computing the higher rate tax liability, of £1,500, of which he retains £375 income tax by deduction at source.

	£
Earned income	22,700
Unearned income	11,000
	33,700
Less: Allowable charge (gross)	1,500
	32,200
Less: Personal allowance	4,375
Taxable Income	27,825

```
                                                    £
        Income tax:
           £
        20,700 @ 25%                                5,175
         7,125 @ 40%                                2,850
        _____                                      _____
        27,825                                      8,025
        _____

           Add:  Basic rate tax retained
                      on charge                       375
                                                    _____
                                                    8,400
                                                    ======
```

If the charge were not allowed at the higher rates the calculation would be:

```
           Taxable Income (as above)                  £27,825
                                                       =======

                                             £              £
           Income tax                                     8,025
           Add: Basic rate tax on charge paid  375
                Benefit of higher rates
                £1,500 @ (40-25)%              225
                                               ___          600
                                                          _____
                                                          8,625
                                                          =====
```

This recognises that, by deducting the charges in the computation, relief has been given at the higher rates; the basic rate element has already been dealt with.

3.7 The offset of charges

Gives the taxpayer the right to offset charges on total income to his greatest advantage.

Statutory income (i.e. income from all sources as computed in accordance with the rules and schedules of income tax) **less** charges, gives Total Income.

4.0 PERSONAL RELIEFS

4.1 General

These are granted for the year of assessment and are treated as a deduction from total income. If they exceed this, the surplus cannot be carried forward.

4.2 Personal allowances

```
(a)  Married allowance    1989/90      £4,375
                          1988/89      £4,095
                          1987/88      £3,795
```

This is given to a husband living with his wife or, if she is not living with him, **wholly** maintaining her voluntarily. In the year of marriage this allowance is proportionately reduced.

(b) Single allowance   1989/90   £2,785
                                 1988/89   £2,605
                                 1987/88   £2,425

An individual, resident in the UK, irrespective of age, who is not married, is entitled to a single personal allowance.

4.3 Wife's earned income relief (WEIR)

Where a married woman is in receipt of earned income she is entitled to a further allowance of the smaller of the amount of her earned income of £2,785 (1988/89 £2,605). The following income, although classified as earned income does not attract WEIR:

(a) national insurance benefits other than a retirement pension received from her own contributions;

(b) any other form of pension income received in respect of a husband's services or contributions.

Invalid care allowance given to a married woman who cares for a person claiming the attendance allowance qualifies as earned income for the purpose of WEIR.

Illustration

Mrs D receives the following income:

	£
Salary	400
Dividends - gross	200

She will be entitled to WEIR of £400.

If her salary were £3,000 the WEIR would be £2,785.

4.4 Dependent relative relief

This is no longer available after 5th April 1988.

4.5 Additional personal allowance

Relief may be claimed for any year of assessment where the claimant has at least one 'qualifying' child, resident with him during part or all of the year. The child does not necessarily have to be the taxpayer's own child, but the relief will not be available where at the beginning of any particular year the child is over the age of 18 years.

The claimant may be either:

(a)   a widow, widower, or other person not eligible for the married person's allowance (other than by reason of any election);

(b)   a married man whose wife is incapacitated physically or mentally throughout the tax year.

The amount of the allowance is £1,590 (£1,490 for 1988/89) irrespective of how many qualifying children there are. A qualifying child is one who is:

(a)   born in the year of assessment; or

(b)   under 16 at the beginning of that year; or

(c)   16 or over at the beginning of that year and who is receiving full-time education;

(d)   and is:

   i)   a child of the claimant, or

   ii)   under 18 and maintained by him at his own expense.

4.6 Housekeeper relief

This is no longer available after 5th April 1988.

4.7 Daughter's and son's services

This is no longer available after 5th April 1988.

4.8 Blind person's allowance

A registered blind person may claim this relief, of £540. If the taxpayer and his wife are both registered blind persons, relief of £1,080 may be claimed.

The son's or daughter's services relief cannot also be claimed.

4.9 Life Assurance relief

Prior to the fiscal year 1979/80, income tax relief in respect of premiums paid on certain life assurance policies was given against the income tax liability of the payer. For 1979/80 and subsequent years, tax relief was given by a reduction of 15% on the premium payable. The assurance company will then recover this 15% from the Inland Revenue. It does not affect the calculation of the income tax liability of an individual except where there is disallowable relief. As from 5th April 1989 the 15% relief is reduced to 12.5%.

The amount of premiums payable on which relief is available is restricted to the greater of:

(a) £1,500; or

(b) one-sixth of total income.

For assurance policies made after 13th March 1984, the relief is withdrawn. For policies already in existence prior to 13th March 1984, the relief continues to be available on premiums paid after this date.

5.0   THE CALCULATION OF TAX

5.1   Income tax

This is calculated at varying rates starting with a lower rate of 25% and a top rate of 40%. A table of rates for 1989/90 is as under:

Band of Taxable Income £	Amount £	Rate	Tax on Band £
0-20.700	20,700	25%	5,175
over 20,700		40%	

6.0   THE FORMAT OF THE COMPUTATION

A suggested layout of a personal computation is as under:

	£	£
Earned income:		
Husband	x	
Wife	x	
	—	x
Unearned income:		
Husband	x	
Wife	x	
	—	x
		x
Less: Charges		x
Total income		x
Less: Personal allowances		x
Taxable income		x
		===

	£
Income Tax	x
Add: Tax on retainable charges	x
	x
Less: Tax credits	x
Tax payable by direct assessment	x
	===

This recognises the fact that, unless a special election is made, a husband and wife are one taxable entity, their income will be jointly assessed to tax, and the husband will be responsible for the tax on both his and his wife's income.

Illustration

Ben, a married man, has the following income for 1989/90:

Self:	Salary	£22,000
Wife:	Salary	£ 3,000
	Schedule A	£ 4,500

	£	£
Earned income: Self		22,000
Wife		3,000
		25,000
Unearned income: Wife		4,500
		29,500
Allowances: Married	4,375	
Wife's earned income	2,785	
		7,160
		22,340
Income tax due:		
25% on £20,700		5,175
40% on £ 1,640		656
		5,831

7.0 THE TAXATION OF HUSBAND AND WIFE

7.1 Joint assessment

For taxation purposes, husband and wife are considered basically as one taxable unit.

Illustration

A.Ford is a sales director employed at a salary of £16,000 per annum plus commission (on sales) which amounted to £2,250 in the year to 5th April 1990. He contributes 10% of his basic salary to his employers' approved superannuation fund.

His employers provide him with a car for which he contributes £200 for private use; his business mileage totalled 2,000 in the year to 5th April 1990. His employers reimburse all other expenses for which he submits approved vouchers.

There is no private petrol paid for by his employers.

In the year ended 5th April 1990 the company made a return of expense payments as follows:

	£	£	£
Car: 150% of Table benefit: £4,100 x 150%		6,150	
Less: private contribution		200	
			5,950
Reimbursed expenses:			
Travelling and hotel expenses in UK		674	
Entertaining UK customers		341	
Agreed business proportion of home telephone		24	
			1,039
			6,989
Subscriptions:			
Club	26		
Professional bodies	16		
British United Provident Association	84		
		126	
Fares and hotel expenses, sales tour to Austria		328	
			454
			7,443

His wife has been a freelance photographer since before their marriage; her adjusted profits have been:

Year to 31st December 1988	£8,580
Year to 31st December 1989	£9,692

The other income of Mr and Mrs Ford has been:

	Years ended 5th April	
	1989	1990
	£	£
Ford: Dividends received	1,134	1,875
National Savings Bank ordinary account interest (account opened June 1988)	90	79
Wife: Interest on 3½% War Loan (paid gross)	1,400	1,400
Dividends received	2,320	4,500
Ford pays interest on a mortgage (under MIRAS)	475(gross)	492(gross)

You are required to calculate the income tax liability for 1989/90.

Earned income:

	£	£	£	£
Mr Ford				
Salary			16,000	
Commission			2,250	
Benefits:				
Car		5,950		
Reimbursed expenses:				
Travelling, etc.	674			
Entertaining	341			
Home telephone	24	1,039		
	—			
Subscriptions:				
Club	26			
Professional	16			
BUPA	84	126		
	—			
Fares and hotel		328	7,443	
		—		
			25,693	
			—	
Less: Expenses Claim:				
Reimbursed expenses		1,039		
Subscriptions to professional bodies		16		
Fares and hotel expenses		328		
		——	1,383	
			——	
			24,310	
Less: Pension scheme contributions -			1,600	
10% x £16,000				22,710
				——
Mrs Ford				
Profits - year ended 31.12.88				8,580
				——
c/f				31,290

		£	£	£	£
	b/f				31,290

Unearned Income
Mr Ford

	£	£	£	£
Dividends		1,875		
+ Tax credit 25/75		625		
			2,500	
NSB interest £(79-70)			9	
(2nd year - actual)				
			2,509	

Mrs Ford

	£	£	£	£
War Loan		1,400		
Dividends	4,500			
+ Tax credit 25/75	1,500			
		6,000		
			7,400	
			9,909	
Less: building society interest paid			492	
				9,417
Total income				40,707
Less: Allowances:				
Personal allowance		4,375		
Wife's earned income relief		2,785		7,160
Taxable income				33,547

Income Tax:

	£		£
20,700	@ 25%		5,175
12,847	@ 40%		5,139
33,547			10,314

	£	£
Add Tax deducted on mortgage interest		123
		10,437
Less: Tax Credits	£	
Mr Ford	625	
Mrs Ford	1,500	2,125
		8,312

In normal circumstances a husband is liable for the tax on his wife's income.

7.2 Separate taxation of wife's earned income (TA 1988, ss.287 & 288)

A husband and wife who are living together may **jointly** elect that the wife's earned income shall be assessed on her as if she were a single person with no other income, her unearned income remaining that of the husband. The conditions for the election are:

(a) it must be made jointly in writing by husband and wife and continues until it is jointly revoked;

(b) it must be made within the period commencing six months before and ending twelve months after the first year of assessment to which it is to apply. It can be revoked within the same time limits.

Wife's earned income for this purpose does not include any pension or superannuation received from her husband's former employment nor any benefits under the National Insurance Acts which do not arise from her own contributions.

The detailed effects of the election are:

(a) charges are deducted from the income of the spouse who pays them. Mortgage interest paid on or after 1st August 1988 can be deducted from the income of the spouses in the most beneficial way - normally from the highest-income-receiving spouse.

   An election for this must be made jointly within 12 months of the end of the fiscal year for which it is first to apply and continues until revoked.

(b) each spouse receives a single person's personal allowance; no married allowance can be claimed by the husband and no WEIR can be claimed by the wife;

(c) any excess personal reliefs on one spouse cannot be carried over against the income of the other;

(d) loss relief is allocated in the following way:

   Husband's loss - against his earned **and** his and his spouse's unearned income;
   Wife's loss - against her earned income.

   This may mean that there is an automatic loss of personal allowances and it may be beneficial to revoke the claim temporarily;

(e) the husband remains entitled to two £70 or one £140 exemption for a joint account in respect of income from the ordinary account in the NSB. A claim under s.287 prevents a claim for age allowance, or a claim for the additional personal allowance for looking after children.

   By making a claim under s.287 savings in tax may be made in those cases where the wife has a substantial earned income.

Illustration

The facts are as for Mr and Mrs Ford, but this time a claim has been made to
have Mrs. Ford's earned income separately taxed:

	Mr Ford	Mrs Ford
	£	£
Earned income	22,710	8,580
Unearned income	9,909	
	32,619	
Less: Mortgage interest	492	
	32,127	
Less: Personal allowances	2,785	2,785
	29,342	5,795

	£	£
Income tax:		
£20,700 :£5,795 @ 25%	5,175	1,449
£ 8,642 @ 40%	3,457	
£29,342		
	8,632	1,449
Tax deducted under MIRAS	123	-
	8,755	1,449

The difference between the tax borne between this and joint assessment is £233,
and it is therefore advantageous to make the election.

8.0 GETTING MARRIED

In the year of marriage the income of husband and wife is not aggregated.

The husband is entitled to a married person's personal allowance scaled down by
one-twelfth of the difference between the married and single personal allowances
for each complete tax month elapsing between 6th April and the date of marriage.
A tax month commences on 6th of one month and ends on the 5th of the next month.
The wife is entitled to a single person's personal allowance but no WEIR.

Non-aggregation of the wife's income in the year of marriage does not prevent
the husband from offsetting excess personal allowances losses and charges against
the wife's post-marriage income.
The wife can offset against her husband's income any excess blind persons
allowance and charges paid on or after the date of marriage.

Illustration

Mr & Mrs J were married on 15th November 1989 and their salaries in the fiscal
year 1989/90 were as follows:

```
                                                              £
Mr J                                                       16,000
Mrs J (Miss H):
to date of marriage                                         3,200
after date of marriage                                      3,250
                                                           ======

They had no other income.


                                                   £          £
Miss H/Mrs J:
Salary to date of marriage                                  3,200
          after marriage                                    3,250
                                                           _____

                                                            6,450
Less: Personal allowance                                    2,785
                                                           _____
      Liable                                                3,665

                                                           ======

Mr J:
Salary                                                     16,000
Less: Personal allowance                        4,375
      Less: 7/12ths of £1,590
      £(4,375-2,785)                               927      3,448
                                               _____    _____
                                                          12,552
                                                          ======
```

Where either party had a child before the marriage it may be possible to claim in
the year of marriage the additional personal allowance given to single persons
claiming child allowance. In the case of a wife, the child must be living with
her before the marriage; in the case of a husband it will prevent him from
claiming the married personal allowance in the year of marriage.

Illustration

Mr Kay, a widower, married Miss Ley on 24th July 1989. He claims the additional
personal allowance for looking after his son Paul, aged 13.

	Claiming Married allowance	Not Claiming Married allowance
	£	£
Personal allowance	4,375	2,785
Less: 3/12ths (£4,375-£2,785)	397	
APA		1,590
	_____	_____
	3,978	4,375
	=====	=====

For the purposes of relief under TA 1988,s.380 the wife's income from the date of marriage is available for relief.

For many couples it is important to decide whether, for tax purposes, to marry or just to cohabit. A man and woman co-habiting are treated as two separate individuals, there is no concept of the 'common law' marriage in taxation.

Points to consider are:

(a)   Couples cohabiting can each obtain mortgage interest relief on a loan of £30,000 provided the loan was taken out before 1st August 1988. After that the loan interest is given on the property and is thus restricted to one allowable loan of up to £30,000. This may be split between the sharers of the property, normally in equal shares. Alternatively each could establish their own main residence;

(b)   if the cohabitees have substantial unearned income non marriage will prevent the woman's unearned income being aggregated with her husband's income which normally occurs even when a claim for separate taxation of wife's earned income is made; substantial tax savings could result;

(c)   if one of the cohabitees was not working the other could transfer income to the other by means of a deed of covenant thus enabling the recipient to recover basic rate tax at no cost to the person covenanting. This is now stopped for deeds entered into after the 14th March 1988;

(d)   If there are children then the cohabitee maintaining the child could claim an additional personal allowance. If there is more than one child then both cohabitees could qualify by maintaining one each.

(e)   Business Expansion Scheme relief of up to £40,000 is available for each co-habitee; a married couple can only obtain relief for one investment of up to £40,000.

9.0 DIVORCE AND SEPARATION

When a couple are divorced or separated they will be treated as two taxable individuals as from the date of the divorce or separation. In the year of separation the husband will continue to obtain the full married allowance, thereafter it will only be available if the husband **wholly** maintains his wife. After the year of divorce, each automatically obtains a single person's allowance.

In the year of separation, the income of the wife will be split on the following basis:

Schedule A   -   Income entitled to be received
                                                       before and after separation.

Schedule B   -   Time basis

Schedule D Cases I, II, III, IV and V	-	The assessment for the year according to the normal rules of assessment, divided on a time basis.
Schedule D Case VI	-	Actual income received.
Schedule E	- -	Salary etc., earned before and after separation.
Dividends and other income taxed at source	-	Dividends, etc. due to be received before and after separation.

After separation the wife will be entitled to a full single person's allowance.

On separating or divorce, one spouse may make maintenance payments to the other or for the maintenance of any children. Up to 1987/88 they were broadly of two types.

(a)   voluntary payments;

(b)   payments made under a legal obligation.

(i)   Voluntary payments had no tax effect, the payer got no tax relief and the recipient was not liable to tax on the receipts.

(ii) Payments made under a legal obligation were allowed as a deductible charge in the case of the payer and were unearned income in the hands of the recipient. Tax was deducted from the payments unless they ranked as 'small maintenance payments'.

Under normal circumstances payments made for the maintenance of children were regarded as income of the recipient spouse. Where the payment was made to the other spouse, in trust for the children, it was normally treated as having created a settlement in favour of the children and the income was treated as that of the settlor. Where the payment was made direct to the children, it was treated as their income provided it was made under the order of the court.

The Finance Act 1988 has significantly changed the tax position of maintenance payments. They are broadly divided into two classes:

(a)   Payments made under a court order or by an enforceable agreement made after 14th March, 1988.

(b)   Payments made by:

   i)   a court order made before 15th March 1988;

   ii)   a court order made before 1st July 1988 on an application made before 15th March 1988.

iii) a legally enforceable agreement made before 15th March 1988 and
received by the Inland Revenue before 1st July 1988;

(a) When the court order or agreement was made after 14th March 1988, the
recipient of the maintenance will not be liable to tax on the income
received. The payment will be made gross and the payer will be able to
claim a deduction from taxable income of £1,590 (the difference between a
single and married personal allowance) or the amount of the maintenance
whichever is less.

In the year of separation it is possible for a husband to claim both the
married allowance and the maximum £1,590 deduction. If he remarries, it
will be possible to claim both allowances if the maintenance payment is
continued.

If the payer supports more than one person, the £1,590 deduction is not
increased.

In the year of separation it is possible for a husband to claim both the
married allowance and the maximum £1,590 deduction. If he remarries, it
will be possible to claim both allowances if the maintenance payment is
continued.

(b) For payment made under existing obligations, any relief available to the
payer is restricted to that available in 1988/89, no allowance will be given
for future increases.   Similarly, the recipient is taxed only on the amount
received in 1988/89, less the difference between the current married and
single personal allowances.

10.0 THE SENIOR CITIZEN

If a taxpayer or his wife is aged 65 years or over at any time during the year of
assessment and his total income does not exceed the following limits for 1988/89
there will be no liability to taxation:

Single taxpayer	£3,400	(£3,180 for 1988/89)
Married couple	£5,385	(£5,035 for 1988/89)

If the taxpayer's statutory total income exceeds £11,400 (£10,600 for 1988/89)
the full age allowance will be reduced by £1 for each £2 of total income over
£11,400 until the allowance is reduced to the original single or married personal
allowance.

Illustration

G, a widower, is 68. He receives a pension of £3,700 and dividends of £225
(excluding tax credit £75) during 1989/90.

		£
Pension		3,700
Dividends £(225 + 75)		300
		4,000
Less: Age allowance		3,400
		600
Tax thereon @ 25%		150
Less: Tax credits		75
Tax to pay		75

Illustration

H is married and aged 66. He receives a pension of £5,900 and his wife receives
Schedule A income of £6,000 for 1989/90.

	£	£
Pension		5,900
Schedule A income		6,000
		11,900
Age allowance	5,385	
Less: 1/2 £(11,900 - 11,400)	250	
		5,135
		6,765
Tax thereon @ 25% on £6,765		1,691

The allowance does not affect the taxpayer's claim to other allowances,
particularly WEIR.

If the taxpayer or his spouse is aged 75 or over at any time in the fiscal year,
a higher age allowance is available, at the following rates:

| Single taxpayer | £3,540 |
| Married couple | £5,565 |

As above, the allowance will be reduced by 1/2 of the statutory total income in
excess of £11,400. The allowance is also available to a taxpayer who but for his
death during the fiscal year would have reached the age of 75 by the end of that
year.

It is important to ensure that the income of the elderly comes from the correct
sources. Investments in building societies and bank deposit accounts should be
avoided if there is likely to be a shortfall of income over personal allowances
as the tax credits attaching to them cannot be repaid, if there is going to be a

shortfall of allowances a deed of covenant could be paid to the senior citizen, and the tax credits are then refundable. A senior citizen without substantial income but with a house could consider a house annuity plan where the house is mortgaged to provide a capital sum to be repaid out of the proceeds of sale on death. The capital of the mortgage is used to purchase an annuity which is used firstly to pay the interest on the mortgage (allowable under MIRAS) with the excess used to provide income.

Tax relief for private medical insurance premiums will be introduced from 5th April, 1990. Broadly, it will be available to single taxpayers aged over 60 or to married couples at least one of whom is over 60. Basic rate relief will be given by deduction at source and higher rate relief will be given in the assessment.

11.0 DEATH

On the death of an individual, the liability to taxation will be calculated as if all sources of income ceased on the date of death. This will involve the cessation basis being applied to certain classes of income such as Schedule D Case I and II etc. Dividends will be treated as receivable before death if they were due before the date of death. Where a widow succeeds to her husband's business on his death the Revenue will allow assessments to be continued on a preceding-year basis if the widow wishes. However, losses made by the husband cannot be carried forward. This does not, of course, affect the widow's right to insist on a discontinuance if greater relief could be obtained. The liability to tax must be settled by the executors who are also liable to any additional tax caused by a revision of assessment on death. The liability to tax on income received after death is that of the executors.

In the year of death, personal allowances will be given as follows:

(a) Husband's death

Full married allowance and wife's earned income relief against income to date of death; widow obtains full single personal allowance for the period from death, widow's bereavement allowance, and possibly additional personal allowance.

Where a man dies in a year of assessment for which he was entitled to the married person's allowance, his widow shall be entitled for that year to a further allowance of £1,590. The allowance is available both in the year of bereavement and the next following year provided that the widow has not remarried before the start of the second year.

(b) Wife's death

Husband obtains full married allowance for year of death, and wife's earned income relief on wife's earnings up to date of death. After that year he is dealt with as a single person.

12.0 INDEPENDENT TAXATION

From 1990/91, the old system of taxation which broadly treated husband and wife as one person will be abolished and each will be treated as a separate taxable person who can claim a personal allowance.

Each spouse will be entitled to a personal allowance equal to a single person's allowance.   The husband will also get a married man's allowance equal to the difference between a single and married personal allowance.   The wife's allowance can be offset against earned and unearned income.

If a husband cannot use his married man's allowance it can be transferred to his wife provided an election is made within 6 years of the end of the relevant tax year.   In ascertaining the husband's income against which allowances can be offset, any deduction for MIRAS interest or BES relief will be ignored.

If property is held jointly by husband and wife, each will be treated as sharing equally in the income. A joint declaration can be made if the asset is held in different proportions and the income will then be assumed to be held in these proportions.   An election can also be made to split mortgage interest in the most beneficial way between spouses.

13.0 NON-RESIDENT BRITISH SUBJECTS (TA 1988, ss.233 & 278)

With certain exceptions all income arising in the UK is liable to tax even if it is paid to a non-resident. UK residents can offset against the income their personal allowances. Non-UK residents do not qualify for personal allowances unless they fall within certain categories:

(a) British subjects;

(b) residents of the Channel Islands or the Isle of Man;

(c) missionaries or current or former Crown employees;

(d) former UK residents now living abroad for health reasons;

(e) where a double tax agreement provides.

Those within these groups qualify for a proportion of their UK allowance.

Relief is given by finding:

(i) the UK tax on the UK income after personal allowances;

(ii) the UK tax on the world (or total) income after personal allowances.

For those purposes, income is classified by where it arises except that income from certain Government securities - notably $3\frac{1}{2}\%$ War Loan - is always considered to be world income. Following **CIR v. Addison 1984** the overseas income of a wife not liable to UK tax should be totally excluded from the computation.

The amount of the tax payable is the **greater** of:

(a) the UK tax on the UK income;

(b) the UK tax on the world income multiplied by the fraction:

$$\frac{\text{UK liable income}}{\text{World liable income}}$$

'Liable' income is income, less charges, but **before** personal allowances.

Illustration

Mr and Mrs N are British subjects who have worked in Europe for many years. Their liable income in the fiscal year 1989/90 was as under:

	£
Arising in UK:	
Rents from house	5,000
Dividends - gross	4,000
3½% War Loan Interest	500
Arising abroad:	
Salaries - Mr N	18,000
Mrs N	10,000
Dividends- Mr N	1,000

Mr N paid mortgage interest of £3,000 on the house to a UK bank. The couple have one child, born in 1981.

	UK Income £	World Income £
Rents	5,000	5,000
Dividends	4,000	4,000
War Loan interest		500
Salary - Mr N		18,000
Mrs N		
Dividends		1,000
	9,000	28,500
Less: Mortgage interest	3,000	3,000
	6,000	25,500
Less: Personal allowances:		
MA	4,375	4,375
	1,625	21,125

	UK Income £	World Income £
Income tax:		
£		
1,625 @ 25%	406	
20,700 @ 25%		5,175
425 @ 40%		170
	─────	─────
	406	5,345

The tax borne will be the **higher** of:

(a)   £406 or

(b) $\dfrac{£\ 6,000}{£25,500}$ x £5,345 = £1,258

But if no personal allowances had been claimed the tax borne would have been:

		£	£
Rents		5,000	
Dividends		4,000	
		─────	
		9,000	
Less: Charges		3,000	
		─────	
	6,000 @ 25%		1,500

A tax credit is not normally available to a non-resident unless he claims s.233 relief or is so entitled under the terms of a double tax agreement.

As from 6th April 1990 there will be no restriction on the personal allowances available to non resident qualifying for S.233 relief.

14.0 DUE DATES FOR THE PAYMENT OF INCOME TAX

The due dates for the payment of income tax are as under:

Type of Income	Due Dates Basic and Higher Rates
Income from a trade, profession or vocation (Schedule D Cases I and II Schedule D Case V - foreign businesses)	One-half on 1st January in year of assessment; one-half on 1st July following year of assessment
Income from employments - Schedule E	PAYE deducted from emoluments when paid
Other untaxed income	1st January in year of assessment
Other income received under deduction of tax	(Higher rates only) 1st December following year of assessment

If the assessment is issued after the due date in the table above, tax will not be due until 30 days after the date of issue of the notice of assessment.

In calculating the tax due charges may be deducted in the most beneficial way. This will normally be against investment income where the tax is due on 1st January in the year of assessment. Personal allowances are deducted primarily against earned income.

Illustration

Mr E has the following income assessable for 1989/90:

	£
Trading profits	16,800
Rents	2,000
Dividends (net)	7,500

He is married and pays allowable interest of £3,000, gross.

	Schedule D I	Schedule A	Dividends
	£	£	£
Income	16,800	2,000	7,500
Add: Tax credit			2,500
			10,000
Less: Charges	1,000	2,000	
	15,800	-	
Less: Personal allowance	4,375	-	
	11,425	-	10,000
	£	£	£

Income tax:
On Schedule DI
@ 25% on £11,425   2,856

Due 1.1.90	1,428
1.7.90	1,428

On Dividends

@ 25% on £9,275	2,319
@ 40% on £725	290
	2,609
Less: Tax credits	2,500
Due 1.12.1990	109

15.0 INTEREST ON OVERDUE TAX

Interest is charged on overdue tax from the 'reckonable date'. This date will depend on whether the assessment giving rise to the tax has been appealed against. The making of an appeal against an assessment does not delay the payment of tax. This will be due on the normal due dates as above, unless an application has been made to postpone the tax payable. The balance of any postponed tax will be due 30 days after the determination of the appeal. The reckonable date for the charging of interest is found as under:

Tax not subject to appeal, the later of:

(a) the normal due date;

(b) 30 days after the date of issue of the notice of assessment.

Tax subject to appeal, the later of:

(a) the normal due date;

(b) 30 days after the date of issue of the notice of assessment;

(c) 30 days after the date of the Inspector's agreement or Commissioner's determination of any amount to be postponed.

The remainder including any increased tax liabilities are due on the later of:

(a) the due date if there had been no appeal;

(b) the later of:

   i)   the date on which the tax would have become due and payable if there had been no appeal;

   ii) the earlier of:

      (1) the date on which the tax becomes due and payable (see above)

      (2) the appropriate date from the following table:

Type of Tax	Relevant date
Tax under Schedules A and D	1st July following the end of the year of assessment
Higher rate tax on income taxed at source	1st June following the December after the end of the year for which assessed

Recent rates of interest have been:

6. 4.1987 to 5. 6.1987	9%	6. 8.1988 to 5.10.1988	9.75%
6. 6.1987 to 5. 9.1987	8.25%	6.10.1988 to 5. 1.1989	10.75%
6. 9.1987 to 5.12.1987	9%	6. 1.1989 to 5. 7.1989	11.5%
6.12.1987 to 5. 5.1988	8.25%	from 6.7.1989	12.25%
6. 5.1988 to 5. 8.1988	7.75%		

Illustration

A is a graphic designer assessed under Schedule D Case I. On 15th November 1989 he received an assessment for 1989/90 showing a tax liability of £30,000. On 10th December 1989 he appealed against the assessment and applied for postponement of £ 12,000 tax. The Inspector agreed to the postponement of £9,000 tax on 2nd January 1990. The Commissioners determined the assessment at an appeal hearing on 28th August 1990 and the final tax due was £35,000. A paid tax as under:

31st March 1990	£10,500
1st August 1990	£10,500
27th October 1990	£14,000

Interest will be charged as under:

Schedule D Case I

1st instalment	£10,500 from 1st February 1990 to 31st March 1990 (Reckonable date 30 days after Inspector's agreement)
2nd instalment	£10,500 from 1st July 1990 to 1st August 1989 (Reckonable date 1st July 1990 - normal due date)
Balance	£14,000 from 1st July 1990 to 27th October 1990 (Reckonable date 1st July 1990)

The Board of Inland Revenue may remit interest of £30, though this will cease to apply from a date to be fixed by statutory instrument.

16.0 REPAYMENT SUPPLEMENTS

A supplement will be paid to an individual taxpayer where he receives a tax repayment of not less than £25 more than twelve months after the end of the year of assessment to which the repayment relates.

The repayment supplement is calculated as interest on the amount repaid, at the rates given above from the 'relevant time' to the end of the tax month in which the repayment order is issued.

The relevant time is the later of:

i)   5th April following the year for which repayment is made;

ii)   the end of the year of assessment in which the tax was paid.

The repayment supplement is tax free.

Illustration

K receives a repayment of tax of £1,000 in respect of 1987/88. The tax was
originally paid by K on 1st July 1988. The repayment order was issued on 14th
February 1990.

The relevant time is 5th April 1989.

The end of the tax month in which the repayment order is issued is 5th March
1990.

The repayment supplement will be calculated as follows:

			£
Period 6.4.89 to 5.7.89	£1,000 @ 11.25% p.a.		28.67
6.7.89 to 5.3.90	£1,000 @ 12.75% p.a.		81.55
			110.22

17.0 ERROR OR MISTAKE CLAIMS

If a mistake has been made in a Return or supporting document (e.g. Accounts) the
taxpayer may make an error or mistake claim and reclaim any tax overpaid in
respect of the previous six complete years of assessment. This relief is only
available in the case of a genuine mistake by the taxpayer and no relief is
available if the Return or statement is made in accordance with the law or
practice applying at the time. The amount of the relief is determined by the
Board of Inland Revenue with an appeal to the Special Commissioners.

CHAPTER TWELVE

Back Duty and Avoidance

1.0 GENERAL

When the Revenue are of the opinion that tax has been lost by the fraudulent or negligent conduct of a taxpayer they adopt a procedure for the recovery of the tax which is generally described as back duty.

The procedure can be broadly divided between the less serious aspects relating to the minor omission of income (i.e. bank deposit interest) and the making of false claims for allowances, and the understatement of business profits, which is regarded with much more gravity. The former cases are normally dealt with at district level by the appropriate inspector of taxes, whereas the second type is always dealt with by a specialist department, such as the Enquiry Branch or an investigation branch.

2.0 COMPLIANCE

S.7 TMA 1970 imposes an obligation on every person liable to income tax who has not delivered a return of income to the Inland Revenue to advise them of income from all sources within 12 months of the end of the year of assessment. Each source of income must be disclosed unless it:

(a) has been dealt with under Schedule E and has suffered PAYE;

(b) has already been taxed;

(c) consists of UK dividends.

The penalty for non-compliance, previously £100 is as from 1988/89 an amount equal to the tax charged by assessments on the non-disclosed income made more than 12 months from the end of the fiscal year.

S.10 TMA imposes a similar duty on companies with the true limit for notification being one year after the relevant accounting period.

S.11A contains parallel provisions for capital gains.

S.8 TMA requires a taxpayer to make a return of income when called upon to do so by the Inland Revenue. The time limit for compliance is 30 days from the date of issue of the notice of assessment. A return of income is treated as validly served on a taxpayer if it is delivered to him or sent to his current or last known place of residence or employment. A person who fails to make a return within the time limit is liable to a penalty of £300 together with an additional penalty of £60 for every day after default has been formally declared by the Commissioners or the Court. In any case failure to submit a return promptly could constitute negligence. Prior to 27th July, 1989, the penalties were £50 and £10 per day respectively.

There are similar provisions for requiring returns of income from a partnership or limited company.

The return made by the taxpayer to the Inland Revenue contains a declaration by him that to the best of his knowledge and belief the information contained therein is complete and correct. This is an important statement and the practitioner must point out its significance to the client before obtaining his signature to the return. S.99 TMA provides for a penalty of an amount not exceeding £3,000 for knowingly assisting in the making or delivery of incomplete returns or accounts. It is important therefore that when the accountant discovers irregularities these are pointed out to the client who is then advised to make full and complete disclosure to the Inland Revenue. If he refuses then the accountant cannot continue to act for the client. S.20 TMA permits an Inspector, on application to a circuit judge, to issue within 12 months a notice to any person who has acted as a 'tax accountant' and against whom a penalty under s.99 has been awarded requiring that person to deliver to the Inspector all his working papers in respect of any client for whom he has acted.

3.0 OBTAINING INFORMATION

The Inland Revenue has considerable powers of obtaining information. The major sources being:

(a)   returns of employees' emoluments on forms P.35, P11D and P9D and details of casual employees.

(b)   returns of fees and commissions paid;

(c)   returns of interest paid.

S.20 TMA gives an Inspector or the Board of Inland Revenue powers to serve a written notice on any person to deliver up documents in his or her possession or to give such particulars which contain information relevant to a tax liability.

An Inspector may also serve a similar notice on certain third parties including spouses and children and, in respect of a business liability, to any person who is carrying on a business.

An Inspector may also require documents relating to unspecified persons, e.g. from the sponsors of tax avoidance schemes as to the contents etc. of the scheme.

An Inspector, but not the Board, requires the consent of a Special or General Commissioner before proceeding. Penalties are required for failure to provide the information requested. Before proceeding with the notice however, an Inspector must give the taxpayer an opportunity to provide the information voluntarily. Normally a taxpayer or other person must be given at least 30 days notice to produce the information required.

S.146 FA 1989 and S.20 TMA enables an officer of the Board of Inland Revenue, on application to a circuit judge, to obtain a warrant authorising him to enter premises within 14 days and to search them and to seize any items which he believes might be required as evidence in proceedings involving serious tax fraud.

A person who falsifies, conceals or destroys a document required by the Inland Revenue is guilty of a criminal offence, punishable by a fine or up to two years imprisonment.

4.0   IN-DEPTH INVESTIGATIONS

In January 1977, a new system of in-depth investigation and review was introduced by the Inland Revenue. This was intended to concentrate time and expertise on those areas which, based on judgement, gave rise to concern. This could be evidenced by:

(a)   unsatisfactory accounts, e.g. those with a qualified audit report, unusual figures for debtors and creditors, drawings etc.;

(b)   low or unusual rates of gross profits;

(c)   the type of trade;

(d)   a bad previous history as to tax matters.

The Inspector will initially review the accounts with the aim of constructing an economic model of business. To enable him to do this, detailed notes on each type of business are prepared which give the Inspector background information on the trade and indicative gross profit percentages. Once this has been done, the Inspector will review the taxpayer individually to see whether the combination of business and personal information links up with the lifestyle and personal circumstances of the taxpayer. In doing this the Inspector might consider:

(a)   the residence of the taxpayer;

(b)   any chargeable assets acquired;

(c)   the pattern and source of other income, etc.

He will be assisted in this by other information including returns of interest paid without deduction of tax, returns of commission, details from other Inspectors, informers' letters and other information from public sources.

After building up this economic picture of the taxpayer, the Inspector will seek to establish information on certain key points and will normally write to the accountant concerned requesting information on these points.   The information given might easily clear up the matter, but if further enquiries are necessary, the Inspector might request an interview with the taxpayer and also seek discovery of books, papers, etc.   Where the records are totally inadequate the Inspector might require the preparation of capital statements.   These statements comprise several separate schedules as follows:

(a)   a statement of the assets and liabilities at the beginning and end of the period under review and at yearly intervals in the interim;

(b)   a statement of income for each year, including legacies and profits on capital transactions;

(c)   a statement of expenditure for each year, including gifts and losses on capital transactions.

The details are compiled on a cash basis, any accruals only being used for the lists of assets and liabilities at the beginning and end of the whole period.

The various schedules are compiled so that Expenditure (per statement)

            plus

Increase in Assets in the year

            less

Income (shown on schedule)

            equals

Undisclosed Income (if any).

The following is an illustration of a capital statement showing the range of enquiries necessary:

NET ASSETS

	1984	1985	at 5th April (Intervening years omitted)	1989	1990
	£	£		£	£
Dwelling house at cost	8,800	8,800		8,800	8,800
Extension thereto, at cost				2,800	2,800
Furniture, at cost	1,850	900		2,250	3,200
Country cottage, at cost		3,000		3,000	
Furniture, at cost		750		1,350	
Business assets (net)	9,000	19,000		38,000	40,000
Investments, at cost		3,000		8,000	12,000
Bank deposit accounts		2,450		8,600	15,000
Bank current accounts	350	700		600	750
	20,000	38,600		73,400	82,550
Creditors	5,000	6,500		8,600	15,200
Mortgage	6,200	5,800		1,800	1,750
	11,200	12,300		10,400	16,950
NET ASSETS	8,800	26,300		63,000	65,600
Increase in net assets (year by year)		17,500			2,600
Living expenses in year		1,800			4,600
Life assurance premiums		140			1,700
Tax Paid		3,800			13,700
Subscriptions, gifts etc.		380			1,700
		23,620			24,300
Legacies received		15,000			
Rights issue sold					600
Matured assurance policy					5,000
Investment income (net)		300			1,900
		15,300			7,500
Deposit interest		39			1,200
Profits on Stock Exchange Transactions		6,000			4,500
Football pool winnings					8,000
		21,339			21,200
Unexplained increases		£ 2,281			£ 3,100

The intervening years would be similarly compiled; some may show deficiencies.

The Revenue would review the taxpayer's circumstances in the light of the statements and, after making any adjustments, agree the tax lost.

5.0 CULPABILITY

In general, there are certain types of 'offence' recognised by the Taxes Acts. They fall into four broad categories:

(a) Innocent mistake

This is where a mistake is genuinely made. S.97 TMA provides that where incorrect returns of income or accounts are submitted and it comes to the taxpayer's notice that they are incorrect then he will not be treated as negligent, provided that the error is pointed out to the Inland Revenue as soon as possible.

(b) Neglect

This is defined in s.118 TMA as 'negligence or failure to give any notice, make any return or to produce or furnish any document or other information required by or under the Taxes Acts'. Negligence may be absolved by reasonable excuse. In general, it is not doing what a reasonable person would do.

(c) Fraud

This is where a false representation has been made knowingly, or without belief in its truth or recklessly careless of whether it be true or not.

After the enquiry is complete, the Inspector may make additional assessments. The time limits are:

(a) Normal

Up to 6 years after the end of the chargeable period to which they relate.

(b) Fraudulent and negligent conduct.

The Inland Revenue can raise assessments at any time within 20 years from the end of the relevant chargeable period.

Assessments on a deceased person's income arising before death must be made within three years after the tax year in which he dies. Assessments for any of the six years preceding death may be made within the same time limit where the assessments are for the purpose of making good tax lost by reason of the deceased person's fraudulent or negligent conduct.

6.0 THE SETTLEMENT

Having agreed the amount of tax lost, the individual will normally be required to sign a 'certificate of full disclosure'. There are no statutory requirements to sign such a certificate but quite clearly to refuse to do so might well arouse suspicions of further matters not yet discovered. A certificate signed in cases where there has not been full disclosure may make the individual liable for fraud.

The amount of duty to be paid must then be agreed bearing in mind the respective liabilities for tax, interest on tax and penalties. The usual procedure is to agree a composite sum taking into account all three aspects, and then for the taxpayer to sign a written undertaking to pay the agreed sum, in consideration of the Revenue forbearing to pursue their rights for penalties. The Revenue may mitigate penalties where they consider it appropriate.

7.0 PENALTIES

The maximum penalties are:

for fraudulent or negligent conduct - 100% of the tax underpaid.

plus in all cases interest at the following rates per annum on the tax lost:

11% from 1st May 1985 to 5th August 1986
8.5% from 6th August 1986 to 5th November 1986
9.5% from 6th November 1986 to 5th April 1987
9% from 6th April 1987 to 5th June 1987
8.25% from 6th June 1987 to 5th September 1987
9% from 6th September 1987 to 5th December 1987
8.25% from 6th December 1987 to 5th May 1988
7.75% from 6th May 1988 to 5th August 1988
9.75% from 6th August 1988 to 5th October 1988
10.75% from 6th October 1988 to 5th January 1989
11.5% from 6th January 1989 to 5th July 1989
12.25% from 6th July 1989

8.0 TAX AVOIDANCE

This is the process of arranging a taxpayer's affairs in such a way that he can, within the law, reduce the amount of tax payable. It differs from evasion which is knowingly breaking the law to reduce a tax liability by the deliberate concealing of income or the false claiming of allowances etc.

In **IRC v. Duke of Westminster (1936)** Lord Tomlin said:

'Every man is entitled if he can to arrange his affairs so that the tax attaching under the appropriate Acts is less than it otherwise would be. If he succeeds in ordering them so as to secure that result, then however unappreciative the Commissioners of Inland Revenue or his fellow taxpayers may be of his ingenuity, he cannot be compelled to pay an increased tax'.

In **Ayrshire Pullman Motor Services v. IRC (1929)** Lord President Clyde said:

'No man in this country is under the smallest obligation, moral or other, so to arrange his legal relation to his business, or to his property as to enable the Inland Revenue to put the largest possible shovel into his stores'.

Over the years attitudes, both judicial and public, appear to have hardened against the tax avoider. In **Latilla v. IRC (1943)** Lord Simon commented that avoiders might prepare schemes that were:

> 'within their legal rights, but that is no reason why their efforts, or those of the professional gentlemen who assist them in the matter, should be regarded as a commendable exercise of ingenuity or as a discharge of the duties of good citizenship'.

To combat this 'digging for wealth in the subterranean passages of the Revenue' (per Lord Denning in **Griffiths v. J.P.Harrison (Watford) Ltd. (1963)**), a mass of anti-avoidance legislation has developed. Unlike some countries, there is no general anti-avoidance legislation, but a series of detailed measures designed to deal with specific instances as and when they arise. Brief details of some of the main anti-avoidance provisions are:

(a) Transactions in securities (TA 1988, ss.703-709)

Where in consequence of a transaction (or transactions) in securities, combined with any special circumstances, a person is able to obtain a tax advantage, the Revenue may make such adjustments as are necessary to correct the advantage. The Revenue must issue a notice of their intentions to correct any advantage and it is open to the taxpayer to contest the Revenue's assertions. The Revenue action will fail if the taxpayer can show that the transactions were made for bona fide, commercial reasons, or in the ordinary course of investment management, and without tax advantages being their main object, or one of their main objects.

The special circumstances referred to above are:

i)   the receipt of an abnormal amount of dividend or other distribution;

ii)   an entitlement to a deduction from profits or gains because of a decrease in the value of securities held;

iii) the receipt of a consideration not taxable as income;

iv)   the receipt, in the form of share capital or securities, of any non-taxable consideration.

It has been held that liquidation may be a transaction in securities. A tax advantage means any relief or repayment (or increase thereof) or avoidance or reduction of a charge or assessment to tax, whether effected by receipts accruing as non-taxable or by deduction from profits or gains.

The taxpayer may protect himself against possible action by the Revenue under these provisions by providing full details of the transactions contemplated or effected and ask for a clearance. The Revenue have 30 days to call for further information or notify their decision as to whether action will be taken.

(b) Transfer of assets abroad (TA 1988,ss.739-746)

Where as a result of a transfer of assets, or of any associated operations,
an individual ordinarily resident in the UK has power to enjoy, forthwith or
in the future, any income of a person resident or domiciled outside the UK
which, if it had been income of that individual received by him in the UK,
would have been liable to tax, it shall be deemed to be his income. These
provisions will not apply if the individual can show that the purpose of
avoiding tax was not the purpose or one of the purposes for which the
transfer or associated operations was effected or that the transfer or
associated operations were bona fide commercial operations not for the
purpose of avoiding liability to tax. The decision in **Vesty v IRC (1980)**
illustrated that only the transferor or his spouse would be liable under
these provisions and, as a result, the provisions have been amended so that
a non-transferor can be liable where benefits are received and income arises
after 9th March 1981.

(c) Transactions between associated persons (TA 1988,s.770)

Where either the buyer or the seller (which may be a body of persons or a
partnership) is controlled by the other party to the contract, or both are
bodies controlled by a third person, a sale, the letting or hiring of
property, the grant or transfer of a right or licence, or the giving of
business facilities at a price other than market price may result in
adjustment by the Revenue of that price to the open market price. This
applies particularly to the transfer of stock between companies at less than
the market valuation. But for these provisions a company could transfer to
a subsidiary abroad stock at less than its true value thereby reducing the
charge to UK tax.

(d) Capital sums received on the sale of income by an individual (TA
1988,s.775)

Where transactions or arrangements are made, having as their main object or
one of their main objects, the avoidance or reduction of income tax, and
which enable some other person to enjoy profits, gains, income, copyrights,
licences or any other rights, deriving directly or indirectly from the
personal activities, past, present or future, which an individual carries on
wholly or partly in the UK, and as a result that individual obtains a
capital amount (i.e. not otherwise taxable) it shall be treated as the
earned income of that individual, assessable under Schedule D Case VI in the
year in which it is receivable.

(e) Artificial transactions in land (TA 1988,ss.776-788)

Any capital gain from the disposal of land or any part of it, which is
realised by the person acquiring, holding or developing it, is treated for
all tax purposes as income of the person realising the gain, assessable
under Schedule D Case VI for the chargeable period in which the gain is
realised, if one of the following conditions is satisfied:

       i)   land (or any property deriving its value from land) is acquired with the sole or main object of realising a gain from disposing of it, or,

      ii)   land is held as trading stock, or,

     iii) land is developed with the sole or main object of realising a gain from disposing of it when developed.

(f)   Sale and leaseback of land (TA 1988,s779)

Where land is transferred by sale, lease, surrender or forfeiture of a lease, etc. and the transferee becomes liable to pay rent or a premium treated as rent, the allowance for the rent will be restricted to the commercial rent of the land concerned. This restriction applies to situations where the rent would normally be allowable, i.e.:

       i)   as a deduction from trading profits;

      ii)   in computing profits or losses under Schedule D Case VI;

     iii) as a management expense;

     iv)   against Schedule E emoluments;

      v)   as deduction in computing profits from woodlands;

     vi)   in computing profits under Schedule A.

Commercial rent means the open market rent of the land taking into account the terms and any special restrictions of the lease.

Where a lease has no more than 50 years to run, when sold, and the period for which the premises are leased back is 15 years or less, the increased rent payable, so far as it does not exceed a commercial rent, is allowable as a deduction from profits. A proportion of the consideration received by the lessee for giving up the original lease, equivalent to one fifteenth of that consideration multiplied by the number of years by which the term of the lease-back falls short of 16 years, will be treated as assessable income and not capital.

CHAPTER THIRTEEN

Introduction to Corporation Tax

1.0 A BRIEF HISTORY

Until 1965 a company was liable to income tax in the same manner as an individual trader. Corporation tax was introduced in FA 1965 but the link with income tax was retained since, unless specifically provided otherwise in the legislation, the amount of income for the purposes of corporation tax was to be computed according to income tax principles. However, the system of corporation tax, as introduced by FA 1965, known as the classical system, tended to discriminate against the payment of dividends (since the company was required to account for income tax on any distributions made as well as accounting for corporation tax on its profits). This, among other reasons, resulted in the introduction of the imputation system of corporation tax as from 1st April 1973; this latter system is intended to be neutral on the subject of distributions.

2.0 THE IMPUTATION SYSTEM - ACT

The basis of the imputation system of corporation tax is a charge, known as advance corporation tax (ACT).

Whenever a company makes a qualifying distribution (normally by paying a dividend) the company must calculate and pay over to the Revenue an amount of ACT, based on the net distribution made. The rate of ACT is fixed for each financial year (year to 31st March) and the rates, which correspond to the basic rates of income tax, have been as follows in recent years:

FY 1986	29/71
FY 1987	27/73
FY 1988	25/75
FY 1989	25/75

Thus, a dividend of £7,500 paid on 1st September 1989 will be multiplied by 25/75 in order to determine the amount of ACT:

	£
Dividend paid to shareholder	7,500
ACT 25/75 paid to Revenue	2,500
Total cash outflow	10,000

The shareholder will be liable to tax on the gross equivalent of the dividend received. The amount of ACT is imputed to the shareholder in the form of a tax credit which satisfies the shareholder's liability to tax at the basic rate.

The amount of ACT paid by a company is treated as a payment in advance of the company's corporation tax liability on its income. The result is intended to be neutral - no matter what amount of dividend is paid the total amount of corporation tax payable should remain the same.

Illustration

A Ltd. has an income liable to corporation tax of £100,000. It distributes alternatively:

(a)   10% of net income;
(b)   100% of net income.

Take corporation tax at 35%. Distributions took place in March 1990.

	Income	Tax	Income	Tax
	£	£	£	£
Profits	100,000		100,000	
Corporation Tax @ 35%	35,000	35,000	35,000	35,000
Net Income	65,000		65,000	
Dividend paid (net)	6,500		65,000	
Retained	58,500		-	
ACT				
25/75 x £6,500		2,167		
25/75 x £65,000				21,667
Balance Payable		32,833		13,333

The balance of corporation tax payable after the offset of ACT is known as Mainstream Corporation Tax (MCT).

Tax is therefore accounted for as follows:

	£	£
ACT	2,167	21,667
MCT	32,833	13,333
Total corporation tax paid	35,000	35,000

3.0   BODIES LIABLE TO CORPORATION TAX

With certain exceptions, corporation tax is chargeable on:

(a)   all companies resident in the UK.
(b)   non-resident companies trading in the UK through a branch or agency.

The term **'company'** includes not only those incorporated under the Companies Act, but also any body corporate or unincorporated association such as a sports or social club.   The profits of the latter which are classified as **mutual profits**, may be excluded from the charge.

After 14th March 1988, a company incorporated in the UK is considered to be UK resident for taxation purposes, unless the terms of a double tax agreement provide otherwise.

Companies incorporated in the UK and carrying on business before 15th March 1988, but which were non UK resident before that date will not be treated as UK resident until:

(a)   15th March 1993; or

(b)   the date on which the company could become resident under existing law,

whichever is earlier.

Companies not incorporated in the UK will only be treated as UK resident under a provision of the existing law.

Existing law provides that a company will be resident in the UK if 'central management and control' occurs within the UK.   (**De Beers Consolidated Mines v. Howe (1906)**). Traditionally, the control is that of the directors rather than the shareholders (**John Hood & Co. Ltd. v. Magee**), and the place of central management has been taken traditionally to be at the place where the board of directors meets.

The case of **Unit Construction Co. Ltd. v. Bullock (1960)**, emphasised that in reviewing where control and management occur, the courts will look to the reality of the position and not merely to the legal documentation such as the Articles of Association.

An Inland Revenue Statement of Practice 6/83 indicates that the Revenue will consider the following factors in determining corporate residence:

(a)   Do the directors actually exercise central management and control?

(b)   If so, where is this control really exercised (not merely where does the board of directors meet)?

(c)   If the directors do not exercise control who does and where is it exercised?

4.0   THE ASSESSMENT OF INCOME

Companies may, subject to the rules laid down by the Companies Act, prepare accounts for any period of time.   This period is known as the **period of account** and can be of any length.

Companies are liable to corporation tax for an **accounting period**; this is the period for which the company's profits are chargeable to corporation tax.   In most cases the period of account and the accounting period will be the same, however TA 1988, s.12 provides detailed rules for ascertaining the beginning and end of the accounting period.

A company's accounting period commences:

(a) when the company first becomes within the charge to corporation tax; or

(b) at the end of the previous accounting period.

A company will come within the charge to corporation tax when it becomes UK resident or first acquires a source of income, etc.

It ends on the first occurrence of any of the following:

(a) the end of the company's period of account if that is twelve months or less in length;

(b) the end of a period of twelve months from the beginning of the company's accounting period if the period of account exceeds twelve months;

(c) the company ceasing to be within the charge to corporation tax;

(d) the commencement or cessation of a trade;

(e) the commencement of a winding-up.

Illustration

B Ltd. commenced trading on 1st January 1988 and made up accounts as under:

                12 months to 31st December 1988
                18 months to 30th June 1990
                 9 months to 31st March 1991
                12 months to 31st March 1992

The company went into liquidation on 30th September 1992.

Each of the above periods forms a period of account but accounting periods are:
                12 months to 31st December 1988
                12 months to 31st December 1989
                 6 months to 30th June 1990
                 9 months to 31st March 1991
                12 months to 31st March 1992
                 6 months to 30th September 1992

Where the company's period of account exceeds twelve months, as in the 18 months to 30th June 1990 in this example, the first twelve months constitute one accounting period and the remaining six months another.

5.0   SPECIMEN CORPORATION TAX COMPUTATION

5.1   The computation of profits

Companies are liable to corporation tax on their profits. Profits are defined
in TA 1988, s.6 as 'income and chargeable gains' and include:

(a)   overseas profits of a UK resident company whether remitted or not;

(b)   profits arising in a winding-up;

(c)   interest received from banks and building societies.

The definition of profits does **not**, however, include dividends and other
qualifying distributions received from other UK resident companies (franked
investment income).

A specimen corporation tax computation is as under:

		Profits
		£
Schedule A		X
Schedule B		X
Schedule D		X
Schedule E (if appropriate)		X
UFII and BSI interest received		X
Capital Gains	X	
Less: Capital Losses	(X)	X
		X
Less: Charges		(X)
		X

5.2   Notes to the computation

(a)   **The application of income tax principles**

Although a company is liable to corporation tax, in determining the income
subject to tax, the same schedules and cases and the general rules of
computation apply as are used for the purpose of income tax. However,
provisions applying solely to individuals, e.g. the exemption of the first
£70 of National Savings Bank ordinary account interest, are not available to
companies. A major difference between the taxation of an individual and a
company is that although the amount of profit of the company is computed by
reference to income tax rules, it is charged to corporation tax on an **actual
basis**.

(b)   **The treatment of capital allowances**

The capital allowance computation of a company broadly follows the same
general form as for an individual. Important differences are:

i)   The basis periods for capital allowances are fixed by reference to twelve-month accounting periods. As there is no preceding year basis of assessment for companies, there are no problems in the opening and closing years. WDA are proportionately reduced if the accounting period is less than twelve months.

ii) For corporation tax purposes capital allowances are treated as a trading expense in arriving at the amount which is taxable in respect of a trade. Thus for a company, trading income will mean the trading profits less capital allowances if appropriate. A balancing charge is added to the Schedule D Case I profits.

iii) There is no private use reduction in the case of a company.

Illustration

A Ltd. commences trading on 1st January 1989 and makes up accounts for an 18-month accounting period to 30th June 1990. It acquires:

Plant and machinery:	
1.3.1989	£6,000
1.2.1990	£6,000
Motor car:	
30.5.1989	£10,000
Industrial building:	
1.2.1989 (excluding land)	£40,000
The trading profits were:	£90,000

AP to 31.12.1989

		P & M Pool General	Car	Industrial Building	Total
	£	£	£	£	£
Cost		6,000	10,000	40,000	
Allowances:					
WDA - 25%		1,500	2,000		3,500
			(Rest.)		
- 4%				1,600	1,600
		4,500	8,000	38,400	5,100

AP to 30.6. 1990

	P & M Pool General	Car	Industrial Building	Total
Additions	6,000			
	10,500			
Allowances:				
WDA	1,313	1,000	800	3,113
	9,187	7,000	37,600	3,113

* In each case WDA for the AP to 30.6.1990 have been reduced by six-twelfths as the accounting period is six months only in length.

The Schedule D Case I profits of the company will be:

		£
AP to 31.12.1989		
Adjusted Profits	12/18 x £90,000	60,000
Less: Capital Allowances		5,100
Schedule D Case I		54,900
AP to 30.6.1990		
Adjusted Profits	6/18 x £90,000	30,000
Less: Capital Allowances		3,113
Schedule D Case I		26,887

(c)   **The treatment of VAT**

Under most circumstances, the income and expenses of the company will be expressed exclusive of VAT. Sometimes VAT paid cannot be recovered and in these circumstances it may be treated as a trading expense or added to the capital cost of the asset, as appropriate.

i)   Non-deductible VAT

VAT which is non-deductible by effect of law, i.e. on entertaining expenses, may be treated as a trading expense. However, UK entertaining expenditure and the associated VAT is never allowed. Where the non-deduction relates to plant and machinery etc., capital allowances may be claimed on the cost inclusive of VAT.

ii)   Partly exempt persons

Where a company is partly exempt, the proportion of VAT non-deductible may be treated as a trading expense or as an addition to the cost of the asset, as appropriate.

iii) Persons not liable to VAT

Where a company is not liable to VAT, perhaps because the turnover is less than £23,600 per annum, the VAT suffered is allowed as a trading expense or an addition to the cost of the asset for capital allowances.

(d)   **The grossing up of income and charges**

Certain income will be received by a company under deduction of income tax such as debenture or loan interest, patent royalties, etc. This income must be grossed up before bringing it into the corporation tax computation.

Illustration

E Ltd. received debenture interest of £750 net on 30th June 1989.

	£
Received	750
Tax deducted 25/75ths	250
Liable to corporation tax	1,000
	=====
Corporation tax thereon @ say 35%	350
	=====

It will be seen, however, that the company will now only have £400 left out of the £750 it has received (£750 - £350). To overcome this, and to ensure that the company only pays corporation tax on its income, a credit for the income tax suffered will be given against the company's MCT. Similarly, to ensure that when a company makes an annual payment under deduction of income tax it does not receive a corresponding tax advantage, income tax deducted from annual payments must be paid over to the Revenue. The detailed procedures for doing this will be considered later, but at this stage it is sufficient to note that any excess of income tax repayable over income tax due will be offset by deduction from the mainstream corporation tax. If it exceeds the MCT any balance will be repaid in cash.

(e)   Capital gains reduction

Companies resident in the UK (and certain non-resident companies) are liable to corporation tax in respect of their chargeable gains. The tax payable is paid as corporation tax and not capital gains tax.

Capital losses of the year or brought forward capital losses, must be deducted from capital gains before charging them to tax.

(f)   Charges on income

The charges paid by a company can be of two classes:

i)   retainable;
ii) non-retainable.

Retainable charges include annual payments in respect of covenants, loan and debenture interest, patent royalties, etc. These will be paid under deduction of basic rate tax and will be treated as a deduction against total profits liable to corporation tax.

Non-retainable charges include interest paid to a UK bank, and short interest, i.e. interest on loans for less than 12 months. These will normally be paid gross. Provided any bank interest is incurred wholly and exclusively for the purposes of the trade it will be treated as a trade expense. In all other cases, it will be treated as a charge against total profits (**Wilcock v Frigate Investments Ltd. (1982)**).

Where the interest paid is treated as a trade expense rather than as a charge on total profits then the interest will be deducted on the accruals basis.

To be deductible as a charge against total profits, the payment must satisfy certain conditions. It must be:

i)   paid out of profits brought into charge to corporation tax in respect of a liability incurred for valuable and sufficient consideration;

ii)   borne by the company;

iii) paid in the accounting period in which a deduction is sought.

It is possible to deduct interest from profits liable to corporation tax even when they have been charged to capital.

Where the payment is interest, then to be deductible as a charge one of the following conditions must be satisfied:

i)   the company must exist wholly or mainly for the carrying on of a trade; or

ii)   the interest must be incurred wholly and exclusively for the purpose of the trade; or

iii) the company must be an investment company.

Illustration

X Ltd. had the following profits for its accounting period to 31st March 1990:

	£
Trading profits	60,000
Rents	5,000
Capital Gains	6,000

It paid the following:

Bank interest on a business loan	2,000	
Debenture interest	6,000	gross
Deed of covenant to Oxfam	1,000	gross

	£	£
Trading profits	60,000	
Less: Bank interest	2,000	
		58,000
Schedule A		5,000
Capital Gains		6,000
		69,000
Less: Charges:		
Debenture interest	6,000	
Deed of Covenant	1,000	
		7,000
		62,000

A UK resident-non-close company can make donations to charities and treat them as charges; for this treatment to apply:

i) the donations must not exceed 3% of the dividends paid on the company's ordinary shares during the accounting period in which the donations are made;

ii) basic rate income tax must be deducted from the payments and accounted for in the normal quarterly accounting under Sch.16 TA.1988.

Despite the fact that neither deeds of covenant to a charity nor donations treated as charges are paid for full consideration, they will still be allowed as a charge against total profits.

(g) **Discounts**

Discounts incurred by a company are dealt with as under:

i) Discounts suffered by a company on bills of exchange are normally allowed as a trade expense if the company is a trading company. Discount on accommodation bills which are drawn by a company, accepted by a bank and discounted by that or another bank or discount house will be allowed as a charge on income. The incidental costs of issuing such bills are allowed as a trade or management expense.

ii) Part of the discount on an issue of deep discount securities after 13th March 1984 is allowed as a charge. A deep discount security is one where there is a difference between the issue price and the amount payable on redemption excluding any interest. A deep discount is one where the discount is more than 15% of the amount payable on redemption overall or ½ % per annum to the earliest possible redemption date and which is not:

   (1) a share; or
   (2) an index-linked stock.

Broadly, the deep discount is treated as accruing evenly over the life of the security. This life is divided into income periods - successive periods of twelve months from the date of issue; however, if the company pays interest, the income periods are the periods for which the company pays interest. The discount accruing in the income periods is called the 'income element'. It is calculated as under:

For the first period $\quad \dfrac{A \times B}{100} - C$

When:

A = the issue price
B = the yield to maturity
C = the interest attributable to the income period.

The yield to maturity and the income elements can be calculated at the outset.

Illustration

A Ltd. issues stock on 1st July 1989 in units of £100 for redemption on 30th June 1999. The redemption price is £200. Interest is 6% per annum payable half-yearly on 30th June and 31st December.
Thus there will be 20 income periods of six months with the first ending on 31st December 1989.

The yield to maturity is, say, 5.72% per income period.

For the first period:

$$\left(\frac{£100 \times 5.72}{100}\right) - £3 = \underline{£2.72},$$

which is then added to the issue price.
For the second period:

$$\left(\frac{£102.72 \times 5.72}{100}\right) - £3 = \underline{£2.88},$$

etc.

The amount of the income element is allowed as a charge against the company's profits of the accounting period in which the income period ends.

Where the owner disposes of a deep discount security, the rolled-up interest is assessed under Schedule D III for the aggregate of the income periods between acquisition and disposal.

If the deep discount security qualifies as a corporate bond any capital gain will be exempt.

Provisions have been introduced to counter the device of coupon stripping. Where this occurs the charge to tax on the holder of the deep discount securities will make him liable on the income element as it accrues rather than only on the redemption or disposal of the securities.

(h) **Periods of account of more than 12 months**

Where the period of account exceeds 12 months in length the profits will be apportioned into the various accounting periods as under:

i)   trading income before capital allowances are apportioned on a strict time basis;

ii)   capital allowances are calculated for the actual accounting periods;

iii) other income is apportioned to the accounting period in which it arises or is due;

iv)   capital gains are allocated to the accounting period in which the disposal occurs;

v)   charges and dividends paid are dealt with in the accounting period in
which they are paid.

6.0 THE CALCULATION OF CORPORATION TAX

6.1 General

The rates of corporation tax payable by a company are fixed for **financial years**.
A financial year runs from 1st April to the following 31st March and is
designated by the calendar year in which it begins.   The financial year 1989
runs from 1st April 1989 to 31st March 1990.   The rates of corporation tax for
current years are as under:

	Normal Rate	'Small' Companies Rate
FY 1984	45%	30%
FY 1985	40%	30%
FY 1986	35%	29%
FY 1987	35%	27%
FY 1988	35%	25%
FY 1989	35%	25%

The application of the small companies rate is explained in 6.2. below.

Special rules apply to close investment companies.

Where a company's accounting period spans two financial years, it will be
necessary to apportion the profits to the respective financial years and
calculate the appropriate amounts of tax.   This apportionment will be made on a
strict time basis.

Illustration

C Ltd. makes up accounts for an 18-month period of account to 30th June 1991.
The trading income liable to corporation tax for that period was £1,200,000.
Assume rates of corporation tax of:

FY 1989	40%
FY 1990	35%
FY 1991	30%

The income of the period to 30th June 1991 will be divided over financial years
as follows:

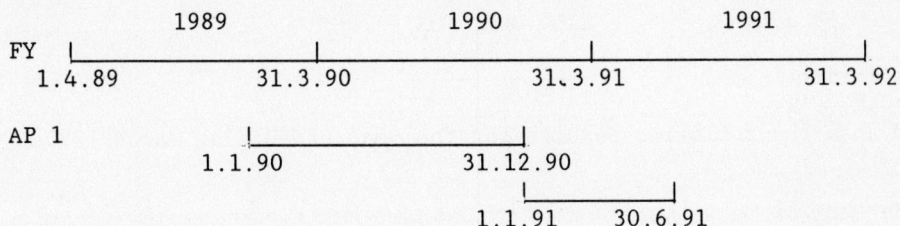

```
              1989              1990              1991
    FY  |_____|_____|_____|
      1.4.89         31.3.90         31.3.91         31.3.92

    AP 1           |_____|
                 1.1.90         31.12.90
                                 |_____|
                               1.1.91      30.6.91
```

AP 1.1.1990 to 31.12.1990:
12/18 x £1,200,000 = £800,000

	£	£
Financial year 1989		
3/12 x £800,000 @ 40%	80,000	
Financial year 1990		
9/12 x £800,000 @ 35%	210,000	290,000

AP 1.1.1991 to 30.6.1991
6/18 x £1,200,000 = £400,000

Financial year 1990		
3/6 x £400,000 @ 35%	70,000	
Financial year 1991		
3/6 x £400,000 @ 30%	60,000	130,000

6.2   Small companies (TA 1988, s.13)

(a)   General

Where a company's profits for an accounting period do not exceed certain limits, its basic profits liable to corporation tax will bear corporation tax at 25%.

Basic profits (BP) are all profits liable to corporation tax less charges.

Profits (P) are basic profits as above plus franked investment income. Franked investment income does not include (for this purpose) dividends received from a more than 50% UK subsidiary company, whether paid under a group election or not.

The limits known as 'the lower maximum', for recent financial years and the rates of corporation tax have been:

FY 1986	£100,000	29%
FY 1987	£100,000	27%
FY 1988	£100,000	25%
FY 1989	£150,000	25%

Illustration

K Ltd. has the following results for the year ended 31st March 1990:

	£	
Trading income	20,000	
Schedule A	1,000	
Debenture interest paid	2,000	gross
Chargeable Gains	3,500	
Dividends received from UK resident company on		
1.12.1989	750	

		£	
DI		20,000	
Schedule A		1,000	
Chargeable Gains		3,500	
		——————	
		24,500	
Less: Charges		2,000	
		——————	
	BP	22,500	22,500
		══════	

	£	
Dividends received	750	
Add: Tax credits	250	
	————	
		1,000
		———————
		£23,500 P
		═══════

Corporation Tax:
  @ 25%   5,625
                                                           ═════

Where a company's profits are greater than the lower maximum, its basic profits will bear corporation tax at the normal rates but an abatement calculated as under, may be deducted if the profits do not exceed an upper maximum:

$$\text{Fraction} \times [(\text{the upper maximum} - P) \times BP/P]$$

where P and BP have the meanings attributed to them as above. The upper maximum and fractions for recent financial years are:

1986	£500,000	3/200
1987	£500,000	1/50
1988	£500,000	1/40
1989	£750,000	1/40

Illustration

L Ltd. makes up accounts to 31st March 1990. It has the following results:

	£
Trading income	198,000
Schedule A income	2,000
Dividends from foreign companies (gross)	1,000
Capital gains	5,400
Capital losses brought forward	2,400
Dividends from other UK resident companies	15,000

It pays: Debenture interest (gross)   8,000

	£	£	£
Schedule DI		198,000	
Schedule A		2,000	
Schedule DV		1,000	
Capital Gains	5,400		
Less: Capital losses	2,400	3,000	
		204,000	
Less: Debenture interest		8,000	
	BP	196,000	196,000

	£		
Dividends received	15,000		
Add: Tax credits	5,000		
			20,000
			216,000 P

Corporation Tax @ 35%	68,600

Less: 1/40 £[(750,000 - 216,000)

$$\frac{196,000}{216,000}$$ 12,114
                                           ~~56,486~~

(b)   Reduction of small company limits

The small company limits of £100,000 and £750,000 referred to above will be
reduced in the following circumstances:

i)   where there are associated companies;
ii)   where the accounting period is less than twelve months;
iii) where the accounting period straddles two financial years.

i)   Associated Companies

When a company is 'associated' with other companies, the small company
limits are divided equally between them. Companies are associated when
one has control of the other or both are under common control.
'**Control**' means having or being able to acquire:

    (1)   more than 50% of the share capital or voting power, or
    (2)   more than 50% of the company's income, or
    (3)   being entitled to more than 50% of the company's net assets in a winding-up.

In this context, it is not necessary for an associated company to be resident in the UK.

Illustration

R Ltd. has two subsidiary companies. The limits for the financial year 1989 for each would be:

       £750,000 divided by 3 = £250,000
       £150,000 divided by 3 = £ 50,000

Companies are treated as associated even if they are associated for part of the accounting period only, but a company which has not carried on any trade or business during the accounting period is ignored.

To avoid effectively splitting the small company limits by subsidiary companies, it may be advantageous to use branches or operating divisions.

ii) Accounting periods of less than twelve months

When a company has an accounting period of less than twelve months the small company limits are proportionately reduced.

Illustration

S Ltd. has an accounting period of six months. The limits for the financial year 1989 will be:

       £750,000 divided by 2 = £375,000 and
       £150,000 divided by 2 = £ 75,000

Should S Ltd. also have an associated company, the limits will be reduced further to:

       £375,000 divided by 2 = £187,500 and
       £ 75,000 divided by 2 = £ 37,500

iii) Accounting periods straddling two financial years

Where the company's accounting period straddles two financial years, income, capital gains and profits are apportioned on a strict time basis with the appropriate small company limits applied to each.

Illustration

T Ltd. makes up accounts for the year to 30th September 1989. The results are as under:

		£	
Trading income		180,000	
Schedule A		14,000	
Patent royalties paid 30.6.1989		5,000 gross	
Capital gains - disposal 31.12.1988		4,457	
Dividends received 1st June 1989		7,500	

			I	
T Limited	£		£	£
Schedule DI			180,000	
Schedule A			14,000	
Capital gains			4,457	
			198,457	
Less: charges			5,000	
			193,457	193,457
Dividend received		7,500		
Add: Tax credit		2,500		10,000
				203,457

Financial year 1988 6/12		
Basic profits	96,729	
Profits		101,729

	£
Small Company Limits:	
Lower 6/12 x £100,000 = £50,000	
Upper 6/12 x £500,000 = £250,000	
Corporation Tax @ 35%	33,855

Less: $1/40 \; £[(250,000 - 101,729) \times \dfrac{96,729}{101,729}]$ 3,525

                        30,330

Financial year 1989 6/12		
Basic profits	96,728	
Profits		101,728

```
                                               £
      Small Company Limits:
        Lower 6/12 x £150,000 = £ 75,000
        Upper 6/12 x £750,000 = £375,000
      Corporation tax @ 35%                    33,855


      Less: 1/40 £[(375,000 - 101,728)
                  x  96,728
                     101,728
                                              6,496
                                             27,359
                                             ======


      Combine                                57,689
                                             ======
```

7.0 INCOME TAX AND ACT

7.1 The quarterly accounting

(a) Income Tax

A company must deduct income tax at the basic rate before making most annual payments. These include:

i)   patent royalties;
ii) debenture and loan interest, other than that payable to a UK bank;
iii) deeds of covenant, and qualifying donations to charities;
iv) mortgage interest, other than that paid to building societies.

A company may similarly receive annual payments under deduction of income tax. These are known as 'Unfranked Investment Income' (UFII). In the corporation tax computation, unfranked investment income and annual payments are included and deducted gross.

(b) The accountability for income tax (TA 1988,Sch.16)

A company must make a return of:

i)   annual payments;
ii) unfranked investment income.

The returns, on form CT 61Z, must be made for 'return periods'. These end on 31st March, 30th June, 30th September and 31st December. If the company's accounting period-end is not co-terminous with one of the above dates, there must be an extra return period up to that date.

Illustration

A Ltd. makes up accounts to 30th April 1990. Its return periods are:

1st May 1989	-	30th June 1989
1st July 1989	-	30th September 1989
1st October 1989	-	31st December 1989
1st January 1990	-	31st March 1990
1st April 1990	-	30th April 1990

14 days after the end of each quarter, the company is liable to pay to the Revenue the tax deducted from annual payments, as reduced by the credit claimed for income tax deducted from unfranked investment income received in the return period. Interest will be chargeable if the payment is not made by the due date. If in a quarter a company's unfranked investment income exceeds its annual payments, the Revenue will refund the tax credit on the excess **but only to the extent that the company has already paid income tax to the Revenue in the same accounting period.**

Illustration

B Ltd. makes up accounts to 31st March 1990 and has the following annual payments and unfranked investment income:

2nd May 1989	Debenture interest paid	£ 6,000 (gross)
31st July 1989	Patent royalties received	£10,000 (gross)
31st October 1989	Debenture interest paid	£ 6,000 (gross)

Return period to	Annual payments £	UFII £	Income Tax Paid £	Income Tax Repaid £	Due Date
30.6.1989	6,000		1,500		14.7.1989
30.9.1989		10,000		1,500	on or after 14.10.1989.
31.12.1989	6,000		500		14.1.1990
	12,000	10,000	2,000	1,500	
	10,000		1,500		
	2,000		500		

Notes

1   The refund of income tax in the second quarter is restricted to £1,500 as that is the amount of income tax that has been paid in the accounting period.

2   In quarter three the balance of £1,000, i.e. 25% of (£10,000 - £6,000) still owing by the Revenue, is deducted from the amount due to them in that quarter.

At the end of the accounting period, there is no further liability to the Revenue.

If in the quarter to 31st March 1990 the company receives further patent royalties of £5,000 (gross) the position would be:

Return period to	Annual payments £	UFII £	Income Tax Paid £	Repaid £	Due Date
30.6.1989	6,000		1,500		
30.9.1989		10,000		1,500	
31.12.1989	6,000		500		
31.3.1990		5,000		500	on or after 14.4.1990
	12,000	15,000	2,000	2,000	
		12,000			
		3,000			

Here the position is reversed. There is a surplus of UFII and a tax credit of £ 750 which has not been repaid to the company. This will be relieved by deduction against the MCT due by the company, and to the extent it exceeds the MCT, the balance will be repaid in cash.

Where a company received building society interest prior to 6th April 1986, the notional tax credits could not be repaid in the quarterly accounting. The notional tax credit was deducted from MCT and if the company had no MCT liability it was repaid in cash. For interest received after 5th April 1986 the tax credits on BSI received may be recovered in the quarterly accounting.

If there is a change in the basic rate of income tax during the accounting period, there is no change in the procedure outlined above. Amounts of income tax will be paid over and recovered, based on the rate of tax which applies to the particular payment or receipt.

Illustration
C Ltd prepared accounts to 30th September annually. In the year to September 1991, it paid and received the following:

15th November 1990   Debenture interest received £8,000 (gross)
16th June 1991   Patent royalties paid   £20,000 (gross)
20th September 1991   Debenture interest received £6,000 (gross)

The rate of income tax was 25% for 1990/91 and 30% for 1991/92.

Return period to	Annual Payments £	UFII £	Income Tax Paid £	Repaid £	Due date
31.12.1990		8,000			
31. 3.1991					
30. 6.1991	20,000		4,000		14. 7.1991
30. 9.1991		6,000		1,800	on or after 14.10.1991
	20,000	14,000	4,000	1,800	

The payment made on 14th July, 1991 is made up as under:

Income Tax due on Patent Royalties: £

       £20,000 @ 30%   6,000

Less: Tax credits on debenture interest
         received:

       £8,000 @ 25%   2,000
                                           £4,000

Unlike previous examples, it is not possible to prove the arithmetic in the return schedules above because of mixing the different rates of income tax.

(c) **Distributions and Advance Corporation Tax (ACT) (s.209TA)**

A company may make a distribution which is defined as either a qualifying or a non-qualifying distribution. The company is only required to account for ACT on qualifying distributions.

Qualifying distributions include:

i)   dividends, including capital dividends;

ii)   interest payable on:
    (1)   a bonus issue of securities;

    (2)   an issue of securities covertible into shares, unless quoted on a recognised stock exchange or issued on terms similar to those applying to quoted securities;

iii) interest in excess of a reasonable commercial rate;

iv)   benefits received by a member on the transfer of assets or liabilities to or from the company, unless the transfer is between members of a 51% group;

v)   the repayment of share capital preceded by a bonus issue (with certain exceptions where the bonus issue was of share capital other than redeemable share capital and the repayment takes place more than ten years after the bonus issue). The repayment is regarded as a distribution up to the amount of the bonus element;

vi)   a bonus issue preceded by a repayment of share capital (with similar exceptions as in (v) above). The bonus issue is treated as a distribution up to the amount of the repayment.

Other qualifying distinctions will be dealt with later.

In all cases, ACT is accounted for in the normal way.

When a company makes a qualifying distribution, the term, Franked Payment (FP), is applied to the amount paid plus the relevant ACT. When a distribution is received by a company, the amount received plus the tax credit is known as Franked Investment Income (FII). To qualify for the description 'franked investment income' both recipient and paying companies must be UK resident.

Where the recipient is an individual, the gross amount (distribution plus tax credit) is treated as unearned income of the individual.

(d) Non-qualifying distributions

There is basically only one major non-qualifying distribution, namely a bonus issue of redeemable shares or securities. On the making of the bonus issue there is no liability on the company but the recipient, if an individual, is liable to higher rate taxes on the actual amount of the issue. When the issue is redeemed, this will be a qualifying distribution ((v) above) and the individual will be liable to income tax on the grossed-up amount. To avoid possible double taxation, the individual can deduct from the tax due on the second event not only the basic rate credit but a credit equal to the tax paid when the bonus issue was received.

For a corporate recipient, the distribution does not rank as FII and is not liable to corporation tax in the hands of the recipient company.

(e) The accountability for ACT (TA 1988,Sch.13)

The accountability for ACT is similar to that for income tax. The return periods are the same, and the return is on the same form. If at the end of the accounting period, there is a surplus of franked payments the associated ACT is available for offset against corporation tax.

Illustration

C Ltd. makes up accounts to 31st March 1990. It gives you the following information:

1st May 1989	Dividend received	£ 7,500
19th September 1989	Dividend paid	£11,250
14th October 1989	Dividend paid	£ 7,500
16th December 1989	Dividend received	£ 750
5th February 1990	Dividend received	£ 1,500

Return period to	FP £	FII £	ACT Paid £	ACT Repaid £	Due Date
30.6.1989	-	10,000	-	-	
30.9.1989	15,000	-	1,250	-	14.10.1989
31.12.1989	10,000	1,000	2,250	-	14.1.1990
31.3.1990	-	2,000	-	500	on or after 14.4.1990
	25,000	13,000	3,500	500	
	13,000		500		
	12,000		3,000		

Notes

1   No refund of the tax credit can be obtained in the quarter to 30th June 1989
     as no ACT has yet been paid by C Ltd. in the accounting period. The credit
     is effectively carried forward and offset against the ACT due in the next
     quarter.

2   In quarter three, franked payments and franked investment income in the
     quarter are netted before calculating the payment made to the Revenue.

3   The company has a surplus of franked payments of £12,000 and can offset ACT
     of £3,000 against its corporation tax.

     Where at the end of the accounting period there is a surplus of franked
     investment income, it will be carried forward into the next accounting
     period and offset against future franked payments. Under normal
     circumstances, the tax credits on a surplus of franked investment income
     cannot be repaid in cash.

Illustration

If, in the previous example, the dividends received in the quarter to 31st
March 1990 were £15,000 the position would be:

Return period to	FP £	FII £	ACT Paid £	ACT Repaid £	Due Date
30.6.1989	-	10,000	-	-	
30.9.1989	15,000	-	1,250	-	
31.12.1989	10,000	1,000	2,250	-	
31.3.1990	-	20,000	-	3,500	on or after 14.4.1990
	25,000	31,000	3,500	3,500	
		25,000			
Surplus FII		6,000			

This will be carried forward into the year to 31st March 1991. In this year, the company has:

1st June 1990	Dividend paid	£22,500
1st March 1991	Dividend received	£ 3,750

Return period to	FP £	FII £	ACT Paid £	ACT Repaid £	Due Date
30.6.1990	30,000				
Less: Surplus FII brought forward	6,000				
	24,000		6,000		14.7.1990
30.9.1990					
31.12.1990 No returns required					

Return period to	FP £	FII £	ACT Paid £	ACT Repaid £	Due Date
31.3.1991		5,000		1,250	
	24,000	5,000	6,000	1,250	
	5,000		1,250		
	19,000		4,750		

The net ACT paid of £4,750 will be offset against the corporation tax liability of the year to 31st March 1991.

Where a company receives unfranked investment income or distributions in a return period but has not made annual payments or distributions in that return period or in preceding return periods (within the same accounting period), the company does not need to make a return to the Revenue.

Where there is a change in the rate of ACT and the company's accounting period straddles 5th April then that accounting period is split into two deemed accounting periods, one ending on 5th April and the other beginning on 6th April. Each of these two periods is treated as entirely separate so that ACT paid in the first period cannot be repaid against FII received in the second and FII received in the first period will be carried forward in the normal way into the second period.

Illustration

D Ltd. makes up accounts to 30th September 1991. In that year it paid and received the following:

```
        1st November 1990   Dividend paid       £ 7,500
        1st March 1991      Dividend received   £11,250
        15th June 1991      Dividend paid        £35,000
        18th August 1991    Dividend received   £ 7,000
```

The rates of ACT are:
```
        1990/91              25/75
        1991/92               3/7
```

Return period to	FP £	FII £	ACT Paid £	Repaid £	Due Date
Deemed AP I 1.10.1990 to 5.4.1991					
31.12.1990	10,000		2,500		14.1.1991.
31.3.1991		15,000		2,500	on or after 14.4.1991.
5.4.1991 – no return					
	10,000	15,000 10,000	2,500 =====	2,500 =====	
Surplus FII		5,000			
Deemed AP 2 6.4.1991 to 30.9.1991					
30.6.1991	50,000				
Less: FII b/f	5,000				
	45,000		13,500		14.7.1991
30.9.1991	45,000 10,000	10,000 10,000	13,500 3,000	3,000 3,000	on or after 14.10.1991
	35,000 ======		10,500 ======		

The ACT of £10,500 is offset against the corporation tax liability of the 12-months accounting period to 30th September 1991.

7.2 The offset of ACT

The basic principle is that ACT can be offset against corporation tax on profits of the accounting period in which the distribution was made. The offset of ACT is restricted to the lower of:

(a) ACT on the surplus of franked payments for the accounting period, or

(b) basic rate income tax on the basic profits liable to corporation tax for the accounting period.

The following are the basic rates that have applied in recent financial years:

1979 to 1985	30%
1986	29%
1987	27%
1988	25%
1989	25%

Illustration

X Ltd. made up accounts to 31st March 1990, and had the following profits:

Trading income	£60,000
Schedule A	£10,000
Capital gains	£ 7,000

It paid the following dividends:

1.6.1989	Final 1988	£35,500
1.2.1990	Interim 1989	£39,500
1.6.1990	Final 1989	£26,800

	£
Schedule DI	60,000
Schedule A	10,000
Capital gains	7,000
	77,000

	£	£
Corporation tax @ 25%		19,250
Franked payments -		
Dividends paid in the accounting period	75,000	
ACT 25/75	25,000	
	100,000	
ACT @ 25%	25,000	
Maximum offset - 25% x £77,000	19,250	19,250
MCT		NIL
Surplus ACT	5,750	

A surplus of ACT may be dealt with in three main ways:

(a)   Carried back and offset against any available corporation tax of accounting
      periods **beginning** within the preceding six years on a LIFO basis.   Priority
      is given to offsetting ACT of the earlier accounting period against that
      period's corporation tax **before** dealing with any carry-back of a surplus.
      The time limit for making a claim to carry-back surplus ACT is two years
      from the end of the accounting period in which the surplus arose.

(b)   Surrendered to a subsidiary - this is dealt with later.

(c)   Unless a claim is made for an alternative treatment, surplus ACT will
      automatically be carried forward and set against the corporation tax
      liability of the next accounting period, and if any is still unrelieved it
      can be carried forward to the next accounting period and so on, without
      limit.   The set-off must be against the first available corporation tax
      liability.

In all cases the ACT (and surplus ACT) offset can never exceed the maximum found
by application of the appropriate percentage, i.e. basic rate income tax
multiplied by basic profits.

Illustration

T Ltd. commenced trading on 6th April 1987 and has the following profits for the
three years ended 5th April:

	1988	1989	1990
	£	£	£
Trading income	54,000	40,000	30,000
Case III	600	700	800
Chargeable gain (after reduction relief where appropriate)	2,000	400	1,500
Debenture interest paid (gross)	8,000	12,000	10,000

During the respective years the company made the following payments:

	Dividends	ACT	Franked Payments
	£	£	£
1988	21,900	8,100	30,000
1989	20,250	6,750	27,000
1990	37,500	12,500	50,000

Small company relief is to be ignored.

	Year ended 5th April		
	1988	**1989**	**1990**
	£	£	£
Trading income	54,000	40,000	30,000
Case III	600	700	800
Chargeable gain	2,000	400	1,500
	56,600	41,100	32,300
Less: charges	8,000	12,000	10,000
	48,600	29,100	22,300

	Year ended 5th April		
	1988	**1989**	**1990**
	£	£	£
Corporation tax @ 35%	17,010	10,185	7,805
ACT paid in year	8,100	6,750	12,500
Maximum offset	13,122	7,275	5,575
ACT originally utilised	8,100	6,750	5,575
MCT originally due	8,910	3,435	2,230
Less: ACT carried back	5,022	525	-
MCT ultimately suffered	3,888	2,910	2,230

Notes

1   The ACT deducted in the year ended 5th April 1990 is restricted to 25% of £22,300 - the profits liable to corporation tax - and this leaves £6,925 (£12,500 - £5,575) as surplus ACT. This can be carried forward or carried back as above.

2   The ACT carried back to the year ended 5th April 1989 is restricted to the following:

	£
Year ended 5th April 1989	
Maximum ACT for set-off (25% x £29,100)	7,275
Set-off as originally paid in the accounting period	6,750
Carried back from year ended 5th April 1990	525

                                                                    £
    Year ended 5th April 1988
    Maximum ACT for set-off (27% x £48,600)   13,122
    Set-off as originally paid in the accounting period   8,100

    Carried back from year ended 5th April 1990   5,022
                                                               ======

3   The surplus ACT of £1,378 not utilised £(6,925 - 525 - 5,022) is carried
     forward against the corporation tax liability on income of the next
     accounting period.

Normally the rate of ACT is fixed in advance; when it is not, the old rate will
continue to be used, with any adjustment made by discharge or repayment of tax or
by a further assessment.

Difficulties can arise when a company's accounting period is not co-terminous
with a fiscal year, and there is a change in the rate of ACT. When this occurs,
the profits will be apportioned over the respective fiscal years and the
appropriate percentage restriction applied to each.

Illustration

Z Ltd. makes up accounts to 30th September 1991. The company has trading income
of £ 60,000 and income from property of £20,000. It pays the following
dividends:

(a)   £75,000 on 1st February 1991;
(b)   £35,000 on 31st August 1991.

Assume corporation tax at 35% throughout and ACT - FY 1990 25/75
                                                 - FY 1991 3/7

                                       £
        Trading income   60,000
        Schedule A   20,000

                                   80,000
                                   ======

                                                    £   £
Corporation tax 35%   28,000
ACT - 1st February 1991
     25/75 x £75,000   25,000

     31st August 1991
     3/7 x £35,000   15,000

                                                  40,000
                                                  ======

Maximum restricted to:
```
    1.10.1990 - 31.3.1991
    25% x 6/12 x £80,000                      10,000
    1.4.1991 - 30.9.1991
    30% x 6/12 x £80,000                      12,000
                                              _____
                                              22,000    22,000
                                                        _____
MCT                                           ======     6,000
                                                        ======

Surplus ACT                                   18,000
                                              ======
```

There are anti-avoidance restrictions in TA 1988, s.245 to prevent the
carry-forward of surplus ACT where there has been either:

(a) within any period of three years a change in the ownership of a company
coupled with a major change in the nature or conduct of a trade or business
carried on by the company, or

(b) a major decline in the activity of the company and a change in its
ownership, before activity revives.

7.3 Using ACT effectively

ACT is effectively a loan to the Inland Revenue until it is offset against a
corporation tax liability. The following factors should be borne in mind to
reduce the effect of this detriment:

(a) Always make a distribution (or annual payment) in a later quarter period
rather than in an earlier quarter. This will postpone the payment of ACT by
at least 3 months;

(b) Remember, however, that this must not be done for distributions made in the
last quarter of an accounting period as this would defer the ACT offset
against corporation tax;

(c) Try to delay paying dividends where it is known that substantial amounts of
FII are likely to be received, until the quarter in which they are to be
received. This will avoid the loss of interest during the period that the
ACT is with the Inland Revenue.

(d) In general it is always better to carry ACT back rather than to carry it
forward (particularly if any of the problems in TA 1988 s.245 are likely to
be encountered).

8.0 COMPREHENSIVE EXAMPLE

Papwood Ltd. was incorporated in 1970, making up accounts to 31st March. The
following is a summary of the profit and loss account for the year ended 31st
March 1990:

	£		£
Salaries and wages	6,003	Gross profit	194,307
Directors' remuneration	17,100	Bank deposit interest	600
Rates,electricity & insurance	620	Dividend on ordinary shares	
Travelling & motor expenses	741	in a UK Co. (including credit)	2,000
Repairs and renewals	480	Profit on sales of shares	250
General expenses	885	Building Soc.interest - gross	100
Audit fee	719	(received 1.6.1989)	
Debenture interest (gross) payable	6,000		
Depreciation	2,764		
Net profit	161,945		
	197,257		197,257

The general expenses consist of:

	£
Stationery,postage and telephone	362
Legal expenses: Bonus issue of shares	30
Staff service agreements	15
Deeds of covenant (gross):	
Employees' benevolent fund	200
Cathedral rebuilding fund	25
Subscription - trade association	21
Staff outing	142
Sundries (all allowable)	90
	885

Repairs and renewals are all allowable.

The debenture interest of £6,000 includes an accrual at 31st March 1990 of £2,000. The dividend was received on 15th July 1989.

Of the profit of £250 on the sale of shares, £162 is the agreed amount of the chargeable gain computed according to the capital gains tax rules after indexation allowance.

The written-down values of plant and vehicles after deducting the capital allowances for the year ended 31st March 1989 were:

	£
Pool	12,117

During the year ended 31st March 1990 the following additional plant and vehicles were bought:

	Cost
	£
21st November 1989 - plant	4,000
1st January 1990 - car (for use by a director, 20% privately)	2,000

Plant which was purchased in 1982 and had cost £280 was sold for £300 during the year and plant which had been bought for £500 in December 1983 was sold for £300.

Recent dividends paid by Papwood Ltd. are:

		£
1st September 1989	For the year to 31st March 1989	11,250
1st September 1990	For the year to 31st March 1990	8,978

REQUIRED: Calculate the corporation tax liability for the year ended 31st March 1990.

PAPWOOD LTD.
Computation of Corporation Tax Liability
AP to 31st March 1990

	£ -	£ +	£
Net profit per accounts		161,945	
Depreciation		2,764	
Debenture interest payable		6,000	
General expenses: Bonus issue of shares		30	
Covenanted payments			
£(200 + 25)		225	
Capital allowances (see computation)	4,384		
Bank deposit interest	600		
Dividend from UK company	2,000		
Profit on sale of shares	250		
Building society interest	100		
	7,334	170,964	
		(7,334)	
Trading income		163,630	
Schedule D Case III -			
Bank deposit interest		600	
Building society interest - gross		100	
Chargeable gains		162	
		164,492	
Less: Charges on income			
Debenture interest paid			
£(6,000 - 2,000)	4,000		
Payments under deed of covenant	225		
		4,225	
		160,267	160,267
Franked Investment Income			2,000
			162,267

	£
Corporation Tax @ 35%	56,093
Less: 1/40 £[(750,000 - 162,267)	
x $\dfrac{160,267}{162,267}$	14,512
	41,581

ACT	£	£	£
Dividend paid	11,250		
ACT - 25/75	3,750		
	15,000		
Less: FII	2,000		
	13,000		
ACT @ 25%		3,250	
MCT		38,331	

Workings: Capital Allowances

	Pool			Total
	General	Cars		Allowances
	£	£		£
WDV b/f at 1.4.1989	12,117			
Additions				
Car		2,000		
Plant	4,000			
	16,117			
Disposal proceeds of				
plant sold	580			
	15,537			
WDA - 25%	3,884	500		4,384
c/f	11,653	1,500		

There is no private use reduction on the motor car though the director may be assessed under Schedule E in respect of a car benefit.

9.0 THE DUE DATE FOR THE PAYMENT OF CORPORATION TAX

(a) Advance Corporation Tax

A company must pay over ACT to the Revenue not later than 14 days after the end of the quarter in which the distribution is made.

(b) Mainstream Corporation Tax

As already mentioned, Mainstream Corporation Tax refers to the basic liability to corporation tax, less the offset for ACT paid.

Prior to 1965, when companies were liable to income tax, the date for payment of tax on income was the same as for an individual (in those days, 1st January in the year of assessment). As a result, the date of the end of the accounting period of the company determined the time interval before the tax was payable.

Illustration

D Ltd. made up accounts alternatively as under:

Year ended 30th April 1964
31st December 1964
31st March 1965

Year ended	Year of Assessment	Due Date	Time Interval
30.4.1964	1965/66	1.1.1966	20 months
31.12.1964	1965/66	1.1.1966	12 months
31.3.1965	1965/66	1.1.1966	9 months

Where the company commenced trading after 31st March 1965, the due date for the payment of MCT is always nine months after the end of the company's accounting period. Thus if E Ltd., making up accounts to 30th June 1986 commenced trading after 31st March 1965, it will pay corporation tax on 1st April 1987.

In order not to prejudice companies existing at 31st March 1965, it was provided that where a company commenced to trade before 31st March 1965 it would retain its old time-interval for the payment of corporation tax. Thus if E Ltd. (above) making up accounts to 30th June 1986 commenced trading prior to 31st March 1965, it would pay its accounts corporation tax on 1st January 1988.

Where a company which commenced trading before 31st March 1965 changed its accounting date, it retained the same time interval after the end of the accounting period as was used before the change.

Illustration

F Ltd. which commenced trading before 31st March 1965, made up accounts to 30th September annually. It changed its accounting date to 31st December and made up accounts for a 15-month period from 1st October 1985 to 31st December 1986.

AP   1.10.1985 to 30.9.1986
due date of MCT   1st January 1988
i.e., a time interval of 15
  months.
AP   1.10.1986 to 31.12.1986
due date of MCT   1st April 1988
still a time interval of 15
  months.

For accounting periods commencing on or after 17th March 1987, steps are being taken to standardise the payment dates of both 'old' and 'new' companies at 9 months after the end of the accounting period. The changes in the payment date are carried out in equal stages over three years. Thus if an 'old' company makes up accounts to 30th June, the 'old' time interval for payment would be 18 months, e.g. the MCT for the year to 30th June 1987 would be due on 1st January 1989.

The difference between the old and the new payment gap is 18 - 9 = 9 months; this will be divided by 3 equalling 3 periods of 3 months. The due dates for payment of MCT will now be:

       AP to 30th June 1988 - 15 months gap - due 1.10.1989
              30th June 1989 - 12 months gap - due 1.7.1990
              30th June 1990 - 9 months gap - due 1.4.1991

In all cases, corporation tax is not payable earlier than 30 days after the date of issue of the notice of assessment.

10.0   INTEREST

10.1 Interest on overdue tax

Interest on unpaid corporation tax is charged at the following rates:

6.4.1987	to 5.6.1987	9%	6.10.1988 to 5.1.1989 10.75%
6.6.1987	to 5.9.1987	8.25%	6. 1.1989 to 5.7.1989 11.5%
6.9.1987	to 5.12.1987	9%	6. 7.1989 onwards 12.25%
6.12.1987	to 5.5.1988	8.25%	
6.5.1988	to 5.8.1988	7.75%	
6.8.1988	to 5.10.1988	9.75%	

The interest must be paid gross and is not deductible as a trade expense or as a charge. The Board of Inland Revenue may remit interest of £30 or less. Interest is charged from the reckonable date. This is:

(a)   Where the tax is not subject to appeal the later of:

   i)   the normal due date, or
   ii)   30 days after issue of the notice of assessment.

(b)   Tax subject to appeal but with no application for postponement or where postponement has been refused; the later of:

   i)   the normal due date in (a) above,

   ii)   30 days after the date of the Inspector's agreement to, or Commissioners' determination of, the amount to be postponed.

(c)   if an application for postponement has been made, and agreed to, the later of:

   i)   the due date for payment under the original assessment, or

   ii)   the earlier of:

      1.   30 days after the final agreement on the tax payable, and

      2.   6 months after the normal due date.

Where an appeal is made or an application for postponement of the payment of tax is made but not agreed to by the Inspector or the Commissioners, the due date for the payment of that tax is 30 days after the date of notification of that decision if that is later than the normal due date.

Where the tax due on an assessment has been increased on appeal, interest on the additional tax becomes payable from the date on which it should have been charged had it been included in the original assessment and dealt with as postponed tax.

Illustration

X Ltd. which commenced trading in 1970, makes up accounts to 31st December 1989. On 2nd August 1990 the Inspector issues a notice of assessment showing tax due of £ 100,000. The company appeals on 15th August and applies for postponement of £40,000 tax. On 12th September the Inspector agrees with the company that £30,000 tax can be postponed pending the appeal hearing. The appeal was heard on 15th April 1991 and the tax due was finally determined as £110,000. The tax payments were:

> £70,000 on 30th October 1990
> £40,000 on 30th April 1991

Interest will be due as under:

(a) On £70,000 from 11.10.1990 to 30.10.1990

(b) On £30,000 from 1.4.1991 to 30.4.1991
On £10,000 from 1.4.1991 to 30.4.1991

Interest on unpaid ACT or income tax due under the quarterly accounting will be chargeable if payment is made later than 14 days after the end of the relevant return period. Again, the Inland Revenue may remit interest of £30 or less.

10.2 Interest on delayed tax repayments

A repayment to the company by the Inland Revenue of corporation tax, ACT or the tax credit on FII, more than 12 months after the material date, carries a tax-free repayment supplement at the same rates as above. The interest runs to the end of the tax month in which the repayment order is issued and starts as under:

(a) Corporation tax originally paid on or after the first anniversary of the material date — At the beginning of the tax month following the next anniversary of the material date after the payment of the tax.

(b) In all other cases — At the beginning of the tax month following the first anniversary of the material date.

Where tax is repaid in respect of corporation tax paid on different dates, it is allocated to that paid to a later date before an earlier one. The material date is the earliest due date for the payment of corporation tax for the appropriate accounting period.

Illustration

Y Ltd. made up accounts to 31st December 1988 and was assessed to corporation tax in the sum of £20,000 on 30th June 1989. The assessment was appealed against and the tax due was paid on the normal due date of 1st October 1989. The Commissioners' hearing took place on 1st December 1989 and agreed the tax due at £25,000. The additional tax was paid on 12th February 1990. For the year to 31st December 1989 a loss is made which is carried back into 1988. This results in a repayment of tax of £8,000 which is received by the company on 30th April 1991. Originally there would have been a liability to interest on £5,000 overdue tax from:

> 31.12.1989 to 12.2.1990
> (31.12.1989 - 30 days after the date of determination, being earlier
>   than 1st April 1990).

This will be repaid by the Collector on a claim being made.
The repayment of £8,000 will be allocated as under:

(1)   To the £5,000 additional payment.
       Paid - 12.2.1990
       Next anniversary of material date - 1st October 1990
       Interest due from 6.10.1990 to 5.5.1991.

(2)   To the original payment of £20,000.
       Interest due from 6.10.1990 to 5.5.1991.

CHAPTER FOURTEEN

Treatment of Losses

1.0 BASIC LOSS RELIEF (s.393(1), (2) and (9))

1.1. General

A corporation tax trading loss is calculated in the same way as corporation tax trading profit, i.e. after deducting capital allowances but before deducting charges paid under deduction of tax.

1.2 Carry Forward TA 1988, s.393(1)

A trading loss may be carried forward and offset against the first available future trading profits of the same trade without time limit.

1.3 Against Other Profits TA 1988, s.393(2)

The trading loss may be offset:

(a) against total profits of the same accounting period. Total profits means **all** income liable to corporation tax, and chargeable gains, but **before** deduction of charges on income; and then, if the company wishes;

(b) against total profits of the immediately preceding accounting period(s) of the same length as that in which the loss was incurred. A claim under (a) above must be made before a claim is made under (b).

Illustration

A Ltd. makes up accounts as follows:

> 12 months to 31.12.1989 - Profit
> 9 months to 30.9.1990 - Profit
> 12 months to 30.9.1991 - Loss

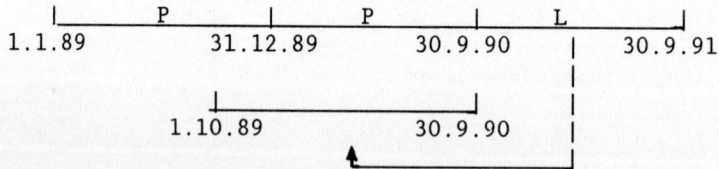

Thus the loss is carried back against the profit of:

(a) The accounting period to 30th September 1990.

(b) 3/12 of the profits of the accounting period to 31st December 1989.

All apportionments of profits are made on a strict time basis.

Before giving loss relief it is important to split any period of account into the appropriate accounting periods.

Illustration

B Ltd. makes up accounts as follows:

> 12 months to 31.12.1988 - Profit
> 12 months to 31.12.1989 - Profit
> 15 months to 31.3.1991 - Loss

In this case the 15-month period is divided up into two accounting periods:

(a)   twelve months to 31st December 1990;

(b)   three months to 31st March 1991

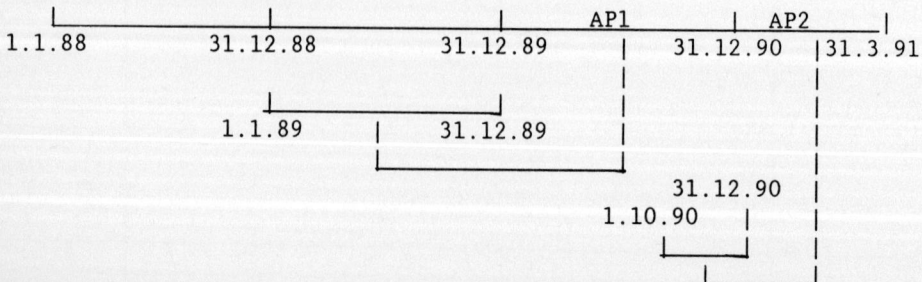

Though relief can be obtained for the loss of AP1, no relief under s.393(2) can normally be obtained for the loss of AP2 as it can only be carried back against three months of AP1 for which there is already a loss. It would, therefore, normally be carried forward.

For relief to be available under s.393(2) the company must:

(a)   be trading on a commercial basis, with a reasonable expectation of profits;

(b)   in the case of companies engaged in farming or market gardening, relief will not normally be available under s.393(2) if in the five preceding years there have been successive trading losses.

Relief is only available by carryback under s.393(2) if the trade producing the loss was also carried on in the accounting period(s) against whose profits the loss is being carried back.

Relief under s.393(2) is not available for Schedule D Cases V or VI losses.

A claim to carry forward losses under s.393(1) must be made within six years of the end of the accounting period in which the loss occurred. A claim to deal with a loss under s.393(2) must be made within two years of the end of the accounting period in which the loss occurred.

In the case of conflict, relief is given under s.393(1) in priority to s.393(2).

Illustration

C Ltd. has the following results:

	Trading Income	**Schedule A**	**Chargeable gains**
	£	£	£
Year ended 31.12.1988	20,000	1,000	2,000
6 months ended 30.6.1989	6,000	500	600
Year ended 30.6.1990	(28,000)Loss	1,200	-
Year ended 30.6.1991	4,000	800	600

Show loss claims under s.393(2) and s.393(1). All capital gains occurred on 30th June in the respective accounting periods.

	£	£
Year ended 30.6.1990		
Trading loss		(28,000)
Schedule A	1,200	
s.393(2)	(1,200)	1,200
	Nil	(26,800) c/f

	£	£
		(26,800) b/f
6 months ended 30.6.1989		
Trading income	6,000	
Schedule A	500	
Chargeable Gains	600	
	‾‾‾‾‾	
	7,100	
s.393(2)	(7,100)	7,100
	‾‾‾‾‾	‾‾‾‾‾
	Nil	(19,700)
	=====	
Year ended 31.12.1988		
Trading income	20,000	
Schedule A	1,000	
Chargeable Gains	2,000	
	‾‾‾‾‾	
	23,000	
s.393(2) Relief restricted		
to 6/12 x £23,000	(11,500)	11,500
	‾‾‾‾‾	‾‾‾‾‾
	11,500	(8,200)
	=====	=====
Year ended 30.6.1991		
Trading income	4,000	
s.393(1) relief	(4,000)	4,000
	‾‾‾‾‾	‾‾‾‾‾
	-	(4,200)
		=====
		s.393(1)
Schedule A	800	
Chargeable Gains	600	
	‾‾‾‾‾	
	1,400	
	=====	

Any apportionments of total profits or losses are made on a strict time basis.

1.4 Charges on income (s.393(9))

So far, relief has been given for losses before the deduction of charges on
income. To the extent that charges on income exceed profits, relief is available
by carry forward and deduction from future trading income. This relief is only
available for those charges incurred wholly and exclusively for the purposes of
the trade. This effectively excludes non-trade charges such as deeds of covenant
to charity, so in order to give maximum relief where there are available profits,
non-trade charges are relieved in priority to trade charges.

Illustration

E Ltd. has the following results:

```
                                                £
            Trading income                   2,000
            Charges on income:
              Debenture interest             3,000
              Covenant to Oxfam                500
```

To ensure maximum relief, charges will be deducted as under:

```
                                                £
            Trading income                   2,000
            Less: Charges:           £
              Covenant to Oxfam        500
              Debenture interest     1,500
                                             2,000
                                             _____
                                                -
                                             ======
            Unrelieved charges              1,500
                                            ======
```

The balance of unrelieved charges, known as **excess charges**, is carried forward and relieved as a deduction against future trading income, in the same way as a s.393(1) loss.

Illustration

F Ltd. made up accounts as under:

	Trading Income £	Schedule D Case III £	Debenture interest paid (gross) £
Years ended:			
31.3.1989	6,000	800	1,000
31.3.1990	(20,000)	1,500	1,000
31.3.1991	8,000	900	1,000

```
Year ended 31.3.1990
  Trading loss                                          (20,000)


Schedule D Case III               1,500
s.393(2)                         (1,500)                  1,500

                                  _____
                                    Nil
                                  ======


                                                          _____

                                                        (18,500)  c/f


(Excess charges £1,000)
```

	£	£	
		(18,500)	b/f
Year ended 31.3.1989			
Trading income	6,000		
Schedule D Case III	800		
	6,800		
s.393(2)	(6,800)	6,800	
	Nil	(11,700)	
Excess charges			
Year ended 31.3.1989	1,000		
Year ended 31.3.1990	1,000		
		(2,000)	
Total available for carry forward		(13,700)	
Year ended 31.3.1991			
Trading income	8,000		
s.393 (1)/(9)	(8,000)	8,000	
	-		
		(5,700)	
Schedule D Case III	900		
Less: Debenture interest paid	1,000		
	NIL	(100)	
Total loss to be carried forward			
s.393(1)/(9)		(5,800)	

1.5 Comprehensive example

X Ltd. has the following information:

	Year to 31.12.88 £	3 months to 31.3.89 £	Year to 31.3.90 £	Year to 31.3.91 £
Trading profit	20,000		8,000	
loss		(32,000)		(9,000)
Schedule A	2,000	3,000	4,000	5,000
Schedule D III	1,000	800	600	400
Capital gains		5,000	4,200	
Capital losses	2,000			2,000
Debenture interest paid (gross)	1,000	1,000	1,000	1,000
Deed of Covenant to charity paid (gross)	200	200	200	200

	£	£	£	£
3 months to 31.3.89				
Trading loss				(32,000)
Schedule A		3,000		
Schedule D III		800		
Capital gains	5,000			
Less: Capital losses b/f	2,000			
		3,000		
		6,800		
s.393(2) relief		(6,800)		6,800
		Nil		(25,200)
Debenture interest paid		1,000 c/f		
Deed of covenant paid		200 lost		
Year to 31.12.88				
Trading profit		20,000		
Schedule A		2,000		
Schedule D III		1,000		
		23,000		
s.393(2) Relief restricted to				
3/12 x £23,000		(5,750)		5,750
		17,250		(19,450)
Less: Charges £(1,000 + 200)		1,200		
		16,050		
Debenture Interest 1989				(1,000)
				(20,450)
Year to 31.3.90				
Trading profit		8,000		
s.393(1)		(8,000)		8,000
		Nil		(12,450)
		£		£
Schedule A		4,000		
Schedule D III		600		
Capital gains		4,200		
		8,800		
s.393(2) brought back		(3,600)		
		5,200		
Less: Charges - Deed of Covenant		200		
		5,000		
Debenture interest		1,000		
		4,000		

Year to 31.3.91	£	£
Trading loss		(9,000)
Schedule A	5,000	
Schedule D III	400	
	5,400	
s.393(2) relief	(5,400)	5,400
	Nil	(3,600)
	=====	
Debenture interest paid	1,000 c/f	
	=====	
Deed of Covenant paid	200 lost	
	=====	
s.393(2) carried back		3,600
		Nil
		=====

To carry forward therefore will be:
  Losses under s.393(1)/(9) £12,450 + £1,000   (13,450)
                                                                   =====

    Capital losses   £2,000
                                                     =====

It is important to recognise the value of the relief that has been obtained for
the loss. Throughout this example, all the companies have been small and the
relief obtained is as under:

Year to 31.12.88
            £5,750 offset against profits - 3/12 x £5,750 @ 27%
                                            9/12 x £5,750 @ 25%

3 months to 31.3.89

            £6,800 offset against profits at 25%

Year to 31.3.90
            £11,600 offset against profits at 25%

Year to 31.3.91
            £5,400 offset against profits at 25%

In general terms the loss should always be relieved to achieve the highest tax
savings.

2.0 TERMINAL LOSSES (TA 1988, S.394)

When a company ceases to trade, any trading loss incurred in the last twelve
months of trading that cannot be relieved under any other loss, relieving
section, can be carried back and offset against the available trading income of
the preceding 36 months, apportioned if necessary on a LIFO basis.

Section 394 provides that terminal loss relief is normally to be given in the last resort, after giving relief under all other loss relieving sections. It is believed that the Revenue interpret this to mean relief under s.393 only and not relief under s. 242 (relief against surpluses of franked investment income) or s.402 (group relief).

Illustration

G Ltd. ceased trading on 30th June 1990. It had the following results:

	Trading Income	Schedule A
	£	£
Year ended 31.12.1988	3,000	500
Year ended 31.12.1989	(20,000)	500
6 months ended 30.6.1990	2,000	-

Here there is the possibility of terminal loss relief as there is a loss in the last twelve months' trading. Before the amount available can be ascertained, all other loss relief must be claimed first.

Year ended 31.12.1989	£	£
Trading loss		(20,000)
Less: Relieved:		
s.393(2) of the year	500	
s.393(2) carried back	3,500	
s.393(1) carried forward	2,000	
		6,000
Loss unrelieved		(14,000)

As six months of the year ended 31st December 1989 fall into the last twelve months, terminal loss relief can be obtained for six-twelfths of the unrelieved loss, i.e. £ 7,000, against 'available trading income' of the three years ended 30th June 1989. The balance cannot be relieved and is lost.

The term 'loss' in respect of terminal loss relief includes:

(a) trading losses;
(b) excess charges on income, wholly and exclusively incurred;
(c) excess capital allowances given by discharge or repayment of tax;

all of which arise wholly or partly within the last twelve months' trading.

As can be seen in the example above, where an accounting period only falls partly into the last twelve months of trading, losses, etc., will be apportioned on a time basis. The term 'available trading income' means the Schedule DI profits of the three preceding years; apportioned if necessary on a strict time basis.

Where in those earlier periods there are trade charges, sufficient profits must be retained to offset those charges. The profits that are retained will be identified as:

(a) other profits; then

(b) trading income;

thus giving the maximum potential relief for terminal losses.

The time limit for claiming terminal loss relief is six years from the date of cessation.

Illustration

H Ltd. ceased trading on 31st December 1990 having made up accounts to 31st December annually. Results for previous years have been as under:

	Trading Income £	Schedule A £	Debenture interest paid £
Year ended:			
31.12.1987	16,000	500	1,000
31.12.1988	8,000	2,000	1,000
31.12.1989	10,000	2,000	1,000
31.12.1990	(30,000)	2,000	1,000

		£	£
Year ended:			
31.12.1990			(30,000)
Schedule A		2,000	
s.393(2)		(2,000)	2,000
		Nil	(28,000)

Year ended:			
31.12.1989			
Trading income		10,000	
Schedule A		2,000	
		12,000	
s.393(2)		(12,000)	12,000
		Nil	(16,000)

Calculation of terminal loss:			
Unrelieved trading loss of last 12 months			16,000
Excess charges of last 12 months			1,000
			17,000

The excess charges of the year ended 31st December 1989 cannot be utilised and are lost.

The terminal loss can then be carried back and offset against the available trading income of the three preceding years on a LIFO basis.

	£	£	£
Terminal loss			(17,000)

Year ended 31.12.1989
   All trading income utilised under s.393(2)

Year ended 31.12.1988	£	£	£
Trading income		8,000	(17,000)
Schedule A	2,000		
Retain for trade charges	1,000		
	1,000		
Terminal loss relief		(8,000)	8,000
			(9,000)
Liable to Corporation tax		1,000	

Year ended 31.12.1987	£	£	£
Trading income		16,000	
Schedule A	500		
Retain for trade charges	500	500	
	-	15,500	
Terminal loss relief		(9,000)	9,000
		6,500	-
Liable to Corporation tax		6,500	

It is important to appreciate that the purpose of retaining sufficient for trade charges is to ensure that there are no unrelieved trade charges which would be incapable of carry forward.

Illustration

	Years to				9 months
	31.12.86	31.12.87	31.12.88	31.12.89	to 30.9.90
	£	£	£	£	£
Trading profit	6,000	4,000	2,000	1,000	(15,000)
Schedule A	600	600	600	-	600
Debenture Interest paid	1,000	400	1,000	-	-
Deed of Covenant to charity	100	100	100	-	-

9 months to 30.9.90

	£	£
Trading loss		(15,000)
Schedule A	600	
s.393(2)	(600)	600
	Nil	(14,400)

	£	£
	Nil	(14,400)

Year to 31.12.89

	£	£
Trading profit	1,000	
s.393(2) restricted to 9/12 x £1,000	(750)	750
	250	(13,650)

Terminal loss as above   (13,650)
Carryback period - 36 months to 30.9.1989:

Period 1.1.1989-30.9.1989
Terminal loss relief against balance of trading
profits of year to 31.12.89 after s.393(2) relief: (250)   250

	Nil	(13,400)

Year to 31.12.1988

	£	£	
Trading profit	2,000		
Schedule A		600	
Retain for trade charges	400	600	
	1,600		
Terminal loss relief	(1,600)		1,600
c/f	Nil		(11,800)

Deed of Covenant to charity £100 lost

Year to 31.12.1987

	£	£	
Trading profit	4,000		
Schedule A		600	
Retain for trade charges		400	
		200	
Terminal loss relief	(4,000)		4,000
	Nil		(7,800)
Less: Deed of Covenant to charity		100	
		100	

Year to 31.12.1986

Trading profit	6,000		
Schedule A		600	
Retain for trade charges	(400)	(600)	
	5,600	-	
	5,600		(7,800)
Terminal loss relief - restricted to 3/12 x £6,000	(1,500)		1,500
	4,100		(6,300)
Less: Deed of Covenant to charity	100		
	4,000		

Note the terminal loss relief in the year to 31st December 1986 is 3/12 x £6,000 **not** 3/12 x £5,600.

The remainder of the terminal loss is unrelieved.

Where there have been sales of assets after cessation of trade, the normal treatment of gains and losses will be:

(a) Sales of stock in trade, etc.   Any profits and losses are dealt with in the last period of account.

(b) Sales of plant and other assets on which capital allowances have been claimed.   Any balancing charges and allowances are dealt with in the last accounting period.

(c) Capital gains, etc.   Assessed in the accounting period in which the asset is disposed of.

3.0   THE EXTENSION OF LOSS RELIEF WHEN THERE IS A SURPLUS OF FRANKED INVESTMENT INCOME (TA 1988, s.242)

In earlier sections the basic forms of loss relief were:

(a) under s.393(2) against total profits of the accounting period;

(b) under s.393(2) against total profits of the immediately preceding accounting period of the same length.

An extension of loss relief is available when there is also a surplus of franked investment income. Where a company has:

(a) trading losses;

(b) charges on income;

(c) management expenses;

(d) capital allowances given by discharge or repayment of tax;

(e) certain capital losses if it is an investment company;

and also has available a surplus of FII of the same accounting period, then the company may elect to treat that surplus of FII as if it were profits liable to corporation tax, so that the losses etc. may be relieved and the tax credit comprised in the FII repaid. Furthermore, the unrelieved losses etc., (but not management expenses or charges on income) may also be set against any surplus FII of the preceding accounting period, of the same length, and the tax credit comprised in that surplus repaid.

The order of set-off is against:

i)   total profits of the accounting period in which loss etc. arises;

ii)   total profits of the preceding accounting period;

iii) the surplus FII of the accounting period in which the loss etc, arises;

iv)   the surplus FII of the preceding accounting period.

For this relief to be claimed the claimant company must be resident in the UK and relief must be claimed:

(a) in respect of trading losses, capital allowances and the investment
     company's chargeable losses - within two years from the end of the
     accounting period in which the loss (or allowance) arose;

(b) in respect of charges on income and management expenses - within six years
     of the end of the accounting period in which the loss arose.

Illustration

L Ltd. is resident in the UK and has the following results:

	Years ended		
	31.3.1988	31.3.1989	31.3.1990
	£	£	£
Trading income	6,000		20,000
Trading loss		(14,000)	
Schedule A	1,000	1,000	1,000
Dividends received	3,796	3,000	2,250
Dividends paid	1,404	1,500	6,000

Show the loss claims for all years - giving relief as soon as possible.
Assume ACT at 27/73 for the financial year 1987 and 25/75 for 1988 and 1989.

		£	£
Year ended 31.3.1989			
Trading loss			(14,000)
Schedule A		1,000	
s.393(2)		(1,000)	1,000
		─────	─────
		Nil	(13,000)
		════	─────
Year ended 31.3.1988			
Trading income		6,000	
Schedule A		1,000	
		─────	
	C/f	7,000	(13,000)
		£	£
	B/F	7,000	(13,000)
S.393(2)		(7,000)	7,000
		─────	─────
		Nil	(6,000)
		═════	

Year ended 31.3.1989

Dividends received	3.000		
Add: Tax credit	1,000		
	─────		
		4,000	
Dividends paid	1,500		
Add: ACT	500		
	─────		
		2,000	
		─────	
		2,000	
s.242 claim		(2,000)	2,000
		─────	
			(4,000)

Tax credit repaid - 25% x £2,000 = £500
                              ═══

Year ended 31.3.1988

Dividends received	3,796		
Add: Tax credit	1,404		
	─────		
		5,200	
Dividends paid	1,460		
Add: ACT	540		
	─────		
		2,000	
		─────	
		3,200	
s.242 claim		(3,200)	3,200
		─────	
		Nil	(800)
		═════	═════

Tax credit repaid - 27% x £3,200 = £864
                              ═══

The effect of a claim under s.242 is to accelerate the repayment of the tax credit attached to surplus FII, thus giving a cash flow advantage. However, had the claim not been made, not only the surplus FII but also the trading loss etc. could have been carried forward for offset against future trading income.   In order to put the company back in the same position as it would have been had a s.242 claim not been made, it is provided in s.242(5) that whenever in a subsequent accounting period there is a surplus of franked payments, the company may treat the lower of:

(a)   the amount of the surplus franked payments, or

(b)   the amount of the s.242 claim

as a trading loss to be relieved against trading income as in s.393(1).

Year ended 31.3.1990	£	£	£
Trading income			20,000
s.393(1)			(800)
			———
			19,200
Franked Payments			
Dividends paid	6,000		
Add: ACT	2,000		
	———	8,000	
FII			
Dividends received	2,250		
Add: Tax credit	750		
		3,000	
	———	———	
Surplus franked payments		5,000	
s.242(5) loss relief		(5,000)	(5,000)
		=====	———
			14,200
Schedule A			1,000
			———
			15,200
			======

	£	£
Corporation tax @ 25%		3,800
ACT - 25% x £5,000	1,250	
Less: Due to Revenue on re-instatement of	1,250	-
trading losses		
	———	———
		3,800
		=====

Notes

1.   Here, the surplus franked payments are less than the amount of the s.242 claim, i.e. £5,200-£5,000 = £200. This has had the effect of reducing the amount of the surplus franked payments (and consequently ACT available for offset) to nil. The amount of £200 not relieved will be carried forward without time limit to be relieved against profits in future accounting periods.

2.   The ACT that relates to the surplus of franked payments is:

                    £5,000 @ 25% = £1,250

If s.242(5) had not been claimed this amount of ACT could have been set off
against the corporation tax liability on income, subject to the usual
limits. However, the tax credit repaid on the original s.242 claim is now
reclaimed by the Revenue, and as a result there will be no set-off of ACT.
The amount of £114 (£1,364-£1250) will be recovered by the Revenue in a
future accounting period.

If the results for the year to 31st March 1991 were:

		£
Trading profits		20,000
Dividends paid		3,750

the position would be:

	£	£
Year to 31.3.1991		
Trading profits		20,000
Dividends paid	3,750	
ACT 25/75	1,250	
	5,000	

Treat the lower of £5,000 or the remaining
s.242 claim of £200 as a s.393(1) loss

			(200)
			19,800
Corporation tax @ 25%			4,950
ACT as above	1,250		
Less: Due to Revenue - balance of	114		1,136
			3,814

Thus the amount of losses received back from the Revenue and the amount of ACT
restored to them precisely balance with the tax credits received from, and the
losses surrendered to, the Revenue in the s.242 claim.

Does it give the same result as if no relief was obtained? If no relief under
s.242 was claimed, at the end of 1989 the position would have been:

	£	£
s.393(1) losses c/f		£6,000
Surplus FII:		
1989	2,000	
1988	3,200	
		£5,200

In 1990 the s.393(1) claim would have been £6,000 to give trading income of
£14,000 instead of £14,200 when s.242 is claimed. The surplus FII would have
been offset against franked payments made in the year to 31st March 1990 and no
ACT would have been payable. However, £5,200-£5,000 = £200 would be carried
forward as surplus FII against future franked payments.

In essence, the claim operates by reducing the loss and releasing the tax credit
under s.242 and giving back the loss and reducing the ACT available for offset
under s.242(5). It is generally worth making when possible, since it means that
extra money is made available straight away - a very important practical factor
when a company is making a loss.

4.0 COMPANY RECONSTRUCTIONS WITHOUT A CHANGE OF OWNERSHIP (TA1988, s.343 & s.344)

Provided certain conditions are fulfilled, where one company ceases trading and
another company commences to carry on its trade, unutilised trading losses of the
first company are transferred to the successor. In addition, fixed assets are
transferred at their tax-written-down values with no balancing adjustments and
capital assets can be transferred at the price which gives neither gain nor loss.

(a)   Both companies must be within the charge to UK corporation tax;

(b)   At least 75% of the trade or of an interest in it (i.e. ownership of the
          ordinary share capital) must belong to the same persons at some time during
          the period commencing one year before the change, and finishing two years
          after it.

If relief is claimed in this way, the company ceasing to trade will not be able
to claim terminal loss relief.

5.0 RESTRICTIONS ON CARRY FORWARD OF LOSSES (TA 1988 s.768 & s.769)

There are anti-avoidance provisions contained in TA 1988, s.768 and s.769
prohibiting the carry forward of losses where:

(a)   within a three-year period there is both a change in the beneficial
          ownership of the company and a major change in the nature and conduct of its
          trade, or

(b)   at any time after a company's trading activities become small or negligible,
          and before they revive, there is a change in the beneficial ownership of the
          company.

A 'major change' includes:

(a)   a major change in the type of property dealt in or services or facilities
          provided in the trade; or

(b)   a major change in customers' outlets or markets of the trade.

A change in the beneficial ownership of the company will generally occur where
one or more persons acquire a majority (more than 50%) shareholding in the
company concerned.

6.0 FOREIGN LOSSES AND SCHEDULE D CASE VI LOSSES

Foreign losses will be considered later, in the section on foreign income. Schedule D Case VI losses may only be offset against future Schedule D Case VI profits with any excess being carried forward and offset against future Schedule D Case VI profits. A claim for relief must be made within six years after the end of the accounting period in which the loss arises.

7.0 USING LOSSES EFFECTIVELY

A loss has been described as a negative asset; like all assets therefore, it is important to use it effectively. Points to bear in mind are:

7.1 General

(a) All other things being equal, a loss should be utilised in such a way as to give the greatest tax savings. This will mean:

    i)   offsetting the loss against marginal profits which bear the highest effective rate of corporation tax;

    ii) then offsetting the loss against profits chargeable at the normal rate;
    iii) lastly offsetting the loss against profits liable at the small companies rate.

(b) Timing is important; it is generally better to obtain loss relief now rather than next year. Thus it may be better to carry the loss back rather than to carry it forward. In doing this however consider the time value of money. It might be better to carry forward a loss if the rate of relief is greater than the indexed value of the relief obtained by carrying the loss back.

(c) Where a loss is carried back there may be the possibility of tax free repayment supplements.

(d) It is a popular misconception to believe that when a loss is offset there will be an automatic repayment of MCT. This will not always be the case, particularly if ACT has already been offset.

Illustration

A Ltd. has the following trading results: £
        Year to 31st March 1989   30,000
        Year to 31st March 1990   (40,000)

        No ACT has been paid.

Before loss relief:	1989	1990
DI	30,000	(40,000)
CT @ 25%	7,500	

If s.393(2) relief is claimed:

DI	30,000	(40,000)
s.393(2)	(30,000)	30,000
	Nil	(10,000)
IR repay	7,500	

If, however, there had been a full offset of ACT the position before loss relief in 1989 would have been:

	£
DI	30,000
CT @ 25%	7,500
ACT offset, restricted to 25% of £30,000	7,500
MCT paid	-

If the loss is now carried back from 1990 there will be no repayment of corporation tax as no MCT has been paid. All the ACT offset will now be thrown into surplus but this does not guarantee a repayment if the maximum offset has already been made in the previous six years.

Where double tax relief is being claimed under the credit system, the offset of a loss may result in the loss of foreign tax credits.

7.2 Terminal loss relief

In maximising this relief remember that the loss qualifying for relief is that of the last 12 months of **trading**. If it is desired to obtain maximum relief the temptation to 'keep going for a little longer to see what the company can do' must be resisted. As there may be substantial capital gains on the disposal of assets, every effort should be made to ensure disposal before the cessation of trade so that any loss arising in the last accounting period can be offset against them.

7.3 S.242 relief

Whilst relief should be claimed as early as possible it is important to remember that there is a restriction on the re-instatement of a loss - i.e. the presence of a surplus of future franked payments. Where there is unlikely to be such a surplus, possibly because of a substantial surplus of FII brought forward, it might be impossible to reinstate the loss under s.393(1) for a substantial period of time. It may be more beneficial therefore, to just consider carrying the loss forward under s.393(1) where the only limiting factor is the presence of future trading profits.

CHAPTER FIFTEEN

Groups

1.0 THE TAXATION OF GROUPS - GROUP RELIEF

1.1 General - the recognition of a group

Like many words in taxation, the word 'group' does not have a single meaning. There are different definitions of the word for separate taxation techniques and it is important initially to have a brief survey of the meanings as far as losses are concerned. Thus for loss relief under ss.402-413 TA 1988 a group will exist if the holding company controls directly or indirectly at least 75% of the ordinary share capital of the subsidiary company.

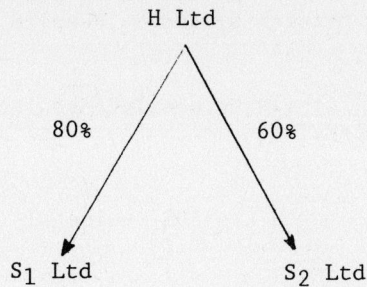

Fig. 3. Group loss relief

In this case S_1 Ltd., but not S_2 Ltd., will be a subsidiary company for group loss relief.

1.2 Groups and group relief - definition

For group relief to be available it is necessary that two basic conditions are satisfied:

(a) all the companies concerned are UK resident;

(b) they are members of a group of companies.

(a) **UK residence**

Most companies will be UK resident if they are incorporated in the UK. If they are not incorporated in the UK, they will be considered to be resident in the UK if the central management and control of their trade or business is exercised in the UK. The traditional test of corporate residence is that it exists at the place where the board of directors meets - **(John Hood & Co. Ltd. v. Magee (1918))**. The case of **Unit Construction Co. Ltd. v. Bullock (1960)** provided that central management and control exists at the place where it actually occurs and not merely where it should occur.

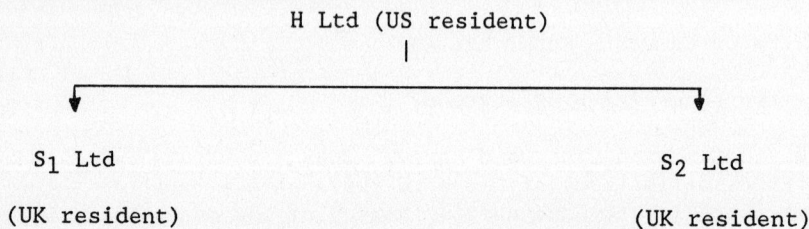

H Ltd (US resident)

S$_1$ Ltd

(UK resident)

S$_2$ Ltd

(UK resident)

Fig.4 US resident holding company

At its most basic, a group consists of a holding company and a subsidiary company. In the above as H Ltd. is not UK resident it will not be possible for losses to be surrendered between S$_1$ and S$_2$ despite the fact that they are both resident in the UK.

To avoid this difficulty, it may be possible to interpose a UK resident intermediate holding company.

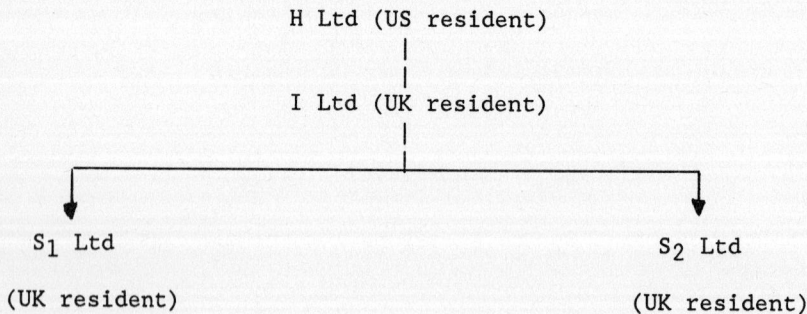

H Ltd (US resident)

I Ltd (UK resident)

S$_1$ Ltd

(UK resident)

S$_2$ Ltd

(UK resident)

Fig. 5. US resident holding company with UK intermediary

In this case it would be possible to surrender losses between I Ltd. and S$_1$ and S$_2$ and also between S$_1$ and S$_2$ as there would now be a UK resident group of holding and subsidiary companies.

This form of structure may well be challenged by the Revenue who will try to show that I Ltd. is not truly UK resident. In particular, problems may be encountered if for example I Ltd. has no independent economic reason for its own existence apart from holding the shares in S_1 and S_2 and thus co-incidentally forming a UK resident group.

(b)   A group of companies

For group relief purposes, companies will form a group when the holding company controls directly or indirectly at least 75% of the ordinary share capital of the subsidiary. Ordinary share capital is defined in TA 1988,S.832(1) as including all shares apart from those paying a fixed rate of dividend. It would thus include participating preference shares.

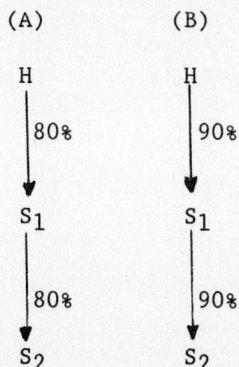

```
           (A)              (B)

           H                H

            | 80%            | 90%
            ↓                ↓

           S₁               S₁

            | 80%            | 90%
            ↓                ↓

           S₂               S₂
```

Fig. 6. Controlling interests

In Case (A), H and S_1 are within a group of companies as H controls 80% directly of S_1. Similarly, S_1 and S_2 are within a group for the same reason. H and S_2, however, are not within a group as H only controls indirectly 80% x 80% = 64% of S_2. Thus losses can be transferred between H and S_1, between S_1 and S_2 but not between H and S_2. In particular it is not possible to surrender losses from H to S_1, and then on from S_1 to S_2.

In case (B), H is clearly the holding company of S_1 and S_1 the holding company of S_2. In addition H controls indirectly 90% x 90% = 81% of S_2.
All these companies are therefore within the same group and losses may be surrendered freely between them.

Indirect holdings through non-UK resident companies must be ignored, so that in (B) above, if S_1 was non-UK resident, S_2 would not be within a group with H.

(c)   Anti-avoidance measures

To deal with situations in which 'artificial groups' were created in order to utilise capital allowances. The basic definition of a group, considered above is extended to include the following additional tests. Thus to qualify as a group the holding company should not only control at least 75% of the ordinary share capital but also:

i)   be beneficially entitled to at least 75% of the profits available for distribution to the equity holders, and,

ii)   be beneficially entitled to at least 75% of any assets of the
subsidiary company available for distribution on a winding up.

1.3   Items available for group relief

Group relief is available for:

(a)   trading losses;
(b)   excess charges, including non-trade charges;
(c)   excess management expenses;
(d)   excess capital allowances given by discharge or repayment of tax.

Trading losses may be surrendered without any prior offset against other
profits; in general the other items can only be surrendered if they exceed the
other profits of the accounting period.

Losses which are caught by the provisions of TA 1988, s.397 ('hobby farming') or
s.393(5) (trading not carried on on a commercial basis) are not available for
group relief.   Nor is it possible to surrender Schedule D Case V losses.

Only items of the current accounting period are available for surrender.
Once a company controls at least 75% of the OSC etc. of the owned company it is
entitled to 100% of that company's losses etc.

1.4   Method of giving group relief

Within the group structure there are two basic types of companies:

(a)   the claimant company - the one that receives the loss, etc.;

(b)   the surrendering company - the one with a loss etc., available for
surrender.

Before a loss etc., can be surrendered by one company to another, detailed
conditions must be satisfied.

(a)   The claimant company

The claimant company may offset losses surrendered to it against total
profits.

Before the loss is offset, however, the claimant company must offset:

i)   losses and charges brought forward under s. 393(1);
ii)   any s. 393(2) losses of the same accounting period;
iii)   charges of the same accounting period.

It must **not**, however, bring back losses etc. from a subsequent accounting period
in priority to giving group relief.

Illustration

J Ltd. is the 100% subsidiary of K Ltd.   It provides the following information
for the year to 31st March 1990:

	£
Trade loss	(1,000)
Schedule A	2,000
Capital gain	3,000
Debenture interest paid	500
Losses brought forward from 1989	(2,000)
Losses of 1991 available for carry back	(2,400)
K Ltd. has a loss of	(10,000)

	£	£
DI		(1,000)
Schedule A	2,000	
Capital Gains	3,000	
	5,000	
s. 393(2)	(1,000)	1,000
	4,000	
Less: Charges	500	
	3,500	

K Ltd. may only surrender £3,500 loss - up to the total of J Ltd.'s profits.

(b)   The surrendering company

There are no specific conditions attached to the surrendering company and in general it may:

i)   surrender as much loss as it wishes to a company up to the maximum of the claimant company's own eligible profits;

ii) spread relief over a number of companies within the group.

In considering the amount of loss that can be surrendered to another group company, the surrendering company would often consider the following factors:

i)   maximisation of loss reliefs;
ii) effective utilisation of ACT;
iii) timing of tax payments;
iv) potential loss of foreign tax credits.

In deciding where to allocate a group loss, then, it will often be necessary to consider a combination of the above factors. In addition possible claims under s.393(2) carry back should always be considered, as a carryback claim may result in earlier relief than that available under group relief.

Illustration

L Ltd. is the wholly-owned subsidiary of M Ltd. Both are resident within the UK. They provide you with the following information about their results:

	Year ended 31st December			
	1987	1988	1989	1990
	£	£	£	£
L Ltd.				
Trading income	1,000		4,000	
Trading loss		(4,000)		(1,000)
M Ltd				
Trading income		500		3,000
Trading loss	(1,000)		(6,000)	
Schedule A	1,500	400	500	1,200

Show suggested loss claims.

L Ltd.		**M Ltd.**	
	£		£
Year ended 31.12.1987			
Trading income	1,000	Trading loss	(1,000)
s. 393(2) c/back	(1,000)	Schedule A (s. 393(2))	1,500
	―――		―――
	-		500
	═══════		═══════
Year ended 31.12.1988			
Trading income	(4,000)	Trading Income	500
s. 393(2) c/back	1,000	Schedule A	400
	―――		―――
	(3,000)		900
Group relief	900		(900)
	―――		―――
C/fwd under s. 393(1)	(2,100)		-
	═══════		═══════

L Ltd.		**M Ltd.**	
	£		£
Year ended 31.12.1989			
Trading income	4,000	Trading loss	(6,000)
s. 393(1) b/f	(2,100)	Schedule A (s. 393(2))	500
	―――		―――
	1,900		(5,500)
Group relief	(1,900)		1,900
	―――		―――
	-	C/fwd under s. 393(1)	(3,600)
	═══════		═══════

L Ltd	£	M Ltd.	£
Year ended 31.12.1990			
Trading loss	(1,000)	Trading income	3,000
		s. 393(1) b/f	3,000
			————
			-
		Schedule A	1,200
Group relief	1,000		(1,000)
	————		————
	-		200
	=====		========
		s. 393(1) loss c/f	(600)

1.5 Non co-terminous accounting periods

The Companies Act provides that normally the accounting periods of all group companies shall be co-terminous. Where they are not it will be necessary to allocate the loss of the surrendering company on a strict time basis into the accounting periods of the claimant company.

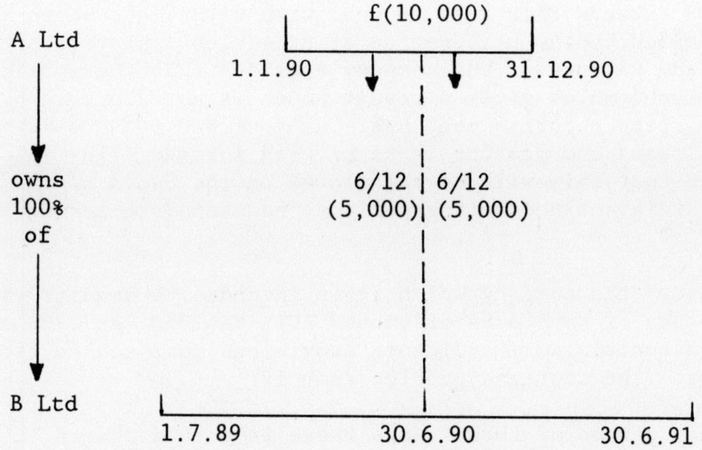

Fig. 7. Co-terminous accounting periods

It is important to remember that losses can only be surrendered if the claimant company has sufficient profits to take those losses. Where accounting periods are not co-terminous it will also be necessary to apportion the profits of the claimant company on a basis to ensure that they are sufficient to take the loss.

1.6 Companies entering or leaving the group

(a) Companies entering the group

When a company enters the group other than at a normal accounting date, an accounting period is deemed to end at the date on which the company enters the group. Losses, and profits if appropriate, will be apportioned using the rules given in 1.5 above.

H Ltd

1.1.90   31.12.90

1.7.90

H Ltd acquired
100% of S Ltd

S Ltd

1.1.90   £(10,000)   31.12.90

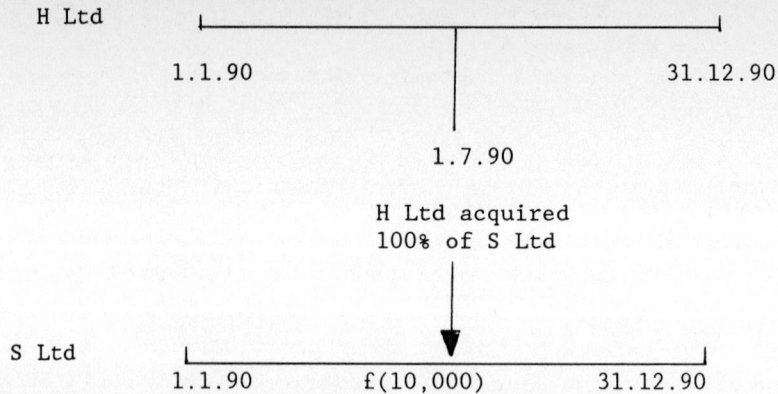

Fig. 8. Companies entering the group

In normal circumstances the loss of £10,000 will be apportioned on a strict
time basis and thus six-twelfths of £10,000 = £5,000 would be available for
surrender from S to H (subject always to H Ltd. having sufficient
profits).

TA 1988, s.409 extends this rule to deal with situations where the relief
had been exploited by the utilisation of exceptional profits and losses.
Where the Inland Revenue or the company consider that the application of the
time apportionment rules gives a result which is unreasonable or unjust then
instead of the time apportionment basis, a just and reasonable method of
apportioning losses and profits is to be used instead. The Inland Revenue
have indicated that this will be calculated on the basis of the profits and
losses of the relevant accounting periods, had separate accounts been drawn
up.

In certain cases, the company which it is intended to acquire will have
unused tax losses or surpluses of unused ACT. TA 1988, ss. 768 and 769 and
TA 1988, s.245 contain anti-avoidance provisions designed to prevent abuse
of these items. The sections provide that if:

i)   within any period of three years there is both a change in the
      beneficial ownership and a major change in the nature or conduct of a
      trade or business carried on by the company; or

ii)   at any time the trading activities of the company are small or
      negligible and before they revive there is a change of ownership of the
      company,

then unused losses or ACT of the company cannot be carried forward beyond
the change of ownership.

(b)   **Companies leaving the group**

Whilst similar provisions as above apply to companies leaving the group, TA
1988, s. 410 provides that a company will not be deemed to be a group member
for group relief purposes throughout any period in which arrangements exist
for that company to leave the group.

The term 'arrangements' is not defined in the legislation and could be extremely wide including for example formal and informal discussions, negotiations, etc. A Statement of Practice (SP 5/80) gives some guidance as to what the Revenue consider to be the meaning of this term. In the case of a normal sale, it will normally be the date of the contract for sale of the subsidiary's shares or the date of the shareholders' meeting giving approval for the sale if that is required.

The effect of this will be that no group relief will normally be available in the accounting period in which the company leaves the group.

1.7 Consortium relief

Consortium relief is not an independent form of relief, but merely an extension of the group provisions described above; for convenience sake, however, it will be referred to as consortium relief in this section. It is important to realise that the basic principles referred to above for groups will also apply to a consortium.

(a) Recognition and definition

The definitions:

A consortium exists broadly in one of the two following circumstances:

(1) Where at least 75% of the ordinary share capital of an owned trading company is held by other UK resident companies, none owning less than 5%;

(2) Where at least 90% of the ordinary share capital of trading companies is owned by an intermediate holding company and at least 75% of that company's own share capital is held by other UK resident companies, again with none owning less than 5%.

These can be expressed diagrammatically:

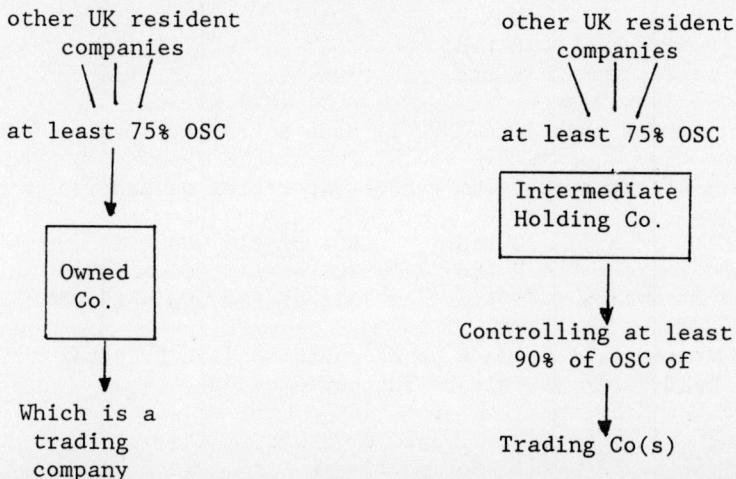

Fig. 9. Consortia

Provided that at least 75% of the OSC is held by UK resident companies then it is possible for a non-resident company or an individual to hold the remaining shares though they will not be entitled to claim any part of the owned company's losses.

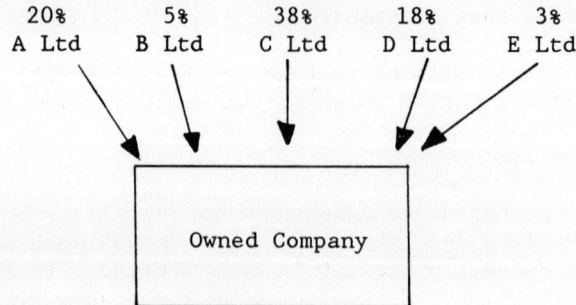

20%	5%	38%	18%	3%
A Ltd	B Ltd	C Ltd	D Ltd	E Ltd

Owned Company

Fig. 10

The owned company is owned by a consortium of A Ltd., B Ltd., C Ltd., and D Ltd., who control 81% of the owned company. E Ltd., because it does not control at least 5% of the OSC is not a member of the consortium.

(b)   Allocation of losses, etc.

Losses, etc., of the owned company will be allocated to the members of the consortium in accordance with their interests in the ordinary share capital of that company. The loss that can be claimed will, as for groups, be restricted by the available profits of the claimant company.

Illustration

P Ltd., a trading company, has the whole of its ordinary share capital owned as under:

$$\begin{array}{ll} \text{Q Ltd.} & 40\% \\ \text{R Ltd.} & 30\% \\ \text{S Ltd.} & 30\% \end{array}$$

In the year ended 30th June 1990 it made a trading loss of £10,000.

The members of the consortium can obtain relief as under:

$$\begin{array}{lll} \text{Q Ltd.} & 40\% \text{ of } £10,000 & = £4,000 \\ \text{R Ltd.} & 30\% \text{ of } £10,000 & = £3,000 \\ \text{S Ltd.} & 30\% \text{ of } £10,000 & = £3,000 \end{array}$$

If, in addition, Q Ltd. made up accounts to 31st December annually, its share of P Ltd.'s loss would be further divided:

$$\text{Year ended 31.12.1989 -} \frac{6}{12} \times £4,000 = £2,000$$

$$\text{Year ended 31.12.1990 -} \frac{6}{12} \times £4,000 = £2,000$$

Where a company owned by a consortium has a trading loss and other profits available in the same accounting period against which a claim could be made under s.393(2) TA 1988 then the loss available for surrender to the consortium will be restricted on the basis that a s.393(2) claim has been made (whether or not in reality it has). This deemed offset does not apply to group loss surrenders. Thus if P Ltd had schedule A income in the year to 30th June 1990 of £2,000 the loss available for surrender would be:

	£	£
Trading loss		(10,000)
Schedule A	2,000	
Potential s. 393(2)	(2,000)	2,000
Available for surrender		8,000

If, in fact, the s.393(2) claim was not made, then again, only £8,000 loss could be surrendered and the balance of £2,000 would be carried forward.

As with group relief, the consortium loss that can be surrendered will be restricted by the profits of the claimant companies.

Ilustration

X Ltd. is owned as under:
   A Ltd 35%
   B Ltd 20%
   C Ltd 30%
   D Ltd 15%

It has a trading loss of £(10,000).

Loss allocated:

	£
A Ltd	(3,500)
B Ltd	(2,000)
C Ltd	(3,000)
D Ltd	(1,500)
	(10,000)

The loss relief may be restricted by the profits of the claimant companies:

	Profit/Loss £	Loss surrendered £	
A Ltd	50,000	(3,500)	
B Ltd	1,000	(1,000)	restricted
C Ltd	180,000	(3,000)	
D Ltd	(20,000)	NIL	restricted
		(7,500)	

It is necessary for all the members of the consortium to consent to a claim for group relief.

Losses may also be surrendered from the owning companies to the owned company. However, the loss that is surrendered may only be offset against the fraction of the owned company's profits attributable to the interests of the various owning companies.

Illustration

If X Ltd. had a profit of £10,000 and the results of the owning consortium were as under:

		Profit/Loss	Appropriate share of profits of X Ltd	Loss surrendered
		£	£	£
A Ltd	35%	(25,000)	3,500	(3,500)
B Ltd	20%	(1,000)	2,000	(1,000) restricted
C Ltd	30%	60,000	3,000	NIL restricted
D Ltd	15%	(30,000)	1,500	(1,500)
				6,000

(c)   **Interrelationship of group relief and consortium relief**

It is possible for a consortium-owned company to give both consortium relief and group relief. Where consortium relief is given however the losses etc. available for surrender will be restricted by any group relief claims that have or could have been made.

Illustration

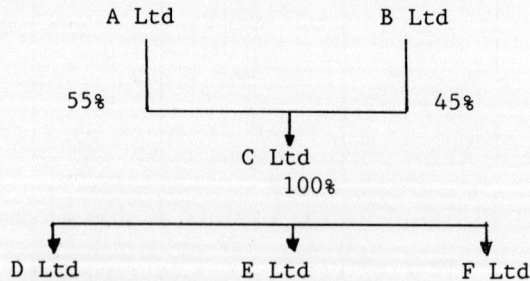

The companies have the following losses and profits:

	£
A Ltd	100,000
B Ltd	80,000
C Ltd	(20,000)
D Ltd	30,000
E Ltd	(150,000)
F Ltd	25,000

The relationships between the companies are:

i)   A Ltd. and B Ltd. are consortium-owning companies of C Ltd., D Ltd., E Ltd. and F Ltd.

ii) C Ltd., D Ltd., E Ltd. and F Ltd. are within a group of companies.

Before any consortium relief is available to A Ltd. and B Ltd. the losses of C Ltd. and E Ltd. must be reduced by any actual or potential group relief. Thus:

		£
Losses - C Ltd.		(20,000)
E Ltd.		(150,000)
		(170,000)

Less: Potential Group Relief -

	£	
D Ltd	30,000	
F Ltd	25,000	55,000
		(115,000)

This loss could then be split:

		£
A Ltd.	55%	(63,250)
B Ltd.	45%	(51,750)
		(115,000)

Where it is wished to surrender losses from the consortium-owning company to an owned company then the profits of that latter company must be reduced in a similar way by any actual or potential group relief that might be available.

Illustration

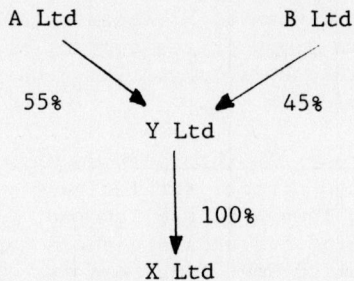

The profits and losses are:

	£
A Ltd.	(20,000)
B Ltd.	(6,000)
Y Ltd.	(4,000)
X Ltd.	40,000

	£
Profit X Ltd.	40,000
Less: Potential group relief	
from Y Ltd.	(4,000)
	36,000

Possible loss relief from:

A Ltd. (£20,000 but restricted	
to 55% of £36,000)	(19,800)
B Ltd.	(6,000)

1.8   Claims

A claim for group relief must have the consent of the surrendering company. It must be made within two years from the end of the relevant accounting period. It is common for a claimant company to pay the surrendering company for the loss surrendered, particularly if there is a minority interest. Provided that such payments are reasonable and do not exceed the amount surrendered they will be totally disregarded for tax purposes.

2.0   INTER GROUP PAYMENTS

2.1   Dividends - TA 1988, s.247(1)-(3)

To avoid difficulties which could arise between a holding company and its subsidiaries it is provided that **dividends** (but not other distributions) may be paid without accounting for ACT when both companies are resident in the UK and either are members of the same group or the company paying the dividend is a trading or holding company owned by a consortium, the members of which include the company receiving the dividends.

A company is a member of a group for this purpose when more than 50% of its ordinary share capital is owned directly or indirectly by its parent company. Holdings through non-resident companies are ignored. A company is owned by a consortium where at least 75% of its ordinary share capital is owned by other UK resident companies, none of which owns less than 5%.

The election does not cover dividends paid to minority interests unless dealt with under the consortium rules, and the company must account for ACT to that extent. The election must be made jointly within three months of the first dividend to which it applies and will continue until revoked.

The dividend when paid without accounting for ACT is termed 'Group Income' of the recipient.

Making the election as such does not save tax; however, it may improve group cash flow. The paying company will not, however, have any ACT to offset against its corporation tax.

Illustration

D Ltd. owns all the share capital of E Ltd. They have profits of £100,000 and £40,000 respectively. E Ltd. pays D Ltd. a dividend of £15,000. D Ltd. pays a dividend of £ 45,000.

If no s.247 election is applied:

	£	D Ltd £	£	E Ltd £
Trading income		100,000		40,000
Corporation tax (at say 35%)		35,000		14,000
ACT on dividend paid:				
25/75 x £45,000 =	15,000			
25/75 x £15,000 =			5,000	
Tax credit on dividend received:				
25/75 x £15,000	5,000	10,000		5,000
MCT		25,000		9,000
If a s.247 election is applied:				
Corporation tax, as above		35,000		14,000
ACT on dividend paid				
25/75 x £45,000		15,000		-
		20,000		14,000

It should be remembered that the legislation merely states that a company **may** pay its dividend without accounting for ACT. There are circumstances when it would be advisable for the company to pay part of the dividend after accounting for ACT and part without, for example, where the subsidiary company itself receives franked investment income. Unless it could offset the tax credit attaching thereto against its own ACT payment, the tax credit would remain unutilised. The subsidiary would therefore pay part of its dividend with ACT attaching, offset the ACT against the tax credit and thus pass it up to its parent company which could offset it against its own MCT liability on dividends to the outside shareholders.

Illustration

F Ltd. has a wholly owned subsidiary, G. Ltd. G Ltd. received a dividend of £750 from H Ltd., another UK resident company. It intends to pay a dividend of £3,000 to its parent company.

G Ltd. should pay part of its dividend with ACT as under:

	£		£
With ACT	750	ACT due 25/75	250
Without ACT	2,250		
	3,000		

Less: Tax credit on FII		250
		-

F Ltd. will now have a credit of £250 to offset against its own ACT due on dividends to outside shareholders. This will thus improve the timing of the tax liabilities of the holding company.

2.2 Charges - TA 1988, s.247(4)

A similar form of election applies to group charges whereby they can be paid gross, i.e. without accounting for income tax. The conditions governing the election are the same as for group income except that the election for group charges covers not only those paid by the subsidiary to the parent but also by the parent to the subsidiary or by one subsidiary to another. However, this extension does not apply to charges within a consortium, which can only be paid gross where they pass from an owned company to the members of the consortium.

3.0 SURRENDERS OF ACT

A UK-resident holding company may surrender ACT paid, in respect of dividends only, to a company which has been its subsidiary company throughout its accounting period. A company will be a subsidiary company where the holding company is entitled to more than 50% directly or indirectly of:

(a) the ordinary share capital;
(b) the profits available for distribution to the equity shareholders;
(c) the assets available for distribution on a winding up.

The ACT which can be surrendered is that of the current accounting period only. A claim to surrender ACT must be made by the surrendering company within six years from the end of the accounting period to which the claim relates and the claimant company must assent to the claim.

ACT surrendered to a subsidiary may be offset against its corporation tax liability. It is subject to the restriction of the appropriate percentage of income liable to corporation tax.

Illustration

J Ltd. owns the whole of the ordinary share capital of K Ltd. They provide you with the following information for the year to 31st March 1990:

	£	£
J Ltd		
Trading income		80,000
Dividends paid	82,500	
Surplus ACT brought forward	6,000	
Interest paid in excess of a reasonable commercial rate - treated as a distribution	1,650	
K Ltd		
Trading income		35,000
Dividends paid	8,250	

			J Ltd		K Ltd	
	£	£	£	£	£	
Trading income			80,000		35,000	
			======		======	
Corporation tax (at say 35%)			28,000		12,250	
ACT: Surplus ACT brought forward		6,000				
On dividends paid:						
25/75 x £8,250				2,750		
25/75 x £82,500	27,500					
On interest in excess of commercial rate -						
25/75 x £1,650	550					
	――――					
	28,050					
Less: Tax credits on dividends received	2,750					
	――――					
	25,300					
Surrender to K Ltd.	6,000	19,300		6,000		
	――――	――――		――――		
		25,300		8,750		
Offset restricted						
K Ltd.: 25% x £35,000					8,750	8,750
J Ltd.: 25% x £80,000		20,000	20,000			
			8,000		3,500	
			======		======	

Note

It is ACT that is surrendered not **surplus** ACT. The amount surrendered to K Ltd. is just enough to give the maximum offset, i.e. 25% x £35,000 though it could have been up to £25,300. J Ltd. has surplus ACT of £5,300.

When the surrendered ACT exceeds the maximum offset in the subsidiary company, the excess may be carried forward and offset against future corporation tax liabilities in accounting periods of the subsidiary throughout which it remains a subsidiary of the holding company or of another company which is also a subsidiary of the holding company. Under no circumstances can a surplus of surrendered ACT be carried back.

Where a subsidiary company has both its own ACT and also surrendered ACT from its holding company the order of offset is:

(1)   surrendered ACT;
(2)   its own ACT.

Any payment made or received in return for the surrender of ACT, not being in excess of the amount of ACT surrendered, is ignored for all corporation tax purposes.

Provisions have been introduced in FA 1989 to restrict the carry forward of surrendered ACT by a subsidiary company where there has been a change of ownership of that company and there has been a major change in the trade of the surrendering company during the six years beginning three years prior to the change of ownership.

4.0   GROUPS AND CAPITAL GAINS

These are dealt with in the section on Capital Gains Tax.

5.0   SUBSIDIARIES OR OPERATING DIVISIONS

Whilst the main thrust of most of the group tax legislation is to treat the group companies as one single corporate entity, it may be more advantageous to operate through a divisional rather than subsidiary structure.   Points to consider are:

(a)   A subsidiary structure will act to fragment the small company limits. Within a divisional structure there is only one company;

(b)   Many of the compliance requirements of both tax and company law will be reduced by operating through a divisional structure.   The number of claims, and many of the restrictions applying to them can be avoided.   Thus payments can be made between divisions without accounting for ACT or income tax and gains and losses on the disposal of capital assets will be automatically matched.

Where divisionalisation is being contemplated it would be best to centralise into the company with the longest possible period between the end of its accounting period and the date of payment of its corporation tax though this advantage is rapidly disappearing.

CHAPTER SIXTEEN

Taxation and the Smaller Company

1.0 CHOICE OF BUSINESS STRUCTURE

One of the first major problems confronting any person intending to set up in business is to decide the type of structure within which he operates. Essentially this provides two alternatives - an unincorporated business including a partnership, or a limited company. In considering this problem it must be emphasised that there is probably no structure which is going to be suitable for all or even a majority of tax payers. In coming to a conclusion the trader may be influenced by:

(a) personal considerations - a limited company even if exempt from certain of the filing requirements of the Company's Act will inevitably require more disclosure than an unincorporated business;

(b) the type of trade - if the trade is risky or speculative then incorporation may be desirable. On the other hand, certain professions are prohibited from incorporation.

A summary of some of the major points to be considered in deciding whether or not to incorporate are:

(a) an unincorporated business will pay income tax on its profits much later than a company with the same accounting date would pay corporation tax. With an accounting date of 30th April 1990 an individual would pay income tax on 1st January 1992 and 1st July 1992; a company with the same accounting date would pay corporation tax on 1st February 1991;

(b) an individual trader who makes a loss can offset it against his other income and in the case of a loss on a commencement can carry it back against the income of earlier years. A loss sustained by a company must be retained within that company;

(c) an unincorporated trader will be taxable on the entire profits that he makes even if he leaves most of the profits within the business; this could attract substantial higher rate liabilities. Within a limited company profits can be sheltered (profits up to £150,000 liable at 25% only) and be released when it is advantageous to the owners of the company;

(d)   the application of the opening and closing assessment rules can mean double
      assessments and 'drop outs' within an unincorporated business. A company,
      being assessed on an actual basis, will have profits assessed once only
      without any 'drop outs';

(e)   National insurance contributions are lower for an individual trader than for
      an employee of a limited company. Note, however, that the use of dividends
      may enable a limited company to distribute its profits without any national
      insurance liability;

(f)   in an unincorporated business expenses relating wholly or partly to private
      purposes will be disallowed; within a company they may be allowed but
      assessed on the directors as a benefit. In certain cases, particularly
      cars, this may be more tax effective to the recipient;

(g)   a trader can make personal pension payments to provide for his retirement.
      These are normally at 17½% of net relevant earnings increasing with age.
      Within a company far more generous contributions to a pension scheme may be
      allowed providing that the Inland Revenue rules dealing with benefits
      deriving from the scheme are not breached;

(h)   a trader who spends a substantial period of time abroad will get no tax
      relief unless he establishes non-resident status. An employee or director
      who spends a qualifying period of 365 days abroad can obtain a deduction of
      100% of assessable emoluments;

(i)   gifts of a minority interest in an unincorporated business will attract
      business property relief of 50%; within a limited company gifts of a
      minority shareholding of not more than 25% may only attract BPR of 30%.

In general it is a useful course of action to commence as an unincorporated
business and then to incorporate if conditions are favourable. If this is done
then:

(a)   there may be a potential 'drop out' of trading profits on the cessation of
      trade giving rise to tax free income;

(b)   potential balancing charges on cessation can be avoided by making an
      election to transfer assets at tax-written-down value.

(c)   unrelieved trading losses may qualify for relief against income received
      from the company under s.386 TA 1988;

(d)   any capital gain may be deferred to the extent that the trader takes shares
      in the company as part of the purchase consideration.

2.0 CLOSE COMPANIES

2.1 General

A close company is a UK resident company under the control of five or fewer
participators with associates or any number of directors with associates. The
Inland Revenue has detailed provisions to restrict the use of such companies as
vehicles to turn retained income into capital gains liable on the owners, at much
lower rates of tax.

2.2 Definitions

(a) 'Control'

A number of alternative tests must be considered in order to determine whether a person, or number of persons, controls a company. **Any one** of the following constitutes control:

i)   ability to exercise control over the company's affairs;

ii)   possession of the greater part of the total share capital or voting power of the company;

iii) possession of rights giving entitlement to the greater part of the company's income if it were distributed;

iv)   possession of rights giving entitlement on a winding-up to the greater part of the assets available for distribution.

In each case it is also necessary to take into account any entitlement to acquire such share capital or rights. The 'greater part' means more than 50%.

In order to determine whether a number of participators have control of a company, there is attributed to a person the rights and powers of others who are:

i)   nominees of the person;
ii)   associates of the person;
iii) companies controlled by the person or by an associate of his.

(b) 'Participator'

A participator is:

i)   a person possessing or entitled to possess share capital or voting rights;

ii)   a loan creditor, other than a bank acting in the normal course of business;

iii) a person entitled to ensure that income or assets of the company can be applied directly or indirectly for his benefit.

(c) 'Associate'

An associate is:

i)   a relative, meaning: a lineal ancestor, lineal descendant, spouse, brother or sister;

ii)   a business partner;

iii) the trustee(s) of a settlement created by the participator himself or a relative as defined in (i) above.

It should be noted that 'associates' do not include associates of associates; thus the participator's wife in his associate but his wife's mother is not his associate.

(d)   'Director'

A director is:

i)   a person occupying the position of director by whatsoever name called;

ii)   a person under whose instructions the board of directors are accustomed to act;

iii) a manager who with associates controls 20% or more of the ordinary share capital.

Illustration

The issued capital of A Ltd consists of 20,000 6% preference shares of £1 each, carrying no voting rights and 35,000 ordinary shares of £1 each with one vote per share.

The shareholdings are as follows:

	Preference shares	Ordinary shares
Arnold (Director)	2,000	3,000
Brian (Director)		1,500
Charles (Arnold's brother)		500
Elizabeth (Arnold's sister)		3,000
David (Director)	2,000	2,000
Fred (Director)		2,500
George	8,000	1,000
Henry		5,000
Ivan		9,000
Joan (Brian's sister)	2,000	5,500
Keith	6,000	2,000
	20,000	35,000

A Ltd is a close company because:

(1)   The directors and their associates control the votes:

	Ordinary shares
Arnold + Charles + Elizabeth	6,500
Brian + Joan	7,000
David	2,000
Fred	2,500
Total possible votes = 35,000	18,000 votes

or:

(2)   Five or fewer participators and their associates control the votes:

	Ordinary shares
They are:	
Ivan	9,000
Brian + Joan	7,000
Arnold + Charles + Elizabeth	6,500
Henry	5,000
Fred	2,500
	30,000

or:

(3)   Five or fewer participators and their associates control the total share capital of £55,000.

	£
Ivan	9,000
George	9,000
Brian + Joan	9,000
Arnold + Charles + Elizabeth	8,500
Keith	8,000
	43,500

If Ivan had been a manager of the company, he would have been considered a director as he controls 20% or more of the ordinary share capital of the company.

Once a person has been associated with another he falls out of account and cannot be associated with anyone else.

Illustration

Two sisters B and C each own 50% of the ordinary share capital of D Ltd.

Once C has been associated with B she falls out of account, otherwise they would be deemed for tax purposes to own 200% of the share capital!

2.3 Exceptions

Certain companies are excluded from categorisation as close companies:

(a)   a company controlled by the Crown;
(b)   a non-resident company;
(c)   a registered industrial or provident society or a recognised building society;
(d)   a company controlled by one or more non-close companies.

Illustration

E Ltd is owned as follows:

	% (1)	% (2)
F Ltd - Non-close	40	48
G Ltd - Non-close	15	-
Others each with 1%	45	52
	100	100

In the first case E Ltd is not close because it is controlled by non-close companies F and G. In the second case, E Ltd. is close; it is not under the control of F Ltd, the non-close company and thus F Ltd is just considered to be a normal participator and with four others will control the company.

The test of closeness is made at the end of the accounting period.

2.4 Quoted companies

A quoted company will not be a close company where:

(a) shares carrying at least 35% of the voting power, not being shares entitled to a fixed rate of dividend with no further participation, have been unconditionally allotted to or acquired by the public and are beneficially held by them, and,

(b) within the last 12 months, the shares have been quoted and dealt in on a recognised stock exchange in the UK or abroad.

'Public' specifically includes:

i)   non-close companies;

ii)   shares held by superannuation funds, retirement schemes, etc., not established for the benefit of employees of the company (sometimes known as **External funds**).

It does not include:

i)   directors or their associates;

ii)   a company under their control or an associated company;

iii) funds, e.g. pension funds, for the benefit of employees and directors and ex-employees and directors of the company concerned (**Internal funds**);

iv)   a principal member.

A principal member is a shareholder who controls more than five per cent of the voting power and who is one of the five largest shareholders.

If more than one shareholder ties for fifth place they will all be principal members.

There is an overriding proviso to this '35% public' exemption that if the principal members (including non-close companies and external funds) between them possess more than 85% of the total voting power, the '35% public' exemption cannot apply and the company will be a close company.

Illustration

F plc is owned as under; the shares are quoted and dealt in on The London Stock Exchange.

	%
A (director)	15
B (his wife)	2
C (director)	23
D (private individual)	11
E (private individual)	4
F (private individual)	3
G (private individual)	3
H Ltd (non-close company)	21
J (pension fund for the benefit of F plc's employees)	6
K (pension fund for the benefit of ICI plc's employees)	12
	100

Analysis of shareholdings:

	Public %	Principal members %
A and B		17
C		23
D		11
E	4	
F	3	
G	3	
H Ltd	21	21
	31	72
K - pension fund	12	12
	43	84

Since 35% or more of the voting power is held by the public, the company is not a close company.

If G sold his shares to C the company would now be close as although 35% or more of the voting power will be held by the public, the principal members would own more than 85%.

3.0 CONSEQUENCES OF BEING CLOSE

3.1 An extended definition of distribution

In addition to the distributions considered earlier, where a benefit (as defined for Schedule E) is provided for a participator or his associate but is not taxed on him under Schedule E, it will be treated as a distribution to the extent that it is not reimbursed by the participator.

The amount to be assessed will be calculated using Schedule E rules. No charge arises when the benefit is provided to the holding of a fellow subsidiary company.

3.2 Loans to participators

Where a close company makes a loan to a participator, it must also pay over a sum equal to ACT on the loan, to the Revenue. The amount is only equal to ACT and not ACT itself so that it cannot be offset against the company's corporation tax liability. It is equivalent to a compulsory loan to the Revenue.

The definition of loan is wide and includes those circumstances where:

(a)   the participator, or his associate, incurs a debt to the company, except for the supply of goods in the normal course of trade unless the period of credit exceeds six months or that normally given to other customers;

(b)   a debt due from a participator or his associate is assigned by the creditor to the company.

It does not however include:

(a)   loans made in the normal course of business by a close company;
(b)   loans made to the participator who is a director or employee of the company, and

    i)   the total loans to that person do not exceed £15,000;

    ii)   he works full time for the company;

    iii) he does not, with associates, own more than five per cent of the ordinary share capital of the company.

On the making of the loan the company must pay over to the Revenue an amount equal to ACT at the rate in force when the loan was made. When the loan is repaid the Revenue will repay all or part of the ACT paid. A claim for repayment must be made within six years of the fiscal year in which the loan was repaid.

Illustration

H Ltd made a loan of £8,030 to B, a participator, on 1st September 1987. He does not qualify for any of the exemptions.

A sum of £2,970, equal to ACT on the loan, must be paid 14 days after the issue of the notice of assessment. If on 30th August 1990 he repays £4,015, the Revenue will repay one-half of the amount paid over, i.e. £1,485.

If the loan is released or written off, the company forfeits the balance remaining with the Revenue and the borrower is treated as having received income equal to the grossed-up equivalent of the amount released. Grossing-up is at the rate of tax existing at the date of release.

Illustration

If, in the illustration above, the balance of the loan is waived when the basic rate of income tax is, say, 25%, the balance of tax with the Revenue of £1,485 is lost. B will be assessed on:

$$\frac{100}{75} \times £4,015 = £5,353$$

and this will be liable to higher rate taxes.

The charge is extended to the situation where, a loan is made, not by the close company in which the borrower is a participator, but by a company controlled by the close company or one in which the close company subsequently obtains a controlling interest.

There is no charge if it can be shown that there is no connection between the making of the loan and either:

(a) the provision of any funds by the company in which the individual is a participator to the lending company; or

(b) the acquisition of control of the lending company by the close company in which the borrower is a participator.

Where the provisions apply, the effect of the legislation is to treat the loan as being made by the company in which the borrower is a participator and not by the one making the loan.

3.3 The apportionment of relevant income

In the absence of the apportionment provisions relating to close companies, such companies could be used to accumulate profits, thereby shielding the shareholders from higher rate tax. The apportionment provisions prevent this by requiring such companies to distribute a minimum amount of their income, determined in accordance with a formula. To the extent that the company fails to satisfy the required level of distributions, the company will be deemed to have made such distribution as is necessary to bring its actual distributions up to the required amount. This deemed distribution will be apportioned between the members, and the tax consequences will be computed as if the deemed distribution had really been made, resulting in possible income tax liabilities in respect of the members and ACT liabilities of the company.

The required level of distribution is known as the **relevant income**.

For accounting periods beginning after 31st March, 1989 apportionment of relevant income has been abolished and is replaced by a withdrawal of small company relief on close investment companies (see later).

(a)   Specimen calculation of relevant income

Relevant Income	Trading Income £	Estate Income £	Investment Income £
Schedule A		X	
B		X	
Schedule D I	X		
Schedule D III			X
Schedule D IV			X
Schedule D V	X or	X or	X
Schedule D VI		X or	X
UFII			X
BSI			X
	X	X	X
Less: charges and losses	(X)3	(X)2	(X)1
	X	X	X
Less: corporation tax on income	(X)	(X)	(X)
	X (T)	X (E)	X
Distributions received and group Income (net)			X
Distributable Income		X +	X
Less: Lower of: (a) £3,000 or (b) 10% of E + T			(X)
			X

Less: Abatement:

$$£75,000 \times \frac{E}{E + T} = a$$

$$\frac{a - E}{2} \qquad\qquad (X)$$

			X

| 50% of balance of Estate Income | | | X |
| Relevant Income | | | X |

Notes

(1)   Trading income is income, which if it was received by an individual would be earned income. Estate income is income arising from property assessed under Schedules A, B and D. Investment income is all other income. Chargeable gains do **not** have to be apportioned.

(2)   Charges and losses [other than s. 393(1) losses] will be deducted:

i)   from investment income, then
ii) from estate income, then
iii) from trading income.

(3)   Where the close company is a 'medium' company, then corporation tax will be apportioned across each column on a pro-rata basis.

(4)   The £3,000 reduction from investment income will be reduced proportionately if the accounting period is less than 12 months. If the company is not a trading company it will be reduced to £1,000, subject to any time reduction.

(5)   The £75,000 abatement figure will be reduced proportionately both if the accounting period is less than 12 months and **also** if there are associated companies. Abatement is not available for non-trading companies.

If the deductions in (4) and (5) above exceed the figure from which they are deductible then that figure will be reduced to nil.

Illustration

E Ltd a trading company with an issued share capital of £12,000, had income charged to corporation tax for the year ended 31st December 1989 which comprised:

	£
Schedule A	30,000
Trading Income	64,000
Schedule A Case III	100
Capital Gains	1,800
Interest on debenture in C Ltd. another	
United Kingdom trading company (in which E Ltd	
also held 1,800 ordinary shares out of a total of	
2,000 issued)	400
Debenture interest was paid of	1,000 gross

A major shareholder received a benefit from the company of £112. He is not a director.

E Ltd received a dividend during the accounting period of £7,677 from H Ltd in which it held 5,000 shares out of a total of 50,000 issued.

Recent dividends paid by E Ltd were:

Date paid	In respect of	£
5.11.1988	Year ending 31st December 1987	2,390
30.10.1989	Year ending 31st December 1988	792
1.6.1990	Year ending 31st December 1989	2,176

Required:

i)   Calculate the amount of corporation tax payable by E Ltd for the year ended 31st December 1989;

ii) Show a detailed calculation of relevant income.

Ignore small company relief.

i) Corporation Tax payable:

	£	£
Schedule A		30,000
Schedule D Case I		64,000
Schedule D Case III		100
UFII		400
Capital gains		1,800
		96,300
Less: debenture interest paid		1,000
		95,300
		£
Corporation Tax @ 35%		33,355

Franked payments:
 dividends -
  £792 x $\frac{100}{75}$ 1,056

 Benefit to shareholder -
  £112 x $\frac{100}{75}$ $\underline{149}$
                                         1,205

FII: £7,677 x $\frac{100}{75}$ $\underline{10,236}$
                                      NIL

ACT   NIL

MCT   33,355

ii) Relevant Income:

	TI £	EI £	II £
Schedule A		30,000	
Schedule D Case I	64,000		
Schedule D Case III			100
UFII			400
	64,000	30,000	500
Less: charges		500	500
	64,000	29,500	NIL
Less: Corporation Tax @ 35%	22,400	10,325	
	41,600(T)	19,175(E)	

| Dividends received | | | 7,677 |
| Distributable income C/f | | 19,175 | 7,677 |

		EI £	II £
	b/f	19,175	7,677

Less: lower of:
    (a) 10% x (£19,175 + £41,600)
       or
    (b) £3,000

	3,000
	4,677

Less: abatement:

$$£37,500 \times \frac{£19,175}{£19,175 + £41,600}$$

$$= \frac{£11,832 - £19,175}{2} \qquad -$$

	19,175

50% thereof   9,588

Relevant income: 14,265

A company must make distributions up to the amount of the relevant income. The following items can be taken into account in arriving at any further distribution that might be required:

i)   dividends declared **for** the accounting period having been paid in the period or within reasonable time after the end of it. A period of up to 18 months may be expected to be regarded as reasonable, and

ii)   other distributions made **in** the period, unless they relate to a previous accounting period under (i) above.

Relevant income less distributions already made is called the **excess of relevant income**. Thus in E Ltd.

	£	£
Relevant income as above		14,265
Less: Dividends paid **for** the accounting period	2,176	
Other distributions paid in the accounting period	112	2,288
Excess of relevant income		11,977

(b)   Apportionments

When there is an excess of relevant income, it will normally be apportioned amongst the participators. No apportionment will be made:

i)   when the company is a trading company or a member of a trading group, if the excess of relevant income is £1,000 or less.

ii)   when the company can justify a retention of income to meet its business requirements, i.e. planned capital expenditure or working capital. (This will be considered later.)

The amount of the excess of relevant income will be apportioned amongst the participators according to their interests in the company. A sum which is both less than 5% of the total amount to be apportioned and, inclusive of a notional amount of ACT, is less than £1,000, will not be assessed on an individual participator. The amount apportioned to an individual is treated as if it were income received on the last day of the accounting period to which it relates. The amount apportioned is grossed-up by a notional amount of ACT and is liable to higher rate taxes as though it was the highest part of the taxpayer's income.

Illustration

The shareholders in E Ltd are:

A	20%
Mrs A	1%
B	68%
C	1%
D Ltd - a close company	10%
	100%

The share capital of D Ltd is owned by E and F, as under:

E	70%
F	30%

To avoid any apportionment, a minimum dividend of £10,977 (£11,977 less £1,000) must be paid. If not, the income will be apportioned as under:

		Amount	Notional Tax credit	Gross
		£	£	£
A	- 20%	2,395	798	3,193
Mrs. A	- 1%	120	40	160
B	- 68%	8,144	2,715	10,859
C	- 1%	120	40	160
D Ltd	- 10%	1,198	399	1,597
		11,977	3,992	15,969

No apportionment will be made on C but one will be made in respect of Mrs. A as she is associated with her husband and jointly they exceed the limits.

Where an amount is apportioned to another close company it must be sub-apportioned until it reaches the individual beneficial shareholders. Thus the amount apportioned to D Ltd will be sub-apportioned as under:

		£	£	£
E	70%	839	280	1,119
F	30%	359	119	478
		1,198	399	1,597

Thus E will be apportioned, but F, as the amount apportioned to him does not exceed the limits, will escape.

Where an apportionment is made, the whole of the excess relevant income must be apportioned, not just enough to leave £1,000.

An appeal can be made by the company, and in certain cases by the participator, against the total and division of the apportioned excess.

The participator is primarily liable for the tax due in respect of the apportioned amount.

The tax is due at the later of:

i)   6th July following the year of assessment, or

ii) 30 days after the issue of the notice of assessment.

If the individual does not pay the tax it may be recovered from the company.

Provisions exist to counter double taxation when in a subsequent accounting period the profits are distributed.

(c) **Accounting for notional ACT**

Although the company cannot avoid an apportionment of excess relevant income it can be seen that the company could possibly avoid accounting for ACT. Notional ACT will, however, be due to the Revenue in respect of the notional distribution at the end of the accounting period. The amount due may be reduced:

i)   by offset against surplus FII of the accounting period; then

ii) by offset against available corporation tax of the accounting period subject to the appropriate percentage restriction; then

iii) by offset against available corporation tax of accounting periods beginning in the six preceding years.

Any balance of notional ACT left is payable in cash to the Revenue. It may then be carried forward and offset against corporation tax liabilities of future accounting periods, as surplus ACT.

(d) Apportionment of other items

TA 1988, s.424 provides that where a company makes annual payments not incurred wholly and exclusively for the purposes of the trade, which have been deducted as charges in the relevant income computation, they may be apportioned amongst the participators in the same way as an excess of relevant income.

(e) Clearances

To avoid the uncertainty of a possible apportionment, a trading company (or any company with estate or trading income) may apply to the Inspector for a clearance, sending to him the adopted accounts, directors' report and any other relevant information. The Inspector has three months to decide whether to make an apportionment or to ask for further information. If he takes the latter course he then has a further three months after receiving the additional information before making his decision. If he does not keep to these time limits he loses his right to make the apportionment unless:

i)   the company has not fully disclosed all the material facts, or

ii) the company ceases to trade or goes into liquidation within 12 months of the end of the accounting period.

(f) Business Requirements

As mentioned earlier, the company can avoid or reduce an apportionment if it can demonstrate the need for a higher retention of profits, by reason of its business needs. The onus is on the Revenue to show that the company can distribute its relevant income without prejudicing its requirements, but the company will need to provide evidence of its requirements. The types of requirement that would be satisfactory to the Revenue would include:

i)   a need for increased working capital;
ii)   a need to invest in business assets, such as buildings, or plant;
iii) the purchase of another trade or business or the purchase of shares in another company in order to expand business opportunities;
iv)   the need to provide for contingent liabilities or known losses which have arisen since the year-end date;
v)   the need to retain funds for research and development.

Examples of requirements which would not be satisfactory are:

i)   repayments of loans or debts incurred for less than full consideration;
ii) artificial or fictitious transactions.

In all cases, a primary requirement in the ability to pay a dividend, is adequate resources to pay. In considering this, the Revenue would consider not only cash balances but also the possession of other liquid resources, particularly investments, which could be easily turned into cash.

Where it is possible to establish such requirements, relevant income becomes so much of the company's distributable income as can be distributed without prejudice to the requirements of the company's business. Under no circumstances can **Relevant Income** calculated in this way exceed that calculated in the normal arithmetic manner.

Illustration

The business requirements for E Ltd have been agreed with the Revenue at:

(a)   £15,000
(b)   £10,000

The alternative calculation of relevant income will be:

| | (a) | (b) |
	£	£
Distributable Income	26,852	26,852
Less: Business Requirements	15,000	10,000
	11,852	16,852

In case (a) the relevant income would now be reduced to £11,852, in case (b) as it exceeds the normal calculation which revealed a figure of £14,265, relevant income will remain at the lower amount.

(g) Effects of an apportionment on the capital gains tax on cost of shares

Where there is an apportionment of relevant income and the tax is paid by the participator not the company, provided the profits are not subsequently distributed, the amount of the tax paid can reduce the capital gain on a subsequent disposal.

Illustration

B acquired 30% of the shares in A Ltd, a close company, on 6th April 1982 for £ 21,000. In 1984 there was an apportionment of relevant income on B of £4,000 gross of notional ACT, on which B was chargeable at 60%. The profits in respect of which the apportionment was made have not subsequently been distributed.

The shares were sold by B on 6th April 1990 for £30,000.

The Indexation allowance is £3,171.

	£	£
Disposal proceeds		30,000
Cost	21,000	
Tax at higher rates		
£4,000 x (60-30%)	1,200	
		22,200
		7,800
Indexation		3,171
		4,629

4.0 CLOSE INVESTMENT HOLDING COMPANIES

The Finance Act 1989 in abolishing the apportionment of relevant income has
placed further burdens on a company which is classed as a close investment
holding company (CIC).   Commencing with the first accounting period beginning
after 31st March, 1989:

(a)   the profits of the CIC will be liable to corporation tax at 35% irrespective
       of the level of the company's profits.

(b)   the repayment of tax credits on dividends paid to individuals may be
       restricted if it appears to the Inland Revenue that there are in existence
       arrangements to create a tax repayment or reduce a tax liability, e.g. one
       shareholder waiving a right to a dividend and so increasing the amount
       payable to other shareholders with unused personal allowances.

A CIC is a close company which is neither a trading company nor a member of a
trading group.   A trading company is one the business of which consists wholly
or mainly of trading on a commercial basis.   Under normal circumstances
companies dealing in land and investments will not be CICs neither will a
property investment company.

CHAPTER SEVENTEEN

Reorganisation and Special Problems

1.0 GENERAL

There are a number of areas in the corporate tax area which present specific problems. A number of these are considered in this chapter.

2.0 ACQUISITION OF A BUSINESS OR SHARES IN A COMPANY

The purchase of a business or shares in a company can present many tax problems and it is common to ask many questions of the vendors, taking warranties, subject to penalty, that the information is accurate. Some of the points for consideration include:

(a) tax payment date;

(b) details of tax-written-down values of assets for capital allowance purposes, and their current values. Details of assets transferred intra group and of assets on hire purchase;

(c) details of items giving rise to a timing difference;

(d) details of any group structure, details of loss transfers and group elections made, etc, the CGT costs of all group assets with details of transferred assets, depreciatory transactions, etc.

(e) details of any rolled- or held-over gains etc.

(f) whether the target of the acquisition has complied with its taxation obligations including:

    i) VAT registration and documentation requirements;
    ii) PIID, dispensations and Schedule E obligations;
    iii) back duty or accounts investigations;
    iv) s.770 obligations.

3.0 MANAGEMENT BUYOUTS

3.1 General

A management buyout is the situation where a holding company wishes to dispose of a subsidiary and offers it to its management and employees. The latter would buy the assets of the organisation or alternatively buy the shares in the company, using, in both cases, a mixture of their own funds and external financing.

3.2 Types of buyout

Whilst there are many forms of buyout, there are two common types:

(a)   Type 1 - in this case the management intending the buyout establish a company - NEWCO providing initial finance in consideration of a share issue. NEWCO then acquires further capital by issues of shares or loan stocks either to individuals or financial institutions. NEWCO then acquires the existing trade from the vendor with the consideration being either cash or a mixture of cash and loan stocks. It can be illustrated as under.

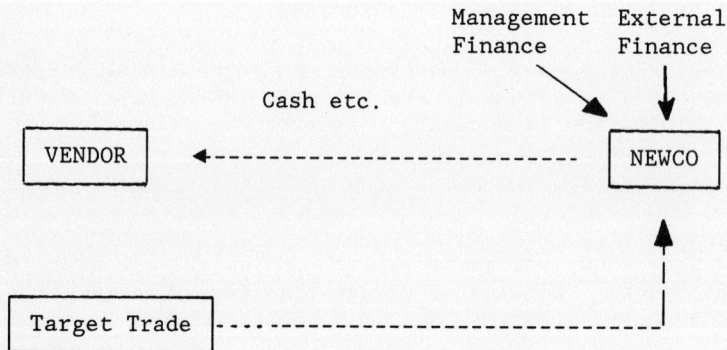

The taxation implications of this type of buyout are:

i)   As the vendor will be disposing of assets this will give rise to:

   (a)   balancing charges or allowances on the plant, industrial buildings, patents etc transferred;

   (b)   capital gains or losses.

ii) The possible loss of unused trading losses relating to the transferred trade.

The vendor company would be able to use the trading losses against any balancing charges and possibly roll over any capital gains against the cost of any qualifying assets it might acquire.

NEWCO will be able to claim capital allowances on the plant etc. transferred. In the case of industrial buildings a reduced tax life could result in accelerated allowances.

(b) Type 2 - in this type, NEWCO acquires the share capital of the company carrying on the target trade. It can be illustrated as under:

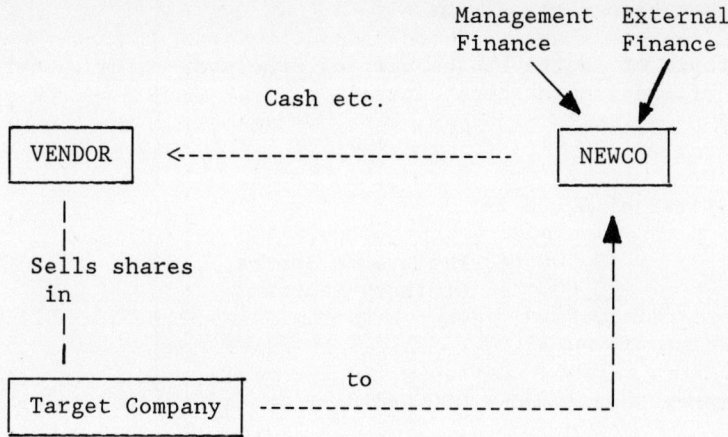

```
                                     Management    External
                                     Finance       Finance

                  Cash etc.                │         │
                                           ▼         ▼
  ┌─────────┐   <----------------------   ┌─────────┐
  │ VENDOR  │                             │  NEWCO  │
  └─────────┘                             └─────────┘
       │                                       ▲
       │                                       │
   Sells shares                                │
      in                                       │
       │                                       │
       │                       to             │
  ┌───────────────┐                           │
  │ Target Company│  -------------------------┘
  └───────────────┘
```

The sale of shares by the vendor may result in a liability to tax on any capital gains.

As far as NEWCO is concerned it will be buying shares rather than assets. This will mean that the acquired company will continue as before subject to:

(a) the change of ownership, coupled with any changes in trade which could affect the carry-forward of any trading losses or surpluses of ACT;

(b) there may be latent tax liabilities, e.g: capital gains rolled over, assets transferred intra group within the preceding 6 years which could affect the purchase price;

(c) there will be no balancing charges, in respect of plant and machinery, industrial buildings, etc. as the assets have not been sold by the company leaving the group.

4.0 COMPANIES PURCHASING THEIR OWN SHARES

Legislation was provided in the 1981 Companies Act which enabled companies to purchase back their own shares. The tax position relating to this was formalised in 1982 and broadly allowed any gain in such a purchase to be treated as a capital, rather than a revenue, gain to the shareholder whose shares were being purchased, subject to detailed conditions being complied with:

(a) the company whose shares are being purchased must be a trading company and be unquoted (shares dealt in on the USM are not regarded as being quoted);

(b) the shareholder must be resident and ordinarily resident in the UK;

(c) the shares must normally be held by the shareholder for at least 5 years prior to the purchase. Where the shares have been inherited, the period of ownership is restricted to 3 years, including any period of ownership by the deceased;

(d) the shareholder must either sell the whole of his shareholding or it must be
materially reduced. It will be so reduced where the proportion of the
company's issued share capital held after the purchase does not exceed 75%
of that held just before the purchase.

(e) after the purchase of shares by the company, the shareholder must not hold
more than 30% of the issued share capital.

Illustration

The issued share capital of A Ltd is:

$$
\begin{array}{ll}
10,000 & \text{£1 Preference Shares} \\
\underline{20,000} & \text{£1 Ordinary Shares} \\
\text{£ } 30,000 &
\end{array}
$$

B owns 3,000 Preference Shares and 9,000 Ordinary Shares. A Ltd is proposing to
purchase from him

i)   3,000 Ordinary Shares, or
ii)   8,000 Ordinary Shares

B's interest in the share capital before the purchase is:

$$\frac{3,000 + 9,000}{30,000} \quad 100 \quad = \quad 40\%$$

After repurchase it is:

Case i)
$$\frac{3,000 + 6,000}{27,000} \quad \times 100 \quad = \quad 33.33\%$$

Case ii)
$$\frac{3,000 + 1,000}{22,000} \quad \times 100 \quad = \quad 18.2 \%$$

Thus in case (i) the holding is not materially reduced and thus any purchase
would be a qualifying distribution. In case (ii) the reduction is material.

(f) in addition to (d) above the person selling shares must also suffer a
material reduction (measured as above) in his entitlement to share in
profits. Thus the proportion of the company's profits to which the vendor
is entitled after the purchase does not exceed 75% of that held just before
the purchase.

The profits available for distribution follow the definitions in the
Companies Act 1985 plus:

a)   £100 and
b)   any fixed distributions - e.g. preference dividends for one year.

In the above illustration assume the distributable reserves are £80,000 and the
preference shares have a dividend paid annually of 12%.

Before the purchase:

	£	**B's entitlement** £
Reserves, and	80,000	36,000
Preference		
Dividend	1,200	360
and	100	45
	81,300	36,405
		44.78%

Assuming in case (ii) of the illustration above that the 8,000 Ordinary shares are purchased for £30,000, the position would be:

	£	**B's entitlement** £
Reserves, and	50,000	4,167
Preference		
Dividend	1,200	360
and	100	8
	51,300	4,535
		8.84%

Again a substantial reduction.

The shareholder's interest in both (d) and (e) must include that of his associates, broadly his spouse, minor children and trustees of settlements created by him.

(g)   the purpose of the purchase must be for the benefit of the trade carried on by the company and not part of a scheme for the avoidance of tax.

The company may apply for a clearance prior to the purchase, which must be made out of reserves available for distribution.

Where shares of the same class are acquired at different times, disposals to the company are identified on a FIFO basis to determine the qualifying period of ownership.

5.0   DEMERGERS

The basic purpose of a demerger is to enable trades formerly carried on together by one company to be managed and owned independently. The intention is that this independence would stimulate the activities of the various parts.

The mechanics of a demerger can take several forms:

(a)   a transfer to any or all of the members of a company of the shares of a 75% subsidiary;

(b)   a transfer of a trade by one company to another or the transfer to that
company of shares in a 75% subsidiary followed in both cases by the issue of
shares in the transferee company to the shareholders of the transferor
company.

The members of a company are holders of the ordinary share capital of that
company.

Where there is a valid demerger:

(a)   the demerger will not be treated as a distribution in the hands of the
transferor company and no ACT will be due; and

(b)   there will be no CGT liability.

The conditions that must be satisfied are:

(a)   The transferor company, any 75% subsidiaries and any recipient company must
be UK resident;

(b)   The transferor company must be a trading company or a member of a trading
group; this must also apply to any 75% subsidiaries;

(c)   The distribution must be made wholly or mainly for the benefit of trading
activities previously carried on by the transferor company and which are now
to be carried on by the recipient company;

(d)   The distribution must not be part of a scheme or arrangement for the
avoidance of tax, the making of any chargeable payments or for the future
cessation of all or part of the trade after the distribution.

There are elaborate provisions designed to deal with avoidance devices.
Companies contemplating a demerger may obtain a clearance from the Revenue.

6.0   COMPANY RECONSTRUCTIONS

The reconstruction of a company or the amalgamation of two or more companies may
have complex taxation consequences not only for the companies themselves but also
for those who are shareholders in those organisations. The terminology is not
clear.   In **Wilde v. South African Supply and Cold Storage Co.** a reconstruction
was considered to be a corporate reorganisation under substantially the same
ownership whilst an amalgamation involved '... a blending of two
undertakings...'. Essentially a reconstruction or amalgamation can consist of one
of the following events:

(a)   the transfer to the shareholders of a company of shares owned in a
subsidiary company - a demerger;

(b)   the amalgamation of companies, perhaps by the setting up of a holding
company to acquire the shares of the companies joining together. The
shareholders in the old companies would exchange their shares for shares in
the new company;

(c)   the transfer of a trade from one company to another.

When any scheme of reconstruction or amalgamation is being considered it is
essential to apply to the Revenue for clearance especially in view of the penal
provisions of TA 1988, s.703. In general this will be given if the Revenue is
satisfied that:

(a)   the scheme is being arranged for bona fide commercial reasons; and

(b)   its main purpose is not the avoidance of taxation.

The demerger has already been considered, the other two main instances are
described below.

6.1   Company mergers

In this case, provided that the company issuing the new shares controls, as a
result of the merger, more than 25% of the ordinary share capital (it will
normally be 100%), then the issue of shares in the acquiring company to the
shareholders in the amalgamating companies will simply be treated as a share for
share exchange. No disposal will be treated as having occurred for CGT
purposes. This may then be followed by a transfer of the trades of the (now)
subsidiary companies to the new holding company. This will be particularly
important in the case of the situation where the holding company is a close
company.

There may be restrictions on the carry forward of losses and ACT. TA 1988,
s.768 provides that where within any period of three years there is both a change
in the ownership of a company and a major change in the nature or conduct of its
trade or, where at any time after the company's trading activities have become
small or negligible and before revival there is a change in ownership of the
company, then:

(a)   unrelieved losses may not be carried forward under s.393(1) to accounting
       periods after the change;

(b)   surpluses of ACT arising before the change may also not be carried forward.

For these purposes an accounting period is deemed to end at the date of the
change in ownership.

6.2   The transfer of a trade

Where a company's business is transferred to another company, there will
normally be a disposal of assets and the cessation of a trade. The consequences
of this may be avoided and no change of ownership will be deemed to have occurred
provided:

(a)   both companies are within the charge to corporation tax; and

(b)   within the period commencing 12 months before and ending 24 months after
       the cessation of the trade by the transferor company, at least 75% of the
       trade is owned by the same persons.

Ownership of the trade is measured by interests in the ordinary share capital of the company and to establish beneficial ownership it may be necessary to pierce the veil of trusts and companies holding shares.
If the conditions are satisfied, then important reliefs are available:

(a)   unused trading losses may be carried forward to the successor company to be offset against **income of the same trade;**

(b)   assets on which capital allowances have been claimed may be transferred across at tax-written-down value.

It it impossible to transfer across capital losses or surpluses of ACT or FII and if the trade is the sole asset of the transferor company it may mean that these items will be lost.   Consideration should therefore be given to their utilisation before cessation of trade.

In the case of capital allowances, relief will be given up to the date of transfer to the transferor company and thereafter to the successor.
Writing-down allowances will be apportioned for periods of less than 12 months.
TA 1970, s.273 will provide relief for CGT as the transferor and successor companies will normally both be within the same 75% group.   There will be a charge under s.278 if the acquiring company leaves the group within six years.

Terminal loss relief is not normally available to the transferor company.

7.0   INVESTMENT COMPANIES

7.1   General

An investment company is any company whose business consists wholly or mainly in the making of investments and the principal part of whose income is derived therefrom.

The calculation of profits liable to corporation tax, proceeds in the normal way.
Dividends received from other UK companies are <u>not</u> liable to corporation tax.   A particular element in the computation is likely to be income from property assessable under Schedule A or Schedule D Case VI.

From the income liable to corporation tax there can be deducted management expenses.   These are normally of three main types:

(a)   pure management expenses which are not specific to any particular type of income, e.g. directors' salaries;
(b)   annual charges;
(c)   capital allowances which are not given specifically against one class of income.

These are aggregated and offset against total profits.   Any unrelieved balance may be carried forward.

A particular feature of this sort of company is that it is likely to have a large amount of franked investment income.   To the extent that there is a surplus thereof, the unrelieved management expenses can be the subject of a s.242 claim.

Illustration

A Ltd is an investment company making up accounts to 31st December annually. It provides you with the following information in respect of the year ended 31st December 1989.

	£
Rents	5,000
Bank deposit interest	500
Dividends received - 30.1.1989	7,500
Expenses:	
Repairs to property	1,200
Rent collection charges	400
Office salaries	4,000
Directors' salaries	1,000
Debenture interest paid (gross)	200
Dividends paid - 28.2.1989	3,000

Schedule A	£	£	£
Rents		5,000	
Less: Expenses:			
Repairs	1,200		
Rent collection	400		
		1,600	
			3,400
Schedule D Case III			500
			3,900
Management expenses:			
Office salaries		4,000	
Directors' salaries		1,000	
Debenture interest		200	
		5,200	
Offset		3,900	3,900
		1,300	Nil

The excess management expenses can either be carried forward and treated as expenses of the next Accounting period or, as there is a surplus of FII, made the subject of a s.242 claim.

Dividends received		7,500	
Add: Tax credit		2,500	
		10,000	
	£		
Dividends paid	3,000		
Add: Tax credit	1,000		
		4,000	
		6,000	
		1,300	(1,300)
s.242			
Surplus FII c/f		4,700	Nil

Repay tax credits
25% of £1,300 = £325

7.2 Close Investment Holding Companies

For accounting periods commencing after 31st March, 1989 profits are liable to
corporation tax at 35% irrespective of their size.

7.3 Losses on unquoted shares in trading companies

If an investment company makes a loss on shares which it has subscribed for in an
unquoted trading company it may treat that loss as a revenue loss and offset it
as in section 7.1 above. The offset will be against the other profits of the
same accounting period and then carried back against total profits of previous
accounting periods ended within the previous twelve months, though if one
straddles the beginning of that period only, the profits which fall within the
twelve-month period (apportioned on a strict time basis) will qualify for relief.

Relief is given after any relief for earlier losses but before deductions for
charges and management expenses.

To obtain relief the investment company making the loss must normally have
traded for six years and must not control or be associated with the company in
respect of which the loss has been sustained.

As an alternative, relief under s.242 is available.

8.0 COMPANIES IN LIQUIDATION

On the passing of a resolution for the winding-up of a company, an accounting
period ends and a new one commences. Thereafter, accounting periods are made up
for periods of twelve months with a final period to the completion of the
winding-up. To avoid delay because the rate of corporation tax is fixed in
arrears, the rate of corporation tax to be used for the company's final
accounting period is normally that fixed for the last financial year.

CHAPTER EIGHTEEN

Overseas Matters

1.0 STATUS IN THE UK

The taxation status of an individual is of great importance in determining his liability to income tax. In general a person will only be liable to UK tax if he is either:

(a) resident in the UK, or

(b) has a UK source of income.

To determine liability certain terms need to be defined.

1.1 Residence

There is no statutory definition of residence and in practice it may be a difficult thing to determine. An Inland Revenue booklet - IR 20 - states the Revenue's view though it must be pointed out that it is selective in its approach and bases its conclusions on those parts of the legislation and case law which favour the Revenue whilst ignoring those which favour the taxpayer.

It is possible to be resident in the UK without having a place of residence, thus a tramp who spent all his life in the UK would be resident even though he had no home in the material sense. Similarly it is not necessary that the taxpayer should intend to be resident in the UK. He may be resident if required to be here because of military service - **IRC v. Inchiquin (1948)** or attendance at school - **Miesagaes v. IRC (1957)**. A person in jail would also be resident in the UK. In deciding whether a person is resident the court would consider:

(a) nationality

(b) physical presence

(c) past history as to residence

(d) family and business ties

(e) the maintenance of a place of abode.

It is important to appreciate that,

> 'Residence is not a term of invariable elements, all of which must be
> satisfied in each instance. It is highly flexible and its many shades of
> meaning vary not only in the contexts of different matters but also in
> different aspects of the same matters'.
> per Rand J in **Thomson v. Minister of National Revenue (1946)**

In general the Revenue in IR 20 propose three basic tests of residence:

(a)   presence in the UK for six months in the fiscal year,

(b)   habitual and substantial visits,

(c)   the maintenance of a place of abode.

   i)   **Presence in the UK for six months in the fiscal year**
           A person who is physically present in the UK for six months (equated by
           the Revenue to 183 days) in the fiscal year will be resident for that
           year. TA 1988,s.336 provides that a person will not, however, be
           resident if he is in the UK for some temporary purpose only and not
           with any intention to become resident. The corollary of this appears
           to be that if a person enters the UK with the intention of becoming
           resident then he will be resident even if physically present for less
           than one-half of the fiscal year.

   ii)   **Habitual and substantial visits**
           Where a person is not resident under (i) above, he may be so if he
           visits the UK year after year and the visits are habitual and
           substantial.

           In **Levene v. IRC (1928)** the taxpayer left the UK in 1919 to stay
           abroad. He did not acquire a place of abode but instead lived in hotels
           or with friends. He also paid substantial visits to the UK amounting
           to an average of five months per year between 1919 and 1925 when he
           acquired a flat abroad. During his visits to the UK he visited his
           relatives, obtained medical treatment and dealt with personal affairs.
           Held that he was resident in the UK. His visits were so habitual and
           substantial as to show that he still was resident here. Per Lord
           Sumner,

           'He changed his sky but not his home'.

           In **IRC v. Lysaght (1928)** Mr. Lysaght had worked for many years in the
           UK as a director of a family business but in 1919 he partially retired
           to Ireland to live on the family estate. He sold his property in the
           UK and had no place of abode in the UK. He continued, however, to
           attend board meetings of the company and for that purpose he visited
           the UK every month staying each time for about a week. During this
           period he stayed in hotels and in no year was he present in the UK for
           more than 101 days. Held that he was resident in the UK.

In considering the above two cases it is important to note that the
question of residence was found as a matter of fact by the
Commissioners and the courts were not prepared to overturn their
findings.

The Revenue equate habitual and substantial to visits of an average
period of three months over four fiscal years. Normally the taxpayer
would only become resident from year five though if he has the
intention of following this pattern of visits he will be treated as
resident from the beginning.

iii) **The maintenance of a place of abode**

Where an individual maintains a place of abode in the UK then he will
be treated by the Revenue as resident if he visits the UK at any time
in the fiscal year. This principle is based on the case of **Cooper v.
Cadwallader (1904)**.

In this case an American attorney leased a hunting lodge in Scotland
and visited it for two months each year. During the rest of the time it
remained empty apart from two servants. Held that he was resident in
the UK in each year in which he visited Scotland.

TA 1988,s.335 provides, however, that where a person carries on a
trade, profession, vocation or employment wholly outside the UK then
the question of residence will be decided without considering the
existence of a place of abode in the UK. Thus in these circumstances
the individual will only be resident if either test (i) or (ii) is
satisfied. The word 'wholly' is interpreted strictly.

In **Robson v. Dixon (1972)** the taxpayer was an airline pilot working for
KLM and based in the Netherlands. He had a place of abode in the UK.
He normally flew from the Netherlands to South America but on a limited
number of occasions he landed at Heathrow en route either to or from
Amsterdam. Held that there was a substantial performance of duties in
the UK.

A UK citizen going abroad will be regarded as still being resident in the UK if
his absence is purely temporary. In practice temporary can extend to a period
of up to one year. It is up to the taxpayer to establish non-residence though in
the case of a person going abroad permanently he may be regarded as absent *ab
initio*.

In the year that an individual leaves the UK for permanent residence abroad or
enters the UK for permanent residence, the Inland Revenue will normally split his
income as under:

(a)   in the period of residence - all income will normally be assessed;

(b)   in the period of non-residence - only the UK-arising income will be liable
      to UK tax.

In the year of leaving or becoming resident in the UK, the full personal
allowances are available.

The residence of companies has been discussed in the section on corporation tax and unlike individuals depends not on physical presence but the concept of place of incorporation or central management and control.

1.2 Ordinary residence

Ordinary residence denotes greater permanence than 'residence'. Using the dicta of Lord Cave in **Levene v. IRC** it denotes residence with 'some degree of continuity' and that of Lord Buckmaster in **Lysaght v. IRC** it

> 'means ... that the residence is not casual and uncertain but that the person held to reside does so in the ordinary course of his life'.

1.3 Domicile

The term domicile denotes as the place of abode of an individual, the country which he regards as his natural home. On birth a person acquires a domicile of origin (normally from his father but from his mother if he is illegitimate). This lasts until the age of 16 when a child is capable of establishing his own independent domicile. This independent domicile, known as the domicile of choice, can be established by the individual abandoning his domicile of origin. Abandonment of the domicile of origin is not an easy thing to establish; it is proved by definite action by the individual to renounce his domicile of origin; he could do this by:

(a) severing all contact with the country in which he is presently domiciled, selling all property there and closing all bank accounts, etc.;

(b) showing himself as subject to the laws of the new domicile; taking nationality in the new country; making a Will according to its laws;

(c) establishing a presence in the new country; buying a residence there or even a burial plot!

From 1st January 1974 a wife does not automatically take the domicile of her husband upon marriage, but can establish her own independent domicile. Women married on 1st January 1974 retain their husband's domicile until they take positive action to change. Whilst a person can be resident or ordinarily resident in more than one country, it is only possible to have one domicile for income tax purposes.

1.4 Appeals

Appeals against the decision of the Revenue on the question of residence, ordinary residence and domicile can be made to the Special Commissioners and then to the courts.

2.0 LIABILITY UNDER SCHEDULE D CASES IV AND V

2.1 Income assessable

Schedule D Case IV - Interest received from foreign securities such as mortgages and debentures.

- Deep discount foreign securities.

Schedule D Case V   -   Income from foreign possessions such as foreign dividends
                         and rents. Foreign pensions and the profits of foreign
                         businesses controlled from abroad are also liable under
                         Case V. Salaries and wages from abroad are liable under
                         Schedule E.

2.2 Basis of assessment

The basis of assessment is normally the same as Schedule D Case III, i.e. the
income arising in the preceding year of assessment whether remitted or not, with
the same rules for the commencement and cessation of a source. In two cases,
however the basis of assessment is the remittances made in the preceding year of
assessment. This basis, known as the 'Remittance Basis', applies to:

(a) persons not domiciled in the UK;

(b) British subjects not ordinarily resident in the UK.

In calculating the amount assessable on the 'arising' basis, a deduction of ten
per cent is made from foreign pensions. Pensions received as a victim of Nazi
persecution are exempt.

Illustration

From the details below calculate the amount assessable under Schedule D Cases IV
or V for the fiscal year 1989/90:

	1988/89 £	**1989/90** £
A - A British subject resident and domiciled in the UK but not ordinarily resident: Interest on a mortgage of property in France:		
Received in the years	40	50
Remitted in the years	10	40
Alternatively, assume he was also ordinarily resident.		

	1988/89 £	**1989/90** £
B - A French citizen temporarily resident in the UK: Share of profits from the Paris partnership:		
Received in the years	1,000	2,000
Remitted in the years	500	1,000
C - A Dutch citizen resident, but not domiciled, in the UK. Income from a pension derived from his former employment in Holland:		
Received in the years	600	900
Remitted to the UK	700	400
Alternatively, assume the recipient was a British citizen domiciled, resident and ordinarily resident in the UK.		

A	(1)	£ 10				D IV
	(2)	£ 40				D IV
B	(1)	£500				D V
C	(1)	£700				D V
	(2)	£600	- 10%	=	£540	D V

Where there is an overseas loss it will be available for relief under s.380 or s.385. When relief is given under s.380 it is only against other foreign income as under:

(a) foreign profits,
(b) foreign pensions,
(c) foreign emoluments assessed under Schedule E.

Illustration

A provides you with the following information: he is resident, ordinarily resident and domiciled in the UK.

Foreign Trade:

Year ended	31.3.1989	£ 6,000 profit
Year ended	31.3.1990	£10,000 loss

Foreign Pension: £
                    1989/90   2,000
                    1990/91   3,000

UK Dividends:
                    1989/90   4,500 (gross)
                    1990/91   7,000 (gross)

Relief for the overseas loss is to be claimed as early as possible.

		Income Earned	Unearned
1989/90			
	£	£	£
D V - Foreign trade		6,000	
D V - Foreign pension	2,000		
Less: 10%	200		
		1,800	
UK Dividends			4,500
		7,800	4,500
D V - Foreign loss - Year to 31.3.1990	(10,000)		
s.380 relief		7,800	(7,800)
		(2,200)	NIL

Total Income: 1989/90   4,500

	£	£	Income Earned £	Unearned £
1990/91				
D V - Foreign trade			NIL	
D V - Foreign pension	3,000			
Less: 10%	300			
	———		2,700	
UK Dividends				7,000
s.380 relief		2,200		
		———	(2,200)	
			———	
			500	

Total Income: 1990/91   7,500
                                                                       =====

The costs of travel to and from the place where the assessee's trade is carried on is treated as a s.74 deduction. Similar provisions as for employees apply to the travel expenses of a spouse and member of the family.

2.3 Unremittable income

Where overseas income is termed 'unremittable', it may be omitted from assessments if the tax-paying company gives written notice to the Inspector before such assessments become final (TA 1988,s.584). Unremittable income is defined as:

(a) such income as cannot, despite reasonable endeavour, be remitted to the UK by reason of the laws of the overseas country, executive action of its Government or the impossibility of obtaining foreign currency, and

(b) such income as the taxpayer has not realised outside the overseas territory for sterling or an unblocked currency.

Where the Revenue consider that these conditions are no longer satisfied, i.e. that the income is no longer unremittable, the income becomes assessable.

2.4 Constructive remittances

A person assessed on the remittance basis may possibly avoid taxation by, for example, obtaining a loan abroad, remitting the proceeds of the loan and using the overseas income to clear the loan. Thus there would be a remittance of capital (non-taxable) rather than income (taxable). TA 1988,s.65 provides that income arising outside the UK shall be treated as having been remitted, and therefore liable to tax if it is applied towards the satisfaction of:

(a) a loan received in the UK:

(b) a loan received outside the UK, the proceeds of which are remitted to the UK.

3.0   SPECIFIC PROBLEMS RELATING TO TRADING

3.1 The problem of trading within, as distinct from trading with, the UK.

FA 1988,2.18 provides that a non-resident will be liable to UK tax on the profits of trading within, as distinct from trading with, the UK.

Trading within the UK was defined by Brett, L J in **Erichsen v. Last (1881)**:

> 'Whenever profitable contracts are habitually made in England by or for a foreigner ... such foreigners are exercising a trade in England even though everything done or supplied by those persons to fulfil the contract is done abroad.'

The mere purchase of goods in the UK for export or resale abroad is not trading within the UK, **Sulley v. Attorney General (1860)**.

The place of the contract is determined according to UK law and is the place where the acceptance of the offer is communicated; thus if acceptance is made by the overseas party by letter, that acceptance is abroad. If communication is by telex, acceptance may be within the UK.

The fact that the foreigner has an employee or representative in the UK will not mean that he carries on a trade here provided that the contracts are concluded abroad, **Greenwood v. Smidth (1922)**.

In **Grainger & Son v. Gough (1896)**, a French champagne house canvassed orders for champagne through the firm of Grainger and Son who would pass on all orders and money received from UK customers to the French company in Rheims. The contracts for sale were made in France and the risk passed there. It was held by the House of Lords that the French company was not trading within the UK.

In **Pommery and Greno v. Apthorpe (1886)**, the London agents of Pommery held stocks of wine in the UK and these were used to satisfy all but large orders. The money collected was paid into Pommery's bank account in the UK. Held that he was trading within the UK.

Although the place of acceptance of the contract was held by Lord Esher in **Werhle v. Colquhoun (1888)** as being the '... foundation of the trade ...', Lord Cave in **Maclaine v. Ecott (1926)** said that there were other factors to be taken into account and disclaimed any exhaustive test. In **Greenwood v. Smidth**, Atkin, LJ asked:

> 'Where do the operations take place from which the profits in substance derive?'

In **Firestone Tyre and Rubber Co. v. Llewellin (1957)**, an American company had a subsidiary of the same name in Brentford, UK. The subsidiary made tyres in the UK and on the directions of its parent supplied them to foreign dealers. The House of Lords held that the American parent was trading within the UK as also was the subsidiary. The location of the master sales agreement in America which governed the trade between the parent and the subsidiary was not conclusive.

The UK tax principles are often affected by the provisions of a double tax convention. Under Article 5 of the OECD draft double taxation agreement, a country cannot impose tax unless the trader is carrying on a business within a territory through the medium of a permanent establishment there. This is broadly defined as a fixed place of business through which the operations of the enterprise are wholly or partly carried on. The term includes a place of management, branch, office, factory or workshop together with an agent with authority to, and who habitually does, conclude contracts in the name of the enterprise. It does not include facilities for the storage, display or delivery of goods or the maintenance of a stock of goods for these purposes.

The profits to be taxed will be limited under Article 7 OECD to those which the enterprise would have been expected to make if it was:

(a)   a distinct and separate enterprise;

(b)   engaged in the same or similar activities;

(c)   under the same or similar conditions;

(d)   dealing independently of the enterprise of which it is a permanent establishment.

This may be more favourable than the provisions for establishing the profits of a branch laid down in TMA 1970,s.79 where the amount assessable would be the amount of profit arising directly or indirectly through or from the branch agency.

TMA 1970,s.81, however, provides that on election the branch or agency may be charged to tax on the profits which might reasonably be expected to be earned by a merchant who had bought from the manufacturer or producer direct.

3.2   The choice of business structure

The profits of a trade carried on wholly abroad are assessed under Schedule D Case V. If part of the trade is carried on in the UK the liability will be under Schedule D Case I.

It is very difficult for a sole trader resident in the UK to show that he is trading wholly abroad. Even though he does not take any part in managing his business in the UK, the mere fact that he could have done so if he wished is enough to show that the trade is not carried on wholly abroad, **Ogilvie v. Kitten (1908)**.

Mr Ogilvie was a manufacturer in Aberdeen and acquired a wool warehousing business in Canada. The Canadian enterprise was operated entirely under local management and Mr Ogilvie never interfered with the conduct of the business. It was held that the profits were assessable under Schedule D Case I because he had the power to manage the business if he had wished and that was enough to show that the operations were not conducted wholly abroad.

Where it is desired to carry on business abroad, a UK trader can do so by either:

(a)   exporting directly;

(b)   licensing an overseas trader to act on his behalf;

(c)   setting up a subsidiary company;

(d)   establishing an overseas branch.

The fundamental difference between a subsidiary and a branch is that the former is a separate legal person from the UK person who creates and owns it. Thus if the overseas operation is likely to be successful, it may be better to set up an overseas non UK incorporated subsidiary as than freedom is maintained over the remittance of profits by way of dividend, subject to the company not contravening the controlled foreign company legislation. This, however, will only be so if it is possible to show that the subsidiary is not UK resident and therefore care must be taken at its establishment to ensure that it is not controlled and managed from within the UK. Conversely, if the overseas operation is likely to produce a loss, then the attraction of a branch is that under the **Ogilvie v. Kitten** principle it will be a mere extension of the UK trade and that the losses will be allowable as a deduction from the UK income. This could of course be achieved via the medium of an overseas subsidiary provided that it was UK resident, i.e. by being incorporated in the UK. However, when operations become profitable it would then be desirable to change the UK residence to a non-UK one, to preserve the non-assessability of profits to UK tax. This will now be impossible following the provisions of FA 1988 making all UK-registered companies UK resident.

In summary therefore the UK tax implications of branches and subsidiaries will be:

(a)   overseas branch of a UK company: the trading profits of such a branch form
       part of the total profits of the UK company subject to UK corporation tax.
       As a result:

       i)   branch profits are taxed in the UK whether or not remitted to the UK;

       ii)   relief is available in the UK for branch losses;

       iii) capital allowances may be claimed in respect of the branch, if
             appropriate.

(b)   overseas subsidiary: the trading profits of a subsidiary are subject to UK
       tax only when a dividend is receivable from the subsidiary. As a result:

       i)   unremitted profits are normally free from UK tax;

       ii)   there is no relief in the UK for the subsidiary's trading losses;

       iii) no UK capital allowances are available in respect of the subsidiary's
             activities.

Care must be taken at the outset to determine the optimum form of structure.

In establishing any business outside the UK there are important non-fiscal matters to be taken into account:

(a)   a branch entails the loss of legal liability and some privacy;

(b)   it also lacks flexibility for mergers etc.;

(c)   the setting-up expenses of a branch and the administration costs often tend to be more expensive than those of a subsidiary;

(d)   a subsidiary may be more satisfactory as regards nationalist sentiments.

3.3 Repatriation of funds/transfer pricing

(a) Repatriation of funds

The following constitute the main methods of repatriation to the UK of profits arising from overseas activities:

i)   dividends

ii)   interest

iii)   rents

iv)   royalties

v)   management charges

vi)   licence fees.

(b)   Liability to UK taxation on repatriated funds

Companies or individuals resident in the UK are subject to UK tax on their world-wide income, irrespective of where those profits arise:

i)   trading profits of a branch established in an overseas country are charged under Schedule D Case I on an arising basis, regardless of whether the profits are remitted to the UK. Exceptionally, trading profits of an overseas branch could be taxed under Schedule D Case V if it could be shown that the trade of the branch was carried on, i.e. managed and controlled, overseas;

ii)   management expenses charged to an overseas operation are charged to tax under Schedule D Case I;

iii)   interest, royalties, etc., are charged under Schedule D Cases IV or V, on an arising basis, regardless of whether the profits are remitted to the UK;

iv)   the sale of know-how, manufacturing rights, selling rights, patents, etc. for a lump sum and/or royalties or licence fees, result in the lump sum or royalties being taxed under Schedule D Cases I or V (TA 1988,ss.524 and 530);

v)   the trading profits of an overseas resident company are not within the charge to UK tax until a dividend is paid by the overseas company to the UK company; a dividend so paid is charged under Schedule D Case V.

With the exception of management charges, these forms of repatriation will generally be subject to a withholding tax in the overseas country. Since management charges are not generally subject to a withholding tax, the imposition of management charges is frequently viewed with disfavour by overseas tax authorities, who consider the use of such charges as a method of extracting profits from their jurisdiction. This may result in management charges being disallowed for tax purposes in the overseas country or alternatively redesignated as a distribution to which a withholding tax may be applied.

(c)   Transfer pricing

Where trading transactions between connected parties are undertaken at other than market price, the price may be adjusted by the Revenue to market price (FA 1988,s.770). In particular where either the buyer or the seller (being a company or a partnership) is controlled by the other party to the contract, or both are controlled by the same persons, any transaction at other than market price can be adjusted so that:

i)   if the price is below market price, market price is substituted in computing the seller's profit (unless the buyer is a UK resident trader and is entitled to deduct the price paid in computing his own profits);

ii)   if the price is above market price, market price is substituted in computing the buyer's profits (unless the seller is a UK resident trader who would thus bring in as a trade receipt the price received).

For this purpose 'control' means the power of a person to secure, by shareholding or voting power (either directly or through another company) or under Articles of Association, that the company's affairs are conducted according to that person's wishes.

The transactions which are brought within the provisions of this section include not only sales, but also 'the letting and hiring of property, grants and transfers of rights, interests or licences and the giving of business facilities of whatever kind'.

As detailed above, the provisions of s.770 apply particularly in connection with transactions between a UK resident company and an overseas company over which it has control (or which are under common control). It is advisable for such transactions to be at arm's length, since otherwise a notional amount may be assessed on one party without any corresponding adjustment to the amount assessed by the overseas tax authorities on the other party to the transaction, and this may be so despite the provisions of a DTA between the two countries. It is also relevant to note that there are provisions similar to s.770 within the tax legislation of most other countries.

Article 9 OECD Draft Double Taxation agreement provides:

ASSOCIATED ENTERPRISES
1   Where

(a)   an enterprise of a contracting State participates directly or indirectly in the management, control or capital of an enterprise of the other contracting State, or

(b)   the same persons participate directly or indirectly in the management, control or capital of an enterprise of a contracting State and an enterprise of the other contracting State, and

conditions, in either case, are made or imposed between the two enterprises in their commercial or financial relations which differ from those which would be made between independent enterprises, any profits which would have accrued to one of the enterprises, but, by reason of those conditions, have not so accrued, may be included in the profits of that enterprise and taxed accordingly.

2   Where a contracting State includes in the profits of an enterprise of that State - and taxes accordingly - profits on which an enterprise of the other contracting State has been charged to tax in that other State and the profits so included are profits which would have accrued to the enterprise of the first-mentioned State if the conditions made between the two enterprises had been those which would have been made between independent enterprises, then that other State shall make an appropriate adjustment to the amount of tax charged therein on those profits. In determining such adjustment, due regard shall be had to the other provisions of this convention and the competent authorities of the contracting States shall if necessary consult each other.

This is wider than UK legislation as it extends to management control or capital without specifying degrees of control. Paragraph 2 refers to the warning in an earlier paragraph. If an adjustment is made by one State to the profits of an enterprise then it is reasonable that the other State makes a corresponding adjustment. The Treaty states that the other State <u>shall</u> make an <u>appropriate</u> adjustment. 'Shall' does not of course mean 'will' and 'appropriate' depends on the individual perception of those concerned.

3.4   Foreign borrowing arrangements

(a)   Payment of interest

When borrowing from overseas, a UK resident company or individual must be aware of the requirements concerning the payment of interest; a tax deduction for the interest payments must also be assured.

A UK resident company paying annual interest on a borrowing is normally required to deduct income tax at the basic rate from the interest payments (TA 1988,s.349). This deduction is not required in certain circumstances:

i)   where the interest is payable in the UK on an advance from a bank carrying on a bona fide banking business in the UK; or

ii)   where the interest is payable to a non-UK resident person, who is resident in a country with which the UK has concluded a DTA which provides that the amount of tax to be deducted from the interest be reduced; or

iii) where the interest is of foreign source (so that the interest is not within Schedule D Case III, a requirement for s.349 to apply).

Circumstances (ii) and (iii) are relevant when considering a foreign borrowing. For (ii) to apply, i.e. for interest payments to be paid with income tax deducted at a reduced or nil rate, permission has to be obtained from the Inspector of Foreign Dividends. Frequently, even where a DTA is available, foreign lenders are not prepared to follow the procedures necessary to obtain permission for deduction at a reduced rate or alternatively, to accept interest payments which are other than gross; this may be because the lender is not in a position to obtain relief for the income tax deducted against its own tax liability. If such is the case, it is necessary to arrange for the interest to be of foreign source, i.e. (iii) above.

There are various procedures which if adopted will generally establish that the interest is of foreign source; these include making the loan document subject to non-UK law, drawing it under seal outside the UK, retaining the document outside the UK. It is advisable to confirm with the Revenue that a proposed loan document will constitute a foreign source.

(b)   Charges on income

The UK resident company will be concerned to obtain a tax deduction for the interest payments. In order to obtain such a deduction, the interest must qualify as a charge on income (TA 1970,s.248 and TA 1988 s.338). The definition 'charge on income' broadly covers yearly interest, other annual payments, and interest payable in the UK on an advance from a bank carrying on a bona fide banking business in the UK, and there are conditions regarding such interest payments which must be satisfied in order for payments to qualify as charges on income (s.338(5) and (6)).

Where interest is paid to a non-UK resident, it will not qualify as a charge on income unless the paying company is UK resident and <u>one of three</u> conditions is satisfied, namely:

i)   income tax is deducted under s.348 (this condition is satisfied if the tax is deducted at a reduced or nil rate under the terms of a DTA), or

ii)   the conditions of s.340 are satisfied; the conditions set out in TA 1988,s.340 are:

   (1)   the interest must be paid by a UK resident company carrying on a trade;

   (2)   the loan agreement must specify that the interest is to be paid, or may be required to be paid, outside the UK;

   (3)   the interest must be paid outside the UK.

(c)   Foreign Lending Arrangements

Where a UK resident company makes a loan to an overseas subsidiary, the UK company must ensure that the interest charged on the loan represents a commercial return; failure to do so could lead to an adjustment under TA 1988,s.770. If the loan agreement could be regarded as a debenture issued by the subsidiary, it will be necessary to obtain Treasury consent under TA 1988,s.765(1)(c).

3.5   Treasury consent under ICTA 1988, s.765

Under s.765 it is necessary to obtain Treasury consent before undertaking any of
the transactions detailed in (a) and (b) below. There is specific provision
within this section for the imposition of penalties of up to two years'
imprisonment and/or a fine up to £10,000 where a UK resident company fails to
obtain Treasury consent when it is required under the section. As far as is
known there have been no prosecutions under s.765. However, a failure to obtain
consent for a relevant transaction could cause enquiry and possible delay in
subsequent dealings with the Treasury or Revenue.

Treasury consent is required:

(a)   where a UK resident company causes or permits a non-UK resident company over
      which it has control to create or issue any shares or debentures; or

(b)   except for the purposes of enabling a person to be qualified to act as a
      director, where a UK resident company transfers to any person, or causes or
      permits to be transferred to any person, any shares or debentures of a
      non-UK resident company over which it has control, being shares or
      debentures which it owns or in which it has an interest.

Applications for consent are required in a format laid down by the Treasury,
requiring certain information. In giving consent the Treasury will be concerned
to ensure that there is not a loss of UK tax as a result of the transaction, and
accordingly if not satisfied to this effect, the Treasury may impose conditions
in giving consent, such as the 100% repatriation of profits to the UK.

A number of general consents have been published; if a transaction falls within
one of these general consents, specific Treasury consent need not be applied for.

FA 1988 provides that a UK registered company cannot change its residence.
Where, however a non-UK registered company which is UK resident because central
management and control take place in the UK wishes to change its residence there
will be a potential charge to Capital Gains Tax. Broadly this will take effect
by a deemed disposal of all its assets just prior to emigration. This charge
will not arise on assets still used in the business of a branch or agency
maintained in the UK. The charge may be postponed if the migrating company
continues to be a 75% subsidiary of a UK resident company.

4.0   DOUBLE TAX RELIEF

4.1   General

Double tax relief is available to individuals and companies; it is given to
ensure that where a UK resident, individual or company receives income from
abroad it is not disadvantaged by being taxed twice, once in the country of
origin and again in the UK. Relief can be in one of two forms:

(a) **Treaty Relief TA 1988,s.788 and 789**

This relief is given in accordance with the terms of a double taxation
agreement negotiated between the UK and another sovereign State. The
Organisation for Economic Co-operation and Development has produced a draft
double tax agreement which is commonly used as a basis for the drawing up of
detailed treaties.

(b) **Unilateral Relief TA 1988,s.790**

This is relief given by the UK Government when there is no double taxation
agreement in existence, or it does not provide relief for a particular class
of income.

4.2 **Types of relief**

There are three basic types of relief:

(a) the foreign tax is deducted from the gross foreign income and the net amount
is assessed to UK tax (TA 1988,s.811). This method may be disadvantageous
and is not normally claimed, unless loss relief is required;

(b) the gross amount of the foreign income is charged to tax in the UK. The
amount of foreign tax is allowed as a tax credit against the UK tax
chargeable on the foreign income. For the purpose of this relief the
foreign income is treated as the top slice of the individual's income; the
amount of relief is the lower of the foreign tax credit or the UK tax borne.
The only foreign tax credits that can be used for relief are those suffered
for direct foreign tax; such direct taxes are often known as withholding
taxes. No relief is available to an individual for foreign indirect, or
'underlying' tax (the credit system);

(c) the foreign income is exempted from tax in the country of origin
(exemption).

Methods (b) and (c) above are specifically referred to in Article 23 OECD. UK
practice is to grant exemption from UK tax to a number of sources of UK income
including:

(a) commercial profits not derived from a permanent establishment;

(b) payments received from overseas by a foreign student;

(c) certain interest and dividends derived from UK sources by a foreign
resident;

(d) pensions derived from UK sources by foreign residents.

4.3 **Types of overseas tax**

(a) withholding (direct) tax - tax which is directly deducted from a foreign
source of income;

(b) underlying (indirect) tax - tax on the profits of which a foreign dividend
forms a part.

4.4 Method of relief - invididuals

CALCULATION OF RELIEF UNDER THE CREDIT SYSTEM

As already mentioned, under the credit system, the overseas income is grossed by the overseas tax before being charged to UK tax. In order to ensure the maximum relief for the overseas tax credit, the taxpayer may treat the overseas income as the 'top slice' of the taxable income. No relief is available to an individual for underlying tax.

Illustration

Mr A is married. In the year 1989/90 he is assessable on:

	£
D I Profits	24,775
Dividends from Ruritania	600 (net)

The dividends had suffered foreign tax of £400 (credit relief is claimed).

D I	24,775
D V - dividend £(600 + 400)	1,000
	25,775
Less: Personal allowance	4,375
	21,400

Income tax:

£20,700 @ 25%	5,175
700 @ 40%	280
21,400	5,455

The credit for the foreign tax is the lower of:

(a)   Foreign tax   £400

(b)   UK tax assuming the foreign dividend to be the top slice of taxable income

	£		
£700 @ 40%	280		
£300 @ 25%	75		
		£355	
			355

UK tax payable	5,100

Where there are several amounts of foreign income, the taxpayer can rank them in such a way as to obtain the greatest relief.

Illustration

Mr B receives the following UK income for 1989/90:

	£
Salary	19,495
Schedule A - Rents	6,000

He also receives the following foreign income:

| Dividends from Ruritania | £ 700 (Ruritanian Tax Credit £300) |
| Dividends from Amazonia | £ 450 (Amazonian Tax Credit £550) |

He pays allowable interest of £2,500 gross and is entitled to personal allowances of £ 4,375.

To obtain the greatest advantage it is important to regard the income that has suffered the greatest amount of foreign tax as the highest slice of income, so that the greatest possible amount of UK tax is available to offset the overseas tax.

	£	£
Salary		21,175
Schedule A	6,000	
Schedule D V:		
Ruritanian Dividend £(700 + 300)	1,000	
Amazonian Dividend £(450 + 550)	1,000	
	─────	8,000
		29,175
Less: Charges		2,500
		26,675
Less: Personal allowances		4,375
		22,300

Income tax:

£20,700 @ 25%	5,175
1,600 @ 40%	640
22,300	5,815

Tax credit relief:

<u>Amazonian Dividend</u>
Taxable income £21,301 - £22,300
Taxed: £1,000 @ 40% = £400

Foreign tax £550		
Tax credit given	400	
	c/f 400	5,815

		£	£
b/f		400	5,815

Ruritanian Dividend
Taxable income £20,301 - £21,300
Taxed: £400 @ 25%   £100
       £600 @ 40%   £240

                     £340
                     ===

Foreign tax £300
Tax credit given   300
                                                   _____   700
                                                              _____
                                                              5,115
                                                              =====

Where foreign dividends are paid through a UK paying agent, the UK agent must, under s.123 TA, deduct UK tax at a basic rate before paying it over to the recipient. Where foreign withholding tax has been deducted the paying agent will normally deduct UK tax at such a rate as will give a total deduction of the UK basic rate. All foreign dividends paid through a UK paying agent are assessed on a current year basis.

	£
Gross dividend	1,000
Less: Withholding tax - 15%	150

	850
Less: UK tax deducted by paying agent - 10% (making 25% in all)	100

Paid to Mrs C	750
	=====

Mrs C will include £1,000 gross in her personal computation with a tax credit of £250, of which only £100 is available for any repayment to which she may be entitled.

As from 26th July 1986, paying agents will not be required to deduct tax at source from foreign dividends etc., which are dealt with through a recognised clearing system, e.g. Euroclear.

4.5 Method of relief - companies

Foreign income received by a UK resident company normally arises under one of three heads:

(a) Schedule D Case I - Income from a trade carried on abroad through a branch etc. by a UK resident company;

(b) Schedule D Case IV - Income from foreign securities such as loans and debentures;

(c) Schedule D Case V - Income from foreign possessions such as royalties, rents, dividends etc.

If a non-resident company carries on business in the UK through a branch or agency then it will be liable to UK corporation tax on:

(a)   trading profits derived from the branch or agency;

(b)   income from property owned by the branch or agency;

(c)   chargeable gains on assets situated in the UK used for the purposes of the branch or agency.

THE APPLICATION OF THE CREDIT SYSTEM

The overseas income will be grossed-up by the foreign withholding tax and the gross assessed to UK corporation tax. The foreign tax is then treated as a credit against the UK corporation tax on the foreign income.

Illustration

D Ltd receives a dividend from Ping-Pong Incorporated of £5,000. This has borne a withholding tax of 15%.

Net amount received	£5,000
Gross for withholding tax - $£5,000 \times \dfrac{100}{85} =$	£5,882

	£
UK corporation tax @ 35%	2,058
Credit for withholding tax	882
UK corporation tax payable	1,176

Underlying tax is the foreign equivalent of corporation tax. It is the tax payable on the profits of which the dividend forms a part. It is only of relevance when considering dividend payments. Relief for underlying tax is limited to UK resident companies which control, directly or indirectly, at least 10% of the voting power of the company paying the dividend.

If in the above illustration D Ltd controls 10% of the voting power of Ping-Pong Incorporated, and Ping-Pong has borne underlying tax at 20%, the gross amount to include in the corporation tax computation is computed as:

Dividends grossed-up for withholding tax	£5,882
Grossed-up for underlying tax - $£5,882 \times \dfrac{100}{80} =$	£7,353

	£	£
UK corporation tax @ 35%		2,573
Less: credit for underlying tax	1,471	
withholding tax	882	
		2,353
UK corporation tax payable		220

As has been illustrated, to avoid double taxation, the amount of the foreign tax borne can be treated as a credit against UK corporation tax on the foreign income. However, the amount of the credit cannot exceed the UK corporation tax borne.

Illustration

B Ltd is a large multinational company which bears corporation tax at 35% on its income. It receives a dividend from a foreign investment of £46,000. The amounts of foreign tax borne are:

(a)   £54,000

(b)   £14,000

	(a)	(b)
	£	£
Dividend received	46,000	46,000
Foreign tax	54,000	14,000
	100,000	60,000
Corporation tax @ 35%	35,000	21,000
Less: Foreign tax credits	54,000	14,000
Corporation tax payable	NIL	7,000
Foreign tax credits lost	19,000	

Where the amount of underlying tax is not given, it will be necessary to calculate it using the principles in **Bowater Paper Corporation v. Murgatroyd (1969).** The formula for calculating the tax is:

$$\text{Overseas corporation tax actually paid on foreign profits} \times \frac{\text{Dividend gross of withholding tax}}{\text{Profits available for distribution per the accounts}}$$

Illustration

F plc is a large UK multinational company. It controls directly 40% of the voting power of Wong Inc. a company resident in Hong Kong. The profit and loss account of Wong Inc. converted into sterling for the year to 31st March 1990 is:

	£	£
Trading profits		600,000
Taxation:		
On current profits	210,000	
Transferred to deferred taxation account	40,000	
	250,000	
Overprovision 1989	20,000	
		230,000
		370,000
Dividends:		
Paid to shareholders	200,000	
Local income Tax	100,000	
		300,000
Retained profits		70,000

The Hong Kong corporation tax actually paid for the year to 31st March 1990 was £190,000.

The underlying tax credit will be:

$$£190,000 \times \frac{£80,000 + 40,000}{370,000} = £61,622$$

The amount chargeable under Schedule D Case V will be:

	£	£
Dividend received		80,000
Foreign tax credits:		
Withholding	40,000	
Underlying	61,622	
		101,622
		181,622

To maximise the utilisation of the foreign tax credits TA 1988, s.797 provides that charges on income, management expenses and other items capable of offset against profits of more than one description may be allocated as the company thinks fit. This will normally be:

(a)   against UK profits;

(b)   against foreign profits.

It also provides that the maximum ACT offset against any class of profits will be an appropriate percentage - presently 25% of that income.

Illustration

F Ltd a UK resident company, has the following income for the year ended 31st
March 1990:

	£	£
Schedule D Case I		35,000
Schedule A		5,000
Chargeable Gains		3,000
Foreign dividend received	23,000	
Foreign tax credits	7,000	
		30,000

The company paid dividends of £112,500 in the accounting period and paid
debenture interest of £4,000 gross. UK dividends received were £75,000.

Corporation Tax Computation

	£	£
Schedule D Case I	35,000	
Schedule A	5,000	
Schedule D Case V	30,000	
Chargeable gains	3,000	
	73,000	
Less: Debenture interest	4,000	
	69,000	
		69,000
FII £75,000 x 100/75		100,000
		169,000
Corporation tax @ 35%	24,150	
Less: 1/40 £(750,000-169,000) $\times \frac{69,000}{169,000}$	5,930	
	18,220	

Calculation of double tax relief:

	UK Profits	Overseas Income
	£	£
Schedule D Case I	35,000	
Schedule A	5,000	
Schedule D Case V		30,000
Chargeable gains	3,000	
	43,000	30,000
Less: Debenture interest	4,000	
	39,000	30,000

			UK Profits	Overseas Income
Corporation tax as above apportioned £39,000:£30,000			10,298	7,922
Less: Foreign tax credits				7,000
				922

		£	
ACT paid: 25/75 x £(112,500-75,000)		12,500	

	£		UK Profits	Overseas Income
Maximum offsets - Against UK profits:				
25% x £39,000	9,750			
Against overseas income: 25% x £30,000 (Restricted)	922	10,672	9,750	922
MCT			548	NIL
Surplus ACT		1,828		

As an alternative to the credit system the company may claim relief under TA 1988,ss.805-811. If this is done, the foreign tax will be deducted from the foreign income and only the net amount will be charged to UK tax. This is not normally advantageous as it means that no relief at all will be received for the foreign tax credits; however, it may be used where the company has a loss.

5.0 CONTROLLED FOREIGN COMPANIES (CFC)

Legislation was introduced in 1984 to prevent avoidance of tax by the use of UK companies maintaining subsidiaries in tax-haven countries. By this means it is possible to keep profits outside the UK jurisdiction and to subject them to reduced or possibly nil rates of tax. Where the Inland Revenue directs, the chargeable profits of a CFC will be imputed to a UK company which satisfies certain conditions. The chargeable profits will not include any capital gains.

The conditions that will trigger an apportionment are that:

(a) the CFC is in a low tax area;

(b) it is controlled by UK resident persons;

(c) the UK company must, together with associates, be entitled to at least 10% of the profits of the CFC.

An area will be a low tax area if the tax paid by the CFC in its country of residence is less than 50% of the UK tax that would be payable on the equivalent profits.

The provisions will not be applied where:

(a) the CFC engages in exempt activities; these are broadly where the company has a real presence in the country in which it is resident and its main activities are not those of leasing or dealing in securities; or

(b) the profits of a CFC for a 12-month period are less than £20,000; or

(c) the CFC remits by way of dividend enough of its profits to satisfy an 'acceptable distribution' test. The dividend received by the UK recipient company will be liable under Schedule D V;

(d) The company is quoted with at least 35% of its voting power held by the public.

To prevent the situation whereby companies sought to avoid tax on the dividend by removing the residence of the overseas company to the UK just prior to payment so that it became non-taxable FII or group income to the recipient, it is now provided that it will only be taken into account for the acceptable distribution test if the paying company was not UK resident at the time of payment.

CHAPTER NINETEEN

Introduction to Capital Gains Tax

1.0 WHEN CAPITAL GAINS TAX STARTED

A comprehensive capital gains tax was introduced in FA 1965 to apply with effect from 6th April 1965 and subsequent amendments have been made by later Finance Acts. These have now been consolidated into the Capital Gains Tax Act 1979 and further amendments have been made since then.

2.0 WHO IS LIABLE? (CGTA 1979, s.2)

All persons (including companies) resident or ordinarily resident in the UK are liable to tax on the disposal of any asset whether situated in the UK or not, but see later for a list of exempt assets. If an individual is not of UK domicile, but resides in the UK, he will only be liable on gains arising in the UK or remitted to this country. A person who is neither resident nor ordinarily resident in the UK but who carries on a trade, profession or vocation in the UK through a branch or agency is liable to CGT on disposals of the assets of that branch or agency.

To prevent avoidance of tax by moving a UK business asset outside the UK prior to disposal, there will be a deemed disposal and reacquisition at market value of UK business assets, if they are moved outside the UK or cease to be used in the UK. The market value used is that at the date the asset is moved outside the UK or that on which the business ceased to be carried on.

Where foreign assets are disposed of outside the UK and the proceeds are incapable of remittance to the UK because of executive action abroad, exchange control restrictions etc., then assessment will be deferred until the proceeds can be remitted. The whole gain will be assessed in the year in which the restrictions are lifted, there is no relating back into the year in which the gain arose.

3.0 WHAT IS A DISPOSAL?

A disposal of an asset, for CGT purposes, does not just mean a sale but also includes the following:

(a)   a gift;

(b)   loss or destruction of an asset;

(c)   provision of use of an asset, e.g. the granting of a lease;

(d)   compensation for damage or injury;

(e)   compensation for forfeiture of rights;

(f)   compensation for not exercising a right.

In addition , where an asset has become of negligible value, the owner may claim to be treated as having disposed of the asset and immediately re-acquired it at its present value. This will enable loss relief to be claimed.

In general terms, an asset is disposed of when an unconditional contract is made for its disposal and not when the proceeds are received. If the contract is conditional, disposal will occur when the conditions are satisfied **(Stanton v. Drayton Commercial Investments Co. Ltd (1982))**. Where a capital sum is received, e.g. as compensation, the disposal occurs when the sum is received.

4.0   BASIS OF ASSESSMENT

The basis of assessment is the actual gains made during the year of assessment or accounting period for a company. Thus, if an individual taxpayer sells an asset on 10th January 1990 he will be liable to tax on any gain he makes in 1989/90 subject to the exempt amount for that year.

5.0   DUE DATE OF PAYMENT

CGT is payable on 1st December following the end of the year of assessment to which it relates or within 30 days of the issue of the final assessment, whichever is later.

6.0   PAYMENT BY INSTALMENTS

Where the disposal proceeds are to be paid by instalments over a period exceeding 18 months and the taxpayer can satisfy the Inland Revenue that it would cause him hardship to pay the tax at the normal due date, then the tax may be paid by instalments over a period not exceeding 8 years, or the period covered by the instalments if shorter.

CHAPTER TWENTY

Method of Calculation

1.0 CALCULATION OF GAIN

The gain arising on the disposal of a capital asset is in general calculated by deducting from the proceeds of sale the allowable costs.

2.0 ALLOWABLE DEDUCTIONS

Those expenses which are available for deduction from the proceeds of sale in order to arrive at the capital gain are as follows:

(a)   cost of the asset;

(b)   incidental costs of acquisition (e.g. advertising for a seller, stamp duty, commission, etc.)

(c)   costs of improving the asset, provided the expenditure is reflected in the nature of the asset at the time of sale;

(d)   costs of defending title to the asset;

(e)   incidental costs of disposal.

For disposals after 5th April 1982 (31st March, 1982 - Companies) the allowable deductions will be increased by an 'indexation allowance'.

2.1 Indexation allowances

FA 1982, introduced measures designed to give relief from the effects of inflation where a chargeable gain arose on an asset held for more than twelve months. The relief took the form of an allowance (known as the 'Indexation Allowance') which was deducted from the gross gain. The allowance was computed by uplifting allowable deductions other than disposal costs by the increase in the retail price index from March 1982 onwards, or the anniversary of the incidence of the relevant allowable expenditure, if later.

Provisions were introduced in FA 1985 to amend and extend the original indexation allowance. In particular it was possible for disposals occurring after 5th April 1985 (31st March 1985 for companies) to:

(a)   obtain relief for increases in the RPI from the date of acquisition (or March 1982 if later) without waiting for 12 months;

(b)   use the indexation allowance to create or augment a loss;

(c)   apply the allowance to the value of assets at 31st March 1982 rather than to original cost, if that is advantageous.

For disposals after 5th April 1988, the indexation allowance is to be calculated by reference to:

(a)   the cost of the asset if it was acquired after 5th April 1982 (31st March 1982 for companies);

(b)   the value at 31st March 1982 if the asset was owned on that date. If, however, cost was larger than the 31st March 1982 value it will be possible to continue indexing cost.

3.0   METHOD OF CALCULATING THE INDEXATION ALLOWANCE

(a)   the indexation allowance is the total of the 'indexed rise' in each element of 'relevant allowable expenditure'.

(b)   'Relevant allowable expenditure' is any item of expenditure taken into account in computing the overall gross gain excluding, generally, costs of disposal.

(c)   The 'indexed rise' in an element of allowable expenditure is computed by multiplying that item by the decimal equivalent of:

$$\frac{(RD - RI)}{RI}$$

RD = The retail prices index (RPI) for the month in which the disposal occurs.

RI = The RPI for March 1982 or if later, the month in which the allowable expenditure was incurred.

The indexed rise is normally calculated to three places of decimals. The indexed rise in an item of relevant allowable expenditure will be nil whenever RD is less than or equal to RI. The RPI has been restated from January 1987 and revised values are used throughout.

Illustration

S sells an antique sofa for £43,800 on 6th June 1989. The sofa had originally cost £15,000 on dates given below:

i)   August 1985
ii)   October 1982
iii) January 1979
iv)   February 1960

Compute the indexation allowance arising in respect of each of the above
acquisition dates on the assumption that the RPI was as follows:

March 1982	79.4
October 1982	82.3
August 1985	95.5
June 1989	115.0

The value of the sofa on 31st March 1982 was £25,000

$$\text{£}$$

i)   £15,000 x $\dfrac{115.0 - 95.5}{95.5}$ =   3,060

ii)   £15,000 x $\dfrac{115.0 - 82.3}{82.3}$ =   5,955

iii) & iv)   As the asset was owned on
               31st March 1982, the indexation
               allowance will be applied to its
               value on that date as this is
               higher than cost.

          £25,000 x $\dfrac{115.0 - 79.4}{79.4}$ =   11,200

4.0 COMPUTATIONS

For disposals after 5th April 1988, the calculation of the capital gain will
depend on when the asset disposed of was originally acquired.

4.1 Assets acquired after 31st March 1982

The method of finding the gain is as under:

	£	£
Disposal proceeds		x
Less: Costs of disposal		(x)
		x
Cost of assets	x	
Other costs (see 2.0 above)	x	(x)
		x
Indexation allowance		(x)
		x

Illustration

A bought a property on 1st January 1983. The cost was £12,000 and solicitors'
fees amounted to £300. It was sold on 5th April 1990 for £50,000, selling
expenses were £2,000.

RPI	January, 1983	82.6.
	April, 1990	120.0.

	£	£
Disposals proceeds		50,000
Less: Cost of Disposals		2,000
		48,000
Cost of property	12,000	
Solicitors' fees	300	12,300
		35,700
Indexation		
£12,300 x $\frac{120.0 - 82.6}{82.6.}$		5,572
Capital Gain		30,128

If the indexation allowance exceeds the gross gain, it will create a loss.

Illustration

Facts as before but the indexation allowance was £40,000 instead of £5,572.

	£
Gain as before	35,700
Indexation	40,000
Capital loss	(4,300)

4.2 Assets acquired between 6th April 1965 and 31st March 1982

In this case, the gain is basically found as in 4.1 above. FA 1988 has, however,
provided that only gains or losses made after 31st March 1982 are relevant
(previously 6th April 1965). A taxpayer may make an election under s.96 FA 1988
whereby all pre-31st March 1982 assets are treated as being acquired on 31st
March 1982 at their value at that date. This election:

(a) covers **all** assets held at 31st March 1982;

(b) is irrevocable;

(c) must be made in writing to the Inspector of Taxes by 5th April 1990 or, if
     later, within 2 years after the end of the year of assessment or accounting
     period in which the first relevant disposal after 5th April 1988 occurs.

Illustration

B bought an investment property on 5th January 1970 for £12,000. He sold it on
5th April 1990 for £100,000. The value at 31st March 1982 is agreed to be
£60,000.

RPI	March 1982	74.0.
	April 1990	120.0.

If the s.96 election is made the gain will be:

	£
Disposals proceeds	100,000
March 1982 value	60,000
	40,000
Indexation	
£60,000 x $\frac{120.0 - 79.4}{79.4}$	30,660
	9,340

If the election under s.96 is not made, the value at 31st March 1982 will still
be used to find the gain unless cost is greater. In this case the greater figure
will be used and indexation will be based on that figure.

Illustration

C sold a property on 5th April 1990 for £150,000. The cost in 1980 was £80,000
and the value at 31st March 1982 was £60,000.

RPI	March 1982	79.4
	April 1989	120.0.

In this case it will clearly be advantageous to calculate the gain using cost
rather than the 31st March 1982 value.

	£	£
Disposal proceeds	150,000	150,000
Cost	80,000	
31st March 1982 value		60,000
	70,000	90,000
Indexation £80,000 x $\frac{120.0 - 79.4}{79.4}$	40,880	40,880
	29,120	49,120

If using cost produces a gain and using 31st March 1982 value gives a loss, or
vice versa, the result will be neither gain nor loss.

4.3 Assets acquired before 6th April 1965

For these assets, the position is potentially more complicated. If the irrevocable election is made under s.96, the calculation of gain or loss is easy. If, however, the election is not made then, as before, the 31st March 1982 will still be used to calculate the gain unless using the old rules for calculating gains give a more advantageous result.

The old rules for finding gains depend on the use of time apportionment. Basically that involves spreading the gain on a strict time basis over the period of ownership of the assets. Only the gain arising after 6th April 1965 was liable to CGT.

Illustration

A bought property on 6th April 1950 for £1,000. It was sold on 5th April 1990 for £20,000. (Ignore indexation).

		£
Disposal proceeds		20,000
Cost		1,000
		——————
		19,000
		══════
Chargeable	$\frac{6.4.65-5.4.90}{6.4.50-5.4.90} = \frac{25}{40}$	11,875
		══════

Where the asset was acquired before 6th April 1945, the gain was time-apportioned only from that date. The gain was, however, still calculated based on the original cost.

Illustration

B bought a property on 1st January 1930 for £1,000. It was sold on 6th April 1990 for £25,000. (Ignore indexation).

		£
Disposal proceeds		25,000
Cost		1,000
		——————
		24,000
		══════
Chargeable $\frac{25}{45}$		13,333
		══════

As an alternative to time apportionment, the taxpayer could elect to calculate the gain by reference to the value of the asset at 6th April 1965. This election, made under CGTA 1979, Sch.5, para. 12, needed to be made within two years of the end of the fiscal year (accounting period in the case of a company) in which the disposal occurs. Once the election was made, it was irrevocable.

Illustration

In the above illustration, the 6th April 1965 valuation was £14,000.

	£
Disposal proceeds	25,000
6.4.1965 valuation	14,000

Chargeable	11,000
	======

B would therefore elect to utilise 6th April 1965 valuation.

The election to use 6th April 1965 value could be used to reduce a gain or to turn a gain based on cost into a no gain/no loss situation if the calculation using 6th April 1965 valuation produced a loss.

Illustration

D bought a property on 6th October 1951 for £8,000; the value at 6th April 1965 and 31st March 1982 were £10,000 and £15,000 respectively. He sold it on 5th April 1990 for £36,000.

RPI	March 1982	79.4
	April 1990	120.0.

	£	£
Disposal proceeds	36,000	36,000
Cost	8,000	
6.4.1965 value		10,000
	------	------
	28,000	26,000
Indexation - based on 31st March 1982 value as as greater than cost or 6.4.1965 value	7,665	7,665
	------	------
	20,335	18,335
Time apportion	------	------
25/38 6/12	13,205	
	======	

No election would be made to use 6.4.1965 value.

Using 31st March 1982 value the position will be:

	£
Disposal proceeds	36,000
March 1982 value	15,000

	21,000
Indexation	
£15,000 x $\dfrac{120.0 - 79.4}{79.4}$	7,665

	13,335
	======

A decision of the Special Commissioners has indicated that time apportionment is to be applied before indexation; this is both logical and advantageous to the taxpayer.

In the above example the calculation based on cost would now become:

	£
Disposal proceeds	36,000
Cost	8,000
	28,000
Time apportion $25/38^{6}/_{12}$	18,182
Indexation	7,665
	10,517

It is understood that the Inland Revenue is appealing the decision to the High Court and thus, throughout the manual, the old method of calculation is used until the position is clarified.

As the old (cost and time apportionment) method gives a lower gain, this will be assessed.

Where the old calculations give a no gain/no loss result, then using the 31st March 1982 value cannot be used to disturb this result.

Illustration

E bought an asset on 6th April 1960 for £10,000; the 6th April value was £12,000 and the 31st March 1982 value was £20,000. It was sold on 5th April 1990 for £21,000.

RPI	March 1982	79.4
	April 1990	120.0.

If no election has been made under s.96 to use 31st March 1982 value the position is:

		£	£
Disposal proceeds		21,000	21,000
Cost		10,000	
6.4.1965 value			12,000
		11,000	9,000
Indexation			
$\dfrac{120.0 - 79.4}{79.4}$ x £20,000		10,220	10,220
		780	(1,220)
Time apportion			
£780 x $\dfrac{25}{30}$		650	

Elect to use 6.4.1965 value, thus no gain/no loss

There will be no comparison with the 31st March 1982 value as it is not possible to amend the no gain/no loss result.

If the election under s.96 was made, the result would be:

	£
Disposal proceeds	21,000
March 1982 value	20,000
	1,000
Indexation	10,220
Allowable loss	(9,220)

Where there has been improvement expenditure on a pre-6.4.1965 asset it is necessary to calculate the gain on the various parts separately.

Illustration

B purchased a property on 6th April 1960 for £22,500. He subsequently incurred expenditure on carrying out improvements on the following dates:

6th April 1970	£6,000
24th May 1982	£2,500

The property was sold on 5th April 1990 for £60,000.

The retail price indices were:

March 1982	79.4
May 1982	81.6
April 1990	120.0

The values at 6th April 1965 were £25,000 and at 31st March 1982 £35,000.

No election has been made under s.96 FA 1988.

		£	£
Disposal proceeds			60,000
Cost 1960		22,500	
Improvements 1970		6,000	
1982		2,500	31,000
			29,000

Indexation:
On March 1982 value

$$£35,000 \times \frac{120.0 - 79.4}{79.4} \qquad 17,885$$

On 1982 improvements:

$$£2,500 \times \frac{120.0 - 81.6}{81.6} \qquad 1,178 \qquad 19,063$$

$$9,937$$
$$\overline{\overline{}}$$

Chargeable gain: £

Cost	£9,937 x	$\frac{£22,500}{£31,000}$	x $\frac{25}{30}$	6,010
Improvement 1	£9,937 x	$\frac{£6,000}{£31,000}$		1,923
Improvement 2	£9,937 x	$\frac{£2,500}{£31,000}$		801

$$8,734$$
$$\overline{\overline{}}$$

Using 6.4.1965 value   £   £

Disposal proceeds		60,000
6.4.1965 value	25,000	
Improvements	8,500	33,500
		26,500
Indexation as before		19,063
		7,437

Lower gain

Using March 1982 value:

Disposal proceeds		60,000
March 1982 value	35,000	
Improvements - May 1982	2,500	37,500
		22,500
Indexation as before		19,063
		3,437

Thus the chargeable gain is £3,437

4.4 Partial disposal

Where part of an asset is sold, it is necessary to find the cost to be used in the CGT computation by the use of the part-disposal formula. This is:

$$\text{Cost x} \quad \frac{\text{Disposal proceeds}}{\text{Disposal proceeds + Market value of the remainder at the date of disposal}}$$

The indexation allowance will be applied to the part cost used in the computation.

Illustration

E bought a property in June, 1983 for £24,000. It was divided into two flats and he sold one on 5th April 1990 for £18,000, when the value of the other flat was £20,000.

RPI	June 1983	84.8
	April 1990	120.0

		£
Disposal proceeds		18,000
Cost £24,000 x £ $\frac{18,000}{18,000 + 20,000}$		11,368
		6,632
Indexation $\frac{120.0 - 84.8}{84.8}$ x £11,368		4,717
		1,915

If the property had been purchased in 1970 and the value at 31st March 1982 was £30,000 this would again have the part disposal formula applied to find the value to be used in the computation.

		£
Disposal proceeds		18,000
31.3.1982 valuation:		
£30,000 x £ $\frac{18,000}{18,000 + 20,000}$		14,210
Gain subject to indexation		£3,790

The indexation allowance will then be applied to £14,210 from March 1982. The part-disposal formula may only be applied to common costs; costs which are specifically attributable to one part of the asset or to another must be allocated to that part. If in the above illustration, additional costs were:

(a)   common conversion costs £2,000;

(b)   cost of an extension to the flat sold £1,200,

the revised gain, subject to indexation, would be:

	£	£
Disposal proceeds		18,000
Costs - Building	24,000	
Conversion	2,000	
	26,000	
	=======	
£26,000 x £ $\frac{18,000}{18,000 + 20,000}$	12,316	
Cost of extension	1,200	
	———	13,516
		———
		4,484
		======

5.0   THE RATE OF TAX

Up to 5th April 1988, the basic rate of Capital Gains Tax was 30%. As from
1988/89 the net capital gains of an individual will be treated as a marginal
addition to his taxable income and charged at the appropriate rate of income tax.
For 1989/90 these rates are:

(a)   basic rate   25%; and/or

(b)   higher rate   40%

The capital gains of discretionary and accumulation and maintenance trusts will
be charged at 35%.

6.0   THE TAXABLE AMOUNT

The 'taxable amount' of an individual must be established for a year of
assessment. The taxable amount is the net chargeable gain, i.e. chargeable gains
less all allowable losses, arising from disposals made in the year.

7.0   CALCULATION OF CGT PAYABLE

For 1989/90 the first £5,000 (1988/89 £5,000) of the taxable amount of an
individual is exempt from CGT; the balance is chargeable as above. For trustees,
in respect of settled property, the exemption is £2,500 (1988/89 £3,300).

8.0   TREATMENT OF LOSSES

If a taxpayer makes losses on the disposal of capital assets he can only obtain
relief by deducting them from capital gains. Except in exceptional
circumstances, capital losses can **never** be set against income or trading profits.

Likewise, except for companies, trading losses can **never** be set against capital gains.

Unutilised allowable losses brought forward may be deducted from the taxable amount. However, the taxable amount need not be reduced by such losses below £5,000 and thus sometimes all or part of the losses brought forward may be preserved for carry forward to some future year assessment.

Illustration

	A £	B £	C £
Unutilised losses at end of 1988/89	(3,000)	(3,000)	(3,000)
1989/90			
Chargeable gains	12,000	5,900	8,500
Less: Allowable losses	1,000	1,000	1,000
Taxable amount	11,000	4,900	7,500
Deduct losses brought forward	(3,000)	nil	(2,500)
Taxable amount	8,000	4,900	5,000
Less: First £5,000	5,000	5,000	5,000
Liable to tax on	3,000	nil	nil
Losses carried forward	nil	3,000	500

CHAPTER TWENTY-ONE

Exempt Assets

1.0 SUMMARY OF EXEMPT ASSETS

Set out below is a brief list of those assets which are exempt or partly exempt and in the following paragraphs some of these are considered in greater depth:

(a)   the taxpayer's own home;

(b)   tangible movable property (chattels) sold for £3,000 or less;

(c)   government securities and qualifying corporate bonds;

(d)   private motor vehicles;

(e)   securities issued under the National Savings Movement (e.g. National Savings Certificates);

(f)   gains on death;

(g)   life assurance policies, unless the person disposing is not the original beneficial owner;

(h)   betting winnings;

(i)   awards for valour, unless purchased;

(j)   foreign currency for personal use of taxpayer outside the UK;

(k)   gifts to charity;

(l)   gifts to the nation;

(m)   cash (sterling);

(n)   tangible movable property which is a wasting asset.

2.0 PRIVATE RESIDENCE

The taxpayer is not liable to CGT on any gains arising from the disposal of his own home, known as his 'only or main residence'. As this implies, the taxpayer can only claim this exemption for one home; if he in fact occupies two, say a town house and a country cottage, he can nominate whichever he prefers as qualifying for the exemption. The election must be made within two years of acquiring the second residence.

A CGT exemption is also available to a taxpayer on the disposal of a residence occupied rent free by a dependent relative of the taxpayer or his wife. Not more than one house may qualify for relief under the 'dependent relative' provisions at any one time. This relief is abolished for disposals after 5th April 1988 unless the relative was occupying the property at 5th April 1988 and continues to occupy it after that date.

If the area of land occupied by the residence and garden exceeds one acre then a proportion of the gain may be liable to tax. Likewise, if any part of the residence is used exclusively for a purpose other than the taxpayer's home this will also give rise to a liability.

Further, if the taxpayer uses the property as his home for part only of the period of ownership then the gain will be apportioned on a time basis to determine how much is chargeable. Provided the taxpayer has physically occupied the property for some time during its ownership, however, the last two years will always be treated as exempt irrespective of the use to which the property was put during those two years.

Illustration

W purchased a house on 1st July 1982 for £50,000 and lived in it until 1st July 1985 when he purchased another house and let his son live in the first. On 1st July 1996 he sold the first house for £170,000 net.

| | RPI | July 1982 | 81.9 |
| | | July 1996 | 140.0 |

	£
Disposal proceeds	170,000
Less: Cost	50,000
	120,000
Indexation $\dfrac{140.0 - 81.9}{81.9}$ x £50,000	35,450
	84,550

Period of ownership		
1.7.82 to 1.7.96	=	14 years

Exempt period	
1.7.82 to 1.7.85 (actual residence)	3 years
2.7.94 to 1.7.96 (last two years)	2 years
	5 years

	£
Gain as above	84,550
Less: Exempt $\frac{5}{14}$ x £84,550	30,196
Chargeable gain	54,354

(a) In addition to the last two years there are other periods of temporary absence during which the taxpayer will be treated as if he had resided in the property, provided:

i) he actually resided there both before and after the period of temporary absence;

ii) he had no other property which would qualify for exemption if he so chose.

Where the period of absence is because of employment abroad or work elsewhere in the UK, then it will not be necessary for the taxpayer to return and reside in the house to validate the last period of absence, (Extra-statutory Concession D4).

(b) The periods of temporary absence are:

i) any period or periods which do not in total amount to more than three years;

ii) any period or periods which do not in total exceed four years if the taxpayer has been forced to move elsewhere in the UK because of his employment;

iii) any period if the taxpayer has gone abroad because of his job.

The Revenue take the view that if these time limits are exceeded, then only the first three or four years as appropriate will be treated as a period of residence with the balance of the gain chargeable.

Illustration

S acquired a house in Croydon in June 1982 at a cost of £15,000 and lived in it until July 1983 when he left for reasons of employment and lived in rented accommodation in Huddersfield where he remained until March 1987. He then went to work abroad for three years. He returned to the house in March 1990 and resided there until May of that year when he acquired another residence. In September 1998 the first house was sold for £75,000.

RPI	June 1982	81.8
	September 1998	145.0

		£
Disposal proceeds		75,000
Cost		15,000
		60,000

$$\text{Indexation} \quad \frac{145.0 - 81.8}{81.8} \times £15,000 \qquad 11,595$$

$$48,405$$

| June 1982 to July 1983 | - | exempt as own residence |
| August 1983 to March 1987 | - | exempt as temporary absence |

(three years for any reason
four years for reason of employment in the UK)

| April 1987 to March 1990 | - | exempt as temporary absence |

(any length of period for reason of employment abroad)

| April 1990 to May 1990 | - | exempt as own residence |

| October 1996 to September 1998 | - | exempt as last two years of ownership and the property has been the taxpayer's only or main residence for some period. |

Thus, the only chargeable period is June 1990 to September 1996, i.e. 76 months out of a total period of ownership of 195 months, and the chargeable gain is therefore:

$$\frac{76}{195} \times £48,405 \quad = \quad £18,865$$

Where the property is let during any periods of absence, then this will not result in the loss of any periods of exemption. Indeed, the provisions of FA 1980,s.80, as amended by FA 1984,s.63(3), allow a further deduction from the assessable gain equal to the lower of:

(a)   the gain attributable to actual or deemed occupation;

(b)   the chargeable gain attributable to the period let;

(c)   £20,000.

Thus, in the above illustration, if the property had been let throughout all the periods of absence the result would be:

		£	£
Gain as above			18,865
Less: lower of:			
(i)	gain attributable to owner occupation (£48,405 - £18,865)	29,540	
		======	
(ii)	gain attributable to letting not already exempt	18,865	
		======	
(iii)	the first	20,000	
		======	18,865
			─────
			NIL
			======

The relief would also be available if a part of the property had been sub-let.

Illustration

J bought a house in December 1971 for £20,000 and sold it in December 1988 for £156,000. During the whole of this period he has let one-third of the house on a commercial basis. The March 1982 value was £40,000 and an election under s.96 FA1988 has been made in respect of all assets held at 31st March 1982. (Ignore indexation).

The gain is £116,000, of which £38,667 is potentially chargeable.

The rule in FA 1980,s.80 exempts the £38,667 to the extent of the lower of:

(a)   £77,333

(b)   £38,667

(c)   £20,000

The chargeable gain is therefore £38,667 - £20,000 = £18,667

When a taxpayer owns a residence and is employed or self employed and lives in other 'job related' accommodation, any gain made on the residence will be exempt so long as he intends to occupy the accommodation as his only or main residence in due course.

Where a lodger occupies part of the taxpayer's residence living as a member of the family by sharing facilities and taking meals with them, etc., then there will be no assessable gain.

The exemptions above not only apply to houses and flats but also to static caravans together with the land that they occupy - **Makins v. Elson (1973)**.

In **Batey v. Wakefield (1980)** buildings appurtenant to the residence qualified for the exemption. Thus it was held that the disposal of a caretaker's cottage occupied rent free and situated within the curtilage of the main dwelling house was not liable to CGT.

It has already been mentioned that where the grounds attached to a residence exceed one acre the excess may be liable to CGT unless the Revenue are satisfied that a larger area should qualify for relief having regard to the size and character of the house etc. Any exemption attaching to the garden or grounds will be lost where the garden is retained after disposal of the house - **Varty v Lynes (1976)**. The Revenue have indicated, however, that they will only take this point where the land retained had development value.

A married couple can only have one residence between them. If ownership of a property has passed between spouses, e.g. on marriage or death then the respective periods of occupation are aggregated in considering the relief available to the spouse disposing of the property.

Where there is the breakdown of a marriage, then one spouse, normally the husband, will leave the matrimonial home. Provided that the remaining spouse continues to occupy the property as his or her main residence then continuity of exemption can be claimed by that spouse. In the case of a divorce, then each person will be treated as an independent taxpayer and may qualify for an individual residence exemption. In the case of a separation, difficulties may be experienced where the spouse leaving the property elects for some other house to be considered as his or her principal residence.

3.0   TANGIBLE MOVABLE PROPERTY (CHATTELS)

Tangible movable property can be defined for the purpose of this chapter as any asset which can be touched or moved. If an asset within this category is sold and the disposal proceeds (before expenses) do not exceed £6,000 (£3,000 pre-6.4.1989) there is no liability to CGT.

Illustration

X bought a ring for £4,000 and sold it for £5,800.

	£
Disposal proceeds	5,800
Cost	4,000
	1,800

Not liable to CGT.

Where the disposal proceeds exceed £6,000 the full gain is liable to CGT but the chargeable gain must not exceed:

$$5/3 \text{ (Disposal proceeds - £6,000)}$$

Illustration

Y bought an antique clock for £1,200 in April 1982. It was sold on 5th April 1990 for either:

(a) £6,600

(b) £14,300

| RPI | April 1982 | 81.0 |
| | April 1990 | 120.0 |

	(a) £	(b) £
Disposal proceeds	6,600	14,300
Cost	1,200	1,200
	5,400	13,100
Indexation $\frac{120.0 - 81.0}{81.0}$	577	577
	4,823	12,523

Gain restricted to:

5/3 (£6,600 - £6,000)   £1,000

5/3 (£14,300 - £6,000)   £13,833

In the case of (a) the maximum assessable gain is £1,000 and in the case of (b) £12,523.

Where the chattel is sold for less than £6,000 and cost £6,000 or less then no capital loss will be allowable. Where the chattel cost more than £6,000 and was sold for less than £6,000 then an allowable loss is available but the disposal proceeds are deemed to be £6,000.

Illustration

An antique coffee pot was sold for £2,600 having cost £6,400 in 1983. Although the taxpayer has incurred an actual loss of £3,800 (£6,400 - £2,600), the loss for capital gains tax purposes will only be £400 calculated as follows:

	£
Deemed disposal proceeds	6,000
Cost	6,400
Allowable capital loss	(400)

This will be increased by any available indexation allowance.

The exemption for gains arising on the sale of tangible movable property where the consideration does not exceed £6,000 would be open to abuse, where sets of articles are concerned, but for anti-avoidance provisions. These require a set to be treated as one asset when disposed of to the same person or to connected persons. Thus it is not possible to sell parts of a set at different times for less than £6,000 and avoid capital gains tax. However, at no stage in the legislation is 'set' identified which, in practice, makes the provisions difficult to enforce.

Illustration

A bought a set of 2 chairs on 1st September 1982 for £700. He sold one on 6th April 1988 to B for £4,200 and the other to B's wife on 6th April 1990 for £4,400. On 6th April 1988 the value of the other chair was £4,300.

$$
\begin{array}{lll}
\text{RPI} & \text{September 1982} & 81.9 \\
           & \text{April 1988} & 105.8 \\
           & \text{April 1990} & 120.0 \\
\end{array}
$$

1988/89

		£
Disposal proceeds		4,200
Cost £700 x $\dfrac{4,200}{4,200 + 4,300}$		346
		3,854
Indexation $\dfrac{105.8 - 81.9}{81.9}$ x £346		101
		3,753

Restricted to:

$$5/3 \; £ \quad 4,200 \; - \left[6,000 \; x \; \frac{4,200}{4,200 + 4,300} \right] \qquad £2,058$$

1990/91

	£
Disposal proceeds	4,400
Cost £(700 - 346)	354
	4,046
Indexation $\dfrac{120.0 - 81.9}{81.9}$ x £354	165
	3,881

Restricted to:

5/3 £(8,600 - 6,000)	4,333
Less: Already assessed	2,058
	2,275

Specifically excluded from the definition of chattels are commodities dealt with on terminal markets, and currency.

4.0 GOVERNMENT SECURITIES

No chargeable gain or allowable loss arises when disposing of marketable government securities, on or after 2nd July 1986.

5.0 QUALIFYING CORPORATE BONDS

Capital gains made on certain qualifying corporate bonds are exempted from CGT if they are disposed of on or after 2nd July 1986.

The exemption is applicable to bonds, debentures, debenture stock or loan stock which are:

(a) quoted on a recognised UK stock exchange or dealt in on the USM or were it is by a company with some of its shares or securities so quoted; and

(b) are a normal commercial loan; and

(c) are expressed in sterling and which are incapable of conversion into another currency.

A qualifying corporate bond is a corporate bond which was:

(a) issued after 13th March 1984, or

(b) issued before 14th March 1984 but acquired after 13th March 1984 unless it was acquired as a gift, or by another no gain no loss transaction, and was not a qualifying corporate bond prior to the disposal.

CHAPTER TWENTY-TWO

Quoted Shares and Securities

1.0 GENERAL

Unlike most other assets, the market value of quoted shares can be easily ascertained. They are an exception to the time-apportionment principle.

2.0 CALCULATION OF MARKET PRICE

The method of calculating market price of quoted shares is as follows:

(a) At 6th April 1965 the higher of:

    i) a figure halfway between the two prices in The London Stock Exchange Daily Official List quotation, or

    ii) a figure halfway between the highest and lowest prices of recorded bargains.

(b) At all other times the lower of:

    i) a figure one-quarter up from the lower of the two prices in the quotation, or

    ii) a figure halfway between the highest and lowest prices of recorded bargains.

3.0 IDENTIFICATION OF DISPOSALS

3.1 Old Rules I - Disposals on or before 5th April 1982 (Companies 31st March 1982)

Disposals were identified with acquisitions as under:

(a) with acquisitions on the same day;

(b)   with acquisitions before 6th April 1965, FIFO;

(c)   with acquisitions after 5th April 1965, in the pool.

Where the liability was being calculated on pre-6th April 1965 acquisitions, it was necessary to compare disposal proceeds firstly with the cost and secondly with the 6th April 1965 value.

Where there were two gains, the lower was assessed and where there were two losses, again the lower was relieved. Where there was one gain and one loss then it was taken as **no gain and no loss (NGNL)** and no gain was assessed nor loss allowed.

In the case of shares acquired post-5th April 1965, they were pooled together and treated as one combined holding of shares. Where shares were sold, a proportionate amount of cost was taken from the pool.

3.2 The CGTA 1979, Sch.5, Para.4 election

Clearly, if the original cost of quoted shares was not known, it was impossible to complete the normal two computations and, in such a case, the Revenue would adopt the circumstances most disadvantageous to the taxpayer. However, there is an election available under CGTA 1979, Sch.5,para.4 to ignore cost altogether and assume that pre-6th April 1965 acquisitions were acquired on 6th April 1965 at the market value on that date, and as a result these shares would be pooled with subsequent acquisitions.

The election needed to be made within two years of the end of the year of assessment in which the first relevant disposal after 19th March 1968 took place. There were two elections available:

(a)   in respect of quoted fixed interest securities and preference shares, and/or

(b)   in respect of other quoted investments, i.e. ordinary shares.

Once an election was made it was irrevocable and applied to <u>all</u> quoted shares and securities of whatever company which were held on 6th April 1965 and had not been disposed of prior to 19th March 1968.

A CGTA 1979,Sch.5,para.4 election could not have the effect of reducing gains and where the market value as at 6th April 1965 was lower than the original cost, it might increase them. It must, however, increase the amounts of allowable losses, or produce such losses in situations where, without the election, a 'no gain, no loss' situation would arise.

It must be emphasised that a Sch.5,para.4 election could only apply to quoted investments and quoted securities. In the case of unquoted investments and securities and other assets held on 6th April 1965 the only election available is under CGTA 1979,Sch.5,para 12.

3.3   Old Rules II - Disposals between 6th April 1982 and 5th April 1985 (Companies 1st April 1982 to 31st March 1985)

Disposals were identified with acquisitions as under:

(a)   transactions in the same Stock Exchange account were matched;

(b)   sales were matched with shares acquired in the previous twelve months, on a 'first in first out' (FIFO) basis;

(c)   sales were then matched with shares acquired more than twelve months before disposal but after 5th April 1982 on 'last in first out' (LIFO) basis;

(d)   acquisitions in the pool purchased between 6th April 1965 and 5th April 1982;

(e)   shares acquired before 6th April 1965 were identified on a LIFO basis.

Indexation was available where appropriate.

Illustration

B acquired ordinary shares in Golf plc as follows:

September 1982	500
October 1982	1,000
November 1982	500
January 1983	500
March 1983	1,000
December 1983	1,500

In December 1983 he sold 3,500 shares in Golf plc in the same Stock Exchange account as his purchase of 1,500 shares.

The 3,500 shares sold in Golf plc were identified as under:

1   Firstly with the 1,500 shares purchased in December 1983; account bargains. No indexation.

2   Then with the 500 shares purchased in January 1983 - no indexation.

3   Then with the 1,000 shares purchased in March 1983 - no indexation.

The purchases in January 1983 and March 1983 were both in the previous twelve months and are dealt with on a FIFO basis.

4   Then with 500 shares purchased in November 1982. As this acquisition took place outside the previous twelve-month period, it is identified on a LIFO basis.

3.4 Old Rules III - Disposals between 5th April 1985 and 5th April 1988 (Companies between 31st March 1985 and 5th April 1988

The Finance Act 1985 provided for pooling to be re-introduced for shares and securities of the same class in the same company.

Shares acquired after 5th April 1982 (Companies 31st March 1982 were pooled using rules which are described in section 3.5 below).

Shares acquired prior to these dates were identified using the following rules:

(1) with the pool of acquisitions between 6th April 1965 and 5th April 1982 (the frozen pool);

(2) with acquisitions pre 6th April 1965 on a LIFO basis.

It is possible to make an election under para. 4 5th Schedule CSTA to transfer pre-6th april 1965 acquisitions into the frozen pool. It covers:

(a) fixed interest securities and preference shares;

(b) equities;

and must be made for <u>all</u> securities in one or both of those classes. The shares covered by the election will enter the 'frozen pool' as they are now deemed to have been acquired on 6th April 1965 at their values on that date. The time limit for making the election is two years from the end of the chargeable period (year of assessment or accounting period) in which the first disposal of any shares in either category occurs after 5th April (31st March) 1985. A group election by the principal company of a group binds that company and all members of the group.

3.5 Disposals after 5th April 1988

The rules cover two major types of acquisition.

(a) shares acquired after 5th April 1982 (Companies - 31st March 1982);

(b) shares acquired before those dates.

Where there are acquisitions after 5th April 1982 (Companies - 31st March 1982) shares are pooled. The rules however identify two types of shares:

(a) those acquired after 5th April 1982 (31st March 1982 - companies) and which are still held at 5th April 1985 (31st March 1985 - companies);

(b) those acquired after 5th April 1985 (31st March 1985 - companies).

The method of pooling is dealt with in accordance with the following steps:

(a) ascertain the number and cost of the shares acquired after 5th April 1982 (31st March 1982 - companies) and which are still held at 5th April 1985 (31st March 1985 - companies). Find the indexation allowances thereon from acquisition to 5th April 1985 (31st March 1985 - companies). The computation then starts with the following format:

	Shares	Cost	Indexed Cost
		£	£
	x	x	x

(b)   every time there is an operative event, increase the indexed cost by the indexation allowance between April 1985 (March 1985 - companies) or the most recent operative event (if later) using the formula:

$$\text{Value brought forward in indexed pool} \quad \times \quad \frac{RE - RL}{RL}$$

where RE is the RPI for the month in which the operative event occurs and RL is the RPI for the month in which the most recent operative event occurred; The indexation allowance is not restricted to 3 decimal places.

(c)   if the operative event is an acquisition, the cost is added to the cost and to the indexed pool;

(d)   if the operative event is a disposal, a proportionate amount of both cost and the indexed pool is removed using the part disposal formula;

(e)   the indexation allowance on a disposal is the difference between the amount removed from the cost and indexed pool columns.

(f)   in practice, of course, the cost column may be completely ignored; the chargeable gain (or allowable loss) is simply the difference between the proceeds and the amount removed from the indexed pool column.

As mentioned above, indexation in the post-5.4.1985 part of the pool is not restricted to three decimal places.

Illustration

X bought shares in ICI plc as under:

7th December 1983	2,000	Cost £7,000
19th July 1984	1,200	Cost £5,100
11 June 1985	600	Cost £2,450

On 30th September 1986 she sold 1,400 shares for £6,000.

RPI	December 1983	86.9
	July 1984	89.1
	April 1985	94.8
	June 1985	95.4
	September 1986	98.3

	Shares	Cost	Indexed Cost
		£	£
7th December 1983			
Cost	2,000	7,000	7,000
Indexation to April 1985			
$\dfrac{94.8 - 86.9}{86.9}$ x £7,000			637
19th July 1984			
Cost	1,200	5,100	5,100
Indexation to April 1985			
$\dfrac{94.8 - 89.1}{89.1}$ x £5,100			326
	3,200	12,100	13,063
11th June 1985			
Indexation to June 1985			
$\dfrac{95.4 - 94.8}{94.8}$ x £13,063			87
			13,150
Cost	600	2,450	2,450
	3,800	14,650	15,600
30th September 1986			
Indexation to September 1986			
$\dfrac{98.3 - 95.4}{95.4}$ x £15,600			474
			16,074
Sale of 1,400 shares	(1,400)		
Cost: £14,650 x 1,400/3,800		(5,397)	
Indexed cost: £16,074 x 1,400/3,800			(5,922)
	2,400	9,253	10,152

If the following transactions then took place:

6th April 1987	800 shares	Cost	£3,600
30th November 1989	1,000 shares were sold for		£5,000
RPI	April 1987		101.8
	November 1989		115.0

the position would be:

	Shares	Cost	Indexed Cost
		£	£
Brought forward	2,400	9,253	10,152

6th April 1987
Indexation to April 1987

$$\frac{101.8 - 98.3}{98.3} \times £10,152$$

	Shares	Cost	Indexed Cost
			361
			10,513
Cost	800	3,600	3,600
	3,200	12,853	14,113

30th November 1989
Indexation to November 1989

$$\frac{115.0 - 101.8}{101.8} \times £14,113$$

	Shares	Cost	Indexed Cost
			1,830
			15,943
Sale	(1,000)		
£12,853 x 1,000/3,200		(4,017)	
£15,943 x 1,000/3,200			(4,982)
	2,200	8,836	10,961

The chargeable gains would be:

	£
Disposal proceeds 30.9.85	6,000
Cost and indexation	5,922
	78

	£
Disposal proceeds 30.11.89	5,000
Cost and indexation	4,982
	18

3.6 Order of identification

If there are shares acquired before 1st April 1982, then gains will be calculated in the normal way and then compared with the result using a 31st March 1982 value.

The full order of identification is that disposals are identified:

(1) with acquisitions on the same day;

(2) with acquisitions in the previous 9 days on a FIFO basis;

(3) with the pool of acquisitions after 5th April 1982;

(4) with the pool of acquisitions between 6th April 1965 and 5th April 1982 (the frozen pool);

(5) with acquisitions pre-6th April 1965 on a LIFO basis.

Acquisitions in (1) and (2) above are not pooled and for (2) no indexation allowance is given.

Illustration

Y bought shares in ICI plc as under:

				£
19th June 1958	600	cost		900
30th December 1963	200	cost		400
11th January 1970	500	cost		1,650
2nd April 1980	1,100	cost		4,000
1st March 1983	400	cost		1,800
31st December 1985	700	cost		3,600
5th April 1990	100	cost		550

The 6th April 1965 value was £2.50 per share and the value at 31st March 1982 was £4.00 per share. He sold 3,000 shares on 5th April 1990 for £18,000.

RPI	March 1982	79.4
	March 1983	83.1
	April 1985	94.8
	December 1985	96.0
	April 1990	120.0

The disposals are identified as under:

(1)	With acquisitions on the same day	£	£
	Disposal proceeds 100/3,000 x £18,000	600	
	Cost	550	
Chargeable gain		50	50

(2)	With post-5.4.1982 pool	Shares	Cost	Indexed Cost
			£	£
	1st March 1983 Cost	400	1,800	1,800
	Indexation to April 1985			
	$\frac{94.8 - 83.1}{83.1}$ x £1,800			254
				2,054
	Indexation to December 1985			
	$\frac{96.0 - 94.8}{94.8}$ x £2,054			26
				2,080
	Cost 31st December 1985	700	3,600	3,600
	c/f	1,100	5,400	5,680	50

		Shares	Cost £	Indexed Cost £	£
	b/f	1,100	5,400	5,680	50

Indexation to April 1990

$$\frac{120.0 - 96.0}{96.0} \times £5,680$$

				1,420
				7,100
Sold 6th April 1990	(1,100)	(5,400)	(7,100)	

Disposal proceeds:
  1,100/3,000 x £18,000   6,600
Cost   5,400
                                                                 ─────
                                                                 1,200

Indexation £(7,100 - 5,400)   1,700
                                                                 ─────

Capital loss   (500)   (500)
                                                                 ─────

(3) <u>With 'frozen pool' of shares
     acquired between 6.4.1965 and
     5.4.1982</u>

Disposal proceeds:
  1,600/3,000 x £18,000   9,600

Cost
  1970   500   1,650
  1980   1,100   4,000
                               ─────   ─────
                               1,600   5,650
Sold   1,600   5,650   5,650
                               ─────   ─────   ─────
                                                         3,950

Indexation

$$\frac{120.0 - 79.4}{79.4} \times (1,600 \times £4.00)$$

                                                         3,270
                                                          680   680
                                                         ═════   ─────

                                              C/Fwd   230

		Cost £	Indexed Cost £	£
(4)	With pre-6.4.1965 acquisitions LIFO			
	B/Fwd			230
	Disposal proceeds:			
	200/3,000 x £18,000	1,200	1,200	
	Cost	400		
	6.4.1965 value		500	
		800	700	
	Indexation			
	$\frac{120.0 - 79.4}{79.4}$ x (200 x £4.00)	409	409	
		391	291	291
				521

Using March 1982 value, the position would be:

Frozen pool:

	£
Disposal proceeds, as above	9,600
Value at 31st March 1982 (1,600 x £4)	6,400
	3,200
Indexation	3,270
	(70)

Compared with the normal calculation giving a gain of £680, the position is now neither gain nor loss.

	£
Pre-6.4.1965 acquisitions	
Disposal proceeds, as above	1,200
Value at 31st March 1982 (200 x £4)	800
	400
Indexation	409
	(9)

Compared with the normal calculation giving a gain of £291, the position is now neither gain nor loss.

Alternatively if an irrevocable election under s.96 had been made for all assets, the position would be:

	£
Disposal proceeds	
$\frac{1,800}{3,000}$ x £18,000	10,800
31st March 1982 value (1,800 x £4)	7,200
	───────
	3,600
Indexation	
$\frac{120.0 - 79.4}{79.4}$	3,679
	───────
Allowable loss	(79)
	═══════

Where shares have been disposed of during the period 6.4.1982 to 5.4.1985 they
will be identified under the old rules.

Illustration

Z bought shares in ICI plc as under:

1st June 1983	600
19th December 1983	1,000
15th April 1984	300

1,500 shares were sold on 31st December 1984.

The shares sold will be identified using the rules existing between 1982 and 1985
(old rules II - see above).

(1) with acquisitions in the previous 12 months FIFO - 300 in April 1984;

(2) with acquisitions outside the last 12 months LIFO - 1,000 in December 1983
     and then 200 from June 1983.

Thus, 400 shares will be left which will be indexed, on disposal from June 1983
to April 1985, to form a new pool.

The election under Para. 4,5th Schedule CGTA has already been introduced in
section 3.2. For most pre-6.4.1965 holdings the time limit for the election had
expired many years ago. A second opportunity has now been provided in FA 1985.
As before it covers:

(a) fixed interest securities and preference shares;

(b) equities

and must be made for **all** securities in one or both of those classes. The shares
covered by the election will enter the 'frozen pool' as they are now deemed to
have been acquired on 6th April 1965 at their values on that date. The time
limit for making the election is two years from the end of the chargeable period
(year of assessment or accounting period) in which the first disposal of any
shares in either category occurs after 5th April (31st March) 1985. A group
election by the principal company of a group binds that company and all members
of the group.

Thus the position if a claim under Para.4, 5th Schedule was made for Y's holding above would be:

£

Frozen pool:
Pre 6.4.1965 acquisitions:

			£
1958	600		
1963	200		
	800	@ 6.4.65 value	2,000
1970	500	cost	1,650
1980	1,100	cost	4,000
	2,400		7,650
Sold	1,800	1800/2400 x £7,650	5,738
	600		1,912

	£
Disposal proceeds	
1,800/3,000 x £18,000	10,800
Cost	5,738
	5,062

Indexation
$$\frac{120.0 - 79.4}{79.4} \text{ x } (1,800 \text{ x } £4) \qquad 3,679$$

1,383

Thus it would not be advantageous to make an election in this particular instance.

If the claim had been made, then, again, it would be necessary to compare with the results using the value at 31st March 1982. As seen earlier, this gives a loss of £79 and thus the position would be neither gain nor loss.

If the s.96 election had been made, it would have been possible to establish a loss of £79.

4.0 BONUS ISSUES AND RIGHTS ISSUES - ITEMS OF THE SAME CLASS

A bonus issue or rights issue is deemed to have been acquired at the same date as the shares, etc., from which it was derived.

4.1 Bonus issues

There will be no increase in the total cost of the holding but on a unit basis the cost per share will be reduced.

Illustration

	£	Unit cost
X bought 2,000 ICI plc shares for	4,000	£2.00

Bonus
 Issue
  1:2   1,000   -

        3,000   4,000   £1.33

It is important when considering a bonus or rights issue to ensure that it is properly attributed to the shares to which it relates.

Illustration

F bought shares in ICI plc as under:

			£
1.9.1962	1,000	cost	3,000
6.10.1971	500	cost	1,900
9.12.1980	800	cost	3,000
7.6.1986	200	cost	690

On 1.12.1989 there was a bonus issue of 1 for 4. F sold 2,400 shares on 6th April 1990 for £20,000. The value of the shares in issue at 31st March 1982 was £4.50; an election has been made under s.96 FA 1988.

RPI	March 1982	79.4
	June 1986	97.8
	April 1990	120.0

Schedule of acquisitions

	Pool Shares		£	June 1986 Shares	£
1962	1,000				
1971	500				
1980	800				
1986				200	690
	2,300	@ £4.50	10,350	200	690
Bonus Issue	575			50	
	2,875			250	
Sold	(2,150)		(7,740)*	(250)	(690)
Retained	725		2,610	-	-

* $\dfrac{2,150}{2,875}$ x £10,350

	£	£	£
Disposal proceeds:			
250/2,400 x £20,000	2,083		
Cost - 1986	690		
	1,393		
Indexation $\frac{120.0 - 97.8}{97.8}$ x £690	157		
			1,236
Disposal proceeds:			
2,150/2,400 x £20,000	17,917		
31st March 1982 value	7,740		
	10,177		
Indexation $\frac{120.0 - 79.4}{79.4}$ x 7,740	3,955		
			6,222
			7,458

4.2 Rights issue

If there is a rights issue, there will be an addition to both the number of shares held and also to the original cost. Although the rights are deemed to have been acquired at the same time as the shares from which they derive, for indexation purposes, the cost of the rights will only be indexed from the date on which it was due or paid whichever is the later.

Illustration

X acquired ordinary shares in ICI plc as under:

| 15.4.1983 | 1,000 | cost | £2,800 |
| 11.4.1984 | 2,000 | cost | £6,400 |

On 1.6.1987 there was a rights issue of 1:4 at £5.00 per share. 2,500 shares were sold on 5th April 1990 for £15,000.

RPI	April 1983	84.3.
	April 1984	88.6.
	April 1985	94.8.
	June 1987	101.9.
	April 1990	120.0.

Ignore the column for unindexed cost.

	Shares	Indexed Cost £
15.4.1983 Cost	1,000	2,800
Indexation to April 1985		
$\frac{94.8 - 84.3}{84.3}$ x £2,800		350
11.4.1984 Cost		
Indexation to April 1985	2,000	6,400
$\frac{94.8 - 88.6}{88.6}$		448
At 5th April, 1985	3,000	9,998
Indexation to June 1987		749
$\frac{101.9 - 94.8}{94.8}$		
1.6.1987 Rights issue	750	3,750
	3,750	14,497
Indexation to April 1990		
$\frac{120.0 - 101.9}{101.9}$		2,575
		17,072
Sold	(2,500)	(11,381)
	1,250	5,691
Disposal proceeds		15,000
Cost and indexation		11,381
		3,619

5.0   BONUS ISSUES AND RIGHTS ISSUES - ITEMS OF A DIFFERENT CLASS

The basic principle of share pooling is that items may only be pooled together
where they are identical. Where this is not so it will be necessary to split up
both cost, 6th April 1965, and 31st March 1982 values, if appropriate. This
division will be made by reference to the market values of the various items on
the first day of dealing in the new issue.

Illustration

G bought 2,000 £1 ordinary shares in ICI plc on 16th December 1970 for £4,200.
On 19th July 1988 there was a rights issue of 1 for 2 preference shares at 88p
each. The market values of the various items on the first day of dealing in the
new preference shares were:

```
              Ordinary shares      £8 each
              Preference shares    90p each
```

The preference shares were redeemed for £1,500 on 6th April 1990

```
        RPI    March 1982          79.4
               July 1988          106.0
               April 1990         120.0
```

The value of the ordinary shares at 31st March 1982 was £6 each. An election has been made under s.96 FA 1988.

```
Cost of holding:                                        £
   2,000 £1 shares - March 1982 value              12,000
   1,000 preference shares - rights issue             880
                                                   _____
                                                   12,880
                                                   =======
```

Thus the combined holding of 2,000 shares and 1,000 preference shares is deemed to have been acquired on 31st March 1982 at a combined cost of £12,880

Split by reference to market values:

```
                                                        £
Shares 2,000 x £8                                  16,000
Preference shares 1,000 @ 90p                         900
                                                   _____
                                                   16,900
                                                   =======
```

Division of cost:

Shares $\quad £12,880 \times \dfrac{£16,000}{£16,900}$ $\qquad$ 12,194

Preference shares $£12,880 \times \dfrac{£\ 900}{£16,900}$ $\qquad$ 686

```
                                                   _____
                                                   12,880
                                                   =======
```

```
Preference shares redeemed at                       1,500
Cost                                                  686
                                                    _____
                                                      814
```

Indexation

March 1982 value -

$£12,000 \times £\dfrac{900}{16,900} \times \dfrac{120.0 - 79.4}{79.4} = £327$

Cost of rights -

$£880 \quad \times £\dfrac{900}{16,900} \times \dfrac{120.0 - 106.0}{106.0} = \underline{\quad 6}$ $\qquad$ 333

```
                                                    _____
                                                      481
                                                    ======
```

A bonus issue of items of a different class would be treated in exactly the same way except that there would be no addition to cost or 31st March 1982 valuation.

6.0 SALE OF RIGHTS NIL-PAID

This is treated as a part disposal. However, where the proceeds are small then they may be deducted instead from cost and 6th April 1965 value if appropriate. This will defer any gain until a subsequent disposal. The proceeds will be regarded as small where they do not exceed 5% of the pre-rights price of the holding from which they derive.

Illustration

H bought 1,000 shares in ICI plc on 2nd January 1986 for £4,000. On 6th April 1990 there was a rights issue of 1:2 shares at £3. She did not take up the rights and sold them alternatively:

(a) for £2 per share

(b) for 20p per share.

Market values of the shares were:

Before receipt of rights	£5.50
At date of disposal	£6.00

RPI	January 1986	96.3
	April 1990	120.0

£

(a)   Sale at £2 per share

Disposal proceeds 500 x £2			1,000
This is material as it exceeds			
5% x (1,000 x £5.50) = £275			

therefore there is a part disposal.

	Shares	Indexed Cost	
2nd January 1986			
Cost	1,000	4,000	
Indexation to April 1990			
$$\frac{120.0 - 96.3}{96.3}$$		984	
		4,984	
£4,984 x $\dfrac{1,000}{1,000 + (1,000 \times £6)}$		(712)	712
Carried forward	1,000	4,272	
			288

	Shares	Indexed Cost	
			£
(b) Sale at 20p per share			
Disposal proceeds 500 x 20p			100

This is immaterial as it does not
exceed £275 and it will be deducted
from cost.

	Shares	Indexed Cost	
As above	1,000	4,984	
Disposal proceeds of rights		(100)	
Carried forwad	1,000	4,884	

Where the disposal proceeds are small and are deducted from the 31st March 1982
value of shares held on that date, then the calculation of the indexation
allowance on a subsequent sale would be:

	£
Indexation uplift on original cost etc. before reduction	x
Less: Indexation uplift on disposal proceeds deducted assuming it to be expenditure incurred on the date the proceeds were received	(x)
Deduct from gross gain	x

Where a capital repayment is received, it is dealt with in the same way as a sale
of rights 'nil paid'.

7.0 TAKEOVERS AND REORGANISATIONS

These fall into two main categories:

(a) paper for paper;

(b) cash for paper.

Where the transaction is paper for paper, i.e. a share exchange, there will
normally be no liability to CGT as none of the gain has been realised.

Where the transaction is cash for paper, then there may be an immediate
liability to CGT in respect of the cash received.

In both cases it will be necessary to split cost and 31st March 1982 value, if
appropriate. This will be done by reference to the market values of the various
items received immediately following the successful takeover bid.

Illustration

J bought 3,000 shares in ICI plc in June 1983 for £8,000. On 6th April 1990 it was taken over by Emile Woolf (International) plc on the following terms:

>   2 Emile Woolf (International) plc ordinary shares
>
>   2 Emile Woolf (International) plc preference shares
>
>   £4 cash

for every 3 ICI shares held.

The market values of the Emile Woolf ordinary shares and preference shares on the first day of dealing following the successful takeover were:

Ordinary Shares	£4	
Preference Shares	90p	
RPI	June 1983	84.8
	April 1985	94.8
	April 1990	120.0

Items received following the takeover:	£
EW ordinary shares 2,000 @ £4 each	8,000
EW preference shares 2,000 @ 90p	1,800
Cash	4,000
	13,800

	Shares	Indexed Cost £
June 1983		
Cost	3,000	8,000
Indexation to April 1985		
$\dfrac{94.8 - 84.8}{84.8}$		944
		8,944
Indexation to April 1990		
$\dfrac{120.0 - 94.8}{94.8}$		2,378
	3,000	11,322

Split indexed cost pro rata to these values: £

        EW ordinary shares $\dfrac{£\ 8,000}{£13,800}$ x £11,322   6,563

        EW preference shares $\dfrac{£\ 1,800}{£13,800}$ x £11,322   1,477

        Cash $\dfrac{£\ 4,000}{£13,800}$ x £11,322   3,282

                                          11,322

As the gain attributable to the cash element has been realised, there will be an immediate assessment.

                                          £

        Cash received   4,000

        Cost   3,282

        Gain before indexation   718

The EW ordinary shares and preference shares will now be carried forward as separate pools.

Where the cash received is less than five per cent of the value of the shares acquired immediately prior to the date of the takeover then there will not be a part-disposal computation in respect of the cash element. Instead the cash received may be deducted from cost or 31st March 1982 valuation, if appropriate. The net amount will then be split pro rata to the values of the other items received.

For indexation purposes, there will be a calculation similar to that on the disposal of shares where an earlier rights issue had been sold **nil paid** for a small amount.

Illustration

Facts as in the previous illustration except that:

(a)   the cash received was only £400.

(b)   the value of the ICI shares prior to takeover was £3.30 each.

The preference shares were sold in April 1991 for £3,000

        RPI   April 1990   120.0
                 April 1991   130.0

Received on takeover: £
        EW ordinary shares 2,000 @ £4 each   8,000
        EW preference shares 2,000 @ 90p   1,800
        Cash   400
                                                 _____
                                                 10,200
                                                 ======

Market value of ICI shares prior to takeover: £

        3,000 @ £3.30   9,900
                                                 ======
                                                    £
        5%   495
                                                 =====

As the cash element is less than £495 it will be deducted from cost.

                                                    £
        Indexed cost brought forward   11,322
        Less: Cash received   400
                                                 _____
                                                 10,922
                                                 ======

Split over:

EW ordinary shares $\dfrac{£8,000}{£9,800}$ x £10,922   8,916

EW preference shares $\dfrac{£1,800}{£9,800}$ x £10,922   2,006
                                                 _____
                                                 10,922
                                                 ======

Preference shares	Shares	Indexed Cost
At 5th April 1990	2,000	2,006
Indexation to April 1991		
$\dfrac{130.0 - 120.0}{120.0}$		167
		_____
		2,173
Sold	(2,000)	(2,173)
		_____
	-	-
	=====	=====
Disposal Proceeds		3,000
Cost and indexation		2,173
		_____
		£ 827
		=====

8.0 UNIT TRUSTS

Disposals of units will be dealt with in a similar way to quoted shares.

CHAPTER TWENTY-THREE

Unquoted Shares and Securities

1.0 GENERAL

Most of the calculations relating to disposals of unquoted shares and securities are similar to those on the disposal of quoted shares and securities.

2.0 MARKET VALUE

In finding market value, there is deemed to be a transaction between a willing buyer and a willing seller. CGTA 1979,s.152 provides that a purchaser is deemed to have available all the information that a prudent purchaser is likely to require from a willing vendor.

3.0 CALCULATION OF THE GAIN OR LOSS

The principles applied to unquoted shares are similar to those applied earlier to quoted shares. Every unquoted share is deemed to be a separate asset, and this will mean that any elections made for one share will not bind future disposals of the same shares in the same company. In practice, when unquoted shares are taken from a pool, the Revenue will normally insist on the part-disposal formula being applied strictly. However, in examinations this may not be so strictly applied and costs on a part disposal can often be calculated in the same way as for quoted shares.

The rules of identification of disposals follow broadly the same rules as for quoted shares. As regards disposals made after 5th April 1988 they are as under:

(a) with acquisitions on the same day or in the previous 9 days;

(b) with acquisitions in the post-5th April 1982 pool (31st March 1982 for companies);

(c) with the pool of acquisitions between 6th April 1965 and 5th April 1982 (31st March 1982 for companies) (the frozen pool);

(d) with pre-6th April 1965 acquisitions (LIFO).

An irrevocable election can be made under s.96 FA 1988 to cover all assets.

Illustration

A bought shares in Unquoted Ltd. as under:

		£
6.11.1972	300	1,200
13.7.1980	100	500
19.6.1982	150	700
15.11.1984	500	5,200

1,000 shares were sold on 6th April 1990 for £14,000.

RPI	March 1982	79.4
	June 1982	81.9
	November 1984	91.0
	April 1985	94.8
	April 1990	120.0

The value of the shares at 31st March 1982 was agreed to be £8 per share. An election has been made under s.96 FA 1988.

	No. of Shares	Indexed Cost £	£	£
Cost - June 1982	150	700		
Indexation to April 1985				
$\dfrac{94.8 - 81.9}{81.9}$ x £700		111		
Cost - November 1984	500	5,200		
Indexation to April 1985				
$\dfrac{94.8 - 91.0}{91.0}$ x £5,200		218		
	650	6,229		
Indexation to April 1990				
$\dfrac{120.0 - 94.8}{94.8}$ x £6,229		1,656		
		7,885		
Sold - April 1990	(650)	(7,885)		
	-	-		

Disposal Proceeds		
$\dfrac{650}{1,000}$ x £14,000		9,100
Cost and indexation		7,885
C/fwd		1,215

	No. of Shares	Indexed Cost £	£	£
B/fwd				1,215
Shares held at 5th April 1982				
November 1972	300			
July 1980	100			
	400			
at 31.3.1982 Value - £8 per share		3,200		
Sold - April 1990	(350)	(2,800)		
	50	400		

Disposal Proceeds

$$\frac{350}{1,000} \times £14,000 \qquad\qquad 4,900$$

Cost	2,800
	2,100

Indexation $\dfrac{120.0 - 79.4}{79.4} \times £2,800$ 1,431   669

                                                     1,884

If no election had been made under s.96 FA 1988 the gain on the pre-6th April 1982 acquisitions would be found in the normal way.

	Shares	Cost £	£
1972	300	1,200	
1980	100	500	
	400	1,700	
Sold	350	1,488	
	50	212	

Disposal proceeds	4,900
Cost	1,488
	3,412
Index on March 1982 value (being greater than cost)	1,431
	1,981

This would be compared with the gain using 31st March 1982 value of £669. As this gives the lower gain, 31st March 1982 value would be used.

4.0 BONUS ISSUES AND RIGHTS ISSUES - ITEMS OF THE SAME CLASS

These are dealt with in the same way as for quoted shares.

5.0   REORGANISATIONS INCLUDING TAKEOVERS AND BONUS ISSUES AND RIGHTS ISSUES OF ITEMS OF A DIFFERENT CLASS

Normally there will be no immediate computation on a reorganisation, unless part of the gain is realised by the receipt of cash. Where part of the new holding is sold, an appropriate amount of cost or 31st March 1982 value is taken using the part-disposal formula.

Illustration

B bought 2,000 £1 shares in Unquoted Ltd. on 1st January 1983 for £5,000. On 30.6.1986 there was a rights issue of 1:2 debentures at 90. £500 debentures were sold at par on 6th April 1990 when the value of the shares was £4 each.

RPI		
January 1983	82.6	
April 1985	94.8	
June 1986	97.8	
April 1990	120.0	

	Shares	Indexed Cost £	£
Cost - January 1983	2,000	5,000	
Indexation to April 1985			
$\dfrac{94.8 - 82.6}{82.6}$		740	
		5,740	
Rights Issue - June 1986:			
Indexation to June 1986			
$\dfrac{97.8 - 94.8}{94.8}$		182	
		5,922	
Cost of rights to £1,000 Debentures		900	
		6,822	
Indexation to April 1990			
$\dfrac{120.0 - 97.8}{97.8}$		1,549	
		8,371	
Disposal Proceeds of debentures			500
Cost £8,371 x $\dfrac{500}{500 + (500 + 8,000)}$		(465)	465
			35
Carried forward		7,906	

CHAPTER TWENTY-FOUR

Wasting Assets

1.0 GENERAL

A wasting asset is one with a predictable useful life of 50 years or less. Land is specifically excluded from the definition.

2.0 TANGIBLE MOVABLE PROPERTY

Where the wasting asset is tangible movable property, there will be no liability to CGT on a disposal. Thus gains will not be assessed nor losses allowed.

An exception to this rule is plant and machinery in respect of which capital allowances have been or could have been given. These will produce a capital gain in the normal way without any wasting away of cost if the disposal proceeds exceed cost, unless they would fall under the chattels rules. In the case of disposal at a loss, any capital allowances claimed are to be excluded from the cost of the plant. If plant was owned at 31st March 1982 any capital allowances made in 1982/83 or subsequent years are treated as made in respect of the 1982 value.

3.0 INTANGIBLE PROPERTY

This type of property is liable to CGT and the cost must be depreciated to take account of the reduction in cost prior to sale. Assets which fall into this category will include:

(a) Options

(b) Copyrights

(c) Trademarks

(d) Certain patents

(e) Life interests in settled property where the expected life of the life tenant is 50 years or less.

441

(f) Short leases (treated separately below).

In all cases, apart from certain options, the cost of the asset must be reduced by the fraction:

$$\frac{\underline{Remaining\ life\ of\ the\ asset}}{Original\ life\ of\ the\ asset}$$

thus writing off the cost on a strict time basis evenly over the life of the asset. Where the asset has a residual value, this will be deducted from cost before making any calculations. Indexation is always calculated on the reduced cost.

Illustration

D acquired the copyright to a book on 6th April 1982. It had 30 years to run at the date of acquisition and cost £24,000. It was assigned to B on 6th April 1990 for £ 19,000.

	RPI	April 1982	81.0	
		April 1990	120.0	

	£
Disposal proceeds	19,000
Cost £24,000 x $\frac{22}{30}$	17,600
	————
	1,400
Indexation $\frac{120.0 - 81.0}{81.0}$ x £17,600	8,466
	————
	(7,066)
	=====

Where the asset is an option, the calculations can be divided into two types:

(a)   traded options;
(b)   other options.

3.1 Traded Options

These are options which are quoted on the London Stock Exchange or in the London International Financial Futures Exchange or on certain overseas exchanges. They include commodity and financial futures and over-the-counter financial options. They are not treated as wasting assets and if the option is abandoned, the cost of the option will constitute an allowable loss. If the option is bought and subsequently sold there will be a chargeable gain or allowable loss according to the rules for quoted shares, etc.

3.2 Other options

These are normally treated as wasting assets. When an option is granted, the grantor is assessed on the full consideration received. The grantee may add the cost of the option on to the cost of the asset to be aquired but if the option is abandoned there will not be an allowable loss. If the option is acquired and subsequently sold it will be necessary to waste away the cost over the life of the option using only the residual cost in the CGT computation.

4.0   SHORT LEASES

Unlike other assets, a short lease is deemed to waste away on a curved line basis. This will mean that each year is given an actuarial value using the tables contained in CGTA 1979, Sch.3. This is given below:

CGTA 1979, SCH.3
SHORT LEASES PERCENTAGE TABLE

Years	Percentage	Years	Percentage
50 (or more)	100	25	81.100
49	99.657	24	79.622
48	99.289	23	8.055
47	98.902	22	76.399
46	98.490	21	74.635
45	98.059	20	72.770
44	97.595	19	70.791
43	97.107	18	68.697
42	96.593	17	66.470
41	96.041	16	64.116
40	95.457	15	61.617
39	94.842	14	58.971
38	94.189	13	56.167
37	93.497	12	53.191
36	92.761	11	50.038
35	91.981	10	46.695
34	91.156	9	43.154
33	90.280	8	39.399
32	89.354	7	35.414
31	88.371	6	31.195
30	87.330	5	26.722
29	86.226	4	21.983
28	85.053	3	16.959
27	83.816	2	11.629
26	82.496	1	5.983
		0	0

Disposal of a leasehold interest can take two forms:

(a)   an assignment,
(b)   a granting.

4.1 Assignments

Where a lease is assigned, the vendor disposes of his entire interest in the lease. It is therefore a disposal. As with other wasting assets it will be necessary to reduce cost by the fraction:

Remaining life of the lease on disposal
Life of the lease on acquisition

but before applying it to the cost, it must be converted to the Sch.3 values.

Illustration

B acquired a lease with 35 years to run for £10,000 on 1st May 1982. He sold it for £ 21,000 on 1st May 1992.

$$
\begin{array}{lll}
\text{RPI} & \text{May 1982} & 81.6 \\
           & \text{May 1992} & 140.0 \\
\end{array}
$$

$$
\begin{array}{lr}
 & \pounds \\
\text{Disposal proceeds} & 21{,}000 \\
\text{Cost £10,000 x } \left(\dfrac{25}{35}\right) \dfrac{81.100}{91.981} & 8{,}817 \\
 & \overline{} \\
 & 12{,}183 \\
\text{Indexation } \dfrac{140.0 - 81.6}{81.6} \text{ x £8,817} & 6{,}313 \\
 & \overline{5{,}870} \\
 & \overline{\overline{}} \\
\end{array}
$$

If the duration of the lease is not in complete years, the table value can be found as under:

(a)   eliminate days by rounding to the nearest month, odd days of 14 or more being rounded up;

(b)   add to the table value for the last full year, one-welfth of the difference between that figure and the next higher in the table for each complete month.

Illustration

A lease has a duration of 34 years 7 months and 25 days. The Sch.3 value is:

$$
\underset{91.156}{34 \text{ years}} + \left(\frac{8}{12} \text{ x } \underset{91.981}{35 \text{ years}} - \underset{91.156}{34 \text{ years}} \right) \text{ rounding 25 days upwards} = \underline{\underline{91.706}}
$$

Where the lease was acquired before 31st March 1982 and a claim under s.96 FA 1988 made, the gain will be found in the normal way but using the value at that date. The lease will thus be deemed to have been acquired on that date for the purpose of depreciation.

Illustration

C acquired a 40-year lease on 6th April 1964 for £30,000. He assigned it on 6th April 1990 for £40,000. The March 1982 value was £30,000 and an election has been made under s.96 FA 1988 for all assets held on 31st March 1982.

$$
\begin{array}{lll}
\text{RPI} & \text{March 1982} & 79.4 \\
           & \text{April 1990} & 120.0 \\
\end{array}
$$

		£
Disposal proceeds		40,000

March 1982 value £30,000 x $\left[\dfrac{16}{24}\right]$ $\dfrac{64.116}{79.622}$ 24,158

                                                      15,842

Indexation $\dfrac{120.0 - 79.4}{79.4}$ x £24,158   12,345

                                                      3,497

Where there has been improvement expenditure, then each part of the original cost and improvement expenditure must be reduced assuming that it was incurred on the first day of a lease which began on the date that the expenditure was incurred and ended on the date that the main lease expired.

Illustration

D acquired a 45-year lease of a property on 6th April 1984 for £20,000. He improved it as under:

Extension	6.4.1985	Cost	£10,000
Extension	6.4.1987	Cost	£8,000

The lease was assigned on 6th April 1990 for £90,000.

RPI	April 1984	88.6
	April 1985	94.8
	April 1987	101.8
	April 1990	130.0

                                              £   £

Disposal proceeds   90,000

Costs:

Original property £20,000 x $\left[\dfrac{39}{45}\right]$ $\dfrac{94.842}{98.059}$ 19,344

Extension 1   £10,000 x $\left[\dfrac{39}{44}\right]$ $\dfrac{94.842}{97.595}$ 9,718

Extension 2   £8,000 x $\left[\dfrac{39}{42}\right]$ $\dfrac{94.842}{96.593}$ 7,855

                                                               36,917

                                                                 53,083   C/fwd

		£	£
			53,083 B/fwd

Indexation

Cost -   £19,344 x $\dfrac{130.0 - 88.6}{88.6}$ 9,034

Extension 1 - £9,718 x $\dfrac{130.0 - 94.8}{94.8}$ 3,605

Extension 2 - £7,855 x $\dfrac{130.0 - 101.8}{101.8}$ 2,176   14,815

                                                              38,268
                                                              ======

Where the lease is a long lease on disposal, it will not be necessary to use the Sch.3 tables and the gain or loss will be calculated as though it were the normal disposal of an asset.

Illustration

E bought a 99-year lease for £50,000 on 1st April 1972. It was assigned on 6th April 1990 for £150,000. The value at 31st March 1982 was £64,000. An election has been made under s.96 FA 1988.

              RPI   March 1982   79.4
                      April 1990   120.0

	£
Disposal proceeds	150,000
March 1982 value	64,000
	86,000
Indexation $\dfrac{120.0 - 79.4}{79.4}$ x £64,000	32,704
Chargeable gain	53,296
	======

If the lease is a long lease on acquisition but a short lease on disposal, the calculation will be as for the disposal of a short lease.

Illustration

F bought a 60-year lease on 1st April 1984 for £20,000 and sold it on 1st April 1998 for £90,000.

              RPI   April 1984   88.6
                      April 1998   150.0

	£
Disposal proceeds	90,000

Cost £20,000 x $\dfrac{46}{60}$ $\dfrac{98.490}{100.00}$

	19,698
	70,302

Indexation $\dfrac{150.0 - 88.6}{88.6}$ x £19,698

	13,651
	56,651
	=====

4.2 Grantings

A granting is the creation of a subsidiary interest out of a superior interest; it is therefore a part disposal. There are three types of grantings:

i)   the grant of a short lease out of another short lease;
ii) the grant of a long lease out of a freehold or another long lease;
iii) the grant of a short lease out of a freehold or a long lease.

(a) The grant of a short lease out of another short lease

This will normally give rise to two tax liabilities:

i)   a liability to income tax under Schedule A on the grant of the short lease.

ii) a liability to CGT on the grant of the right.

The CGT liability is calculated as under:

	£
Disposal proceeds	x

Cost x $\dfrac{\text{Duration of headlease on grant of sublease} - \text{Duration of headlease at end of sublease}}{\text{Duration of the headlease when originally acquired}}$

			(x)
			x
<u>Less:</u> Indexation			(x)
			x
		£	
<u>Less:</u> Assessable Premium:			
Premium		x	
Less: $2 \left[\text{Duration of sublease} - 1 \text{ in years} \right]$ % thereof		(x)	(x)
Balance of gain assessable			x
			===

The assessable premium will be liable in full even if it exceeds the chargeable gain. If it does, then the chargeable gain will be reduced to nil - it will not turn it into a loss.

Illustration

G acquired a 40-year lease on 6th April 1985 for £30,000. On 6th April 1990 he granted a 20-year sublease for a premium of £28,000 and a rent of £1,000 per annum.   RPI April 1985 94.8
April 1990 120.0

		£	£
Disposal proceeds			28,000
Cost £30,000 x $\dfrac{35 - 15}{40}$			
x $\dfrac{91.981 - 61.617}{95.457}$			9,543
			18,457
Indexation $\dfrac{120.0 - 94.8}{94.8}$ x £9,543			2,538
Chargeable gain			15,919
Assessable premium:			
Received		28,000	
Less: 2(20 - 1)% x £28,000		10,640	
			17,360
Chargeable gain assessed			Nil

No capital loss

(b) The grant of a long lease out of another long lease or a freehold

As the lease granted is long there will be no Schedule A liability. The gain will be calculated using the normal part-disposal formula in which the market value of the remainder will be made up of two elements:

i)   the capital value of the rents to be received measured at the date of granting;

ii) the value of the reversionary interest.

Illustration

H bought a 125-year lease on 6th April 1983 for £25,000. He granted a 60 year lease to J on 6th April 1990 for £30,000 and a rent of £1,000 per annum. The capital value of the rents was calculated at £17,641 and the value of the reversionary interest was fixed at £22,000.

RPI   April 1983   84.3
April 1990   120.0

	£
Disposal proceeds	30,000

Cost £25,000 x $\dfrac{£30,000}{£30,000 + (17,641 + 22,000)}$ 10,770

                                                                   19,230

Indexation $\dfrac{120.0 - 84.3}{84.3}$ 4,556

Chargeable gain   14,674

(c) The grant of a short lease out of a long lease or a freehold

Again there will be a liability to Schedule A on the premium. The calculation of the chargeable gain will be:

	£
Premium	x
Less: 2 years of duration % thereof of lease - 1	x
Liable under Schedule A	x
Disposal proceeds	x

Cost x $\dfrac{\text{Disposal proceeds}}{\text{Total Premium + Capital value of the rents and value of the reversionary interest}}$

	x
	x
Indexation	x
Chargeable gain	x

Illustration

K acquired a freehold property on 19th June 1985 for £40,000. He granted to L a 21-year lease on 6th April 1990 for a premium of £30,000. The value of the reversionary interest was £16,000 and the capital value of the rents was estimated at £28,000.

RPI   June 1982   95.4
        April 1990 120.0

	£
Premium	30,000
<u>Less</u>: 2(21 - 1)% x £30,000	12,000
	18,000
Disposal proceeds	12,000

$$\text{Cost } £40,000 \times \frac{£7,200}{£18,000 + £(16,000 + 28,000)} \qquad 4,645$$

$$\qquad\qquad\qquad\qquad\qquad\qquad\qquad\qquad\qquad 7,355$$

Indexation

$$£4,645 \times \frac{120.0 - 95.4}{95.4} \qquad\qquad\qquad 1,198$$

Chargeable gain   £6,157

(d) Relief for premiums paid

In all the above examples, the method of acquiring the lease was left open.
When a person acquires a lease it may be either by assignment from an
earlier owner or by the grant of a new lease or sublease. Where a short
lease has been granted then the landlord will be assessed under Schedule A
and the grantee will be able to obtain relief for the chargeable amount of
the premium paid by deduction from either:

i)   trading profits
ii)   rent received from the grant of a sublease.

The method of giving relief is calculated by the following formula:

$$\frac{\underline{\text{Chargeable amount assessable on landlord}}}{\text{Duration of lease}}$$

The amount of relief given as above will reduce cost on a subsequent
disposal.

Illustration

L granted to M a 40-year lease for a premium of £30,000 on 1st January 1983. On
31st December 1990 M assigned the lease to N for £60,000. M was a trader and
prepared accounts to 31st December annually.

	RPI	January 1983	82.6
		December 1990	125.0

	£	£
Disposal proceeds		60,000
Cost £30,000 x $\left[\frac{32}{40}\right] \frac{89.354}{95.457}$	28,082	
C/fwd	28,082	60,000

		£	£
b/f		28,082	60,000

Relief for premium paid to L:

	£
Premium paid	30,000
<u>Less:</u> 2(40 - 1) % x £30,000	23,400
	6,600

Annual relief £6,600/40 = £165

Relief already obtained £165 x 8		1,320	
			26,762
			33,238
Indexation $\dfrac{125.0 - 82.6}{82.6}$ x £26,762			13,729
Chargeable gain			£19,209

CHAPTER TWENTY-FIVE

Business Problems

1.0 RETIREMENT RELIEF

Where a taxpayer aged over 60 has a material disposal of business assets which include:

(a) the whole or part of a business;

(b) shares or securities in a family company (which can either be a trading company or the holding company of a trading group)

then 'retirement' relief may be available. Full relief is available provided that the person retiring:

(a) is aged over 60;

(b) has a qualifying period for relief of at least ten years.

It is not necessary to retire to qualify for relief; so long as the person disposing of the asset is aged over 60 he may retain his business interests.

The full relief available is the aggregate of:

(a) £125,000 and

(b) one-half of the gains between £125,000 and £500,000.

Illustration

O, aged 64 years, retired and sold his business premises for £694,000. The premises had cost him £90,000 in 1983. His chargeable gain (ignoring indexation) will be:

		£
Disposal proceeds		694,000
Less: Cost		90,000
		604,000
Less: Retirement relief	£	
a) Full	125,000	
b) $\frac{1}{2}$£(500,000 - 125,000)	187,500	312,500
		291,500

Where the qualifying period is less than ten years the amount of retirement relief will be proportionately reduced.

Illustration

M, aged 64, retired from his business after eight years. He sold the goodwill for £350,000. It had cost him £10,000 eight years ago in 1983. (Ignore indexation).

		£
Disposal Proceeds		350,000
Cost		10,000
		340,000
Retirement Relief -		
Maximum available	£	
a) full - 8/10 x £125,000	100,000	
b) 1/2 relief -		
£(340,000 - 100,000) x 1/2	120,000	220,000
		120,000

The maximum limit for half gain relief is 8/10 x £500,000 i.e £400,000. If the gain on the goodwill was £540,000, the relief would be:

		£	£
Gain			540,000
Retirement Relief -			
a) full - 8/10 x £125,000		100,000	
b) 1/2 relief -			
£(400,000 - 100,000)		150,000	250,000
			290,000

No retirement relief is available unless the qualifying period is at least one year.

Where the taxpayer retires before the age of 60, retirement relief may still be available provided the retirement was due to ill-health. This will be decided by the Inland Revenue.

A qualifying period is one during which the taxpayer was either:

(a) in business; or

(b) owned shares in, and was a full-time working director of, a family company.

1.1 Disposal of a business or an interest in a business

Relief will be given on the disposal of business assets. For this purpose, these may consist of all or part of a business and an interest in a partnership. The calculation of the relief is as under:

	£
Gains, **less** losses on chargeable business assets	x
Less: Retirement relief	x
	x

A chargeable business asset is an asset (including goodwill but not including shares, securities or other assets held as investments) which is used for the purpose of a trade, profession or vocation carried on by the individual concerned. For full relief the taxpayer must have traded for a qualifying period of at least 10 years.

Illustration

Y had been trading since 6th April 1970 as a sole trader in a grocery business. On 6th April 1990 he retired, aged 62, and sold his entire business as a going concern to Z.   The assets sold were:

	Cost	Date of acquisition	31.3.82 value	Disposal proceeds
	£		£	£
Land and buildings	10,000	6.4.1970	100,000	350,000
Leasehold shop	30,000	6.4.1985		45,000
		(40-year lease)		
Goodwill	-	-	14,000	60,000
Plant - no item worth more than £3,000	12,000	6.4.1983		6,000
Debtors				15,000
Stock				32,000
Cash				19,000

In addition, creditors of £14,000 were taken over by Z.

Election has been made under s.96 FA 1988 i.e. 31st March 1982 value to be used throughout.

```
            RPI      March 1982      79.4
                     April 1985      94.8
                     April 1990     120.0
```

Chargeable Business Assets sold	£	£	£

Land and buildings:

		£	£
Disposal proceeds		350,000	
March 1982 valuation		100,000	
		250,000	

Indexation $\dfrac{120.0 - 79.4}{79.4}$ x £100,000

		£	£
		51,100	
		198,900	198,900

Leasehold shop:

		£	£
Disposal proceeds		45,000	
Cost £30,000 x $\left[\dfrac{35}{40}\right]$ $\dfrac{91.981}{95.457}$		28,908	
		16,092	

Indexation $\dfrac{120.0 - 94.8}{94.8}$ x £28,908

		£	£
		7,690	8,402

Goodwill:

		£	£
Disposal proceeds		60,000	
March 1982 valuation		14,000	
		46,000	

Indexation $\dfrac{120.0 - 79.4}{79.4}$ x £14,000

		£	£
		7,154	
		38,846	38,846

	£
	246,148

Less: Retirement relief	£	£
Full	125,000	
1/2 £(246,148 - 125,000)	60,574	
		185,574
		60,574

The goodwill is deemed to have been acquired for nil consideration and built up over the period of ownership of the business.

1.2 Disposal of shares in a family company

To obtain relief:

(a) the company must be a trading company or the holding company of a trading
     group; a company will be a trading company if it exists wholly or mainly for
     the purpose of carrying on a trade;

(b) the taxpayer must be a full-time working director of the company. A
     full-time working director is one who is required to devote all, or
     substantially all, of his time to the company in a managerial or technical
     capacity;

(c) the company must be a family company. This is one in which:

     i)   the taxpayer controls at least 25% of the voting power personally, or

     ii) he controls at least 5% of the voting power personally and more than
          50% of the voting power is held by members of the family including him.

     Family includes the husband or wife of an individual, and a relative of the
     individual or of the individual's husband or wife. A relative means
     brother, sister, ancestor or lineal descendant.

Calculation of the relief: £

(1) Find the gains on the shares disposed of   x (A)
                                                                           =

(2) Find the gain attributable to the chargeable business assets:

$$\text{Gains on shares} \times \frac{\text{Chargeable business assets}}{\text{Total chargeable assets}} \qquad \text{x (B)}$$

     Chargeable Assets are all the company's assets except those
     which would not be liable to CGT (i.e. cash, stocks, debts,
     etc.).

     Chargeable Business Assets are all assets, including goodwill,
     (but not including shares or securities or other assets held as
     investments), which are used for the purposes of the company's
     trade and are chargeable assets.

(3) Deduct Retirement Relief   (x)
                                                                           __
                                                                            x

(4) Assess the remainder of the gain (A - B)   x
                                                                           __
                                                                            x
                                                                           =

For full relief the conditions in (a),(b) and (c) above must all be satisfied for
a qualifying period of at least 10 years.

Illustration

X retired on 6th April 1990 and sold all his shares in his family trading company for £75 each. He had acquired his shares as under:

16.12.1968	1,000 shares cost	£1,000
6.4.1970	1,000 shares cost	£2,000
6.4.1976	1,000 shares cost	£3,000

The balance sheet of the company at 6th April 1990 was:

	£		£
Share Capital 10,000 shares of £1	10,000	Freehold property	80,000
Profit and Loss account	200,000	Goodwill	20,000
		Plant and machinery	15,000
	210,000	Motor cars	8,000
Creditors	12,000	Stock	12,000
		Debtors	30,000
		Investments	40,000
		Cash	17,000
	222,000		222,000

It was agreed that all the assets were valued at proper market values apart from the freehold property which was worth £100,000. The plant was a single item of machinery.

X was aged 61 years at the date of his retirement.

RPI	March 1982	79.4
	April 1990	120.0

The value of X's shares at 31st March 1982 was agreed at £20 each and an election has been made under s.96 FA 1988.

Gains on shares:	£
Disposal proceeds	225,000
March 1982 value	60,000
	165,000
Indexation $\frac{120.0 - 79.4}{79.4}$	30,660
	134,340

Attributable to Chargeable Business Assets:

£

$$£134,340 \times \frac{£ \ (100,000 + 20,000 + 15,000)}{£(00,000 + 20,000 + 15,000 + 40,000)}$$ 103,634

Less: Retirement relief   125,000
                                                                          _____
                                                                            NIL
Remainder of gain £(134,340 - 103,634)   30,706
                                                                          _____
                                                                          30,706
                                                                          ======

Where an individual has been involved in two or more businesses, then provided that the relevant conditions are fulfilled, the qualifying periods may be aggregated in order to determine the amount of retirement relief due, provided that any gap between them does not exceed 2 years.

Retirement relief is also available in certain circumstances on disposals by trustees and by directors or employees, of assets held for the purposes of his office or employment.

2.0   TRANSFER OF A BUSINESS TO A LIMITED COMPANY

On the transfer of the business of a sole trader or a partnership to a limited company there will often be a transfer of business assets (e.g. land, building and goodwill) which is a chargeable event for CGT purposes.

Relief is given for this gain provided that:

(a)   the business is transferred as a going concern together with all its assets, or all assets other than cash;

(b)   the business is transferred wholly or partly for shares issued by the company to the transferor;

(c)   the transferor is not a company.

If the transfer is for shares only, the total gain is deferred until the shares are finally sold. This gain is brought into charge at the date of sale by reducing the cost of shares by the amount of the gain.

The calculation of the deferral will be:

£
(1)   Find gains on assets transferred   x

(2)   Defer the amount of the gain, found by the fraction:

$$\text{Gains on assets} \times \frac{\text{Value of shares}}{\substack{\text{Value of total consideration,} \\ \text{i.e. net assets transferred}}}$$ x
                                                                               ___
      Assess   x
                                                                               ===

Illustration

Assume the facts of Y above except that instead of retiring, Y transferred his entire business to Y Ltd for a consideration of:

> £50,000 cash
> 150,000 £1 Ordinary Shares fully paid

	£
Gain on assets transferred	246,148
Deferred £463,000 £513,000	222,157
Immediate Assessment	23,991

Note: The value of the assets transferred is the total value of assets less the creditors.

The deferred gain will be deducted from the value of the shares:

	£
Value of shares	463,000
Less: Gain deferred	222,157
Revised cost	240,843

3.0 ROLL-OVER AND HOLD-OVER RELIEF

If a taxpayer disposes of a business asset and replaces it within the period commencing one year before the date of the disposal and ending three years after that date, he is permitted to deduct the chargeable gain made on the disposal from the cost of the replacement asset thereby postponing the chargeable gain until a subsequent disposal. This procedure can be repeated for as long as one business asset is replaced with another asset provided the assets are within the following categories:

(a) Land and buildings. Furnished holiday lettings under FA 1984,s.50 are also eligible for roll-over relief where the new asset is disposed of after 5th April 1982;

(b) Fixed plant; satellites, space stations and spacecraft;

(c) Ships;

(d) Aircraft;

(e) Goodwill;

(f) Hovercraft;

(g) Milk and Potato quotas.

The first asset does not have to be replaced by a similar asset. Thus a ship can be sold and the gain rolled-over against the purchase of, say, goodwill.

The first asset and the replacement asset must be used for the purposes of the taxpayer's trade. If the taxpayer, either successively or at the same time, carries on two or more trades, those trades are treated as a single trade for the purposes of this relief.

Illustration

Charles Wilson sold his freehold factory (which cost £30,000 in June 1982) for £40,000 on 1st June 1986 and invested the whole amount in the freehold of a similar factory which he acquired on 1st January 1987. He sold the factory for £48,000 on 1st December 1989 and did not reinvest the proceeds.

RPI		
	June 1982	81.9
	June 1986	97.8
	January 1987	100.0

The capital gains tax position, assuming roll-over relief is claimed will be:

<u>On disposal of factory 1</u>

	£
Sale proceeds	40,000
Less: Cost	30,000
Chargeable gain	10,000
Indexation $\frac{97.8 - 81.9}{81.9}$	5,820
	4,180

As the proceeds of sale were fully reinvested within three years of disposal by purchasing an eligible asset, the chargeable gain may be rolled-over and deducted from the cost of the new asset so that the gain on the disposal of that asset will be correspondingly increased, thus, assuming RPI for December 1989 to be 115.0, the position will be:

	£
Cost of factory 2	40,000
Gain rolled-over	4,180
Revised cost for CGT purposes	35,820
Disposal proceeds factory 2	48,000
Cost	35,820
	12,180
Indexation $\frac{115.0 - 100.0}{100.0}$	5,373
Chargeable gain	6,807

Where the taxpayer does not reinvest all the disposal proceeds, there will be an immediate liability to CGT on the non-reinvested gain equal to the proceeds not reinvested. The balance of the gain may then be rolled-over. Thus, if in the above illustration, factory 2 cost £37,000 instead of £40,000 the position would be:

	£	£
Immediate assessment:		
Disposal proceeds		40,000
Less: Cost of factory 2		37,000
		3,000
Disposal proceeds factory 2		48,000
Cost	37,000	
Less: Balance of gain rolled-over	1,180	
		35,820
		12,180
Indexation		5,373
Chargeable gain		6,807

The intention of the rebasing rules in FA 1988 is broadly to exclude from taxation, gains arising pre-31st March 1982 and to charge gains made after that date (for individuals) at higher rates of tax. This could produce difficulty where for example an asset was acquired before 31st March 1982 and disposed of after that date but before 6th April 1988. In this situation:

(a) the pre-1st April 1982 gains would continue to remain in charge;

(b) no rebasing at 31st March 1982 would be possible as disposal took place before 6th April 1988;

(c) The pre-1st April 1982 gain might be liable at the higher marginal rate of 40% (for an individual).

To remedy this situation, where any deferred gains relate in whole or in part to a period before 31st March 1982, they will be halved.

Illustration

R bought a freehold property on 1st April 1975 for £30,000 and used it in her trade as a manufacturer. She sold it on 15th April 1987 for £100,000 and claimed full roll-over relief against another qualifying asset which was still held at 5th April, 1988. The March 1982 value was considered to be the same as cost.

```
          RPI       March 1982     79.4
                    April 1987    101.8
```

	£
Disposal Proceeds	100,000
Cost	30,000
	70,000
Indexation $\dfrac{101.8 - 79.4}{79.4}$	8,460
Qualify for deferral	61,540
But deferral reduced to	30,770

Thus the remaining part of the gain becomes free of tax.

The deferred part of the gain will reduce the cost of the new qualifying asset.

Where part of the asset is not used for trading purposes, then the gain attributable to that part will not qualify for roll-over relief.

Illustration

A bought a freehold factory on 1st January 1983 for £200,000. He used 90% of it in his manufacturing business and sublet the remainder. He sold it on 6th April 1990 for £400,000 and immediately reinvested £350,000 in another freehold factory.

RPI	January 1983	82.6
	April 1990	120.0

	£	
Sale of Factory 1:		
Disposal proceeds	400,000	
Cost	200,000	
	200,000	
Indexation $\dfrac{120.0 - 82.6}{82.6}$	90,600	
	109,400	

	£	£
Analysis of gain:		
Available for roll-over 90%	98,460	
Immediately assessed 10%	10,940	10,940
	109,400	

c/f		10,940

	£	£
b/f		10,940
Assessment of proceeds not reinvested:		
Proceeds	400,000	
Less: 10%	40,000	
	360,000	
Reinvested	350,000	10,000
Immediate assessment		20,940
Cost of second factory	350,000	
Less: Gain rolled-over	88,460	
Revised CGT cost	261,540	

Capital allowances (if appropriate) will be available on the full purchase cost less non-qualifying expenditure.

Where the replacement asset is a depreciating asset, the rolled-over gain is not deducted from the cost of the replacement asset since this cost is depreciated and it would therefore effectively mean that the postponed gain is depreciated. The charge to CGT on the gain deferred is postponed until the earliest of the following events:

(a)   the passing of ten years from the date of acquisition of the replacement asset;

(b)   the sale of the replacement asset;

(c)   the cessation of trade, or the cessation of the use of the asset in the trade.

The postponed gain will be deemed to arise during the year of assessment (or accounting period) in which the earliest of these events takes place and the capital gains tax will be calculated according to the rates ruling in that year of assessment etc.

A depreciating asset is one with a predictable life of 50 years or less or one which will have a life of 50 years or less at any time within ten years of acquisition. Instead of roll-over the term hold over is applied to this situation. The term will normally cover all the qualifying assets referred to in classes (a) to (g) above except freehold and leasehold property with a life of more than 60 years and goodwill.

Illustration

Z bought a freehold factory in June 1983 for £30,000. He sold it on 19th June 1989 for £50,000 and immediately reinvested £46,000 in fixed plant. This was sold on 6th April 2002 for £100,000.

		RPI	June 1983	84.8
			June 1989	112.0
			April 2002	200.0

	£	£
1988/89		
Sale of factory:		
Disposal proceeds		50,000
Cost		30,000
		20,000
Indexation $\dfrac{112.0 - 84.8}{84.8}$		9,630
		10,370
Immediate assessment on:		
£50,000 - £46,000		4,000
Cost of plant		46,000
Gain held over	6,370	
1999/2000		
Held-ver gain assessed at expiration of 10 years from acquisition	6,370	
2002/2003		
Disposal proceeds of plant		100,000
		54,000
Indexation $\dfrac{200.0 - 112.0}{112.0}$		36,156
Chargeable gain		17,844

Where, within the hold-over period, the taxpayer acquires a non-depreciating asset he may elect to substitute the hold-over claim for a roll-over claim against the cost of the non-depreciating asset. This will have the effect of converting a temporary deferral into one which is semi-permanent. To obtain full relief the cost of the non-depreciating asset should be at least equal to the disposal proceeds of the first asset. If this is not so, then only part of the held-over gain can be converted.

4.0 RELIEF IN RESPECT OF LOANS TO TRADERS

Where a loan has been made to a trader after 11th April 1978, and that loan later becomes irrecoverable, then any loss will be treated as an allowable loss for CGT purposes. To obtain relief, the loan must be a qualifying loan, which is one where:

(a)   the money lent is used by the borrower for the purpose of carrying on a trade other than the trade of moneylending;

(b)   the borrower is UK resident;

(c)   the debt is not a debt on security.

The Revenue must be satisfied that the debt is irrecoverable.

Relief will be obtained in the fiscal year or accounting period in which the claim for relief is made. It is, however, possible to backdate the claim for up to two years provided that at that time the debt was irrecoverable.

If the debt is recovered either wholly or partly, there will be a chargeable gain equal to the amount recovered which will be assessed in the year of recovery.

The relief also applies to payments made under a guarantee.

5.0 PARTNERSHIPS AND CAPITAL GAINS

Dealings in partnership assets are treated as those of the individual partners and not those of the firm. The CGT liability will be assessed on the partners individually. The treatment of partnership gains is set out in a Revenue press release of January 1975, as amended by other Statements of Practice.

5.1 Nature of the asset liable to tax

As far as the partnership assets are concerned, each partner is treated as owning a fractional share of each asset. Where it is necessary to find the value of a partner's share in an asset for CGT purposes, it will be taken as a fraction of the value of the total partnership interest in the asset with no discount for the size of the share. When a new partner joins the partnership, he will be treated as acquiring a share in the partnership assets from the other partners.

Illustration

A was a sole trader. On commencement of trade in 1983 he acquired goodwill for £20,000. In 1986 he took B into partnership at which time the goodwill was valued at £ 30,000. The partnership business was sold in 1990, goodwill realising £50,000.

The agreement between A and B provided that profits and losses were to be shared equally. Ignore indexation.

In 1986, A will be treated as having sold one-half of the goodwill to B.

	£
Disposal proceeds:	
½ x £30,000	15,000
Cost - ½ x £20,000	10,000
Chargeable gain	5,000

In 1990, each partner will be treated as having sold his share of the goodwill:

	A	B
	£	£
Disposal proceeds	25,000	25,000
Cost	10,000	15,000
Chargeable gain	15,000	10,000

To give a liability to CGT, there must normally be a disposal. A mere revaluation of assets with a credit to the partners' capital accounts in profit-sharing ratio will not constitute a disposal. Where, on the admission of a partner, there is no revaluation of assets, then there will not normally be any liability to CGT as the incoming partner will only be paying the other partners an amount equal to their share of the cost of the asset.

Thus, if in the above illustration, the goodwill was not revalued on the admission of B, the position would be:

	£
On admission of B:	
Disposal proceeds	
½ x £20,000	10,000
Cost - ½ x £20,000	10,000
	-

	A	B
On sale of the goodwill:	£	£
Disposal proceeds	25,000	25,000
Cost	10,000	10,000
Chargeable gain	15,000	15,000

A liability to CGT will also arise when there is a change in partnership profit-sharing ratios including changes arising from a partner joining or leaving the partnership. In these circumstances, a partner who reduces or gives up his share in asset surpluses will be treated as disposing of part or the whole of his share in each of the partnership assets and a partner who increases his share will be treated as making a corresponding acquisition. The normal disposal consideration will be a fraction of the current balance sheet value of each chargeable asset. Where no upward revaluation is made of the asset values, there will only be an adjustment to the original cost of the asset.

Illustration

A, B and C have been in partnership since 1983 sharing profits in the ratio 3:2:1. As from April 6th 1990 they decide to share profits equally. All the assets of the partnership are properly valued, apart from the freehold premises which cost £50,000 and which are presently worth £110,000. It has been decided not to make an upward revaluation. Ignore indexation.

	A	B	C
Current profit-sharing ratio	50%	33 1/3%	16 2/3%
New ratio	33 1/3%	33 1/3%	33 1/3%
Increase/(decrease)	(16 2/3)	-	16 2/3

Chargeable gain - A		£
Disposal proceeds	16 2/3% x £50,000	8,333
Cost	16 2/3% x £50,000	8,333
		Nil

Adjustments to cost:	A	B	C
	£	£	£
Original	25,000	16,667	8,333
Disposal	(8,333)		
Acquisition			8,333
	16,667	16,667	16,666

If the revaluation were made:

Chargeable gain - A		£
Disposal proceeds	16 2/3% x £110,000	18,333
Cost	16 2/3% x £ 50,000	8,333
Chargeable gain		10,000

Adjustments to cost:	A	B	C
	£	£	£
Original	25,000	16,667	8,333
Disposal	(8,333)		
Acquisition			18,333
	16,667	16,667	26,666

Where an asset is disposed of by the partnership to a third party, each of the partners will be treated as disposing of his fractional share of the asset. Similarly, if a partnership makes a part disposal of an asset, each partner will be treated as making a part disposal of his fractional share. In finding gains and losses, disposal proceeds will be allocated between the partners in the ratio of their shares in asset surpluses at the time of the disposal. Expenditure on the acquisition of assets by the partnership will be allocated between the partners in the same way, at the time of acquisition. This allocation may require adjustment, as above, if there has been a subsequent change in the partnership sharing ratios.

Illustration

D, E and F have been in partnership for many years sharing profits 5:4:3 throughout. In 1974 the firm acquired a freehold office block for £210,000 and sold it on 6th April 1990 for £960,000. The value at March 1982 was £400,000; an election has been made under s.96 FA 1988 by all parties.

RPI	March 1982	79.4
	April 1990	120.0

	D (5)	E (4)	F (3)
	£	£	£
Disposal proceeds	400,000	320,000	240,000
March 1982 value	166,667	133,333	100,000
	233,333	186,667	140,000
Indexation $\dfrac{120.0 - 79.4}{79.4}$ x £400,000	85,167	68,133	51,100
	148,166	118,534	88,900

Illustration

G, H and J are in partnership sharing profits 3:2:1. In 1970 the firm acquired a property for £30,000 and sold it on 6th April 1990 for £90,000. In 1985 J had been admitted as a partner in place of I who had retired. The profit-sharing ratio as between G, H and I was maintained on the admission of J. J paid £10,000 to I in 1985 for his share of the property. (Ignore indexation).

1970	G £	H £	I £	J £
Cost of property	15,000	10,000	5,000	
1985				
Disposal proceeds/cost to J			10,000	10,000
			————	
Chargeable gain			5,000	
			======	
1990				
Disposal proceeds	45,000	30,000		15,000
	————	————		————
Chargeable gain	30,000	20,000		5,000
	======	======		======

6.0 COMPANIES

6.1 General

Where a company disposes of a capital asset, the same rules of computation apply as for an individual in determining the amount of the chargeable gain or allowable loss. Reliefs specifically applying to individuals (e.g. the £5,000 annual exemption) are ignored. Instead of CGT, a company pays corporation tax on the chargeable gain.

Chargeable gains, after deducting allowable (capital) losses of the current period and any unrelieved capital losses brought forward, and after reduction by the specified fraction, if appropriate, form part of the total profits of the company subject to corporation tax. As such, chargeable gains may be used to relieve a trading loss where claims under TA 1988 are made. Capital losses may not be offset against trading profits.

6.2 Groups and capital gains

(a) Definition. A group is one consisting of a principal company and all its 75% subsidiaries. If a subsidiary has its own 75% subsidiary, then the latter company will also be a member of the group. Thus, if the following arises:

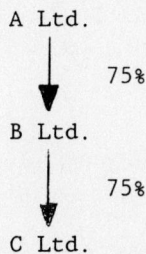

A Ltd.

↓ 75%

B Ltd.

↓ 75%

C Ltd.

all the companies will be within a group.

Restrictions have been introduced in ss.135-138 FA 1989 to prevent avoidance
by the creation of artificial groups by providing that to be within a group
the subsidiary company must be an effective 51% subsidiary of the principal
company.   Broadly this will mean that the principal company must be
beneficially entitled to more than 50% of the profits of the subsidiary
available to the equity holders of the subsidiary, and also to be
beneficially entitled to more than 50% of any of the assets of the
subsidiary available for distinction on a winding up.

Group holdings are still relevant if held through a non-resident company.
Within a group, assets will be transferred at such a price as will give
neither gain nor loss. This will normally be the cost plus any indexation
allowance. For the calculation of any subsequent allowances, the date of
acquisition of the transferor will be deemed to be that of the transferee.
Thus a capital gain will normally only arise where the asset is disposed of
outside the group. Where the holding company owns less than 75% of the
ordinary share capital of the subsidiary, any transfer of an asset is deemed
to be at market value.

Where an election is made to base indexation on the value of an asset at
31st March 1982, the acquiring company will base future indexation
calculations on original cost plus indexation calculated on the March 1982
value.   Elections under s.96 will be made by the principal company and will
bind the group.

(b) Companies leaving the group. Where a group member leaves the group, and
within the six years prior to leaving has acquired an asset from another
group member at original cost, then the company leaving will be deemed to
have made a chargeable gain equal to the difference between the cost and
market value of the asset at the date of the original transfer. Not the
date on which the company left the group.

Illustration

A Ltd. acquired a building for £50,000 in June 1983. In November 1985 it
was transferred to B Ltd., another group company, when its market value was
£90,000.   In 1987 B Ltd. was sold to another group and in April 1990 it sold
the building for £130,000.

    RPI   June 1983   84.8
             November 1985   95.9
             April 1990   120.0

Liabilities:

1985   A Ltd.   No effect; transferred at original cost plus indexation.

                                            £
    Cost   50,000

    Indexation $\frac{95.9 - 84.8}{84.8}$ 6,550
                                        _____
                                        56,550
                                        ======

1987   B Ltd.   At the time of leaving the group a gain equal to the
                difference between the original cost and its value at the
                date of transfer to B Ltd. is deemed to be made and treated
                as a gain of 1985.

	£
Market value	90,000
Cost and indexation	56,550
	33,450

	£
1990 B Ltd. Disposal proceeds	130,000
Deemed acquisition cost	90,000
	40,000
Indexation $\dfrac{120.0 - 95.9}{95.9}$	22,590
	17,410

If the asset was orginally acquired before 31st March 1982 and transferred
into group before 6th April 1988 then, as in roll-over relief, one-half of
any potentially deferred gain will not be charged to tax on a potential
disposal.

(c) Depreciatory Transactions. Where the value of a subsidiary's share is
materially reduced as a result of a depreciatory transaction, any capital
loss arising on the subsequent disposal of the subsidiary's shares may be
reduced. A depreciatory transaction can include:

i)   intragroup disposals of assets at less than market value;

ii)   any other intragroup transaction.

Illustration

C Ltd. acquired 100% of the share capital of D Ltd. for £100,000. The major
asset of D Ltd. was a freehold property which cost £20,000. After
acquisition, D Ltd. transferred the property to C Ltd. at cost, when its
market value was £ 75,000. One year later C Ltd. sold the shares of D Ltd.
for £30,000. Ignore indexation.

The transfer of the property to C Ltd. is a depreciatory transaction to the
extent of:

	£
Value at transfer	75,000
Consideration	20,000
	55,000

The loss on the disposal of the shares in D Ltd. will be restricted by this amount:

	£
Disposal proceeds	30,000
Cost	100,000
	(70,000)
Less: deducted as above	55,000
Allowable loss	15,000

As the amount of the loss on disposal of D Ltd.'s shares has been reduced by £ 55,000, it follows that double taxation could occur if on disposal of the property by C Ltd. the cost was taken as £20,000. To avoid this, an equivalent deduction is made in calculating any chargeable gain of C Ltd.

Following the rebasing to 31st March 1982, depreciatory transactions taking place before that date are ignored.

(d)   Group Roll-Over. It is possible to roll-over gains on the disposal of qualifying assets by one group company against the cost of assets acquired by another.

Illustration

D Ltd. and E Ltd. are members of a group of companies. D Ltd. disposes of a factory which had been acquired in 1984 for £100,000 on 1st July 1987, realising a gain of £20,000. E Ltd. acquires a light aircraft on 30th September 1989 for £95,000.

i)   the replacement asset has been acquired within the 3-year period commencing 1st July 1987, so that hold-over relief is available;

ii)   not all the proceeds of disposal have been reinvested, so only a portion of the gain may be held-over:

$$£95,000 - (£100,000 - £20,000) = £15,000$$

The balance of D Ltd.'s gain, £5,000, is chargeable in D Ltd.'s accounting period which includes 1st July 1987;

iii) the asset acquired by E Ltd. is a wasting asset, and thus the held-over gain of £15,000 will crystallise on the earliest of:

(1)   the cessation of E Ltd.'s trade;

(2)   the disposal of the aircraft;

(3)   ten years from acquisition of the aircraft, i.e. 30th September 1999.

As in general roll-over and balance relief, one half of any deferred gain on assets acquired before 31st March 1982 and sold before 6th April 1988 will be taken out of account.

(e) Trading Stock. When an asset is transferred by one group company to another which appropriates it as trading stock, the asset passes at cost and then the acquiring company is treated as appropriating it into stock at market value. The gain or loss may be either:

   i)   assessed or relieved in the normal way; or

   ii) be deducted from the 'cost' of the stock in the case of a gain, or added to 'cost' in the case of a loss. Thus, effectively, the assets are being taken into stock at their original cost plus indexation allowance to the transferor company.

(f) Group Relief for Capital Losses. There is no group relief for capital losses. Thus it is important to match gains and losses by either holding assets within one company or transferring assets to one company before they are sold.

(g) Non-Resident Companies. A company not resident in the UK is not within the charge to corporation tax unless it is carrying on a trade in the UK through a branch or agency. In such a case it will be liable to corporation tax on chargeable gains on the disposal in the UK of assets used in the trade. A deemed disposal will also arise on assets moved outside the UK or on cessation of trade in the UK.

(h) Close Companies. Where there is an apportionment of relevant income which has resulted in a liability to higher rate taxes or investment income surcharge, the tax thus paid will be allowable as a deduction in finding the gain on a subsequent disposal of shares.

Illustration

B acquired 30% of the shares in Alpha Ltd., a close company, on 6th April 1983 for £21,000. On 6th April 1990 he sold them for £50,000. In 1984 there was an apportionment of relevant income on B of £4,000 gross of notional ACT, on which B was chargeable at 75%. The profits subject to the apportionment have not subsequently been distributed. The basic rate of income tax in 1984 was 30%.

RPI	April 1983	84.3
	April 1990	120.0

	£	£
Disposal proceeds		50,000
Cost	21,000	
Tax at higher rates and investment income surcharge on apportionment		
£4,000 x (75% - 30%)	1,800	
		22,800
		27,200
Indexation $\dfrac{120.0 - 84.3}{84.3}$ x £21,000		8,883
		18,317

If a close company transfers an asset to any person at a value less than its
market value and the person receiving the asset is not liable either under
Schedule E or on a qualifying distribution, i.e. as an employee or as a
shareholder, then the amount of the undervalue will be apportioned amongst
the participators and will reduce the cost of their shares for CGT purposes.

Thus, if Alpha Ltd. had previously transferred a property worth £25,000 to
the friend of one of the shareholders for £15,000 then the amount of the
undervalue of £10,000 would be apportioned between the participators and B
would have to deduct from the cost of his shares 30% x £10,000 = £3,000 so
reducing his cost down to £18,000.

Following rebasing, such transactions taking place before 31st March 1982
are ignored.

7.0 RELIEF FOR LOSSES ON SHARES IN UNQUOTED TRADING COMPANIES

TA 1988,ss.574-576 provide that where a person **subscribes** for shares in an
unquoted trading company and makes a capital loss on disposal it is possible to
offset that loss against income.

The loss is calculated as for CGT purposes and may be offset against any income
in the fiscal year in which disposal takes place and/or the next fiscal year.
The order of offset is as for s.380; however, s.574 takes priority over s.380.

A qualifying trading company is an unquoted company which:

(a) is a trading company at disposal or which ceased to be such a company not
     more than three years before the disposal;

(b) is resident in the UK;

(c) has traded for at least six years prior to the date of disposal, subject to
     certain conditions.

Companies which do not trade on a commercial basis or which trade in stocks and
shares, lands or commodity or financial futures are not eligible for relief. The
disposal must normally be at arm's length or by way of distribution in a
winding-up.

If the subscriber for shares is an investment company, then it may offset the
loss against the other income in the same way as a loss under s.393.

If relief cannot be claimed under s.574, then normal CGT relief is available.

Where there are several acquisitions of shares of the same class some by
subscription and some by purchase, for s.574 purposes any disposal is identified
on a LIFO basis.

Illustration

X acquired shares in Alpha Ltd., an unquoted trading company as under:

15.10.1982	2,000 shares subscribed for at £4 each	£8,000
19.12.1984	1,500 shares purchased for	£3,700

On 6th April 1990 2,500 shares were sold for £3,000.

RPI	October 1982	82.3
	December 1984	90.9
	April 1985	94.8
	April 1990	120.0

For CGT purposes the disposal is identified in the normal way, in this case with the post-5.4.1982 pool.

	Shares	Unindexed cost	Indexed cost
		£	£
15.10.1982 Subscription	2,000	8,000	8,000
Indexation to April 1985; $\frac{94.8 - 82.3}{82.3}$			1,216
19.12.1984 Purchase	1,500	3,700	3,700
Indexation to April 1985; $\frac{94.8 - 90.9}{90.9}$			159
	3,500	11,700	13,075
Indexation to April 1990; $\frac{120.0 - 94.8}{94.8}$			3,476
			16,551
6.4.1990 Sale	(2,500)	(8,357)	(11,822)
	1,000	3,343	4,729

	£
Disposal proceeds	3,000
Cost and indexation	11,822
Capital loss	(8,822)

For s.574 purposes the disposal is identified on a LIFO basis:

(1)   with   1,500 shares purchased in 1984

(2)   with   1,000 shares subscribed for in 1982.

On the latter the loss would be:

	£
Cost	4,000
Indexation to April 1985: $\dfrac{94.8 - 82.3}{82.3}$	608
	4,608
Indexation to April 1990: $\dfrac{120.0 - 94.8}{94.8}$	1,225
	5,833
Disposal proceeds 1,000/2,500 x £3,000	1,200
Available for relief	4,633

The remainder of the loss of £8,821 - £4,633 qualifies for capital loss relief.   £4,188

CHAPTER TWENTY-SIX

Miscellaneous Matters

1.0 COMPENSATION AND INSURANCE PROCEEDS

Where an asset is destroyed, this will be a disposal for CGT purposes. Where compensation is received, then a gain or loss must be calculated in the normal way. Where, however, the whole of the compensation is applied within twelve months of receipt, or such longer period as the Revenue may direct, towards the acquisition of a replacement asset then any gain may be deducted from the cost of the replacement asset.

Illustration

A bought a piece of jewellery on 1st April 1983 for £20,000. It was stolen and on 6th April 1990 insurance compensation of £40,000 was received. This was used to acquire a replacement piece on 1st June 1990 which cost £44,000.

	RPI	April 1983	84.3
		April 1990	120.0

	£
Compensation received	40,000
Cost	20,000
	———
	20,000
Indexation $\dfrac{120.0 - 84.3}{84.3}$	8,460
	———
Chargeable gain	11,540
	======
Cost of replacement asset	44,000
Less: gain deferred	11,540
	———
Revised cost	32,460
	======

As a result of rebasing, if the jewellery had been acquired before 31st March 1982 and the compensation was received before 6th April 1988, only one half of the gain will be used to reduce the cost of the replacement asset.

Where the asset has been damaged and compensation is received this will be a part disposal; however if the compensation is wholly applied towards restoration of the asset, then there will be no assessment of any gain.

Illustration
B bought a painting for £8,000. It was later damaged by fire and compensation of £2,500 received. The cost of restoration was £3,000.

	£
Original cost	8,000
Cost of restoration	3,000
	──────
	11,000
Less: Compensation	2,500
	──────
Revised cost	8,500
	══════

Where compensation is received, but not all of it is spent on restoration, there will be a part disposal computation. If the amount not spent is small then it will be deducted from cost, thus deferring any gain. 'Small' in this context means not more than 5% of the compensation received or the value of the asset.

Illustration

C bought a Chippendale commode for £18,000 in 1983. It was damaged and compensation of £8,000 was received. The amount spent on restoration was:

(a)   £7,700

(b)   £6,000

The value of the commode after restoration was £23,000.   (Ignore indexation)

	(a)	(b)
	£	£
Compensation received	8,000	8,000
Amount spent	7,700	6,000
	─────	─────
	300	2,000
	═════	═════

5% of compensation = £400

Thus in (a), the amount not spent is small. It is less than 5% of the compensation. The position will be:

	£
Cost	18,000
Spent on restoration	7,700
	25,700
Compensation received	8,000
Revised cost	17,700

In the case of (b) however the amount not spent is substantial and there will be a part disposal computation.

	£
Amount not spent	2,000
Cost £18,000 x $\dfrac{£\ \ 2,000}{£2,000 + £23,000}$	1,440
Chargeable gain	560

The cost to be used in any future computation will be:

	£
Cost	18,000
Less: used in part disposal	1,440
	16,560
Spent on restoration	6,000
	22,560
Less: Compensation received	6,000
	16,560

2.0 RELIEF FOR GIFTS FA 1980 s.126

A gift is deemed to be made at market value for CGT purposes and this may result in a liability to tax on the donor.   Where, however, both donor and donee are individuals and the donee is resident or ordinarily resident in the UK, then relief may be claimed if the disposal is of a qualifying asset.   The relief is given by allowing the chargeable gain arising on the disposal to the donee to be deducted from the donee's cost for CGT purposes.   This will defer possible assessment of the gain until a future disposal by the donee.

A qualifying asset includes:

(a) Assets used for the purposes of a trade, profession or vocation carried on by:

    i)   the transferor; or

    ii)   his family company; or

    iii) a member of a trading group of which his family company is the trading company.

(b) Agricultural property not falling in (a) above (because it is not used for the purposes of a trade) but which qualifies for agricultural relief for inheritance tax purposes either at the 50% or 30% rates.

(c) Shares and securities in an unquoted trading company or the unquoted holding company of a trading group.

(d) Shares and securities in a company which is the individual's family company.

If the transferor is the trustee of a settlement, relief is available for broadly similar classes of assets.

Family company has the same meaning as in retirement relief.

If the gift is one of shares, relief will be restricted if the company's chargeable assets do not consist wholly of chargeable business assets.   If at any time within 12 months prior to the disposal the transferor can exercise 25% or more of the voting power or the company is his family company, the gain capable of deferral will be:

$$\text{gain} \times \frac{\underline{\text{chargeable business assets}}}{\text{Total chargeable assets}}$$

all expressed at market value.

Illustration

A bought a business property on 1st January 1983 for £10,000. He gave it to B on 6th April 1989 when its market value was £25,000.

RPI January 1983 82.6
April 1989 115.0

	£
Market value on disposal	25,000
Cost	10,000
	15,000
Indexation $\dfrac{115.0 - 82.6}{82.6}$	3,930
Chargeable gain	11,070

The cost to B would be:

	£
Market value on acquisition	25,000
Less: A's gain deferred	11,070
	13,930

This will be the cost used on a subsequent disposal. Indexation will be available from the date of the gift. Thus if B sold the property on 6th April 1990 for £40,000, the position would be:

RPI April 1990 120.0

	£
Disposal proceeds	40,000
Cost	13,930
	26,070
Indexation $\dfrac{120.0 - 115.0}{115.0}$	599
Chargeable gain	25,471

Where any part of the gain is realised, there will be an immediate liability to CGT on that amount and only the balance of the gain may be deferred. Thus, if in the above illustration of A's gift to B, A had instead sold the property to B for £14,000 the position would be:

	£
Chargeable gain as before	11,070
	======
Amount realised:	
Disposal proceeds	14,000
Cost	10,000
Immediate assessment	4,000
	======

The balance of the gain may be deferred.
   The cost to B would be:

	£
Market value of property at date of acquisition	25,000
Less: Gain deferred (£11,070 - £4,000)	7,070
	17,930
	======

The gain that may be deferred will be the final chargeable gain, i.e. after deducting retirement relief etc.

Illustration

C retired on 6th April 1990 as a full-time working director in a qualifying trading company. He was aged 63 and had satisfied all the conditions for a full amount of retirement relief. On retirement he gave his shares to his son D. The cost of the shares on 6th April 1970 was £10,000 and the market value on 6th April 1990 was £390,000. The value of the shares at 31st March 1982 was £100,000. Election is made under S.96 FA 1988 for all assets.

RPI	March 1982	79.4
	April 1990	120.0

	£
MV of shares	300,000
March 1982 value	100,000
	290,000
Indexation $\dfrac{120.0 - 79.4}{79.4}$ x £100,000	51,100
	238,900

Less: Retirement relief	£	
First	125,000	
1/2 £(238,900 - 125,000)	56,950	
		181,950

Chargeable gain	56,950
	========

Cost to D:	£
MV of shares	390,000
Less: gain deferred	56,950
	333,050
	========

If the sale at an undervalue is of an asset in respect of which retirement relief has been claimed then there will only be an assessment if the realised gain exceeds the retirement relief given. Thus, if in the illustration of C and D above, C had, instead of giving the shares to D, sold them to him for:

(a) £190,000

(b) £300,000,

the position would be:

	(a) £	(b) £
Disposal proceeds	190,000	300,000
March 1982 value	100,000	100,000
Realised gain	90,000	200,000
Less: Retirement relief	181,950	181,950
Immediate assessment	NIL	18,050
Original gain	56,950	56,950
Assessed as above	NIL	18,050
Available for deferral	56,950	38,900

If the original asset was acquired before 31st March 1982 and was gifted before 6th April 1988 any half of the gain made will reduce cost on a subsequent disposal.

Where there was also a CTT or IHT liability in respect of the gift, then the donee's cost on a subsequent disposal will be increased by the amount of the CTT or IHT paid (whether by transferor or transferee). The addition of the CTT or IHT can result in a smaller gain but cannot turn a gain into an allowable loss.

Illustration

E gave to F a property on 6th April 1985 when its value was £50,000. It had cost £ 12,000 on 6th April 1982. The CTT paid on the transfer was:

(a) £50,000

(b) £90,000

F sold the asset on 6th April 1990 for £80,000.

RPI	April 1982	81.0
	April 1985	94.8
	April 1990	120.0

	£
MV of property at date of gift	50,000
Cost	12,000
	38,000

Indexation $\dfrac{94.8 - 81.0}{81.0}$ 2,040

35,960

Cost to F:

	£
Market value	50,000
Less: Gain deferred	35,960
	14,040

On the sale by F:

	(a)		(b)	
	£	£	£	£
Disposal proceeds		80,000		80,000
Cost	14,040		14,040	
Indexation $\dfrac{120.0 - 94.8}{94.8}$	3,735		3,735	
	17,775		17,775	
CTT paid on gift	50,000	67,775	90,000	107,775
Chargeable gain		12,225		NIL

Deferral is also available when an individual transfers assets into a settlement, and also when assets are transferred out of a settlement by the trustees to the beneficiary. In all cases, a joint election is required except for transfers into a settlement.

Where deferment has been claimed and the donee ceases to be resident or ordinarily resident within six years of the claim for relief, there will be a clawback of the relief given immediately before the donee ceases to be resident or ordinarily resident in the UK.

Before 6th April, 1989 gift relief was broadly available for transfers of any asset between UK donors and donees.   If the asset gifted no longer qualified for deferral relief, CGT due can be paid by equal annual instalments over 10 years.

The assets which qualify for the instalment option are:

    i)   land;

    ii)   a controlling holding of shares or securities in any company;

    iii) minority holdings of shares or securities in companies which do not
         have a full listing or which are not quoted on the USM.

Although the tax can be paid by instalments, interest will be added on the full
amount outstanding.

The first instalment will be due on the normal due date for a payment of tax.

3.0 TRUSTEES

Where assets are transferred into a settlement there will be a disposal at
market value by the settlor. It is possible to defer the gain if gift relief is
claimed.   If the trustees dispose of trust assets in the normal course of
administration then they will be liable to CGT in the normal way but gains of
only £2,500 will normally be exempt. Where assets are transferred out of the
settlement to a beneficiary, then, again provided that gift relief is claimed,
any gains on the transfer of the assets at market value may be deferred, by
deduction from the cost to the beneficiary.

Where after 5th April 1982, the life tenant of the settlement dies the assets
will pass to the trustees at market value. There will be no liability to CGT
unless gift relief had previously been claimed on the transfer of the assets into
the settlement; if it had previously been claimed it will crystallise on death.
The assets will normally pass to the beneficiaries at the value at which they
pass to the trustees.

4.0 HUSBAND AND WIFE

Transfers between husband and wife living together are treated as being made at
such a value as gives no gain and no loss.

Relief similar to roll-over relief described earlier is available to mitigate the
potential additional liability on transfers of assets acquired pre-31st March
1982 but transferred intra spouse before 5th April 1988.

Where the spouse acquiring the asset appropriates it as trading stock, the
transfer will be treated as being made at market value and any subsequent gain on
disposal will be liable under Schedule D Case I or II.

The gains and losses of each spouse will be aggregated and the combined amount
will be liable to CGT. There is only one annual exemption available to a
married couple.

The net gain is liable as the top slice of the husband's income.

Illustration

Mr. and Mrs. A have the following gains and losses for 1989/90.

		Mr.A	Mrs.A
	£	£	£
Gains		5,600	3,900
Losses		600	400

Mr. A		
Gains	5,600	
Less: Losses	600	
		5,000
Mrs.A		
Gains	3,900	
Less: Losses	400	
	3,500	
		8,500
Less: Annual exemption		5,000
		3,500

If Mr. A already has taxable income after personal allowances of £18,700. The tax due will be:

		£
£20,700 - £18,700	£2,000 @ 25%	500
	£1,500 @ 40%	600
		1,100

Husband or wife may elect for separate assessment. If this is done, the individual gains are still aggregated and tax is calculated as before. The tax will be divided between husband and wife in proportion to their net gains. In the above this would be:

	Husband £	Wife £
Gains as above	5,000	3,500
Annual exemption - apportioned pro rata	2,941	2,059
	2,059	1,441

3,500

Tax as before   1,100

Apportioned:

$$£1,100 \times £ \frac{2,059}{3,500}$$ 647

$$£1,100 \times £ \frac{1,441}{3,500}$$ 453

1,100

A separate election can be made by 6th July following the year of assessment by either spouse that his/her net losses of a fiscal year are not offset against the gains of the other spouse.

In the year of marriage, the spouses are treated as though they were separate individuals in the same way as for income tax.

In the year of separation, husband and wife are treated as one person up to the date of separation. After separation, the wife will be treated as a separate taxable person. Up to the date of separation, the annual exemption will be apportioned between husband and wife in proportion to the husband's total gains in the fiscal year and the wife's gains up to the date of separation. After separation, the wife will be treated as a separate taxable person with her own annual exemption.

From 6th April 1990 each spouse will be assessed separately and entitled to an individual annual exemption. The losses of one spouse will not be transferable to the other, though disposals between spouses will still be treated as made on a no gain/no loss basis.

5.0 DISPOSALS TO CONNECTED PERSONS

Where a disposal is made to a connected person which is not on an arm's length basis, then the market value of the asset will be substituted for the consideration (if any).

Connected persons are broadly:

(a)   a person's spouse or relative (brother, sister, lineal ancestor or descendant) or a relative of the spouse, separated spouses are connected, divorced spouses are not;

(b)   the trustees of a settlement set up by the person;

(c)   persons in partnership with that person;

(d)   a company controlled by that person, or that person and other persons connected with him or her.

If the disposal to the connected person at market value results in a loss, that loss may only be offset against future gains on other disposals to the same connected person.

When assets which form part of a set are disposed of within a 6-year period to a connected person, then the value of the assets transferred will be the greater of:

(a)   a proportion of the market value of the total of the assets transferred in the series (taken at the end of the series);

(b)   the value of each asset if taken together they exceed the value in (a).

Illustration

X purchased a set of two candelabra on 1st July 1983 for £22,000. He sold one candelabra to his son on 6th April 1986 for £18,000 which was agreed to be its market value. The value of the other was agreed to be £15,000. He sold the other to his son on 6th April 1990 for £17,000 which was again agreed to be its market value. The value of the set to the son at 6th April 1990 was agreed to be £45,000.

RPI	July 1983	85.3
	April 1986	97.7
	April 1990	120.0

£

First disposal:

	£
Disposal proceeds	18,000
Cost £22,000 x $\dfrac{£18,000}{£18,000 + £15,000}$	12,000
	6,000
Indexation $\dfrac{97.7 - 85.3}{85.3}$ x £12,000	1,740
	4,260

    Second disposal: £

Disposal proceeds	17,000
Cost (£22,000 - £12,000)	10,000
	7,000
Indexation $\dfrac{120.0 - 85.3}{85.3}$ x £10,000	4,070
	2,930

However, as the total value to the son is £45,000 at 6th April 1990 and this exceeds £ 35,000 (£18,000 + £17,000) the Inland Revenue will require the gains to be recalculated using total disposal proceeds of £45,000. These will be split on a just and reasonable basis.

First disposal - gain recalculated:

	£
Deemed disposal proceeds - say	22,500
Cost £22,000 x $\dfrac{£22,500}{£22,500 + £15,000}$	13,200
	9,300
Indexation $\dfrac{97.7 - 85.3}{85.3}$	1,914
	7,386

Second disposal - gain recalculated:

	£
Deemed disposal proceeds	22,500
Cost £22,000 - £13,200	8,800
	13,700
Indexation $\dfrac{120.0 - 85.3}{85.3}$	3,582
	10,118

CHAPTER TWENTY SEVEN

Value Added Tax

1.0 GENERAL PRINCIPLES

Value Added Tax (VAT) is chargeable on the supply of goods or services in the UK where that supply is a taxable supply made by a taxable person in the course or furtherance of any business carried on by such a taxable person. In addition, tax is chargeable on the importation of goods and some services.

The basic principle of VAT is fairly simple - a supplier of chargeable goods or services adds VAT at 15% to the price he charges to customers and pays the total tax added over to the Commissioners of Customs and Excise (CCE) quarterly. This VAT is known as **output tax**. In making the payment to CCE, the supplier is entitled to deduct the VAT he has suffered on chargeable goods and services supplied to him. This VAT is known as **input tax**. Thus each quarter the supplier is paying to CCE his output tax minus his input tax.

As chargeable goods move from manufacturer to wholesaler to retailer to ultimate consumer, each **trader** in the chain pays input tax when he buys and charges output tax when he sells. The ultimate consumer pays the tax when he buys and has no one to pass the tax on to, and so finally bears the burden of the tax.

Illustration

A Ltd manufacturers a sewing machine and sells it to:

B Ltd, a wholesaler, for £100 plus 15% VAT	=	£115
B Ltd sells it to C Ltd. for £140 plus 15% VAT	=	£161
C Ltd sells it to D, the final consumer for £200 plus 15% VAT	=	£230

The effect on each of them is shown in the following table:

Transaction	Input Tax	Output Tax	Paid to CCE	Ultimate effect
	£	£	£	
A Ltd sale to B Ltd				
A Ltd		15	15	A Ltd - nil
B Ltd	15			
B Ltd. sale to C Ltd.				
B Ltd		21	6	B Ltd - nil
C Ltd	21			
C Ltd. sale to D				
C Ltd.		30	9	C Ltd - nil
D	30			D suffers the £30

It can be seen that A Ltd. collects £15 from B Ltd and pays it over to CCE (no
effect on A). B Ltd. suffers that £15 but collects £21 from C Ltd, and pays the
difference of £6 to CCE (no effect on B). C Ltd suffers the £21 but collects
£30 from D, and pays the difference of £9 to CCE. D suffers the £30 and stays
suffering.

1.1 Sources of the law and its interpretation

VAT was introduced by FA 1972 and came into force on 1st January 1973. Since
that time the tax has been amended and the legislation has been consolidated in
the Value Added Tax Act 1983 (VATA 1983), although further amendments have been
enacted by subsequent Finance Acts.

All statutory references are to the VATA 1983, unless otherwise stated.

VAT is administered by HM Customs and Excise.

Unlike other taxes, many detailed rules have been subordinated to Orders, Rules
and Regulations in the form of Statutory Instruments.

In addition, the Acts and the Regulations frequently allow for the Customs and
Excise to be provided with a discretion (**J.H. Corbitt (Numismatist) Ltd. v. CCE**)
in their implementation.

An indication of the likely attitude of the Customs and Excise can be obtained
from the various notices and leaflets published by them and obtainable from their
offices.

With certain exceptions (e.g. Notice 727 (Special schemes for retailers)), these
notices have no legal effect and should not be relied on when considering the
application of the law to specific transactions.

It must also be borne in mind that EEC law will prevail where there is a conflict
between that and UK law.

2.0 REGISTRATION

2.1 Introduction

A person who is or who ought to be registered as a taxable person and taxable
supplies made by that person carry with them the obligation to charge and account

for VAT. Unless registration is actually effected VAT cannot be charged so that
the VAT to be accounted for is determined by treating the consideration for the
supplies as inclusive of VAT.

It is therefore advisable that the regulations regarding the requirements for
registration are considered carefully.

Where the supplies are zero-rated the Customs and Excise have discretion to
exempt the person from having to register.

A person's liability to register dates from the time that he should have
registered rather than the time he actually does register.

2.2 Registration limits

A person is liable to register for VAT if his taxable turnover exceeds certain
limits specified in Schedule I. These are, if the turnover (exclusive of VAT)
exceeds:

(a)   £8,000 for the last calendar quarter; or

(b)   £23,600 for the last four calendar quarters.

A person is also required to register if there are reasonable grounds for
believing that the taxable turnover for the next twelve months will exceed
£23,600. Exempt supplies (see later) do not count towards the limit, nor do
supplies of capital goods.

A 'person' includes a self employed individual, limited company, partnership,
club, etc., who carries on a business activity, profession or vocation.

It is the person who is to be registered and not the business (CCE v.
Glassborrow), accordingly it is the aggregate supplies of all businesses carried
on by a person that is considered for registration purposes, restriction on input
tax, etc.

To prevent the artificial separation of business activities to avoid
registration, e.g. a husband runs a licensed public house whilst his wife
operates the catering in the premises as a separate concern so that she will be
under the registration limit, S.10 FA 1986 gives CCE powers to direct that the
separate businesses be treated as one for VAT registration etc. purposes. Before
doing this CCE must be satisfied that:

(a)   each person performs part of the activities of the overall business and
      makes taxable supplies in respect of that part;

(b)   the taxable turnover of the overall business exceeds the registration
      limits;

(c)   a major reason for the separation of activities is the avoidance of the
      liability to register for VAT.

In general, it is not possible to transfer registration from one person to
another, however, if a business is transferred as a going concern then CCE may
under s.33 VATA cancel the transferor's registration and register the transferee

with the same number. The consequences of doing this are laid down in form VAT
68 and effectively transfers the VAT obligations of the transferor to the
transferee. This will _inter alia_ include any liability to account for unpaid
VAT.

Partnership registration is in the name of the partnership.

A person liable to register must obtain form VAT 1 and submit it to the CCE no
later than 30 days after the end of the relevant quarter. Registration will then
be effective from the end of the month in which the 30th day falls or from such
other date as is agreed with the CCE. Advance registration is allowed provided
that the person can satisfy the CCE that his future turnover will exceed the
registration limits.

There are penalties for late registration, for notification up to 9 months late,
the penalty is 10% of the overdue tax. For notification over 9 months but up to
18 months late, the penalty is 20% and for notification over 18 months late, the
penalty is 30%. The minimum penalty is £50.

2.3 Voluntary registration (Sch.I, para 11)

Registration may be effected voluntarily where persons can satisfy CCE that they
are making taxable supplies even though the turnover limits have not been
exceeded. This will be desirable where, for example, the customers are all
registered persons able to reclaim the VAT charged on any supplies. Inability to
register in such circumstances would mean that the actual cost to customers may
be increased as the supplier's costs will include VAT for which no relief is
available.

The trader must notify CCE within 30 days if he ceases to make taxable supplies.

2.4 Group and divisional registration

Companies resident in the UK who are members of a group may elect to be treated
for VAT purposes as a single person. The registration need not cover all of the
companies in the group and provides opportunities for tax planning. The
principal advantages relate to reduction of administration, possible avoidance of
restrictions on input, tax credit due to the making of exempt supplies and in
cash flow.

The representative member is responsible for maintaining records, making
returns, etc., but the responsibility for the tax due is a joint and several
liability.

The application for group registration must be made at least 90 days before the
date on which it is to have effect although the Customs and Excise do have
discretionary power to accept a late claim.

A claim for group treatment means that:

(a) intra-group supplies of goods or services can be disregarded;

(b) any other supply of goods or services to or from a group member is deemed to
     be made to or from the representative member only and that this member is
     also liable for any tax payable on the importation of goods.

Companies will be within a group where the holding company controls more than one-half of its ordinary share capital.

It is also possible to apply for divisional registration if a company is split into autonomous accounting units.

2.5 Deregistration

A person may deregister for VAT if the expected taxable turnover excluding VAT in the next 12-month period will not exceed £22,600.

A person who ceases to make taxable supplies must notify CCE and the CCE will deregister him. Application for deregistration is not compulsory and a taxpayer may retain his registration if he wishes.

Deregistration is compulsory and notification must be given to CCE within 30 days if:

(a)   the business is closed down or sold;

(b)   taxable supplies are no longer made;

(c)   a business is incorporated, or a company disincorporated.

CCE must also be informed if there is no longer a need for voluntary registration or advance registration was applied for and given but taxable supplies are no longer to be made.

On deregistration VAT is due on any retained stocks of goods for resale and equipment. These must be accounted for on the last VAT return. VAT is due on all sales up to deregistration in the normal way. Normally no VAT is due on goods in respect of which no VAT has been reclaimed. VAT due on deregistration is remitted if it is £250 or less.

2.6 Changes in registration

The following changes in registration particulars must be notified to the local VAT office within 30 days:

(a)   changes in the trading name of the business and any changes in names and addresses of any partners in the business;

(b)   changes in the address of the principal place of business;

(c)   changes in trade classification;

(d)   changes in bank accounts;

(e)   changes in the composition of a partnership.

3.0 OUTPUT TAX

3.1 General

Tax chargeable on supplies is known as **Output Tax**. There are currently two
rates of tax - the standard rate of 15% and the zero rate.

3.2 Supply

Supplies of goods or services made in the UK are liable to tax. The UK
comprises England, Wales, Scotland, Northern Ireland and the territorial sea of
the UK.

As from 1st April 1980 the Isle of Man and the UK form a single VAT area
although the Isle of Man provides for its own collection and administration.

The term includes:

(a) sales, whether made directly or by an agent, on hire purchase, auction, cash
     or credit sale;

(b) hiring, leasing, rental, loan or exchange of goods;

(c) goods provided as gifts or as promotional items,

and as far as services are concerned any service provided for money or money's
worth.

Certain events are or may be deemed to be supplies:

(a) self supplies: where a person acquires or produces goods or does anything
     for the purpose of that business which would be a supply of services if made
     for a consideration - those goods or services are deemed to have been both
     supplied to and by him. Orders have been made in respect of printed
     material and cars;

(b) the private use or disposal of assets is deemed to be a supply of services
     or goods respectively.

Certain supplies are not considered to be supplies for VAT purposes:

(a) the sale of certain repossessed goods;

(b) transactions within a VAT group of companies;

(c) goods lost or destroyed (this does not cover the situation where cash is
     stolen as the supply will already have occurred).

The rescission of a voidable contract **(HB Litherland & Co. v. CCE)** annuls the
supply. However, the disposal of stolen goods **(CCE v. Oliver)**, or sale subject to
reservation of title **(Vermitron v. CCE)**, are considered to be supplies.

3.3 The time of the supply - tax point

The obligation to account for VAT on a supply is determined by the prescribed accounting period in which the tax point falls.

For VAT purposes the time when a supply of goods or services takes place can have far-reaching effects not only because it may determine whether a person is liable to register himself, but also because it helps to dictate the amount of VAT he must pay in a particular period. The time at which a supply of goods or services is deemed to take place is known as the 'tax point', i.e. the point at which VAT becomes chargeable.
There are special rules governing the time of supply. Subject to certain alternative rules (which are described below), the supply of goods will be treated as taking place:

(a) if the goods are removed, at the time of the removal;

(b) if the goods are not removed at the time when they are made available to the person to whom they are supplied.

A supply of services will be treated as taking place when the services are performed.

The 'basic tax point' above will be overridden in the following circumstances:

(a) if before the time of supply mentioned above, the person making the supply issues a tax invoice in respect of it, the supply will, to the extent covered by the invoice, be treated as taking place when the invoice was issued;

(b) if before the time of supply mentioned above, the supplier receives a payment. The supply will, to the extent covered by the payment, be treated as taking place at the time the payment is received;

(c) if the supplier issues a tax invoice within a period of fourteen days following the date otherwise applicable in (a) and (b) above, the supply will be treated as taking place at the time the invoice is issued. Customs and Excise can extend the fourteen-day period (e.g. monthly invoicing).

Where goods are supplied on hire, it is provided generally that the supply will be treated as having taken place when a payment under the agreement is received.

3.4 Value of supply

Where no mention of VAT is made the consideration is deemed to be VAT inclusive. In particular where:

(a) consideration is in the form of money: the value of the supply is that amount which together with VAT thereon at the appropriate rate (governed by the rate applicable at the tax point), amounts to the consideration;

(b) consideration is not or not wholly in money: the value is taken as its market value.

Where discounts are offered, the consideration is taken to be the amount reduced by the available discount whether or not, in fact, it is taken. If discount is available at varying rates the lowest discounted value is to be taken:

Illustration

A supplies goods to B at a price of £5,000 + VAT. A discount is available of 5% for payment within 30 days. Whether or not the discount is taken, the VAT due is:

	£
Price	5,000
Less: 5% discount	250
	4,750
VAT @ 15%	712
Consideration	5,462

3.5 Special types of outputs

3.5.1 Motor cars

Where a motor car has been used in a business no VAT is due on a disposal where the disposal proceeds are less than the purchase price. Where they exceed the purchase price VAT is due in respect of the margin, which is regarded as being VAT inclusive.

Illustration

B acquired a motor car for use in his trade as a manufacturer. The cost in 1985 was £ 8,000 and because of a demand for that particular model it was resold in 1990 for £ 11,200. VAT is due on the margin as under:

$$£11,200 - £8,000 = £3,200 \times 3/23 = £417$$

3.5.2 Gifts

A gift of business assets is a supply of goods and VAT is due on the cost of those goods. No VAT will normally be due where the gift is:

(a) of goods costing less than £10 and not forming part of a series of gifts to the same person;

(b) free meals to employees.

Gifts to charities are normally exempt. The provision of trade samples would not normally be considered to be a gift and thus would not normally be liable to VAT. Prizes of goods are treated as gifts.

Gifts of services are not liable to VAT.

3.5.3 Private use

Where the proprietor of the business or an employee takes goods out of the business for personal use there is a supply and VAT will be due on the cost of those goods.

3.5.4 Loss, theft, etc.

No VAT is chargeable where the trader can satisfy CCE that goods which belong to him have been accidentally lost or destroyed. Where goods have been sold and the cash stolen, VAT will still be due.

Where goods are stolen or obtained by fraud, the trader may be able to claim relief provided that:

(a) the theft is reported to the police, and

(b) a conviction is obtained.

3.5.5 Salaries and wages

These are not liable to VAT.

3.5.6 Sales on hire purchase

These are supplies of goods and tax is due in the normal way. The hire purchase finance charge is exempt. Where goods are repossessed because of the default of the purchaser this is not treated as a supply of goods. A sale of repossessed goods by the person who repossessed them is generally a supply of goods and VAT will be due unless:

(a) the goods are covered by one of the secondhand schemes, e.g. cars, antiques, caravans, etc., and

(b) the goods are sold by the repossessor in substantially the same condition as when they were acquired.

If these conditions are satisfied then the disposal will be outside the charge to VAT.

3.6 Local and national authorities

Goods and services supplied to a national or local authority are liable to VAT in the normal way. Where such an authority provides goods or services liable to VAT then the tax must be charged and a VAT invoice provided in the normal way.

3.7 Exports

Exports are zero rated, and thus no VAT will be chargeable. The exporter will need to satisfy CCE that export has occurred. This can be done by producing when required:

(a) the customer's order;

(b) the exporter's copy invoice;

(c) copies of the airfreight documents or bills of loading for sea freight etc.;

(d) evidence of payment by the customer.

Exports on sale or return or transfers of goods by a UK trader to a place of business abroad are not taxable supplies.
A retail export scheme is available for overseas visitors who purchase goods in the UK and who intend to leave the UK within 3 months of purchasing the goods and who have not been in the UK for more than 365 days out of the two years preceding the purchase of the goods. Certain goods are not eligible including motor cars, motor cycles and motor caravans; to qualify for zero rating these must be exported direct. To qualify, the visitor must be asked to provide evidence that he qualifies for zero rating - normally by producing his passport. Once the supplier is satisfied he will charge VAT in the normal way but provide the visitor with VAT form 407 describing with registration or identification marks the goods purchased. When the visitor leaves the UK, he will produce the form and goods to customs at the port of embarkation who will certify it. The form will then be returned to the supplier who will refund the VAT charged.

3.8 Relief for bad debts

Relief for bad debts can be claimed if the customer has been made bankrupt or entered into a scheme of arrangement.

The goods and services supplied must not have been supplied for more than market value, and the supplier must have accounted for the output tax.

In making the calculation:

(a) specific payments on account are allocated to the invoices to which they relate;

(b) general payments on account are allocated to earlier debts rather than to later debts;

(c) amounts due to the customer are set off against amounts due from him.

Illustration

An individual has made standard and zero rated supplies to XYZ Ltd. XYZ Ltd has recently gone into liquidation and will be unable to pay its creditors.

Invoices have been issued as follows:

Tax Point	Net	VAT Rate	Gross
	£		£
17th April 1990	25,000	nil	25,000
11th May 1990	12,234	15%	14,069
19th August 1990	18,197	15%	20,926
7th November 1990	11,500	nil	11,500

XYZ Ltd has made a payment of £3,000 on account of the invoice dated 19th August 1990, and general payments on account of £17,000 and £9,600. On a separate contract, the individual owes XYZ Ltd £1,056.

	Total Debt £	Specific Allocation £	General Allocation £	Amount Unpaid £	VAT Rate	VAT Repayment Claim £
17.4.90	25,000		25,000	-	Nil	
11.5.90	14,069		2,656	11,413	$\frac{15}{115}$	1,489
19.8.90	20,926	3,000	-	17,926	$\frac{15}{115}$	2,338
7.11.90	11,500			11,500	Nil	
	71,495	3,000	27,656	40,839		3,827

	£
Amount received	17,000
Amount received	9,600
Set-off	1,056
	27,656

	£
Claim from Customs & Excise	3,827
Claim from liquidator	37,012
	40,839

Note: It is not possible to reduce the amount of outstanding debt by the issue
of credit notes.

Where a dividend is subsequently received there are no provisions to claw back
any of the VAT recovered.

In the case of an overseas bad debt then the VAT charged cannot be recovered.

3.9 The cash accounting scheme for small businesses

As from 1st October 1987, traders with a turnover of not more than £250,000 will
be allowed to account for and recover VAT on a cash basis. Tax invoices will
continue to be issued in the normal way but VAT will only be due when payment is
received; similarly, input tax can only be recovered when the invoice is paid.
As no VAT will be due until payment is received, the new system will give
automatic relief for bad debts.

3.10 Annual accounting

Commencing on 1st July 1988, businesses which have been registered for at least
12 months and whose turnover is less than £250,000 will be able to apply for VAT
to be calculated on an annual basis. Only one VAT return will be submitted each
year but the business would make nine agreed payments on account by direct debit
with a balancing payment accompanying the 10th payment and annual return, which
must be submitted within two months after the end of the accounting period.

The payment on account will be based on the previous year's liability.

4.0   INPUT TAX

4.1   Introduction

Input tax is the tax on the supply to a taxable person, of goods or services and
on the importation of any goods used or to be used for the purposes of any
business carried on or to be carried on by him.

Relief is granted to taxable persons for input tax, primarily by set off against
VAT to be accounted for on supplies made.

Where the input tax exceeds the output tax in any prescribed accounting period
the excess is refunded to the taxable person.

Although it is any taxable person who is entitled to relief, not just registered
persons, claims by non-registered persons are likely, in practice, to be met with
resistance.

Section 23, however, provides for relief to be granted to a person carrying on a
business in the EEC but not in the UK whereas s.21 provides for relief to
do-it-yourself house-building ventures.

VAT on non-business goods or services received will not be recoverable. This
will include items acquired for private use or supplied to the trader for the use
of another person. Where there is partial private use CCE will restrict the
recovery of input tax.

Illustration

C incurs repairs on a building used partly for his residence and partly for business. The agreed ratio is 40:60. The repair bill is £1,000 + VAT.

The recoverable VAT will be:

    £1,000 x 15% = £150 x 60% = £90

4.2   Irrecoverable input tax

Certain input tax suffered is irrecoverable whether or not the expense relates to the business; it includes:

(a) business entertaining:

    VAT suffered on entertaining is always disallowed unless it relates to food or accommodation provided to staff.

(b) motor Cars:

    Tax on private cars, but not on vans, lorries, London taxis, etc., cannot be recovered. If the vehicle is a private car then no recovery is permissible even if the vehicle is wholly used for business purposes. VAT on repairs and maintenance can be reclaimed in full even if the car is used partly for private motoring.

    As from 6th April 1987, traders can recover all the input tax on petrol irrespective of business or private use. Instead the petrol used by the proprietor or employee will be deemed to be a supply to him and VAT will be due. The deemed value of the supplies of fuel will be:

	VAT inclusive supply		VAT Due	
cc of vehicle	Quarterly	Monthly	Quarterly	Monthly
	£	£	£	£
Up to 1400 cc	120	40	15.65	5.21
1401 - 2000 cc	150	50	19.56	6.52
2001 cc and over	225	75	29.34	9.78

Where business mileage exceeds 4,500 per quarter or 1,500 per month the value is reduced by one-half.

Where VAT cannot be recovered it will increase the revenue or capital cost which may then be treated as a trade expense or qualify for capital allowances as appropriate.

4.3 Imports

VAT on importation is chargeable and payable as if it were a customs duty.
Prior to 1st October 1984 a registered taxable person could adopt a postponed
accounting system whereby the VAT is shown on the return in which that VAT is
claimed - it is treated as both an output and an input. Effectively therefore,
VAT was not paid until the goods were sold, when VAT on the full consideration
was accounted for. Since 1st October 1984, VAT must be paid on imports and the
postponed accounting system has been abolished.

A number of reliefs are available:

(a) where goods would otherwise be zero rated (s.16);
(b) where Customs and Excise legislation in respect of customs duties is
     extended by s.24;

(c) by Treasury Orders and Regulations (in respect of goods used for
     demonstration, personal goods of small value imported from the Isle of Man
     or the EEC).

After 31st May 1985, provided ownership is not transferred to the processor,
taxable persons need not pay VAT on importation in respect of:

(a) goods temporarily imported for repair or renovations and re-exported with
     the same identity (i.e. goods restored to their original condition); and

(b) goods temporarily imported for modifications or processing and re-exported
     with the same identity. The relief will not apply to materials for
     manufacture into other goods or goods imported only for warehousing, or
     minor handling such as re-packing.

Also from 1st June 1985, goods which have been temporarily exported and are
re-imported after repair, process or adaptation, will bear VAT only on the value
of the repair etc., plus freight and insurance, provided the goods are
re-imported by, or on behalf of, the original exporter and property in the goods
has not been transferred.

5.0 EXEMPTION AND ZERO RATING

5.1 Exemption

Certain supplies are either exempt or zero rated.

If a trader's supplies are totally exempt then he is not liable to register for
VAT irrespective of the size of his turnover. As he is not registered, however,
he will not be able to reclaim input tax. The main categories of exempt
supplies are:

(a) land - the grant, assignment or sale of land or of an interest in land is
     exempt. This will not cover the provision of accommodation in a hotel etc.,
     holiday accommodation, car parking fees, etc. From 1st August 1989, the
     vendor has an option to tax land at the standard rate;

(b) insurance;

(c)   postal services provided by the Post Office;

(d)   betting, gaming and lotteries;

(e)   finance charges;

(f)   education provided by schools, universities-polytechnics and other
      non-profit-making bodies;

(g)   the provision of health care by a registered medical practitioner or in
      certain hospitals etc. The provision of certain goods and appliances;

(h)   burial and cremation, the funeral of a pet is not exempt;

(i)   subscription to professional bodies, learned societies, trades unions and
      trade associations.

(j)   certain disposals of heritage property where neither IHT nor CGT is
      chargeable

5.2 Partial exemption

Where a person makes both taxable - normal or zero rate - and exempt supplies
then he may not be able to recover all the input tax suffered.

As from 1st April 1987 a partially exempt trader will not normally be able to
recover any exempt input tax. This is defined as input tax which is
attributable wholly or partly to exempt supplies.

Broadly:

(a)   input tax suffered on supplies which are subsequently reflected in taxable
      outputs can be recovered in full;

(b)   input tax suffered on supplies which are subsequently reflected in exempt
      outputs cannot be recovered;

(c)   input tax not directly attributable to either taxable or exempt supplies -
      the remaining input tax - will be apportioned and recovered in a reasonable
      way. This will be by agreement with CCE but would normally be on a suitable
      pro rata basis. Methods indicated by CCE would include:

Remaining input tax   x   tax wholly attributable to taxable supplies
                                total input tax on taxable, exempt and
                                partly exempt supplies

It will be possible to recover all exempt input tax where it is less than
any of the following:

(a)   £100 per month on average; or

(b)   both £250 per month on average and 50% of all input tax;

(c)   both £500 per month on average and 25% of all input tax.

5.3 Zero rating

A person making zero rated supplies is a taxable person if his turnover exceeds
the registration limits and will be liable to register despite the fact that no
VAT is chargeable on his outputs. This will be advantageous to him because he
can now recover VAT on inputs.

The major zero rated supplies are:

(a) food and drink - This is zero rated if it is provided for human
     consumption unless it is supplied in the course of catering, for
     consumption on the premises where the supply was made or is hot take-away
     food. Sweets, crisps, alcoholic and many non-alcoholic soft drinks are
     standard rated. Animal feeding stuffs, but not pet food, are zero rated;

(b) the provision of water and sewerage services other than services to industry
     from 1st July 1990;

(c) books, newspapers, maps, music, etc.;

(d) talking books and wireless sets, and recording apparatus for the blind;

(e) fuel and power other than petrol; from 1st July 1990 fuel and power supplied
     to commercial concerns will be standard rated;

(f) the sale of land and the construction of new domestic buildings other than
     professional fees, hire of goods etc. Repairs are generally standard rated
     unless they relate to a protected building;

(g) passenger transport in a ship, vehicle or airplane designed to carry 12 or
     more persons. Commercial freight services outside the UK or transport to or
     from a place outside the UK;

(h) mobile caravans and houseboats;

(i) gold and bank notes;

(j) drugs, medicines and certain supplies made to a sick or disabled person;

(k) certain imports and exports;

(l) certain supplies to charities;

(m) clothing and footwear for young children and certain protective clothing;

(n) certain commodity transactions on a terminal market.

6.0 SPECIAL SCHEMES FOR RETAILERS

Normally a taxable person has to account for VAT each time he supplies goods or
services to a customer. This is called output tax. To account for output tax in
the **normal VAT way**, the taxable person needs to have a record of every separate
transaction. Most retailers cannot keep a record of that kind for all their

sales, because they do not usually issue invoices to their customers or make any written record at the time when a sale takes place. The special schemes for retailers allow retailers to calculate output tax (or most of it) in other ways, which vary according to the particular scheme.

A retailer for this purpose can include anybody whose business consists mainly of supplying goods or services direct to the public without tax invoices.

There are nine different schemes for retailers to choose from. Some of them are suitable only for certain types of business and some have conditions or limits in them which mean that not every retailer is allowed to use them.

7.0 ADMINISTRATION

7.1 General

The Board of Commissioners - a Chairman, two Deputy Chairmen and Commissioners - are responsible for the management, administration and collection of VAT. The local VAT offices are in direct contact with taxable persons. Control visits are made every two to three years, usually by prior appointment.

The VAT (General) Regulations make provisions obliging taxable persons to notify the Customs and Excise of changes in their circumstances. Customs and Excise are empowered to request any information they may require about any goods and supplies of goods or services such as the consideration or the name and address of the recipient of the supply.

Samples may be taken (Sch.7), books and documents may be removed and Customs and Excise are empowered to require security before a supply can be made where, for example, they have reason to believe that VAT will not be accounted for.

Customs and Excise are empowered to exchange information with the Revenue.

In extreme cases the Customs and Excise have the power of entry and search (Sch.7, para.10) and to distrain goods and chattels where tax has not been paid after it had been demanded by the Collector.

7.2 Returns

At regular intervals a taxable person must render accounts of input and output tax and return them to the Revenue on Form VAT 100. This will show the net amount of VAT payable by or repayable to him. The period for which a return is made is known as the tax period and the standard period is three months. Where, however, a taxable person expects his input tax to regularly exceed his output tax, he may have a tax period of one month. In order to spread the flow of returns evenly over the year, the three-month return periods are staggered. Where the net tax payable is £1 or more, the full amount must be paid at the same time that the return is made. Similarly, when the net tax repayable is £1 or more the Customs and Excise will make a refund of the amount due. If the tax due or repayable is under £1 then a return must still be made, but the payment or repayment is waived. If a registered person fails to make a return when it is due, or if he makes an incomplete return the Customs and Excise have power to make estimated assessments. These will be made under Schedule 7, in the following circumstances:

(a) the absence of proper information;

(b) failure to make returns;

(c) failure to keep proper records;

(d) where it appears to the Customs and Excise that a submitted return is incomplete or incorrect.

The time limits for the making of estimated assessments are:

(a) two years after the end of the prescribed accounting period, or

(b) one year after the evidence of facts sufficient in the opinion of the Customs and Excise to justify the making of the assessment, comes to their knowledge.

Further assessments may be made if an estimated assessment proves to be insufficient, so long as they are based on further information that has come to light.

The normal time limit for the making of assessments is six years after the end of the prescribed accounting period. In the case of fraud, wilful default or neglect, the assessment can, with the leave of the VAT Tribunal, be made at any time. An appeal to a VAT Tribunal can be made against any assessment.

In winding-up or bankruptcy proceedings, VAT limited to that which has become due within a period of twelve months ending at the relevant date, enjoys the same priority as other taxation liabilities.

Distress may be levied on a trader's goods under a warrant signed by a Collector of Customs and Excise if the trader refuses or neglects to pay any actual or estimated amount of tax due from him.

Records

Every taxable person must keep such records as the Commissioners of Customs and Excise may require (currently for six years). These will consist of the following:

(a) tax invoices relating to inputs;

(b) evidence of tax on imported goods;

(c) copies of tax invoices attributable to outputs;

(d) details of credits allowed to customers and received from suppliers;

(e) details of errors and adjustments requiring collection;

(f) details of any self supplies.

Special requirements are provided by the Value Added Tax General Regulations 1980, as to the issue and content of VAT invoices. As a general requirement a taxable person when making a taxable supply to another taxable person must supply him with a tax invoice. The invoice must include all the following items, although the exact order and layout are immaterial:

(a) the name, address and VAT registered number of the supplier;

(b) the date of the supply;

(c) the number of the invoice;

(d) the name and address of the person to whom the goods or services are supplied;

(e) the type of supply;

(f) a description sufficient to identify the goods or services supplied ;

(g) the amount payable before VAT for each of the descriptions;

(h) the rate of any discount offered;

(i) the rate and amount of tax chargeable.

In the case of retailers it is recognised that the task of making out separate tax invoices would be extremely burdensome. It is provided therefore that such a person is not generally required to provide a tax invoice. If, however, he is requested to do so, and the value of the supply is under £50 inclusive of VAT, then the tax invoice need only contain the following details:

(a) the name, address and registration number of the retailer;

(b) the date of the supply;

(c) a description sufficient to identify the goods or services supplied;

(d) the total amount payable including tax;

(e) the rate of tax in force at the time of making the supply.

The tax invoices do not have to accompany the VAT return but must be kept available for inspection for six years,

If, in addition to supplies taxable at one or more positive rates of tax, a tax invoice includes zero rated or exempt supplies, it will be necessary to show clearly which items bear no VAT charge.

Special rules apply to traders who adapt the till rolls produced by their cash registers to serve as tax invoices.

7.3 Computers

Taxable persons are able to forgo the need to provide tax invoices and instead
opt for the necessary information to be recorded in a computer and to be
transmitted to the customer electronically (directly from computer to computer).

It is a condition of the legislation that the Customs and Excise be given at
least one month's notice for the person to comply with any conditions that the
Customs and Excise might impose. In this respect it should also be noted that
all records may be maintained on a computer provided it can be readily converted
into a form capable of inspection by the Customs and Excise on request.

The Customs and Excise should be consulted at the design stage when considering
using computer-based accounting systems for VAT.

7.4 Accounts

It is necessary to summarise taxable transactions and record the VAT in an
appropriate account. This is to enable the Customs and Excise officers to check
the accuracy of the returns. The Commissioners of Customs and Excise require
records to be kept for such period as they may require. This is normally six
years. The records may be kept in bound books or by such other means (i.e. in a
computer) as the Commissioners may approve. An example of a specimen VAT
Account may appear as follows:

SPECIMEN VAT ACCOUNT FOR FULLY TAXABLE PERSONS

	£	£		£	£
Input Tax (inclusive of tax on imported goods and goods from bonded warehouses):			Input Tax		
August	849.10		August		1,199.00
September	870.30		September		1,096.10
October	816.90		October		932.00
		2,536.30			3,228.00
			Tax due on imported goods and goods from bonded warehouses:		
			August	70.20	
			September	40.30	
			October	72.80	
					183.30
Overdeclaration and/or overpayments of tax in respect of previous periods:			Underdeclarations and/or underpayments of tax in respect of previous periods:		
Notified by Customs and Excise	Nil		Notified by Customs and Excise	Nil	
Other	271.60		Other	213.70	
		271.60			213.70
TOTAL TAX DEDUCTIBLE		2,807.90			
By credit transfer		817.10			
TAX PAYABLE		3,625.00	TOTAL TAX DUE		3,625.00

The officers of the Customs and Excise have considerable powers as to the obtaining of information, copies of records and samples of goods. In the obtaining of these items, the officers may at any reasonable time enter the premises used in connection with the carrying on of a business. Powers of forcible entry, seizure and search are available on the granting of a warrant by a Justice of the Peace.

Where an authorised person removes any documents etc., he must, on request, provide a record of what has been removed. The officer in overall charge of the investigation must, on request, allow access to such documents etc., and allow them to be photocopied unless he has reasonable grounds for believing that to do so would prejudice any investigation or criminal proceedings.

7.5 Penalties

Criminal penalties involving fines and imprisonment are available for certain tax offences including:

(a) fraudulent evasion of tax;

(b) furnishing or producing with intent to deceive, false documents or making knowingly or recklessly false statements;

(c) making false returns;

(d) dealing in goods or services upon which tax has not been paid.

Civil penalties are also chargeable in addition to those above for a number of offences including:

(A) tax evasion involving dishonesty;

(B) serious misdeclarations or neglect resulting in understating tax due or overclaiming recoveries;

(C) failure to notify a liability to register;

(D) the unauthorised issue of VAT invoices;

(E) breaches of regulations.

A taxable person who fails to submit a return or pay the tax shown on a return within the required time is in default. If the default continues for more than two return periods in any 12-month period then the CCE may serve a surcharge liability.

The liability surcharge is the greater of:

(a) £30; and

(b) 5% of the outstanding tax for the first default period, 10% for the second default period up to a maximum of 30% for the sixth and any later period.

No civil penalty under (B) or (C) above arises where the person satisfies CCE or a tribunal that there is reasonable excuse for his conduct. A tribunal has no general power to vary the amount assessed as a penalty.

From December 1989 a serious misdeclaration penalty will apply where a taxpayer's true VAT liability is understated by more than 30% of the true amount of the tax, or the greater of:

(a)   5% of the true amount of the tax, or

(b)   £10,000.

The penalty is 30%; it can be mitigated or avoided if there is reasonable excuse.

7.6 Repayment supplements

A repayment supplement of 5% of the amount repaid or £30 whichever is the greater will be applied to repayments provided the return is received by CCE no later than 2 months after the end of the prescribed period.

7.7. Appeals

7.7.1 General

Appeals can be made against decisions of the Commissioners of Customs and Excise in respect of the following:

(a)   registration or cancellation of registration;

(b)   assessments;

(c)   tax chargeable;

(d)   tax deductible, and certain other items;

(e)   civil penalties.

On an appeal against an assessment to a penalty, etc., the burden of proof that tax has been evaded and that conduct involves an element of dishonesty, lies upon the Commissioners.

An appeal will not normally be entertained until a taxpayer is up to date on all returns and tax payable by him. In the case of items (b) and (c) above, the Commissioners may require that part or all of the tax due must be paid over before the appeal can commence. If it is subsequently discovered that it is not due then it will be repaid with interest.

Provisions similar to s.54 TMA 1970 are made for the Commissioners and an applicant or his agent to settle appeals by agreement, subject to repudiation by the appellant within 30 days.

Where an appellant notifies the Commissioners of his intention of withdrawing his appeal, unless the Commissioners object to the withdrawal within 30 days, the parties are treated as having agreed that the decision under appeal should be upheld without variation.

7.7.2 VAT Tribunals

To hear VAT appeals VAT Tribunals have been set up in major cities in the UK.
Unlike certain tribunals, they have been brought under the direct supervision of
the Council on Tribunals. This has the effect of ensuring that all alterations
in the workings of the Tribunal can only be made with the approval of the
Council.

7.7.3 Staff

The executive head of the Tribunals is the President. He is appointed by the
Lord Chancellor and must be a solicitor or barrister of at least ten years'
standing. The President may retire at any time, and can be removed by the Lord
Chancellor for incapacity or misbehaviour. His remuneration is fixed by the
Treasury.

The other members of a Tribunal consist of Chairman and members. Both are
chosen from a panel. The quorum for a tribunal is normally three but where only
two members are present the Chairman has a casting vote. Chairmen are normally
full-time and paid a salary. Other members are normally part-time and paid a fee
only.

7.7.4 Conduct of an appeal

To be effective a notice of appeal must be served at the appropriate tribunal
centre. It must be served by or on behalf of the appellant and must be signed by
him or his agent. _Inter alia_ it must state:

(a)   his name and business address.

(b)   the grounds of the appeal.

The normal time limit for the making of an appeal is 30 days after the date of a
letter from the Commissioners containing the disputed decision. This may be
extended in certain cases. When an appeal is received at the Tribunal Centre an
acknowledgement will be sent.

Within 42 days of the notification of the appeal the Commissioners of Customs
and Excise must serve at the Tribunal Centre a copy of the disputed decision and
their reasons for making it. A copy of these reasons will be forwarded to the
person making the appeal. If the Commissioners consider that an appeal does not
lie they once again must serve a notice of their reasons at the appropriate
Tribunal Centre and a copy must once again be sent to the appellant. Each party
to the appeal must deliver to the Tribunal Centre a list of the documents that
he intends to produce at the hearing together with a list of the witness
statements. He must indicate a reasonable time and place for the inspection of
these documents by the opposing party. All the documents must be available at
the Tribunal hearing. The witness statements must contain details of the
evidence proposed to be given by any witness together with his name, address and
description. If a witness is unwilling to come forward then a summons may be
issued requiring his attendance.

The appeal will normally be held in public unless the Tribunal decides that all
or part of it would be best held in private.

The taxpayer or any person whom he may appoint for the purposes is entitled to conduct his case at the hearing. A similar right applies to the Commissioners.

Where on the hearing of an appeal, no party is represented, the Tribunal may dismiss the appeal. If only one party is present then the Tribunal may proceed in the absence of the other party. In both cases the Tribunal is empowered to reinstate the appeal or set aside their decision on such terms as may be just.

7.7.5 Procedure

The procedure before the Tribunal is for the appellant to address the Tribunal and to call and examine witnesses. The opposing party can also address the Tribunal and call and examine witnesses. Both sides have the opportunity of cross-examination. Witnesses before a Tribunal are examined under oath or affirmation.

7.7.6 Decision

At the end of a hearing the decision may be announced by the Chairman. In all cases, however, a written notice of the decision is sent to both parties. This is signed by the Chairman and contains all findings of fact and the reasons for the decision.

7.7.7 Costs

Costs may be awarded by the Tribunal. These normally follow the event.

7.7.8 Appeals from the Tribunal

Under the Tribunals and Inquiries Act 1971, a party dissatisfied with a decision of the Tribunal on a point of law may appeal to the High Court, or under certain cases direct to the Court of Appeal.

7.7.9 Penalty for failure to comply with directions etc., of Tribunals FA 1985

A person who fails to comply with a direction or summons issued by a VAT Tribunal is liable, subject to appeal, to a penalty not exceeding £1,000.

CHAPTER TWENTY EIGHT

Inheritance Tax

1.0 INTRODUCTION

For many years, the major charge to tax on transfers of capital was Estate Duty. Introduced in 1894, this was widely regarded as an "avoidable tax" as careful estate planning coupled with gifts made many years before death could easily result in no charge to tax.

FA 1975 introduced capital transfer tax (CTT) to bring into taxation both lifetime and death transfers of property, thereby replacing the old estate duty legislation which was essentially a tax on death transfers only. The FA 1976 made substantial changes to the legislation, and the FA 1981 altered the future basis of charge. Other enactments have introduced minor alterations and increases in the CTT rates.

The Capital Transfer Tax (Consolidation) Act 1984 brought together all the legislation enacted.

FA 1986 introduced major changes to the legislation; the tax has now been renamed Inheritance Tax and the CTTA has been renamed the Inheritance Tax Act 1984. The major change introduced by IHTA has been to remove most lifetime transfers of goods or property from the charge to IHT provided that they are made more than 7 years before death.

2.0 LIABILITY TO TAX

2.1 General

IHT is chargeable whenever a chargeable transfer of value has been made. A transfer of value is any disposition which results in a loss in value to the transferor's estate and which is not an exempt transfer.

2.2 Scope of the tax

If the transferor is domiciled in the UK, he is liable to IHT on transfers of assets made anywhere in the world. If he is not domiciled in the UK, he is only liable on transfers of assets situated in the UK.

(a) **Situation of property**: Subject to any double-taxation agreements the following rules apply to determine where property is situated:

i) tangible property is situated where it is physically located. (<u>Note</u>: a work of art in the UK solely for public examination, cleaning or restoration will not be treated as situated in the UK if it is normally kept outside the UK);

ii) land, whether freehold or leasehold, is situated where it is physically located;

iii) registered shares and securities are situated in the country where they are registered, i.e. where the register is required to be kept;

iv) bearer securities are situated where the document of title is located at the time of transfer;

v) bank accounts are situated at the branch where the money is payable;

vi) business assets (including goodwill) are situated where the business is carried on (this includes an interest in a partnership);

vii) debts are situated in the country where the debtor resides;

viii) life policies are situated in the country where the proceeds are payable;

ix) currency is situated where it is physically located, not in the country of issue;

x) trust property is situated according to the above rules, regardless of the appropriate trust law or the residence of the trustees.

(b) **Domicile**: The general definition applies (i.e. a person's domicile is the place in which he has his fixed and permanent home, and to which, whenever he is absent, he has the intention of returning).

However, for IHT purposes a person will also be deemed to be domiciled in the UK, if at the time of a transfer:

i) he was domiciled in the UK on or after 10th December 1974 and at any time within the three years immediately preceding the transfer; or

ii) he was resident in the UK for tax purposes on or after 10th December 1974 and in at least seventeen of the twenty years of assessment ending with the year of assessment in which the transfer is made.

3.0   EXEMPT, CHARGEABLE AND POTENTIALLY EXEMPT TRANSFERS

3.1   General

IHT is chargeable when a person makes a chargeable transfer of value. A
transfer of value is any disposition which reduces the transferor's estate. A
chargeable transfer of value is a transfer of value which is not an exempt
transfer. The measure of a transfer of value is the loss to the transferor's
estate; not necessarily the gain to the transferee.

The new IHT regime divides transfers into three main categories:

(a)   exempt transfers;

(b)   chargeable transfers (CLT);

(c)   potentially exempt transfers (PET).

3.2   Exempt transfers

Certain transfers, provided that they satisfy the appropriate conditions will be
exempt from IHT.

They include:

3.2.1   Normal expenditure out of income

Where lifetime gifts are made out of income they are wholly exempt from IHT
provided that the transferor can show that:

(a)   the transfer was part of his normal expenditure. Normal is equivalent to
      typical or habitual and would entail such expenditure recurring for at least
      three years. However, the first payments on a life assurance policy or a
      deed of covenant are treated as normal, and retrospective exemption may be
      given for other gifts once normality is established; and

(b)   taking one year with another the gift was made out of income. 'Income' is
      net income after income tax and the exemption is not lost merely because of
      fluctuations in yearly income; and

(c)   he was left with sufficient income to maintain his usual standard of living;
      this being the personal standard normally maintained by the transferor
      himself.

In practice, a transferor with an established pattern of gifts (of say £1,000
per annum) is likely to be able to claim the exemption in respect of such gift
even if it is made to a new transferee.

3.2.2   Small gifts

Outright lifetime gifts are exempt from IHT provided they do not exceed £250 to
any one individual in any one tax year. A transferor may, thus, make any number
of gifts below £250 (say fifty gifts of £200 each) to different donees, and each
of them would be exempt.

3.2.3 Transfers on marriage

Gifts in consideration of marriage are exempt from IHT up to a limit which is
dependent on the relationship between the transferor and the parties to the
marriage. The gifts (whether outright or settled) must be made or promised
before and in consideration of a particular marriage, which must take place. The
exemptions are:

(a)   £5,000 if the transferor is a parent of one of the parties to the marriage;

(b)   £2,500 if the transferor is a grandparent or remoter ancestor of one of the
      parties to the marriage;

(c)   £2,500 if the transferor is one of the parties to the marriage;

(d)   £1,000 if the transferor is any other person.

The exemption is given to each transferor in respect of any one particular
marriage, and so the four parents of the bride and groom (if alive) can each give
an exempt £5,000. If an individual gift is over £5,000, the annual exemption
might be applied to all or part of the balance. By concession, a spouse may put
his partner in sufficient funds to enable both parents to claim the £5,000
exemption without the associated operations provisions being invoked.

3.2.4 Annual Transfers up to £3,000

Lifetime gifts, which are not exempted or relieved under any other provision, are
exempt up to a total of £3,000 per transferor in any one tax year. Where the
gifts in any tax year exceed the exemption limit, they are counted towards the
limit in chronological order, the later gifts receiving less or no exemption
allowance. If the gifts in any tax year are below the exemption limit, the
unused balance may be carried forward into the following year, but no further.
The current year's exemption allowance must be fully utilised before any
brought-forward allowance can be used.

Illustration

Calculate the transfers in respect of the following gifts made by Edward if they
were made within 7 years of his death:

June 1989	£200 to his friend Alice
November 1989	£6,000 to his daughter on her marriage
January 1990	£1,500 to his niece
July 1990	£3,200 to his now closer friend Alice

		£	£
June 1989	Gift to Alice		200
	Less: small gift exemption		200
November 1989	Gift to daughter		6,000
	Less: marriage exemption	5,000	
	annual exemption 89/90	1,000	
			6,000
January 1990	Gift to niece		1,500
	Less: annual exemption 89/90		1,500
July 1990	Gift to Alice		3,200
	Less: annual exemption 90/91	3,000	
	annual exemption 89/90	200	
			3,200

(<u>Note</u>: The unused annual exemption of £300 from 1989/90 is lost.)

Where a transferor makes more than one gift on the same day the exemption is apportioned between them in proportion to the amounts that would otherwise be chargeable to tax.

Illustration

Assuming that on 10th June 1990 Edward made three more gifts to each of his grandchildren, of £1,000, £3,000 and £6,000 respectively, the transfers as a result of his death within 7 years would be:

	£	£
Gift 1	1,000	
Less: annual exemption £ $\frac{1,000}{£10,000}$ x £3,000	300	
		700

	£	£
Gift 2	3,000	
Less: annual exemption £ $\frac{3,000}{£10,000}$ x £3,000	900	
		2,100
Gift 3	6,000	
Less: annual exemption £ $\frac{6,000}{£10,000}$ x £3,000	1,800	
		4,200

If in the same year there is a potentially exempt transfer and a chargeable transfer, the latter is always deemed to be made first and will thus take the annual exemption.

3.2.5 Gifts between husband and wife

A husband and wife are each entitled to the various exemptions and reliefs in their own right (i.e. each party can claim the £3,000 annual exemption etc.), and in general, transfers between them are completely exempt from IHT. However, if the transferee is not UK domiciled, the exemption is limited to a cumulative total of £ 55,000. This prevents the transfer of UK property to a non-UK domiciled person and so creating excluded property. Where both spouses are UK domiciled or where both are non-UK domiciled the full exemption applies.

3.2.6 Gifts to charities

Outright gifts (and gifts in trust subject to anti-avoidance provisions) to UK charities are wholly exempt from IHT.

3.2.7 Gifts to political parties

Outright gifts to political parties are wholly exempt from IHT.

In order to qualify for the exemption a political party must either:

(a) have had two members elected to the House of Commons at the last general election before the gift; or

(b) have had one member elected and 150,000 votes cast for all its candidates.

3.2.8 Gifts for national purposes

Gifts of funds or property to national institutions which exist wholly or mainly for the purpose of preserving (for the public benefit) any collection of scientific, historic or artistic interest and which are approved by the Treasury, are exempt. Such institutions include:

(a) the National Gallery;

(b) the British Museum;

(c) other approved art galleries and museums;

(d) the National Trust;

(e) the Nature Conservancy Council;

(f) any library serving the needs of teaching and research at a UK university;

(g) any local authority;

(h) any UK university or university college;

(i) any government department.

The exemptions considered above are available on lifetime and death transfers as under:

	Lifetime	Death
Normal Expenditure	✓	
Small gifts	✓	
Marriage	✓	
Annual transfers up to £3,000	✓	
Gifts between husband and wife	✓	✓
Gifts to charities	✓	✓
Gifts to political parties	✓	✓
Gifts for national purposes	✓	✓
Gifts for the public benefit	✓	✓
Transfers into employee trusts	✓	✓

3.3 Chargeable transfers

All other transfers which are neither exempt nor potentially exempt are
chargeable transfers. These will need to be included in the IHT computation
when they are made and tax calculated thereon. These transfers could include:

(a)   transfers to trustees, if not exempt or partially exempt, e.g. a transfer
      into a discretionary settlement;

(b)   a transfer involving a company, e.g. a transfer of an asset at an undervalue
      by a close company.

The IHT due on a lifetime chargeable transfer will be at one-half the normal
rate.   Additional IHT may be chargeable on the death of the donor within 7 years
of making the transfer.

3.4   Potentially exempt transfers

A potentially exempt transfer (PET) is a transfer of value made by an individual
which, if certain conditions apply, might be exempt from IHT.   They broadly
comprise three main types of transfers:

(a)   to another individual;

(b)   to an accumulation and maintenance trust and with effect from 17th March
      1987 to an interest in possession trust;

(c)   to a disabled trust.

A PET will become a chargeable transfer if the donor dies within 7 years of
making it and IHT may be charged, subject to tapering relief.   If the donor
survives for 7 years after making the PET it will become an exempt transfer.
Under normal circumstances the tax on a PET becoming chargeable will be due from
the donee, subject to a right of recovery from the personal representatives of
the deceased. On death therefore additional tax may be due on a chargeable
lifetime transfer and tax may be due on a PET which has been made within the
preceding 7 years.
The tax due will be that which applies at the date of death of the donor, less
the tapering relief given in the following table and in the case of a CLT, the
tax originally paid when it was made.

Years between date of PET or CLT and date of death	Percentage of tax charged
0 - 3	100
3 - 4	80
4 - 5	60
5 - 6	40
6 - 7	20

3.5   Dispositions which are not transfers of value

Subject to the various conditions being met certain transfers, which are not
exempt, will not be considered to be transfers of value.   These will include:

3.5.1 Gifts for family maintenance

Lifetime gifts for the maintenance of family dependants will not be liable to IHT in certain circumstances:

(a) a gift for the maintenance of a spouse or former spouse is unconditionally exempt;

(b) a gift for the maintenance, education or training of a child of either party to the marriage is exempt up to the age of eighteen or until the completion of full-time education if later. This exemption is also available for any child not in the care of its parents or who is illegitimate, adopted or a step-child;

(c) a gift to make reasonable provision for the care and maintenance of a dependant relative of the transferor or his spouse is exempt if the relative is incapacitated by old age or infirmity from maintaining herself/himself (or is the widowed, divorced or separated mother of the transferor or his wife, whether incapacitated or not).

3.5.2 Gifts in the course of trade

Gifts made in the course of trade, such as Christmas gifts to staff, small gifts to customers, **ex gratia** retirement pensions to ex-employees, are exempt from IHT provided that they are an allowable deduction in arriving at the adjusted profit for income tax purposes.

3.5.3 Waivers of dividends and remuneration

A person who waives any dividend within twelve months before any right to the dividend has accrued is not treated as making a transfer of value. A general waiver of all future dividends is only effective for dividends payable within twelve months after the waiver.

A waiver of remuneration is not a transfer of value where, had the remuneration not been waived (or repaid), it:

(a) would have been assessable to Schedule E income tax;

(b) would have been deductible in computing the employer's profits for tax purposes.

3.5.4 Gifts for the public benefit

Gifts of certain national heritage property to a non-profit organisation are exempt from IHT where approved by the Treasury. This exemption applies to property comprised in a settlement as well as assets owned by individuals and covers:

(a) land of outstanding scenic, historic or scientific interest;

(b) buildings approved for preservation as being of outstanding historic, architectural or aesthetic interest, together with the cost of preservation;

(c)   land used as the grounds of any building within (b), and any object which is
      normally kept in and which is given with, a building within (b);

(d)   any print, picture, book, manuscript, work of art or scientific collection
      which is of national, scientific, historic or artistic interest;

(e)   property given to be a source of income for the upkeep and maintenance of
      any of the above to the extent that it produces no more income than is
      required.

If necessary, undertakings to ensure reasonable public access and the
preservation of the property may have to be given.

3.5.5   Transfers into employee trusts

A lifetime or death transfer of shares in a company by an individual into a
trust for the benefit of the employees of that company is exempt from IHT
provided that:

(a)   the shares are held on trust for the benefit of the majority of all
      employees of the company;

(b)   any participator who is entitled to five per cent or more of any class of
      shares in the company or to five per cent or more of its assets on a
      winding-up, cannot benefit under the trust;

(c)   at or within twelve months of the transfer, the trustees hold more than half
      of the ordinary shares in the company and have voting control of the
      company.

3.6   Gifts with reservation

A person may make a transfer of value and yet retain some interest in the
property transferred. A common example would be the gift of a taxpayer's
residence to his children subject to retaining the right to live there for the
remainder of his or her life. This type of transfer is called a gift with
reservation.

S.102 IHTA provides that a gift with reservation is one where the individual
makes a gift and either:

(a)   possession and enjoyment of the property is not bona fide assumed by the
      donee at or before the beginning of the relevant period, or

(b)   at any time in the relevant period, the property is not enjoyed to the
      entire exclusion or virtually to the entire exclusion, of the donor and of
      any benefit to him by contract or otherwise.

The relevant period is the seven years prior to the death of the donor.

If the gift is subject to the provisions, the asset will be taxed as though it
was still beneficially held by the donor.

The provisions may be avoided where:

i)   In the case of a chattel or land, the donee pays a market rent for the enjoyment of the asset, or

ii)   the occupation by the donor was unforseen and was brought about by his old age, infirmity or otherwise and is a reasonable provision for his maintenance.

3.7 Excluded property

Certain assets are ignored for IHT purposes and do not enter any IHT computation. Such excluded property includes:

(a)   property situated outside the UK if the person beneficially entitled to it is domiciled outside the UK;

(b)   settled property situated outside the UK provided the settlor was domiciled outside the UK at the time of making the settlement. This exclusion applies even when the beneficiaries of the trust property are UK domiciled on death;

(c)   certain Government securities which are exempt from income tax if owned by a person neither domiciled nor ordinarily resident in the UK (the deemed domicile provisions are ignored). Such securities comprised in a settlement also qualify as excluded property if the person beneficially entitled to an interest in possession in them is neither domiciled nor ordinarily resident in the UK.

Tax-free Government securities include certain issues of:

i) $3\frac{1}{2}\%$ War Loan;

ii)   Funding Loan;

iii) Treasury Loan;

iv)   Convertible Stock;

v)   Exchequer Stock;

(d)   certain savings held by a person domiciled in the Channel Islands or the Isle of Man. These savings are:

i)   War Savings Certificates;

ii)   National Savings Certificates;

iii) Premium Savings Bonds;

iv)   Deposits with the National Savings Banks or with a Trustee Savings Bank;

v)   Certified contractual savings schemes (e.g. SAYE).

(e) assets of a member of the armed forces passing as a result of death from
     wounds, accident or disease while on active service (or in Northern
     Ireland). Although technically an exemption, this provision is included here
     for convenience;

(f) emoluments and tangible moveable property of members of visiting forces and
     staff of allied headquarters posted to the UK;

(g) cash options under approved retirement annuity schemes;

(h) foreign currency accounts at UK banks (or the Post Office) owned by a person
     neither domiciled, resident nor ordinarily resident in the UK at the time of
     his death;

(i) a reversionary interest in settled property. A reversionary interest is a
     future interest in trust property, such as that of the remainderman of a
     trust. Although a reversionary interest could be valued actuarily, it is
     excluded for IHT purposes, provided that:

     i)   it has not been acquired at any time for a valuable consideration;

     ii) neither the settlor nor his spouse is or has been beneficially entitled
          to the reversionary interest at any time.

3.8 Omissions to act

Where a person's estate is reduced in value while another's estate is increased
in value as a result of the former's deliberate omission to exercise a right, he
is treated as having made a PET at the latest time that he could have exercised
the right. An omission benefiting a discretionary trust will be treated as a
chargeable transfer of value. This provision is designed to prevent, for
example, shareholders with control from surrendering control by failing to take
up rights issues (and so reducing the value of their holdings for IHT purposes).

4.0 CALCULATION OF THE TAX

4.1 Rates of Inheritance Tax

Death Scale:

Transfers 18th March 1986 to 16th March 1987

Cumulative chargeable transfers (gross) £	Rate %	IHT on band £	Cumulative IHT £	Rate on net
0 - 71,000	NIL	-	-	-
71,001 - 95,000	30	7,200	7,200	3/7
95,001 - 129,000	35	11,900	19,100	7/13
129,001 - 164,000	40	14,000	33,100	2/3
164,001 - 206,000	45	18,900	52,000	9/11
206,001 - 257,000	50	25,500	77,500	1
257,001 - 317,000	55	33,000	110,500	1 2/9
over 317,000	60			1 1/2

Transfers from 17th March 1987 to 14th March 1988

Cumulative chargeable transfers (gross) £	Rate %	IHT on band £	Cumulative IHT £	Rate on net
0 - 90,000	NIL	-	-	-
90,001 - 140,000	30	15,000	15,000	3/7
140,001 - 220,000	40	32,000	47,000	2/3
220,001 - 330,000	50	55,000	102,000	1
over 330,000	60			1 1/2

Transfers from 15th March 1988 to 5th April, 1989

Cumulative chargeable transfers (gross) £	Rate %	IHT on band £	Cumulative IHT £	Rate on net
0 - 110,000	NIL	-	-	-
over 110,000	40			2/3

Transfers from 6th April 1989

Cumulative chargeable transfers (gross) £	Rate %	IHT on band £	Cumulative IHT £	Rate on net
0 - 118,000	NIL	-	-	-
over 118,000	40			2/3

Chargeable lifetime transfer scale:

Transfers 18th March 1986 to 16th March 1987

Cumulative chargeable transfers (gross) £	Rate %	IHT on band £	Cumulative IHT £	Rate on net
0 - 71,000	NIL	-	-	-
71,001 - 95,000	15	3,600	3,600	3/17
95,001 - 129,000	17½	5,950	9,550	7/33
129,001 - 164,000	20	7,000	16,550	1/4
164,001 - 206,000	22½	9,450	26,000	9/31
206,001 - 257,000	25	12,750	38,750	1/3
257,001 - 317,000	27½	16,500	55,250	11/29
over 317,000	30			3/7

Transfers from 17th March 1987 to 14th March 1988

Cumulative chargeable transfers (gross) £	Rate %	IHT on band £	Cumulative IHT £	Rate on net
0 - 90,000	NIL	-	-	-
90,001 - 140,000	15	7,500	7,500	3/17
140,001 - 220,000	20	16,000	23,500	1/4
220,001 - 330,000	25	27,500	51,000	1/3
over 330,000	30			3/7

Transfers from 15th March 1988 to 5th April, 1989

Cumulative chargeable transfers (gross) £	Rate %	IHT on band £	Cumulative IHT £	Rate on net
0 - 110,000	NIL	-	-	-
over 110,000	20			1/4

Transfers from 6th April 1989

Cumulative chargeable transfers (gross) £	Rate %	IHT on band £	Cumulative IHT £	Rate on net
0 - 118,000	NIL	-	-	-
over 118,000	20			1/4

Where a chargeable lifetime transfer is made, the person with primary liability to pay IHT is the transferor. As the measure of the transfer is the reduction in value of his estate, as the result of making the transfer it will be gift plus the tax. To find the tax it is necessary to gross-up the transfer.

Illustration

A makes a transfer to a discretionary trust on 30th June, 1987 of £145,000 (Ignore any exemptions).

This is a 'net' transfer and it is necessary to gross-up. Using the net cumulative chargeable transfers from the lifetime table, find the net amount nearest beneath the transfer:

£	£
132,500 net =	140,000 gross
12,500 difference	
—————	
145,000	
—————	

The difference is grossed-up as though it had suffered tax at the rate applying to net transfers between:

£132,500 and £196,500

$$£ 12,500 \times \frac{100}{100 - 20}$$ 15,625

155,625 gross

The IHT payable is:

$$£155,625 - £145,000 = £10,625$$

An alternative method of finding the tax is:

		£
Tax on	£132,500 net is	7,500
on	£12,500 x 1/4 is	3,125
		10,625

If, alternatively, the transfer was made into the discretionary trust on the understanding that the trustees would bear the IHT themselves, the reduction in value of the transferor's estate would be only £145,000. This would be a 'gross' transfer and tax could be found on the £145,000 directly without any grossing up:

		£
Tax on	£140,000	7,500
on	£ 5,000 @ 20%	1,000
		8,500

Had the transfer been made on 30th June 1990, the tax due had it been a net transfer would be:

£	£	
118,000 net =	118,000	gross
27,000 difference	33,750	
$\times \dfrac{100}{100 - 20}$	151,750	gross

The IHT payable being:

£151,750 - £145,000	£6,750

Altneratively:

		£
Tax on	£118,000 net is	NIL
on	£ 27,000 x 1/4 is	6,750
		6,750

If the trustees were to pay the tax - the gift being a 'gross' gift, the tax due would be:

		£
Tax on	£118,000	NIL
on	£ 27,000 @ 20%	5,400
		5,400

On death, the value of the estate increases the amount of the chargeable lifetime transfers. Tax is calculated using the rates on death.

Illustration

A died on 31st July 1994. The value of his estate was £200,000; assume the earlier transfer was made on 30th June 1990.

	£
Transfers within the previous 7 years	151,750
Value of the estate	200,000
	351,750

IHT payable using death scale:

	£
On £118,000	NIL
£233,750 @ 40%	93,500
	93,500

Less: IHT on transfers within the previous 7 years on death scale - £151,750

on £118,000	NIL	
£ 33,750 @ 40%	£13,500	
		13,500

Payable by executors		80,000

As A has died within 7 years of the earlier transfer, additional tax is due. This will be the difference between the IHT (if any) already paid on the transfer and the tax chargeable on it using the IHT rates at the date of death. The tax found will then be reduced by tapering relief as under:

Years between date of earlier transfer and date of death	Percentage of tax charged
0 - 3	100
3 - 4	80
4 - 5	60
5 - 6	40
6 - 7	20

	£
Tax on death scale	13,500
	======
60% thereof	8,100
Less: tax paid when transfer made	6,750
	_____
	1,350
	======

Where a potentially exempt transfer has been made, no tax calculation takes place when the transfer was made. On a death within 7 years, tax will be calculated in the same way as before and abated by tapering relief at the appropriate rate.

Illustration

On 1st January 1990 B gave £140,000 to her son on his marriage. She had not made any earlier transfers. On 15th April 1993, B died; her estate was valued at £100,000.

The transfer to B's son was a potentially exempt transfer. As a result of death its value on 1st January 1990 was:

	£	£
Gift		140,000
Less: Marriage exemption	5,000	
Annual exemption -		
1989/90	3,000	
1988/89 b/f	3,000	
	_____	11,000
		_____
		129,000
		========

On B's death the tax will be calculated as under:

	£
Transfer within previous 7 years	129,000

IHT thereon at death rates -	
on £118,000	NIL
£ 11,000 @ 40%	4,400
	4,400

Payable by B's son - 80% thereof	3,520

IHT on estate:

Transfers within previous 7 years	
as above	129,000
Value of estate	100,000
	229,000

	£
IHT thereon:	
on £118,000	NIL
£111,000 @ 40%	44,400
	44,400
Less: IHT on £129,000	4,400
Payable by personal representatives	40,000

Frequently there will be a number of previously chargeable or partly exempt transfers, and it will be necessary to calculate the IHT payable in respect of each of them.

Illustration

C died on 31st December 1995. She had made the following transfers during her lifetime:

30th June 1989	to a discretionary trust	£130,000
30th June 1990	to her daughter on her marriage	£ 50,000
15th December 1991	to her son	£ 25,000

The value of her estate on death was £150,000.

The schedule of transfers made within the 7 years before death will appear as under:

		£	£	£
30th June 1989	to trustees		130,000	
	Less: Annual exemption -			
	1989/90	3,000		
	1988/89	3,000		
			6,000	
			124,000	
	IHT thereon:			
	on £118,000		NIL	
	£ 6,000 x 1/4		1,500	
			1,500	

This was a net transfer as the trustees have not paid the tax themselves.

The gross transfer is thus   £125,500

		£	£	£
30th June 1990	Daughter		50,000	
	Less: Marriage exemption 5,000			
	Annual exemption -			
	1990/91	3,000		
			8,000	
				42,000
15th December 1991	Son		25,000	
	Less: Annual exemption -			
	1991/92		3,000	
				22,000

On the death within 7 years additional tax will be due on the chargeable transfer into the discretionary trust, and the potentially exempt transfers will become chargeable.

	£	£	£
Transfer to discretionary trust		125,500	
IHT - on £118,000	NIL		
on £ 7,500 @ 40%	3,000		
£125,500	3,000		3,000
		125,500	3,000
Transfer to daughter		42,000	16,800 @ 40%
		167,500	19,800
IHT - on £118,000	NIL		
on £ 49,500 @ 40%	19,800		
£167,500	19,800		
Transfer to son		22,000	8,800 @ 40%
		189,500	28,600

The IHT payable will be:

Trustees	£3,000 x 20%	600
	Paid already	1,500
	To pay	£ NIL

| Daughter | £16,800 x 40% | £6,720 |

| Son | £8,800 x 60% | £5,280 |

The tax payable on the estate would be:

	£
Total chargeable transfers	189,500
Value of estate	150,000
	339,500

IHT - on £118,000	NIL
on £221,500 @ 40%	88,600
£339,500	88,600
Less: IHT on £189,500	28,600
	60,000

Transfers made under the CTT regime prior to 17th March 1986 will be aggregated with transfers made within the following seven years. There will be an additional liability to IHT on the excess of IHT over any CTT paid, if death occurs within 3 years of making the earlier CTT transfer.

Illustration

In February 1986, N gave to his daughter O a freehold house. After deducting available exemptions the chargeable transfer amounted to £120,000. O obtained a bank loan and paid the CTT of £8,375 on the due date.

In December 1989 he made further gifts as follows:

December 3   £10,000 cash to his son P on his 25th birthday to expand the business P set up in 1984.

December 5   £40,000 cash into a discretionary trust for his four grandchildren.

December 18   A new £9,000 car to his wife M on her birthday.

December 21   A watch valued at £200 to his godson.

December 23   A £35,000 flat into a trust, his sister being life tenant.

December 30   £2,000 cash to his goddaughter on her marriage.

The schedule of chargeable lifetime transfers is:

		£	Gross £	IHT £	Net £
Chargeable transfer b/f at 17.3.1986			120,000		
IHT thereon at lifetime rates prior to the date of the first gift				400	119,600
Dec. 3 Transfer to P	PET				
Dec. 5 Transfer to discretionary trust		40,000			
Less: AE 1989/90	3,000				
1988/89	3,000	6,000	42,500	8,500	34,000
(As transferee is not paying the tax - gift is net)					
			162,500	8,900	153,600

£	Tax £
118,000	NIL
35,600 x 1/4	8,900
153,600	8,900

Dec. 18 - Car to wife	9,000	
Less: Spouse exemption	9,000	
Dec. 21 - Watch to Godson	200	
Less: Small gift exemption	200	
Dec. 23 - Flat into trust	PET	
Dec. 30 - Cash to goddaughter	2,000	
Less: Marriage exemption	1,000	
PET	1,000	

If N died on 31st January 1990, leaving an estate worth £200,000, the position would be:

	Gross	IHT
	£	£
Chargeable transfers b/f	120,000	
Dec. 3 P	10,000	4,000
	130,000	
(No annual exemption allocated. Whilst AE are normally allocated to transfers on a FIFO basis, if the exemptions have been allocated to a CLT already in the same fiscal year, that allocation will not be upset - see also note).		
Dec. 5 Discretionary Trust	42,500	17,000 @ 40%
	172,500	
Dec. 18 Exempt		
21 Exempt		
23 Flat into Trust	35,000	14,000 @ 40%
	207,500	
Dec. 30 Goddaughter	1,000	400 @ 40%
	208,500	
Value of Estate	200,000	80,000 @ 40%
Totals Tax	408,500	

IHT will be payable by:

	£	£
Personal representatives		80,000
Goddaughter		400
Trustees of trust		14,000
Trustees of discretionary Trust	17,000	
Less: Paid when CLT	8,500	8,500
P		4,000

Note: If an annual exemption has been brought forward and offset against a CLT in year 2 and as the result of a subsequent death an earlier PET in year 1 becomes chargeable, the exemption must be removed from the CLT and brought back into year 1 for offset against PET.

Where there has been a change of rates it will be necessary to recalculate the IHT on the total transfers before the change of rates in order to find the IHT on the later gifts. There will be no reduction in the IHT due on the earlier transfers.

Illustration

X made CLTs as under:

15.12.1987	£ 150,000
19.6.1988	£ 100,000

Ignore exemptions:

The IHT due will be:

	Gross	IHT
	£	£
15.12.1987	150,000	9,500

15.12.1987

£	Tax £
140,000	7,500
10,000 @ 20%	2,000
150,000	9,500

15.3.1988 - Recalculate tax:

£	Tax £
110,000	NIL
40,000 @ 20%	8,000
150,000	8,000

8,000

19.6.1988

	100,000	20,000 @ 20%
	250,000	28,000

In finding the tax due on death only PETs made within the preceding 7 years enter into the computation to find the IHT due on the value of the estate. The starting-off point in the computation is to take the date 7 years before death and to accumulate all chargeable lifetime transfers made 7 years before that date. These earlier transfers will drop out of the computation on their seventh anniversary and thus will not affect the tax due on the estate. They may, however, affect the tax due on PETs made within the 7 years prior to death.

Illustration

Y made the following transfers (after all exemptions):

		£
1.10.1981	Chargeable	120,000
1.7.1985	Chargeable	80,000
1.10.1987	PET	50,000
1.12.1989	Chargeable	70,000

He died on 31st December 1991.

The cumulation would be:

Lifetime:

	£
1.10.1981	120,000
1.7.1985	80,000
	200,000
1.10.1988 Remove transfer made on 1.10.1981	(120,000)
	80,000
1.12.1988	70,000
	150,000

On death:

	£
Transfers made in 7 years before 31.12.1984	120,000
1.7.1985	80,000
	200,000
1.10.1987 PET becomes chargeable	50,000
	250,000
1.10.1988 Remove transfer made on 1.10.1981	(120,000)
	130,000
1.12.1988	70,000
	200,000

Thus the PET made on 1.10.1987 will be affected by the chargeable transfers made within the preceding 7 years. The PET which is now chargeable will increase the tax due on the CLT made on 1.12.1988.

Illustration

D transfers £120,000 into a discretionary trust on 31st December 1986. The trustees pay any IHT thereon. He transfers £50,000 to his son on 31st December 1989 and dies on 30th June 1994 leaving an estate of £170,000. (Ignore any exemptions).

IHT on gift to son:

	£	£			
		£			
Transfer to son		50,000			
Transfers within previous 7 years		120,000			
		───────			
		170,000			
		───────			

IHT - on £118,000   NIL
      on £ 52,000 @ 40%   20,800
      ─────────   ───────
      £170,000   20,800

Less: IHT on £120,000
      ════════

      on £118,000   NIL
      on £ 2,000 @ 40%   800   800
                                                   ───────

                                                  20,000   x 60%   £12,000
                                                  ═══════   ══════

IHT on estate:
                                                      £
Transfer within 7 years of death   50,000

Value of estate   170,000
                                                  ───────
                                                  220,000
                                                  ───────

IHT thereon   40,800

Less: IHT on £50,000   NIL
                                                  ───────
      Due from personal representatives   40,800
                                                  ═══════

4.2 Quick succession relief (QSR)

Where a person's estate is increased by a transfer received and not more than
five years later IHT arises as a result of a second transfer made, then a
proportion of the IHT or CTT on the first transfer will be allowed as a credit
against the IHT on the second transfer. The relief will only apply where the
second transfer occurs on death, or is of settled property in which the
transferor is entitled to an interest in possession.

The IHT payable on death is reduced by a percentage of part of the tax payable on the earlier transfer received, the percentage varying according to the time period between the two transfers:

Not more than 1 year	100%
More than 1 year but not more than 2 years	80%
More than 2 years but not more than 3 years	60%
More than 3 years but not more than 4 years	40%
More than 4 years but not more than 5 years	20%

The relevant percentage is applied to the IHT attributable to the **Net Value** of the property which had increased the deceased's estate. In other words:

$$QSR = \text{tax paid on first transfer} \times \frac{\text{net gift}}{\text{gross gift}} \times \text{relevant percentage.}$$

The relief is given whether or not the particular property which had been received is owned by the deceased on his death. If it is owned, then its value on that death is completely irrelevant. If there is more than one transfer subsequent to the original chargeable transfer (e.g. two deaths in lquick succession'), the credit will be given against the earliest of these. However, if the whole of the tax credit is not used, subsequent transfers may benefit - so long as they fall within the five-year period.

Illustration

In June 1985, Justin (gross chargeable transfers of £116,000) gave Mary shares worth £ 10,000 (no exemptions being available). Mary died in May 1990 and included in her estate were the shares, now worth £12,000.

Assuming that Mary had paid the CTT due in 1985 (i.e. £10,000 @ 20% = £2,000), QSR would be:

$$£2,000 \times \frac{8,000}{10,000} \times 20\% = £320$$

Assuming that Justin had paid the CTT due in 1985 (i.e. £10,000 x $\frac{20}{80}$ = £2,500), QSR would be

$$£2,500 \times \frac{10,000}{12,500} \times 20\% = £400$$

The QSR is deducted from IHT chargeable on Mary's death, and if not fully used may still be available if the shares are again transferred on the death of Mary's beneficiary (within five years of the first transfer). The credit is calculated by deducting the QSR used on the second transfer from the QSR available on the third.

4.3 Liability to pay IHT

The Inland Revenue can collect IHT from a number of people, some of whom have a primary liability to pay the tax while others have a secondary liability (and are only approached on the default of a person with a primary liability):

chargeable event	primary liability on	secondary liability on
Chargeable transfers	the transferor	(i) the transferee (ii) any other person in whom the property has become vested.
Additional IHT on chargeable transfers (within seven years of death)	the transferee	the personal representatives and any other person in whom the property has become vested.
Free estate (passing on death)	the personal representative	any person in whom the property is vested after death.
Potentially exempt representatives and any	the transferee	the personal other person in whom the property has become vested.
Settled property (on the termination of an interest in possession)	the trustee(s)	(i) any person with an interest in possession (ii) any person to whose benefit the property (or income) is applied (iii) if the termination (or transfer) is during his lifetime - the settlor.

It is also necessary to distinguish between who pays the tax (i.e. as shown above) and who actually bears it (i.e. the person whose property is reduced by the payment). In the case of:

(a)   lifetime gifts, the IHT is borne by the person responsible for the payment;

(b)   the free estate:

   i)   the IHT on personalty is paid out of the residue of the estate, and so is effectively borne by the residuary legatees (whose benefit is reduced);

   ii)   the IHT on realty is borne by the residuary legatees.

   Naturally, a deceased person's Will may indicate responsibility for bearing IHT other than that prescribed by law (e.g. a legacy of shares subject to any IHT attributable to the gift);

(c) settled property, the IHT is paid out of the trust capital and is therefore borne by the remaindermen.

Where IHT is not paid on land and certain other property, an Inland Revenue charge will attach thereto until the tax is paid.

5.0   VALUATION

5.1   Introduction

The value of property for IHT purposes is determined by the amount the transferor's estate is reduced by the transfer. In effect his estate should be valued immediately before and immediately after the transfer, and the difference is the transfer of value. However, as this is both impractical and unnecessary,

> 'the value at any time of any property shall for the purposes of IHT be the price which the property might reasonably be expected to fetch if sold in the open market at that time; but that price shall not be assumed to be reduced on the ground that the whole property is to be placed on the market at one and the same time.'

The valuation must be at the price which would be negotiated between unconnected persons seeking to strike an arm's length bargain, producing the best possible price for the vendor. Regard must be had to any other property comprised in the transferor's estate which, if sold together with the property under consideration, would enhance its price. If there are any restrictions on the freedom to dispose of property (e.g. limitations on the transferability of shares or the disposal of a share in a partnership), the value of that property may be reduced. Another consideration is the possibility of property values being affected by the existence of related property, and before dealing with specific items, it is necessary to explain the meaning of this term.

5.2 Related property

The value of any property in a person's estate is found by taking **related property** into account where by so doing a higher value for all or part of the property in his estate would be obtained. Property is related to that in a person's estate if:

(a) it is comprised in the estate of his spouse (including trust property in which either party has an interest in possession); or

(b) it is or has been, within the previous five years, the property of a charity, charitable trust or one of the political, national or public bodies to which exempt transfers may be made, as a result of an exempt transfer made by the taxpayer or his spouse.

The related property provisions may apply, for example, to the joint ownership of a house by the husband and wife, or to valuable chattels whose ownership is divided (e.g. a set of five rare prints may be worth more collectively than the sum of the values of two prints owned by the husband and three prints owned by the wife when valued separately). However, the most important aspect of the related property provisions is in respect of shares in private companies.

Illustration

The shares in a private company are held as follows:

Mr. D	40%
Mrs. D	35%
Junior D (their son)	20%
Charity (shares given by	
Mrs. D three years ago)	5%

Mr. D transfers 50% of his holding to his son, the estimated values for different levels of holdings being:

	£
	£
5%	5,000
20%	23,000
35%	45,500
40%	52,000
60%	86,000
80%	120,000

The transfer of value by Mr. D is not £23,000, or even £29,000 (i.e. the difference between the value of a 40 per cent holding and a reduced holding of 20 per cent), as related property must be taken into account.

The related property before the transfer amounts to a holding of 80 per cent, (i.e. 40% + 35% + 5%) valued at £120,000, while after the transfer it amounts to 60 per cent (i.e. 20% + 35% + 5%) valued at £86,000. The transfer of value by Mr. D is calculated as follows:

		£
Holding before the transfer:		
$\frac{40}{80}$ x £120,000	=	60,000
Holding after the transfer:		
$\frac{20}{60}$ x £86,000	=	28,667
Transfer of value (loss to transferor's estate)		31,333

If Mr. D had gifted all his shares, or they had passed on his death, their value would have been £60,000.

The value of property passing on death is usually increased as a result of the related property provisions. If, within three years of death, the whole or part of that property is sold by the personal representative or beneficiary at arm's length to an unconnected person (with no right of repurchase) for a lower price, a claim for relief may be made. The relief is given by revaluing the property sold as at the date of death ignoring the related property provisions; then recomputing the IHT payable, and reclaiming any overpaid IHT. For example, if the 40% of shares owned by Mr. D passed on his death (at a value of £60,000 - see above), and were sold within three years by his PR for £55,000, relief could be claimed. The shares would be revalued at £52,000 (the value ignoring related property provisions) and the IHT recomputed. However, where this relief is claimed, there may also be a reduction in the amount of business property relief or agricultural relief available. The adverse effects of this may make it worthwhile not to claim for the reduced valuation.

5.3 Unlisted investments

Unlisted shares and securities are valued at the price they would fetch in the open market in an arm's length transaction between a willing buyer and a willing seller. The prospective purchaser is assumed to have available all the information that a prudent purchaser might reasonably require (e.g. prospective take-over bids, flotations etc). To some extent, this is an artificial basis of valuation as, of course, there is no open market in unlisted investments, and agreement must be reached with the Inland Revenue.

5.4 Listed investments

Listed shares and securities are valued at the lower of:

(a) one-quarter up on the difference between the lower and higher closing prices on the Stock Exchange (**the quarter-up rule**); or

(b) half-way between the highest and lowest recorded (<u>or marked</u>) bargains for the day.

Units in an approved unit trust scheme are valued at the manager's buying price, which is the lower of the two prices published.

Where the transfer takes place on a day the Stock Exchange is closed, the valuation is made using the prices quoted or bargains marked on the day previous, or the day following the transfer, whichever produces the lowest result on the property transferred.

Illustration

E transferred 1,000 ordinary shares in R plc to his son on Saturday 25th June. On Friday 24th June the shares were quoted at 150-158 with recorded bargains of 150, 151, 152 and 156. On Monday 27th June the shares were quoted at 150-156 with recorded bargains of 151, 154 and 156. The four valuations, in the order given, are:

1	1,000 @	152	=	£1,520
2	1,000 @	153	=	£1,530
3	1,000 @	151½	=	£1,515
4	1,000 @	153½	=	£1,535

The value of the PET is, therefore, based on the quotations for Monday 27th June.

5.5   Accrued income and payments in advance

Regular income such as rent, or interest accrued to the deceased's date of death, is included in a person's estate with apportionment being made to the nearest day (including the date of death). Adjustments are not usually made for rent paid in advance, although accrued liabilities may be deducted. For examination purposes apportionment is usually made to the nearest month.

As regards listed investments:

(a)   if the quotation is cum div, accrued income is already included in the valuation;

(b)   if the quotation is ex div the whole amount of the next impending dividend (or interest net of tax) must be added to the ex div price. For example, if on Herbert's death, £2,000 10% National Stock in his estate was quoted 80-84 ex div (interest payable half-yearly), the IHT valuation would be:

	£	£
£2,000 10% National Stock @ 81		1,620
Interest - ½ x 10% x £2,000	100	
Less: income tax @ 25%	25	
	───	
		75
		─────
		1,695
		═════

This calculation is only made in respect of transfers on death as the interest will form part of the deceased's estate when received.

The statutory apportionment of dividends or interest for executorship or trust purposes has no effect on the IHT valuation of the listed investments. However, if the deceased was a life tenant of a trust, care must be taken to include any income accrued up to the date of his death in the free estate and not as part of the settled property. Although the total IHT liability in respect of his death remains the same, more tax will be borne by the free estate and less by the settled property.

5.6   Fall in value of listed investments

Where qualifying investments are included in a deceased person's estate and are sold (by the PR or any other person responsible for paying the IHT on them) within twelve months after death for a price lower than the valuation at death, relief may be available. Qualifying investments include shares and securities quoted on the Stock Exchange, holdings in authorised unit trusts, and shares in a common investment fund (e.g. managed by the Public Trustee). The gross sale prices (before deduction of expenses) may be substituted for the death valuations, but all investments sold within the period must be revalued in this way and not just those which have fallen in value. The reduction in value of the listed investments does, of course, reduce the total value of the estate passing on death, thereby reducing the IHT rate applicable to other property.

The relief is restricted if listed investments are purchased within two months after the last sale in the twelve-month period. The loss on sale is reduced by the fraction:

$$\frac{\text{total purchase prices}}{\text{total sale prices}}$$

-   the expenses of sale or purchase being excluded.

Illustration

F died on 1st January 1990 leaving an estate valued at £118,000, including quoted investments valued at £50,000. Eight months after F's death his PR sold the investments for £40,000, but within two months of the sale purchased other quoted investments for £30,000.

The revised IHT computation at death would include the listed investments valued as follows:

	£	£
Other property		60,000
Listed investments:		
Value for probate	50,000	
Proceeds of sale	40,000	
Loss on sale	10,000	
Less: $\frac{£30,000}{£40,000}$ x £10,000	7,500	
	2,500	
New valuation		
£(50,000 - 2,500)		47,500
		107,500

Note that the computation is laid out to show the allowable fall in value as a deduction from the original probate value of the investment.

5.7 Land and buildings

Land and buildings, like other property, have to be valued at an open market price. The transferor, or his PR, would normally employ a professional valuer and ultimately reach agreement with the Inland Revenue's own district valuers. When valuing agricultural estates, any farm cottages occupied by agricultural workers are valued as **agricultural cottages** and not as potentially more valuable second homes etc.

Where land and buildings are included in a deceased person's estate and are sold within three years after death, relief may be available. The gross sale proceeds, if lower, may be substituted for the value at the date of death, but all sales of land by the person(s) acting in a particular capacity must be revalued in this way and not just those which have fallen in value.

No claim can be made where the difference between the two values is less than the lower of £1,000 or five per cent of the value on death, and also where the sale is to a beneficiary or one of his near relatives. The relief is restricted if land is purchased between the date of death and four months after the last sale in the three-years period. The loss on sale is reduced by the fraction:

$$\frac{\text{total purchase prices}}{\text{total sale prices}}$$

- the expenses of sale or purchase being excluded.

Illustration

G died on 30th April 1990. His total estate was £250,000 and included the following:

	£
Property A	15,000
B	28,000
C	47,000

The properties were sold on 30th June 1990 to pay IHT and realised:

	£
Property A	14,500
B	20,000
C	50,000

The loss on Property A can be ignored as the loss is lower than the smaller of:

(a)   £1,000; or

(b)   5% x £15,000 = £750

The loss and gain on Properties B and C are both material and so the value of the estate would be reduced by:

	£
Loss on Property B	(8,000)
Gain on Property A	3,000
	(5,000)

12   Pierre Gaston was born in France in August 1928. He qualified as an engineer and worked for a major French company until 31st December 1963. On 1st January 1964 he came to the UK, at the request of the French company, to set up a UK subsidiary operation. Prior to coming to the UK, he married a French girl, Monique, and she came to the UK with him.

It has always been the intention of Pierre and Monique Gaston to return to France in their later years and spend the rest of their lives there.

The following points arise:

(a) Pierre wishes to sell a large shareholding in a French company, and with the proceeds purchase a villa in the South of France. He will go there for occasional holidays and during the rest of the year he will let it for a substantial rent.

(b) Monique's mother, who had been living in France, has recently died leaving her an expensive painting. Monique is thinking of gifting the painting to her old art teacher in France. The painting has always been held in France.

(c) Monique's mother has also left her a bank account of £100,000. Monique would like to leave the money to earn interest in France, but would occasionally like to bring over sums of money to the UK for her own use.

Required:

Discuss these points, explaining whether or not UK tax will arise. (Ignore any possible French taxation.)   (15 marks)

13   THE OLIVIA AERO ENGINE CO LTD

Profit and Loss Account for the 65 weeks ended 31st March 1990 (i)

	£	£
Turnover		1,262,000
Net trading profit after charging: 351,500		
Directors' remuneration	42,000	
Auditors' fees and expenses	4,600	
Hire of plant and machinery	5,400	
Depreciation of fixed assets (ii)	31,400	
Amortisation of 50-year lease of premises	6,500	
Patent royalties (gross) (iii)	16,000	
Provision for bad debts through insolvency of major customer	25,000	
Income from investments:		
Dividends from UK companies (iv)	17,080	
Rents received (v)	24,250	41,330
		392,830

	£	£
Net profits before interest, taxation and extraordinary items		392,830
Interest payable: On bank overdraft	6,100	
On debentures repayable		
August 1994	10,500	(16,600)
Corporation tax	110,000	
Less: Over-provided in 1988	4,500	(105,500)

Extraordinary items:

Surplus on sale of shares held as an investment (vi)	13,520
Payment for infringement of patent (iii)	(4,500)
Capital sum to establish profit-sharing scheme for employees (vii)	(18,900)
Expenses of loan stock issue (viii)	(1,224)
Net profit for the accounting period	259,626
transferred to reserve to redeem 9% Debenture Stock	(10,000)
Dividends paid and proposed (ix)	(72,670)
Unappropriated profit carried forward	176,956

Notes

i)   The company's accounting date was changed to be more in accord with   its pattern.

ii)   Depreciation -

	£
Plant and machinery	16,400
Buildings (including sales office not qualifying for capital allowances £1,950)	15,000

iii)   Patent royalties are calculated on certain sales. Owing to a legal dispute payment for the twelve months to 31st December 1988 (£9,000) was withheld and paid on 1st September 1989. The payment for the period to 31st August 1989 (a total of £4,600) was made on 31st January 1990. Royalties due at 31st March 1990 (£11,400), though not yet paid, have been reserved in the profit and loss account.

On 1st July 1989 OAEC Ltd paid £4,500 as a penalty for an infringement of the UK patent.

iv)   Dividends received:

- from ordinary shares   £6,650 on 31st May 1989
- from 9% cum. pref. shares   £10,430 on 15th November 1989.

The cumulative preference dividend represented arrears unpaid for 1987 and 1988.

v)   Rental income includes:

(a) Rents from residential properties let to tenants on a 14-year
     lease at £ 10,800 per year payable quarterly until 1993.
 Rent owing from a previous tenant of £2,500, which was
written off in 1982, was received from his executors on 1st
December 1989 and is included in the accounts. Relevant
allowable expenditure, £800 per quarter, has already been
charged in the trading account of OAEC Ltd.

(b) The remaining rent is received on a monthly basis.

vi)   Shares in the Tornado Engine Co. plc, acquired for £10,500 on 7th
April 1965, were sold on 8th April 1989 for £24,020 (net of
incidental expenses) to provide cash as working capital. Their
market value at 31st March 1982 was £15,000. Capital losses
brought forward are £10,000.

vii)   The company's profit-sharing scheme was given Revenue approval on
6th April 1989. The fund was formally set up on 6th May 1989.

viii)   On 31st March 1990 the company made an issue of £30,000 loan stock
at 12¼%, redeemable in 1994 or convertible into ordinary shares at
that time.   Included are secretarial and printing costs £364,
solicitor's fees £410, stamp duty £450.

ix)   Dividends   £   Declared   Paid

Preference shares   6,300   20.12.88   2.5.89
Ordinary shares   37,500   28. 2.89   6.6.89
Ordinary shares   53,500   31.10.89   1.3.90
Preference shares   6,300   21.12.89   4.1.90
Ordinary shares   12,870   10. 4.90   31.5.90

x)   The following information appears in the notes to the balance
sheet at 31st March 1990:

Fixed assets - additions: £
  Machinery   12.1.89   38,000
  Machinery   29.4.89   25,500 (see note (v)(b))
  Buildings   21.3.89   25,200
    (Extension to research laboratory)
  Motor cars   30.3.89:
    Managing Director   12,000
    Three sales representatives   18,000

(The capital allowance written-down value for plant/machinery,
other than that shown above, is £26,000: for cars £4,280 (bought
June 1987) at 31st December 1988.

Debenture interest (£8,400 pa) is paid on 15th December annually. The
company is not a close company for corporation tax. The company
commenced to trade on 1st January 1934.

RPI   March 1982   79.4

April 1989   110.0

Required:

Compute the mainstream corporation tax payable by the company.

(29 marks)

14

(a) Q Ltd which commenced to trade on 1st December 1987, is a wholly-owned
     subsidiary of T Ltd. Trading results are as follows:

	Q Ltd	T Ltd
	£	£
Year to 30.11.88		
Trading profit (loss)	-	(5,000)
Year to 30.11.89		
Trading profit (loss)	(12,000)	10,000
Bank interest received	-	5,000
Debenture interest (gross) paid	-	2,000
Year to 30.11.90		
Trading profit (loss)	(5,000)	(10,000)
Bank interest received	-	5,000
Debenture interest (gross) paid	-	2,000

Required:

Illustrate how loss relief is claimed and why you make your
particular form of claim in these circumstances. Explain how
unrelieved losses and charges may be dealt with.

(9 marks)

(b) The issued share capital of Z Ltd is 80,000 £1 ordinary shares.
     48,000 are owned by A Ltd, 24,000 by B Ltd and 8,000 by C Ltd.
     Trading results of all companies, which are resident in the UK, for
     the year to 30th June 1990   are:

		£
Z Ltd	profit	50,000
A Ltd	profit	40,000
B Ltd	loss	(60,000)
C Ltd	profit	10,000

Explain fully how and in what conditions B Ltd's loss may be relieved.

(6 marks)

(Total 15 marks)

15   Bandroyal Limited has the following sources of income for the year ended 31st March 1990:

	£
Schedule D, Case I	400,000
Rental income	40,000
Dividend from overseas subsidiary	see below
Capital gains	240,000

It paid debenture interest of £50,000 on 1st August 1989, and a dividend of £641,000 on 1st January 1990.

During the year, Bandroyal received a dividend from its wholly-owned subsidiary in Ruritania amounting to £144,000, after withholding-tax of 10% had been deducted by the Ruritanian tax authorities.

The subsidiary company had paid 20% tax on its profits as they arose.

Required:

Calculate the mainstream corporation tax payable by Bandroyal Limited for the year ended 31st March 1990, clearly showing the utilisation of foreign tax and ACT paid.

(10 marks)

16   A Ltd has the following results for the year ended 31st March 1990:

	£
Trading Income	50,000
Bank interest received	20,000
Rental income less outgoings	10,000
Capital gains	9,000
Dividends received (net)	1,400
Charges paid (gross)	16,000
Dividends paid (net)	58,800

The company has also received a dividend of £10,800 from its wholly-owned subsidiary in Ruritania (a foreign country). The dividend has suffered withholding-tax of 10%. The rate of tax paid on corporate profits in Ruritania is 40%.

Calculate the company's liability for mainstream corporation tax, for the year ended 31st March 1990, indicating clearly the amount of foreign tax wasted and ACT carried forward. Take corporation tax at 35% throughout.

(15 marks)

17   Verity Spinners Ltd is a non-close company engaged in the textile industry;   it also owns residential properties which are let.   The company owns 60% of the ordinary share capital of Langridge Ltd, which operates retail shops.

For many years Verity Spinners Ltd has made up accounts to 31st March, and in the year ended 31st March 1988 the company incurred a loss of £96,100 (including capital allowances) in its trade.   Claims for relief were made against the profits of that year and the previous year, the amount of loss so used being £47,448.

The profit and loss account for the year ended 31st March 1989 may be summarised as follows:

	£
Profit on trading	102,846
Rental income (net of related expenses)	13,220
Investment income	9,290
Surplus on a sale of a residential property	16,130
	141,486

Items charged in arriving at the profit on trading include the following:

	£
Depreciation (including amortisation of lease)	20,800
Patent royalties (gross)	7,850
Repairs at Kirkstall Mill:	
Alterations to accommodate new machinery	3,200
Replacement of fencing	6,970

The patent royalties were payable under an agreement entered into in August 1988.
The amount charged in the accounts includes £1,440 accrued, but not yet paid, at 31st March 1989.

The investment income, which was all received during the accounting period, consists of the following items:

	£
Interest on bank deposit	2,340
Dividend from Langridge Ltd (paid under a group election to pay dividends without accounting for advance corporation tax)	5,250
Dividends from other UK companies (including tax credit)	1,700
	9,290

The surplus on sale of a residential property relates to a house sold for £46,350 on 16th February 1989;   the house had been bought for £26,220 in March, 1983.   The Retail Price Index was 83.6 for March 1983 and 120.0 for February 1989.   The main premises of Verity Spinners Ltd are at Kirkstall Mill, which has been occupied since 1st May 1982 under a lease for 20 years;

a premium of £55,000 was paid for the lease. The lessor had acquired the land for £9,000 in 1972 and completed construction of the mill on 1st January 1977 at a cost of £124,500. In February 1984, with the permission of the lessor, Verity Spinners Ltd incurred expenditure of £31,600 on an extension to the building for the purpose of storing raw materials.

On 1st June 1988 the company purchased Park Mill in order to increase production capacity, paying £115,000 (including £17,500 for land) to another company which had used the building continuously as a mill since construction was completed on 1st June 1977. The original cost was £10,000 for land and a further £62,650 for construction.

On 10th March 1989 Verity Spinners Ltd paid £26,500 for the extension of an existing small laboratory in the grounds of Park Mill for the purposes of technical research into matters connected with the trade.

The pool value of the company's plant and machinery on 1st April 1987 was nil. During the year ended 31st March 1989 purchases of new machinery totalled £104,700 and sales realised £6,100; no item was sold for more than it cost.

The last dividend paid by Verity Spinners Ltd was in August 1987.

<u>You are required to calculate:</u>

the corporation tax payable by Verity Spinners Ltd for the year ended 31st March 1989.

(15 marks)

18

(a)   The ordinary share capital of North Yorkshire Plastics Ltd is acquired by the Mendips Investment plc in July 1990. NY Plastics operated specialist manufacturing processes. Owing to changes in market patterns its trade had begun to diminish from about 1987. By July 1988 it had unrelieved corporation tax losses of £420,000, surplus ACT of £75,000 and capital losses of £36,000. Mendips Investment plc contemplates extending the design function of NY Plastics for use by other companies within its group and to diversify somewhat the range of NY Plastics' manufacturing activities. Four of the seven directors of NY Plastics will retire.

You are required to comment on any taxation difficulties that may arise from this proposal.

(7 marks)

(b)   Recent legislation introduced 'demerger' provisions to make easier the splitting of a larger unit into smaller units.

<u>Required</u>

Explain:

i)   what are the two principal problems which caused obstacles to demergers?

ii)   what solutions are contained in the legislation?

iii) what are the main conditions for exemption under the legislation?

(8 marks)

(Total 15 marks)

19   Jardine, who was born on 23rd October 1917, is resident and ordinarily resident in the UK. During the year ended 5th April 1990 he carried out the following capital transactions, none of which was with a connected person:

(a)   On 1st December 1989 he sold 3,000 unquoted ordinary shares in Townsend Ltd for £ 13,500.
Before the sale he owned 4,000 shares, which he had bought as follows:

8th June 1956	1,500 shares for	£4,200
3rd April 1962	2,500 shares for	£12,800

You are informed that in both 1963 and 1964 Townsend Ltd suffered substantial losses and accordingly it is likely that the market value of the shares on 6th April 1965 was only about £2 each. The market value of the shares at 31 March 1982 was £4 each.

(b)   On 3rd April 1990 he sold all his unquoted ordinary shares in Clark (Winchester) Ltd for £40,700. Jardine had been a full-time director of the company, which sells video equipment, since he bought the shares for £11,500 on 29th June 1987, and his holding carried 10% of the voting rights. The other voting rights were exercisable 10% by Jardine's sister, 35% by his son and 45% by a merchant bank.

The market values of the company's assets on 3rd April 1990 were agreed as follows:

	£
Freehold premises	95,000
Goodwill	64,500
Investments	5,500
Stock, debtors and bank balance	48,400
	213,400

(c)   Jardine made the following sales of 10% Treasury Stock 1992, which is included in Capital Gains Tax Act 1979, Sch. 2 as being exempt from capital gains tax in certain circumstances:

9th May 1988	£8,000 stock for	£6,850
21st December 1988	£20,000 stock for	£17,360

His purchases of this stock were as follows:

6th October 1987	£6,000 stock for	£4,420
8th December 1987	£9,000 stock for	£7,065
17th March 1988	£14,000 stock for	£13,540
1st February 1989	£5,000 stock for	£4,150

All transactions in Treasury Stock were carried out through the Stock Exchange.

Retail Price Index figures include the following:

March 1982	79.4	December 1989	115.0
June 1986	97.8	April 1990	125.0

Jardine also asks for your advice in connection with potential liability to capital gains tax and inheritance tax on a house with a current market value of about £ 50,000 which he bought for £8,000 in 1968. It has never been his residence, having been let throughout his ownership, and has no development value.

He wishes to transfer the house early in 1991 to trustees for the benefit of his infant grandchildren. He has made no gifts since 26th March 1974.

You are required to:

(a) prepare a statement showing Jardine's capital gains tax position for 1989/90. An election has been made under s.96 FA1988.

(8 marks)

(b) list the points relating to capital gains tax that you would bring to his attention in connection with the proposed transfer of the house.

(4 marks)

(Total 12 marks)

20   Hans Schmidt, an Austrian national, aged 36, has approached you for tax advice regarding a large legacy he has recently inherited in the UK. The legacy comprises a plot of land with substantial development value, and various bank and building society accounts. The following points arise:

(a) He is thinking of disposing of the plot of land with substantial development value to a property developer in the near future. Hans wishes to ascertain what taxes may be payable as a result of the sale.

(b) He would like to retain some of the moneys in the UK in his own name for possible use in the future, but is concerned about the adverse impact of IHT in the event of his early death. He wishes to know whether he can minimise his exposure to IHT.

Required:

Draft short notes for your discussions with Hans Schmidt.

(15 marks)

21   The share capital of Hallsvalla Ltd, a trading company, is owned as follows:

	Shares
John Stephens	630
Mary Stephens (John's wife)	140
Jim Stephens (John's brother)	230
	1,000

The shares have been held for many years.

John's son, Philip, joined the business on 17th May 1989 and on that date John gifted Philip 280 shares in the company. Jim gifted Philip 140 shares.

The Revenue have agreed the following share valuations:

75 - 100%	£53 per share
50 - 74%	£37 per share
26 - 49%	£23 per share
10 - 25%	£11 per share
0 - 9%	£ 4 per share

Calculate the value of the potentially exempt transfer made by both John and Jim on the gift of the shares.

(Ignore capital gains tax)   (13 marks)

22   Nichols died on 8th February 1990. He was a widower, domiciled in England, and his assets were valued for probate as follows:

	£
Freehold house in Essex	86,500
Foreign assets	31,900
Quoted investments	261,690
Personal chattels	18,100
Bank balance	33,600

The debts due by Nichols at the date of his death amounted to £6,850 and funeral expenses were £490. The foreign duty on the foreign assets is £3,833.

His wife had died in 1971 leaving her entire estate in trust to Nichols for life with remainder to their only child, a son, born in 1968. The total value of the trust fund on 8th February 1990 was £178,450.

Nichols was also life tenant of a family trust in which his interest had commenced on the death of an aunt on 15th March 1989 when the value of the trust fund was £ 41,800; inheritance tax of £7,420 was payable by the trustees as a result of the aunt's death. The value of the fund on 8th February 1990 was £37,350.

By his Will, Nichols made charitable bequests totalling £30,000. The residue of his estate was left in trust for his son, who was to become absolutely entitled to the capital of the estate on reaching the age of 25.

During his lifetime, Nichols had made chargeable transfers of value totalling £ 21,400. No tax was payable on these transfers, which were within 7 years of death.

All the IHT payable as a result of the death of Nichols was paid on 30th September 1990, no claim for deferment of any tax being made.

On 19th October 1990, his executors purchased quoted shares for £7,440. They still own this stock.

Since obtaining probate the executors have made the following sales of quoted investments owned by Nichols at the time of his death:

	Probate value £	Gross proceeds £	Selling expenses £	Net Proceeds £
21st October 1990	160,500	142,800	1,150	141,650
14th November 1990	41,800	43,200	450	42,750

The remaining quoted investments which were owned by Nichols at the time of his death are still owned by the executors on 15th December 1990 and all have current values higher than probate values.

You are required to:

(a) Calculate the total IHT payable as a result of the death of Nichols;

(7 marks)

(b) Calculate the potential repayment of IHT resulting from the transactions in quoted investments.   (3 marks)

(c) List the points relating to IHT that you would bring to the attention of the executors in connection with any future transactions in quoted investments.

(3 marks)
(Total 13 marks)

23 VAT

In relation to value added tax explain:

i)   what is meant by and the importance of the term 'tax point'.

ii) the rules for determining the tax point on an outright sale of goods.

24 VAT

With regard to value added tax:

(a) outline the different effects where a person makes supplies which are:

i)   zero rated only
ii) exempt only

(b) A tax invoice is often regarded as one of the most important documents in the operation of VAT. State the items which must be contained in such an invoice.

Ephraidge A. T. Rinomhota

25   VAT

Comment and advice on the VAT position on each of the following:

(1)   John Downs decided to act as a part-time consultant in the construction
       industry.   he **expects** his fees to be about £20,000 in his first year.
       If he does not register for VAT purposes he would have to add
       approximately 10% of his fees chargeable to cover the VAT which he is
       charged.   Most of his clients are large businesses supplying goods
       liable to VAT.

(2)   Michael has carried on a business as a newsagent for several years and
       is registered for VAT.   however, over the years administrative work in
       respect of VAT returns etc. has increased and he finds that he cannot
       cope.   his turnover for the past years has been on average, £17,000 per
       annum and because of the declining number of people living in the area,
       he does not expect his turnover to increase.

(3)   Julie, whose husband dies two years ago, decided to use her home as a
       residential hotel during the summer months.   She expects that her
       takings for the first year - 1990 will be approximately £16,800.   She
       also expects the figure for 1991 to increase only with inflation.

(4)   Adam runs a business supplying only exempt goods.   Sandra, his sister,
       runs a business supplying only zero rated goods.   Adam and Sandra do
       not charge any VAT to customers though both has a turnover of £24,600
       per annum.

       How, if at all, do their positions differ?

26   VAT

(a)   How are tax periods determined for value added tax?

(b)   outline the records to be kept and returns to be made by a taxable
       person.

Suggested Answers to Examination Questions

| 1 | | MOUNTAIN |

(a) <u>Income tax chargeable on compensation payment</u>

		£	£
Income excluding compensation:			
Earned income: Schedule E			18,920
Investment income: UK dividends - Mr Mountain	6,510		
Mrs Mountain	2,235		
		8,745	
Less: mortgage interest		1,480	
			7,265
			26,185
SPA			2,785
Taxable income ignoring compensation			23,400
Compensation received			60,000
Less: exempt			30,000
Taxable			30,000
			£
Tax thereon at 40%			12,000

(b)   <u>Mrs Mountain</u>

Income tax payable:
1st October 1989 to 5th April 1990   £   £   £

<u>Earned income</u>

Business profits £(3,278 + 6/12 x 7,804)   7,180
Pension   9,545

                                                                16,725

<u>Investment income</u>:

UK dividends   2,905
Foreign dividends   795
UK and foreign taxes deducted (25/75)   265   1,060

                                                       3,965
Estate of Mountain deceased   5,840

                                                       9,805

<u>Less</u>:   Loan interest and charges paid -

             interest   1,235
             covenant   260   1,495   8,310
                                          ------   -------   -------

Statutory Total Income   25,035

Personal allowance   2,785

Additional personal allowance   1,590

Widows' Bereavement allowance   1,590   5,965
                                                      -------   -------

Taxable Income   19,070
                                                                 ======

                                          £   £
£19,070 @ 25%   4,767

Add: Basic rate on charges:
       Mortgage interest
          £1,235 x 25%   309
       Deed of covenant
          £260 x 25%   65   374
                                          ------   -------

Income Tax Payable
   (before tax credits)   4,393
                                                                 ======

2   **ROBERTS**

(a) <u>Computation showing effect of Wife's Earnings Election 1989/90</u>

	£	Total £	Mr Roberts £	Mrs Roberts £
Mr Roberts: Schedule E		21,750	21,750	
Mrs Roberts:				
Schedule D Case II	6,624			
Capital allowances	619	6,005		6,005
		27,755	21,750	6,005
<u>Unearned Income</u>				
Mr Roberts: Dividends		7,445	7,445	
Mrs Roberts: Schedule A		1,835	1,835	
		37,035	31,030	6,005
<u>Charges</u>				
Mortgage £(1,221 x 100/75)		(1,628)	(1,628)	
Deeds of Covenant				
£(438 x 100/75)		(584)		(584)
<u>Allowances</u>				
MA		(4,375)		
WEIR		(2,785)		
SPA			(2,785)	(2,785)
<u>Taxable Income</u>		27,663	26,617	2,636

	Total £	Mr Roberts £	Mrs Roberts £
Basic and Higher Rates £			
20,700 x 25% 2,636 x 25%	5,175	5,175	659
6,963 x 40%	2,785		
5,917 x 40%		2,367	
Income tax borne	7,960	7,542	—
Add: Basic Rate on charges			
Mortgage £1,628 x 25%	407	407	
Deed of Covenant			
£584 x 25%	146		146
Income tax payable	8,513	7,949	805

£8,754

The wife's earnings election will result in an increase in income tax payable of £241.

(b) <u>Advice in connection with the personal pension premium</u>

i)   As Mrs Roberts is aged 31, she can pay a premium of up to 17½% of her net relevant earnings, and have the payment allowed against her marginal rate of tax.

ii) Unused relief can be carried forward for up to six years and utilised on a FIFO basis in a year when the premium paid for that year exceeds the limit for that year.

iii) The maximum premium payable by Mrs Roberts for 1989/90 is £1,398, calculated as follows:

	Schedule D Case II £	Capital Allowances £	Net Relevant Earnings £	17½% £
1988/89	2,208	225	1,983	347
1989/90	6,624	619	6,005	1,051
	=====	===	=====	
Maximum PPP payable				1,398
				======

iv) The payment of the premium for 1989/90 will have an effect on the wife's earnings election as follows:

	Total £	Mr Roberts £	Mrs Roberts £
Income tax payable (as before)	8,513	7,949	805
Premium:			
£ 1,398 x 40%	(559)		
£1,398 x 25%			(349)
	─────	─────	──
	7,954	7,949	456

£8,405

Hence it would be even more beneficial <u>not</u> to have a wife's earnings election.

Mr Roberts
Schedule E

	£	£	£
Salary			19,375
Car benefit	3,850		
Less: 50%	1,925	1,925	
Fuel benefit	900		
Less: 50%	450	450	2,375
			21,750

Mrs Roberts
Schedule D Case II

1988/89 first year.

1989/90 first 12 months = $\frac{12}{13}$ x £7,176 = £6,624

Capital Allowances

	£	
Purchase of car		
Open market value	3,600	
1988/89 WDA 25% x $\frac{4}{12}$	300	x 75% = £225
	3,300	
1989/90 WDA 25%	825	x 75% =£619
	2,475	

Rental income

	TRL A £	LFR B £	LFR C £
24th June 1989	500	550	-
29th September 1989	500	550	250
	1,000	1,100	250
25th December 1989	500	-	250
25th March 1990	500	650	250
	2,000	1,750	750

Expenses	£		£		£	
Agents' Commission	117		130		190	
Advertising	-		205		40	
Ground Rent	48		-		-	
Repairs - while let	-		980		730	
- while empty	-		840		-	
		165		2,155		960
		1,835		(405)		(210)

The loss on an LFR cannot be set against the profit on a TRL.

Note:

Repairs while empty not allowed on 'C' as this was not a void period within the required definition.
It is assumed that the repairs are of a revenue nature, in spite of their relative size.

3   **VALENTINE**

(a)   Schedule D assessments for 1988/89 to 1990/91

	1988/89 £	1989/90 £	1990/91 £
Schedule D Case I (working 1)	29,250	44,900	62,600
Averaging adjustment (working 1)		6,150	(6,150)
	29,250	51,050	56.450
Less: Agricultural buildings allowances (working 2)	9,982	13,266	13,266
Net Schedule D Assessments	19,268	37,784	43,184

Workings

(1) Opening year assessments and averaging adjustment

	£
1988/89 Actual	29,250
1989/90 First twelve months (£29,250 + 3/12 x £62,600)	44,900
1990/91 PY - year ended 31.3.90	62,600

(Valentine will not elect under s.62 as profits are rising)
Although the first year cannot enter an averaging claim, such a claim is available for 1989/90 and 1990/91.

£ 44,900 > 70% of £62,600
        < 75% of £62,600

Therefore marginal relief applies.
Averaging adjustment 3(H-L) - 75% H
= 3£(62,600 - 44,900) - 75% (£62,600) = £6,150

(2) Agricultural buildings allowances

	1988/89 (restricted to 9/12) £	1989/90 £	1990/91 £
Year ending			
31.3.79 £11,800 x 10% WDA	885	-	-
31.3.81 to 31.3.87			
£114,600 x 10%	8,595	11,460	11,460
31.3.88 £16,750 x 4%	502	670	670
31.3.89 £28,400 x 4%		1,136	1,136
	9,982	13,266	13,266

(b) Mrs Valentine - Income Tax Borne 1989/90

Earned income: £
        Schedule E: Salary   7,944
                     Commission   1,646
                     Benefits in kind: Travelling   2,540
                                  Car benefit £950 x $\frac{10}{12}$ 792

                                  Fuel benefit £600 x $\frac{10}{12}$ 500

                                  (not insubstantial as £2,300 >
                                   £2,500 x 10/12)
                                  BUPA subscription   134

                              13,556
        Less: s.198 relief   2,540

                 c/f   11,016

		£
	b/f	11,016

	£	£
Unearned Income:		
UK dividends £3,820 x 100/75	5,093	
Schedule D V (remittance basis - 2nd year actual)		
£1,000 x 10/8	1,250	6,343
		———
STI		17,359
Less: Personal allowances:		
SPA	2,785	
APA	1,590	4,375
		———
Taxable income		12,984
		======
Tax borne: £12,984 x 25%	3,246	
Less: DTR	250	
UK income tax borne	2,996	
	======	

4

R ROBB

Taxable Income 1989/90

	£	£	£
Schedule E - Salary			40,000
Less: Superannuation (4%)			1,600
			———
			38,400
Benefits in kind:	2,950		
Less 50%	1,475	1,475	
	———		
Fuel	900		
Less 50%	450	450	
	——		
TV - Video (20% x £800)		160	
Foreign accommodation		1,000	3,085
		———	———
Schedule E			41,485
Schedule D Case V (£750 x 90%)			675
			———
Less:			42,160
Mortgage interest £25,000 x 5% x $\frac{5}{12}$		521	
Interest (Rose Boutique Ltd) £8,000 x 12% x $\frac{6}{12}$		480	1,001
		———	——
Less:			41,159
Marriage allowance		4,375	41,159
Business expansion scheme		10,500	14,875
		———	
Taxable income			26,284
			======

(1) Car Benefit
     The car benefit is the scale figure, less 50% as business mileage is
     more than 18,000 miles per year.

(2) Fuel Benefit
     The fuel benefit is per table, less 50% reduction as business mileage
     is more than 18,000 miles year.

(3) TV-Video
     The benefit is 20% of market value at the time it is first provided by
     the employer for the employee.

(4) Foreign Accommodation
     Reimbursed expenses for travel are allowable where the employee is
     performing the duties of his employment outside the UK for a period of
     not less than 60 consecutive days. Accordingly, only the accommodation
     is a chargeable benefit.

(5) Housing Scheme
     It was held in **Hochstrasser v. Mayes (1960)** that for a benefit to be
     taxable, it must be made by reason of the duties of the employment
     rather than just because he is an employee. Accordingly, a
     compensation for the loss in value of the house was held not to be
     taxable.

(6) Beneficial Loan
     As the loan is for a qualifying purpose, no benefit-in-kind arises on
     the beneficial loan.

(7) Business Expansion Scheme
     The investment in Rose Boutique Ltd qualifies for relief under the
     Business Expansion Scheme.

5   **JERRY**

(a) i)   Retirement Provision
          So long as the pension scheme is approved by the Revenue, payments
          made by Jerry are deductible from his Schedule E income and
          payments by the employer are fully allowable and are not treated
          as a benefit.
          If the scheme is not approved, no deduction is available to the
          employee and the employer's payment is assessable as a benefit in
          kind.

     ii) Golden Handshake
          For the favourable rules on termination payments to be applied the
          payment must not be remuneration for services past, future or
          present.
            It is likely that the Revenue would argue that the entitlement
          to the 'golden handshake' (e.g. in the employee's contract or
          under the company's Articles of Association) will be treated as
          ordinary Schedule E remuneration.

If there is no contractual right to the payment, special rules apply in taxing the payment. The first £30,000 is exempt; the excess is taxable in full.

iii) **'Gilt-Edged Securities'**
The income from the gilt-edged securities will be liable to UK income tax - no exemption from income tax can be claimed whilst Jerry is resident and ordinarily resident in the UK.

If the interest payments are made gross (e.g. War Loan) the assessment will be under Schedule D Case III (on a preceding-year basis). If the interest payments are made net, the assessment will be on an actual basis. No relief is available on the capital cost of the security against the individual's income tax liability.

When the gilt-edged securities are sold any capital gain made is exempt from tax. Conversely any loss is not allowable.

5(b) 1998/91

	£	£	£	£
Salary		50,000		50,000
Less: Pension contribution	2,000		2,000	
Additional	-		4,500	
		2,000		6,500
		48,000		43,500
Marriage allowance		4,095		4,095
Taxable Income		43,905		39,405

Basic and Higher Rates:

20,700 x 25%	5,175	5,175
23,205/18,705 x 40%	9,282	7,482
	14,457	12,657
	12,657	
Tax saving	1,800	

6   **WALTERS, MITCHELL AND BARNETT**

(a)   Amounts to be included in total income in respect of the partnership
      for 1989/90.

	Total £	Walters £	Mitchell £	Barnett £
Net profit for year to 31.7.88	4,010			
Add back: depreciation	1,630			
drawings	10,500			
Schedule D Case I	16,140			

	Total £	Walters £	Mitchell £	Barnett £
6.4.89 to 31.7.89 (4 months)				
= $\frac{4}{12}$ x 16,140	5,380			
Salaries (4/12)	3,500	1,000	2,500	
PSR 55:45	1,880	1,034	846	
	5,380	2,034	3,346	
1.8.89 to 5.4.90 (8 months)				
= $\frac{8}{12}$ x £16,140	10,760			
Salaries (8/12)	8,000		4,000	4,000
PSR 60:40	2,760		1,656	1,104
	10,760		5,656	5,104
Total	16,140	2,034	9,002	5,104
Less: TA 1988 s.385		(2.034)	(565)	
			8,437	
Annuity received/paid: (2 payments in year) 60:40		2,500	(1,500)	(1,000)
Amounts to be included in income		2,500	6,937	4,104

Calculation of loss available under s.385

(1) Allocation of loss 1987/88	Total	Walters	Mitchell
	£	£	£
Loss of year to 31.7.87	2,850		
Add: Capital allowances	15,450		
	18,300		
Salaries	10,500	3,000	7,500
PSR 55:45	(28,800)	(15,840)	(12,960)
	(18,300)	(12,840)	(5,460)

	Total	Walters	Mitchell
	£	£	£
(2) Assessments for 1987/88 and 1988/89			
1987/88 Schedule D I (y/e 31.7.86)	16,200		
Less: Capital allowances	2,600		
	13,600		
Salaries	10,500	3,000	7,500
PSR 55:45	3,100	1,705	1,395
	13,600	4,705	8,895
Add: Investment income		2,425	
Deduct: Interest			(4,000)
Income		7,130	4,895
Less: TA 1988 s.380		(7,130)	(4,895)
1988/89 Investment income		2,760	
Less: TA 1988 s.380		(2,760)	

(3) Summary of Loss Utilisation	Walters	Mitchell
	£	£
Loss for the year 1987/88	(12,840)	(5,460)
Less: s.380 relief: 1987/88	7,130	4,895
1988/89	2,760	
Carried forward under s.385	2,950	565

Note: Walters wastes £916 of the loss relief (£2,950 - £2,034 in 1989/90)

(b) <u>Effect of annuity payments on income tax liabilities of Walters and the continuing partners</u>

i)   Annuities are accounted for on a paid basis; no accruals are brought into the calculations.

ii)   The annuity payments are not an expense within Schedule D Case I; they are added back and allowed in each partner's computation.

iii) So long as a partner retires through age or ill health and payments are made under a partnership agreement for his benefit then up to a certain limit the annuity will be treated as earned income in the hands of the recipient (Walters) and as a deduction from the earned income of the paying partners.
     The limit referred to is 50% of the average of the partner's share of the profits for the best three out of the last seven years in which the partner worked for the partnership (including 1987/88 in the case of Walters).
     The profit shares are indexed by the retail prices index in December of each year to December in the year of retirement.
     The yearly limit is also indexed by the retail prices index in December prior to the year of payment to December in the year of retirement.

iv) The annuity is paid net of basic rate income tax; higher rate relief is given in the paying partners' personal computations.

(c) On the change in the personnel of an existing partnership, the assessment for the tax year of the change <u>and the following three years</u> are to be on actual profits. The options normally available in the second and third years of a new business will apply to the fifth and sixth years. The new rule applies to partnership changes occurring from 20th March 1985. The option to elect within two years of the date of the change for the continuation basis remains in force.

7   ALEX, BERT AND CHARLES

Each partner can deal with his share of the loss in the manner most beneficial to him.

<u>Alex</u> (£12,590)

The options available to Alex are:

    s.380 (set-off against total income)
    s.388 (terminal loss relief)

As Alex's other income in 1989/90 is £2,100 this is covered by his personal allowance for the year. Hence, there is no advantage in making a claim under s.380.

Accordingly, the only claim that can beneficially be made by Alex is under s.388.

The claim would be:

	1986/87 £	1987/88 £	1988/89 £
Original Schedule D Case I Assessments	7,500	7,216	3,846
Terminal Loss Relief £(12,590)	(1,528)	(7,216)	(3,846)
Revised profits	5,972	-	-

Bert and Charles (£7,554 and £5,036)

The options available to Bert and Charles are:

    s.388 (terminal loss relief)
    s.386 (carry forward against income from company).

As most of the trading profits assessable on Bert and all of the assessable profits on Charles for 1986/87 to 1988/89 are covered by charges and personal allowances, a terminal loss relief claim will be wasted:

	1986/87 £	1987/88 £	1988/89 £
Bert			
Schedule D Case I	4,500	4,330	2,308
Charges	(1,500)	(1,500)	(1,500)
Allowances	(3,655)	(3,795)	(4,095)
Effective TLR	-	-	-
Charles			
Schedule D Case I	3,000	2,887	1,539
Charges	(1,150)	(1,150)	(1,150)
Allowances	(3,655)	(3,795)	(4,095)
Effective TLR	-	-	-

Accordingly, Bert and Charles should claim relief under s.386 against the income derived from the company instead (so long as the company continues the same trade and Bert and Charles continue to own the shares).

The relief would be:

	Bert £(7,554)		Charles £(5,036)	
	1988/89 £	1989/90 £	1988/89 £	1989/90 £
Schedule E	3,333	6,667	7,333	16,667
s.386	(3,333)	(4,221)	(3,333)	(1,703)
	-	2,446	-	14,964

Loss incurred in 1989/90

£

$$6.4.89 - 31.7.89 = \frac{4}{12} \times £3,300 = \qquad 1,100$$

$$1.8.89 - 31.1.90 = \frac{6}{6} \times £26,280 = \qquad (26,280)$$

$$\underline{(25,180)}$$

The loss is shared by Alex, Bert and Charles in their profit-sharing ratio,

i.e. Alex	£12,590
Bert	£ 7,554
	£ 5,036
	£25,180

Schedule D Case I Assessments

	Normal	s.63	
1989/90	Nil		

1988/89	£	£	£
PY - y/e 31.7.87	10,340		
Actual 6.4.88 - 5.4.89:			
6.4.88 - 31.7.88		$\frac{4}{12} \times £16,480 = £5,493$	
1.8.88 - 5.4.89		$\frac{8}{12} \times £3,300 = £2,200$	7,693

<u>1987/88</u> PY - y/e 31.7.86
Actual 6.4.87 - 5.4.88   11,240

     6.4.87 - 31.7.87 $\frac{4}{12}$ x £10,340 = £3,446

     1.8.87 - 5.4.88 $\frac{8}{12}$ x £16,480 = £10,987   14,433

                     21,580   22,126

The Revenue will revise the assessments to actual under TA 1988, s.63.

Division of assessments between partners:

	Total £	Alex £	Bert £	Charles £
1989/90 None	-	-	-	-
1988/89 (Actual)	7,693	3,846	2,308	1,539
1987/88 (Actual)	14,433	7,216	4,330	2,887
1986/87 (PY)	15,000	7,500	4,500	3,000

8   **JOHN, BOB AND TOM**

(a)   <u>Schedule D Case I Assessments and Capital Allowances for new Partnership</u>

<u>Schedule D Case I</u>
<u>1988/89</u>   £   £

Actual 1.10.88 to 5.4.89 = $\frac{6}{12}$ x £57,218 =   28,609

                                   28,609

<u>1989/90</u>

Actual 6.4.89 to 3.5.89 = $\frac{1}{12}$ x £57,218 =   4,768

        4.5.89 to 5.4.90 = $\frac{11}{12}$ x £66,184 =   60,669   65,437

1990/91

Actual 6.4.90 to 3.5.90   = $\frac{1}{12}$ x   £66,184   =   5,515

      4.5.90 to 5.4.91   = $\frac{11}{12}$ x   £77,424   =   70,972   76,487

1991/92

Actual 6.4.91 to 3.5.91   = $\frac{1}{12}$ x   £77,424   =   6,452

      4.5.91 to 5.4.92 = $\frac{11}{12}$ x   £60,012   =   55,011   61,463

Capital Allowances

Basic Periods
1988/89: 1.10.88 - 5.4.89
1989/90: 6.4.89 - 5.4.90
1990/91: 6.4.90 - 5.4.91
1991/92: 6.4.91 - 5.4.92

	Plant	Scientific Research	Allowances
	£	£	£
1988/89			None
1989/90			
Purchase	6,250	7,250	
WDA (25%)	1,563		1,563
	4,687	7,250	1,563
Scientific Research (100%)		7,250	7,250
		-	8,813

1990/91

Purchase	3,128		
	————		
	7,815		
WDA (25%)	1,954		1,954
	————		=====
	5,861		

1991/92

WDA (25%)	1,465		1,465
	————		=====
	4,396		

(b) **Taxable Income of John, Bob and Tom 1988/89 and 1989/90**

	Total £	John £	Bob £	Tom £
1988/89				
Schedule D Case I	28,609			
	======			
Salaries $\frac{6}{12}$	6,500	4,000	2,500	
Profits	22,109	5,527	7,738	8,844
	————	————	————	————
	28,609	9,527	10,238	8,844
	======			
Less: Capital Allowances b/f		(1,863)	(3,492)	
Losses b/f		(4,145)	(1,262)	
		————	————	————
		3,519	5,484	8,844
Schedule D Case V				8,000
Dividends		10,000	-	-
		————	————	————
		13,519	5,484	16,844
Less: Charges $\frac{6}{12}$ x £4,200 = £2,100		(525)	(735)	(840)
Allowances		(4,095)	(2.605)	(2,605)
		————	————	————
		8,899	2,144	13,399
		=====	=====	======

<u>1989/90</u>
Schedule D Case 1   65,437
Capital Allowances   8,813
                                           ───────
                                           56,624
                                           ───────

Salaries	13,000	8,000	5,000	-
Profits (25:35:40)	43,624	10,906	15,268	17,450

	56,624	18,906	20,268	17,450

Schedule D Case V   10,000
Dividends   10,000

		28,906	20,268	27,450
Less: Charges £4,200		(1,050)	(1,470)	(1,680)
Allowances		(4,375)	(2,785)	(2,785)
Taxable income		23,481	16,013	22,985

9   **CHARLES REDD AND TOM WOOD**

(a) <u>Income Tax</u>

The transfer of the business to a limited company causes a cessation of the partnership.

i) <u>TA 1970, s.118</u>

<u>1989/90</u>	<u>Normal</u>	<u>Actual</u>
	£	£
	160,000	160,000

<u>1988/89</u>

PY - y/e 31st March 1988	120,000	
Actual - y/e 31st March 1989		150,000

<u>1987/88</u>
PY - y/e 31st March 1987	100,000	
Actual - y/e 31st March 1988		120,000
	220,000	270,000

The Revenue will revise the assessments for 1986/87 and 1987/88 to actual.

ii) Capital Allowances

A balancing charge will arise on the transfer of the factory and plant to the limited company. The balancing charge will be calculated by taking market value of the asset at date of transfer (subject to this value not exceeding cost) over the tax-written-down value.

However, an election can be made under FA 1971, Sch. 8, para. 13 for the assets to be transferred at the tax-written-down value, as the buyer (the company) and seller (the partnership) are connected persons.

When such an election is made, the partnership can claim capital allowances in the final year of trading.

(b) Capital Gains Tax

i)   A charge to capital gains tax will arise on the sale of the chargeable assets of the partnership to the new company.

	Factory £	Goodwill £
Consideration	222,000	76,000
Cost	100,000	30,000
	122,000	46,000

Indexation (based on 31.3.82 market values):

$$\frac{120.0 - 79.4}{79.4}$$

	Factory	Goodwill
	51,100	15,330
	70,900	30,670 = £101,570

ii) As all the assets of the business are being transferred to the company, an election can be made under CGTA 1979, s.123 to deduct the chargeable gain arising on the transfer from the cost of the shares acquired, to the extent that the consideration is satisfied by shares.

	£	£
Chargeable gain	101,570	101,570
Transfer wholly for shares	101,570	
Transfer partly for shares		
Relief limited to £200,000 x £101,570	72,550	280,000
Chargeable to CGT (1989/90)	Nil	29,020
Market value of shares transferred	280,000	200,000
Gains deferred. (CGTA 1979 s.123)	101,570	72,550
	178,430	127,450

10   SOLOMON MATTHEWS

(a) The due dates are:

       i)   £4,500 (first instalment) (½ x £9,000)
              later of 1st January 1989 and
              26th February 1989

              i.e.   26th February 1989

       ii)   £4,500 (second instalment)
              later of 1st July 1989
              26th February 1989

              i.e.   1st July 1989

       iii) £8,000 (balance)   12th September 1989

(b) The reckonable dates are:

       i)   £4,500 (first instalment)   26th February 1989
       ii) £4,500 (second instalment)   1st July 1989
       iii) £8,000 (balance)   1st July 1989

(c) Interest on overdue tax is:

                                                                            £

       i)   £4,500 x 8.5% x $\frac{217 \text{ days}}{365 \text{ days}}$ =   227.40

       ii)   £4,500 x 8.5% x $\frac{92 \text{ days}}{365 \text{ days}}$ =   96.41

       iii) £8,000 x 8.5% x $\frac{92 \text{ days}}{365 \text{ days}}$ =   171.39

       Total interest on overdue tax   495.20

11   MR AND MRS H VAN RIJN

The pattern of visits to the UK suggests that under normal Revenue practice, Mr and Mrs Van Rijn are not resident and not ordinarily resident in the UK.
  As regards domicile, Mr Van Rijn would appear to have a domicile of origin in the Netherlands with no indication that this has changed. Mrs Van Rijn is also almost certainly domiciled in the Netherlands either by the domicile of dependence rule (marriage prior to 1st January 1984) or by her acquiring a domicile of choice in the Netherlands.

(a) Consultancy Engagement
It is necessary to determine whether the consultancy engagement was an employment or self-employment. If this was an employment (a contract of service), it will be liable to UK income tax under Schedule E Case II.
    If this was a self-employment (a contract for services), it will be liable under Schedule D Case II or possibly Case VI.

(b) Rental Income
Mr Van Rijn is assessable under Schedule A in respect of the rents arising in the UK.

(c) Sale of Farm
As Mrs Van Rijn is neither resident or ordinarily resident in the UK, and the farm was not being used for trade being carried on by her (through a branch or an agency in the UK), there is no liability to UK capital gains tax.
    The rental income from the farm would have been assessed under Schedule A.

(d) Government Securities
Under TA 1988, s.47, where certain British Government securities are beneficially owned by persons not ordinarily resident in the UK, income arising thereon is exempted from UK income tax.
    Both the 3½% War Loan and the 15½% Treasury Loan 1998 are such British Government securities.

12   PIERRE AND MONIQUE GASTON

It is clear that Pierre and Monique Gaston are resident and ordinarily resident in the UK. It is also almost certain that in view of their intentions to return to France, they have remained domiciled in France.

(a) Sale of Shares in France and Purchase of Villa
As Pierre is resident and ordinarily resident in the UK, he is liable to capital gains tax on gains made anywhere in the world.
    However, when an individual is not domiciled in the UK a gain made on an overseas asset is only chargeable if it is remitted to the UK.
    Accordingly, as Pierre is not domiciled in the UK and the overseas gain is not being remitted to the UK, no liability to capital gains tax arises.   (Note: it has been held that income or gains do not lose their character by being invested overseas and then remitted to the UK. Accordingly, if Pierre subsequently sells the villa and then remits the proceeds to the UK, he will have remitted the original gain on the sale of shares and will pay tax accordingly.)
    Income tax will be due on the rental income under Schedule D Case V. As Pierre is not domiciled in the UK, he will be liable only on a remittance basis.

(b) Gift of Painting
Although Monique is not domiciled in the UK, as she has been resident in the UK for 17 out of the previous 20 tax years, she is deemed to be domiciled for inheritance tax purposes and may be liable to inheritance tax on worldwide transfers if she dies within 7 years.

Accordingly, although the painting is an overseas asset, Monique will be making a transfer on the gift to her art teacher.

She may be able to utilise her annual exemptions for the current year and the previous year if these have not yet been utilised.

Any chargeable transfer must be reported to the Revenue.

(c) Bank Accounts
The interest on the bank accounts will be assessable under Schedule D Case V. As Monique is not domiciled in the UK, she will be liable only on a remittance basis.

Where some remittances are made out of a mixed capital and income source, the Revenue will argue that remittances are made first out of income (which are liable to UK tax) and then out of capital (which are not liable to UK tax).

As Monique intends making occasional remittances, she would be best advised to have the capital of £100,000 kept in one bank account, with the interest earned being credited to a separate bank account. Any remittance can then be made out of the capital account and can clearly be demonstrated not to have been a remittance of income.

13   THE OLIVIA AERO ENGINE CO LTD

Mainstream Corporation Tax Liability

	12 months to 31.12.1989		3 months to 31.3.1990	
	£	£	£	£
Schedule D Case I (W1)		258,131		72,181
Schedule A (W4)		14,200		3,550
		272,331		75,731
Less: Charges paid:				
Patent Royalties	9,000		4,600	
Debenture interest	8,400	17,400	-	4,600
		254,931		71,131
Corporation tax (W6)		79,822		21,987
Less: ACT (W3)		11,058		17,782
Mainstream Corporation Tax Liability		68,964		4,205

Workings

(1) Adjustment of profit for 15-months period of account to 31.3.1990

		£
Net profit per accounts		259,626
Add: Depreciation		31,400
Amortisation		6,500
Patent royalties		16,000
Debenture interest		10,500
Corporation tax		105,500
Stamp duty on loan stock issue		450
Payment for infringement of patent		4,500
Rented property expenses		4,000
		———
		438,476

	£	
Deduct: UK dividends	17,080	
Rental income	24,250	
Surplus on investment	13,250	
	———	54,850
		———
Adjusted trading profit before capital allowances		383,626
		═══════

CAP	y/e 31.12.89	3 mths to 31.3.90
	£	£
Profits	306,901	76,725
Less: Capital allowances (Note 2)		
on plant	(23,570)	(4,544)
on research equipment	(25,200)	-
	———	———
	258,131	72,181
	═══════	═══════

(2) Capital allowances

  i) On plant used in the trade

	Expensive car	Car Pool	Pool	Capital allowances
	£	£	£	£
CAP y/e 31.12.89				
Tax WDV b/f	-	4,280	26,000	-
Additions	12,000	18,000	30,000	
		———	———	
		22,280	64,000	
WDA @ 25% (max)	(2,000)	(5,570)	(16,000)	23,570
	———			═══════

	Expensive car £	Car Pool £	Pool £	Capital allowances £
CAP 3 months to 31.3.90				
Tax WDV	10,000	16,710	48,000	
WDA @ 25% x 3/12 (max)	(500)	(1,044)	(3,000)	4,544
Tax WDV c/f	9,500	15,666	45,000	

ii) On expenditure for scientific research
     CAP y/e 31.12.89 100% relief on research laboratory expenditure,
        £25,200.

(3) <u>Advance corporation tax</u>

CAP y/e 31.12.89:   £

Dividends paid: 2.5.89   6,300
                 6.6.89   37,500
                                                                    _____
                                                                    43,800

                                                    £
Less: Dividends received: 31.5.89   6,650
                            15.11.89   10,430
                                                _____
                                                                    17,080
                                                                    _____
                                                                    26,720
                                                                    _____

ACT thereon @ 25/75   8,907

Surplus ACT from 3 months to 31.3.90 carried   2,151
  back (see below)
                                                                    _____
                                                                    11,058
                                                                    _____

CAP 3 months to 31.3.90:
  Dividends paid: 1.3.90   53,500
                  4.1.90   6,300
                                                                    _____
                                                                    59,800

ACT thereon @ 25/75   19,933

Maximum set-off 25% x £71,131   17,782
                                                                    _____

Surplus ACT c/back   2,151

(4) <u>Rents from property</u>

	12 months to 31.12.89	3 months to 31.3.90
	£	£
Rents	10,800	2,700
Less: Expenses	3,200	800
	7,600	1,900
Other Rent	6,600	1,650
	14,200	3,550

(<u>Note</u> Rents recovered of £2,500 will normally be assessed in the year they were receiveable though where accounts are prepared the IR may accept recovered rents as assessable in the AP in which received.

(5) <u>Capital Gains</u>
Investments sold 8.4.89

	£	£
Proceeds	24,020	24,020
Less: Cost	10,500	
31st March, 1982 rate	-	15,000
Gross gain	13,520	9,020
Less: Indexation allowance:		
£15,000 x $\frac{110.0 - 79.4}{79.4}$	5,775	5,775
Take lower gain	7,745	3,245
Less: Capital losses b/f	======	3,245
		-
		======

(6) <u>Year ended 31.12.89</u>

	Total	FY 1988 3/12	FY 1987 9/12
	£	£	£
Income	254,931	63,733	191,198
FII £ 17,080 x $\frac{100}{75}$	22,773	5,693	17,080
	277,704	69,426	208,278
	======	======	========

	£	£
FY 1988: £63,733 @ 35%	22,307	
Less: Small companies relief:		
$\frac{1}{40}$ £(125,000 - 69,426) $\frac{63,733}{69,426}$	1,275	21,032
FY 1989: £191,198 @ 35%	66,919	
Less: Small companies relief:		
$\frac{1}{40}$ £(562,500 - 208,278) $\frac{191,198}{208,278}$	8,129	58,790
		79,822

3 months ended 31.3.90

	£	£
Income: £71,131 @ 35%	24,896	
Less: Small companies relief:		
1/40 £(187,500 - 71,131)	2,909	21,987

14

(a) <u>Q Ltd</u>
Group relief can be surrendered in the same period in which the loss is incurred.
  Group relief is claimed after all other reliefs (including charges, except for reliefs due from a later accounting period).

<u>T Ltd</u>
<u>Year to 30.11.1988</u>
Loss can be carried forward under s.393(1).

<u>Year to 30.11.1989</u>

	£
DI	10,000
Less: s.393(1)	(5,000)
	5,000
DIII	5,000
	10,000
Less: Charges paid	2,000
	8,000
Group Relief	8,000
	-

Year to 30.11.1990

	£
DI (Loss)	(10,000)
DIII (s.393(2)).	5,000
	(5,000)

The loss of £5,000 is carried forward against future profits of the same trade under s.393(1).

The debenture interest of £2,000 is also carried forward against future profits of the same trade (under s.393(9)).

Q Ltd
Year to 30.11.1989

	£
DI (loss)	(12,000)
Surrendered to T Ltd	8,000
	(4,000)

The loss of £4,000 must be carried forward against future profits of the same trade under s.393(1).

Year to 30.11.1990

	£
DI (loss)	(5,000)

The loss of £5,000 must be carried forward against future profits of the same trade under s.393(1).

(b) Z Ltd

Z Ltd is owned by a consortium, as all the companies are resident in the UK, and at least 75% is owned by UK resident companies.

Since 1981, consortium relief can pass in either direction pro rata to the shareholding.

Accordingly, B Ltd can set part of its loss against the profits of the consortium company.

The relief is limited to the lower of proportionate share of profits and proportionate share of losses.

	£
Profit share $\frac{£24,000}{£80,000}$ x £50,000	15,000
Loss $\frac{£24,000}{£80,000}$ x £60,000	(18,000)
Maximum relief is	15,000

<u>B Ltd</u>	£
Loss	(60,000)
Consortium relief	15,000
(as above)	
	(45,000)

The loss of £45,000 must be carried forward against future profits of the same trade in B Ltd under s.393(1).

The claim for consortium relief must be made with the written consent of the consortium members within two years of the end of the surrendering company's accounting period to which the claim relates.

15   **BANDROYAL LTD**
                 <u>Year ended 31st March 1990</u>

<u>Mainstream corporation tax payable</u>

	UK Profits	DV
	£	£
DI	400,000	
Schedule A	40,000	
Capital Gains	240,000	
Overseas dividend		200,000
	680,000	200,000
Less: charges	50,000	
	630,000	200,000

	UK Profits	DV
	£	£
Corporation tax @ 35%	220,500	70,000
DTR	-	56,000
	220,500	14,000
Less: ACT set-off (restricted)	157,500	14,000
	63,000	-

The mainstream corporation tax liability is £63,000.

<u>ACT carried forward</u>

	£
ACT paid £641,000 x 25/75	213,667
ACT utilised	171,500
ACT carried forward	42,167

Calculation of Schedule D Case V and Foreign Tax

		£	Foreign Tax £
Dividend received		144,000	
Withholding tax (10) (90)		16,000	16,000
		160,000	
Underlying tax (20) (80)		40,000	40,000
Schedule D Case V		200,000	56,000

16   A LTD

(a) Mainstream Corporation Tax Liability Year Ended 31st March 1990

	Source	Charges	Net	CT @ 35%	DTR	ACT	MCT
	£	£	£	£	£	£	£
DI	50,000						
DIII	20,000	16,000	73,000	25,550		18,250	7,300
A	10,000						
Gain	9,000						
DV	20,000		20,000	7,000	7,000		
				32,550	7,000	18,250	

Mainstream corporation tax liability   7,300

(b) Schedule D Case V and Foreign Tax

	£	Foreign Tax £
Dividend received	10,800	
Withholding tax (10) (90)	1,200	1,200
	12,000	
Underlying tax (40) (60)	8,000	8,000
Schedule D Case V	20,000	
Total foreign tax available		9,200
Utilised		7,000
Foreign tax relief wasted		2,200

(c)   ACT Carried Forward

	£
Dividends received	1,400
Dividend paid	58,800
Net	57,400
ACT at 25/75	19,133
Utilised	18,250
	883

17   VERITY SPINNERS LTD

(a)   Corporation Tax Payable Year Ended 31st March 1989

	£
Schedule D Case I (Schedule 1)	76,102
Less: B/f (s.393(1)) £(96,100 - 47,448)	48,652
	27,450
Schedule A	13,220
Schedule D Case III	2,340
	43,010
Chargeable gains	8,724
	51,734
Less Charges:	
Patent Royalties £(7,850 - 1,440)	6,410
	45,324
FII	1,700
Profits for Small Companies' Rate	47,024
Corporation tax £45,324 x 25%	11,331

SCHEDULES
Year ended 31st March 1989

		£	£
(1)	Schedule D Case I		
	Trading profits		102,846
	Add: Depreciation	20,800	
	Patent Royalties	7,850	
	Alterations	3,200	
			31,850
			134,696
	Less: Capital allowances (Schedule 2)	56,889	
	Lease amortisation	1,705	58,594
	Schedule D Case I		76,102

(2) Capital Allowances

(a) IBA on Park Mill = $\dfrac{£62,650}{14 \text{ yrs.}}$ 4,475

(b) IBA on Extension at Kirkstall Mill
          £31,600 x 4%   1,264

(c) Scientific Research 100% x £26,500   26,500

(d)

(d)	(d)	Plant: brought forward	(NIL)	
		Additions (£104,700 + 3,200)	107,900	
		Sales	9,300	
			98,600	
		WDA - 25%	24,650	
				24,650
				56,889

(3) Relief for Lease Premium Paid   £

Premium   55,000
Less: 2% (20 - 1) x £55,000   20,900

Schedule A   34,100

Annual Equivalent $\dfrac{£34,100}{20}$ 1,705

(4) <u>Chargeable Gain on Sale of House</u>   £

Consideration   46,350
Cost   26,220
                                                                 _____

Gross Gain   20,130

Indexation $\frac{120.0 - 83.6}{83.6}$ = 0.435 x £26,220   11,406
                                                                 _____
                                                                  8,724
                                                                 ======

18

(a) <u>North Yorkshire Plastics Ltd</u>

A company is a distinct legal entity; hence normally there is no effect
on the corporation tax position of the company if the ownership of the
company changes.

   However, the following points should be noted in connection with the
change:

i)   <u>Trading losses</u>
     Under TA 1988, s.393(1), a trading loss can be carried forward
     against future profits of the same trade. So long as the same
     trade is being continued by the company (a question of fact), loss
     relief will not be denied.
        However, where there is <u>both</u> a change in ownership and a major
     change in the nature of conduct of the trade (including the type
     of property dealt in, customers, outlets or markets), or within a
     period of three years a company's trade has become negligible and
     before there is a considerable revival of the trade, there is a
     change in the ownership of the company, loss relief under s.393
     can be withheld (TA 1988, s.768).

ii) <u>Advance corporation tax</u>
     Under TA 1988, s.245 the carry forward of ACT can be restricted in
     the same circumstances.

iii) <u>Capital losses</u>
     There is no statutory provision restricting the amount of capital
     loss available to be carried forward against future gains of the
     company.
        It is, however, worth pointing out that under the House of
     Lords' decision in the **Ramsay** case, the **Burmah** case and **Furniss
     v. Dawson (1983)**, if the transactions are carried out purely for
     tax avoidance purposes with no commercial reason for the
     transactions, loss relief can be denied.

iv) <u>Retirement of directors</u>

The retirement of the directors on its own does not have any adverse tax effect.   If the company is to make compensation payments, it will have to demonstrate that these are wholly and exclusively for the purposes of the company's trade, for them to be an allowable deduction.

(b) <u>Demergers</u>

i) The two principal problems which caused obstacles to demergers were (1) on division of the group or company, a distribution took place, with adverse income tax and ACT consequences, and (2) a disposal or part disposal took place for capital gains tax purposes.

ii) So long as the demerger was an exempt distribution, no income tax or ACT arose and the shareholder was exempted from any CGT liability in a reorganisation, at the point of transferring the shares.

iii) The main conditions for exemption are:

(1)   The transaction must be one which would otherwise be a distribution within TA 1988, s.209.

(2) The company making the distribution must be a trading company (or a member of a trading group).

(3) The transaction must be wholly or mainly to benefit some or all of the trading activities involved in the demerger.

(4) It is intended that the newly demerged trade should be left free to operate under its new independent management - quite separate from the former parent.

(5) All the companies involved must be resident in the UK at the time of the distribution.

(6) The demerger must not be part of a scheme or arrangement for the avoidance of tax.

(7) If the transfer is of shares, these must not be redeemable, and the shares must constitute, substantially, the whole of the distributing company's holding and voting rights in the 75% subsidiary's share capital.

19   **JARDINE**

Hence BDV not beneficial and no election is made.

	£	£
		(3,876)

ii) 3.4.90 Sale of shares in Clark (Winchester) Ltd:

	£	£
Proceeds	40,700	
Less: Cost 29.6.87	11,500	
Gross gain	29,200	

Less: Indexation:

$$£11,500 \quad \times \quad \frac{125.0 - 97.8}{97.8} \qquad 3,197$$

Net chargeable gain   26,003

Less: Retirement Relief:
As Jardine has been a full-time working
director for 2 3/4 years the maximum
retirement relief available to him at
the 100% rate is:

$$\frac{2\frac{3}{4}}{10 \text{ years}} \quad \times \ £125,000 \ = \ £34,375$$

Gain Eligible for Retirement Relief

$$£26,003 \times \frac{£95,000 + £64,500}{£95,000 + £64,500 + £5,500} = £25,136 \quad £25,136 \qquad 867$$

(iii)   Sale of 10% Treasury Stock 1992 - Exempt   -

Overall allowable loss for 1989/90   (3,009)

(b) Points to note in connection with proposed transfer of house:

Capital gains tax
The transfer of the house to trustees is a chargeable disposal for
capital gains tax. The gain will be computed as the difference between
its market value and original cost with relief for indexation from
March 1982 to the month of transfer. The chargeable gain may not be
held over but any tax payable may be by instalments.

21   HALLSVALLA LTD

John Stephens
Gift in May 1989   £
        Estate before:
                    630 x £53   33,390
        (related property = 770 shares)
        Estate after:
                    350 x £23   8,050
        (related property = 490 shares)   _____

                                                        25,340

        Less: BPR 50%   12,670

        Transfer of value   12,670
                                                        ======

Jim Stephens   £
Gift in May 1989

Estate before:
                    230 x £11   2,530
Estate after:
                    90 x £4   360
                                                        _____

                                                        2,170
Less: BPR 30%   651
                                                        _____

Transfer of value   1,519
                                                        =====

22   **NICHOLS**

(a) <u>Inheritance tax paid on death of Nichols</u>

   Date of Death 8th February 1990.

	£	£
<u>Estate</u>		
Freehold house		66,500
Foreign assets		31,900
Quoted investments		261,690
Personal chattels		18,100
Bank balances		33,600
		————
		431,790
Less: Debts	6,850	
Funeral expenses	490	
	————	
	7,340	
		————
		424,450
Less: Charitable bequests		30,000
		————
		394,450
Life interest in family trust		37,350
		————
Estate on Death		431,800
		=======

	Gross £	IHT £
Chargeable lifetime transfers (at death rates)	21,400	-
Estate on death	431,800	134,080
	————	————
	453,200	134,080
	=======	=======

IHT on death estate

                                                £
                                        134,080 (estate rate
                                                 31.0514%)

Less: Quick succession relief on trust:

       100% x £7,420 x £34,380   (6,103)
                       £41,800   _____

                                                 127,977

Less: Double taxation relief   (3,833)   (3,833)

       (foreign tax rate = £ 3,833 = 12.02%
                           £31,900
       which is less than estate rate, hence all   _____
       can be offset)   124.144
                                                     ========

(b)   <u>Potential repayments of inheritance tax through transactions in</u>
       <u>securities</u>

       Net loss on sale within 12 months:

	Probate Value	Gross Proceeds
	£	£
12th October 1990	160,500	142,800
14th November 1990	41,800	43,200
	_____	_____
	202,300	
	186,000	186,000
	_____	

       Net Loss on Sale   (16,300)

       Reinvestment Restriction:

            £ 7,440   x £16,300 =   652
       £142,800 + £43,200   _____

       Reduction in Estate   (15,648)
                               ======

       IHT Marginal Rate 40%   £6,259
                               ======

       Potential Repayment of IHT £6,259
                                  ======

(c) <u>Points in connection with future transactions in quoted investments</u>

    i)   No further sales should be made of quoted securities showing a profit over their probate value until 9th February 1991.

    ii) No further purchases of quoted securities should be made within two months of the last sale. (If no further sales are made, this date is 14th January 1991.)

    iii) The securities purchased in October 1990 can be sold by the executors, with no further effect on the relief.

23

i)   VAT is charged on the supply of goods or services and the tax point is the date on which the supply is deemed to have been made. The rate of VAT in force at this date is the rate chargeable and the VAT payable must be accounted for by reference to the prescribed accounting period in which the tax point falls.

ii)   The basic tax point is the date when the goods are made available to the purchaser which, if the goods are to be removed, will be the time of removal, or if the goods are not removed, the date on which they are made available.

If within 14 days after the basic tax point the person making the supply issues an invoice then, unless he elects otherwise, the date of the issue of the invoice will become the tax point of the supply.
   If invoicing or payment take place before the goods are removed or made available and such invoicing or payment is prior to the basic tax point, the tax point will be the earlier of the invoice date or the date of payment.

24

(a) Goods which are zero rated are still treated as a taxable supply but the rate of tax charged is, of course, nil. A registered person making zero-rated supplies is therefore fully within the VAT system and can reclaim any input tax suffered, which may result in him receiving a repayment from Customs and Excise.

    Where a supply is made of an exempt item it is not regarded as a taxable supply for VAT purposes and therefore no VAT is chargeable. The supplier will not be able to reclaim input tax suffered which must be borne consequently by the business. He does not have to register with the Customs & Excise or keep the required records which a zero-rated supplier would have to maintain.

(b) Where a registered taxable person (except zero-rated supply) makes a supply (other than a zero-rated supply) to another taxable person he must normally provide him with an invoice which contains the following particulars:

i)   an identifying number;

ii) the date of supply;

iii) the name, address and registration number of the supplier;

iv) the name and address of the person to whom the goods or services are   supplied;

v)   the type of supply, i.e. sale, cash sale, hire etc.;

vi) a description of the goods or services;

vii) for each description the quantity of goods or the extent of services, the rate of tax, the amount payable excluding tax;

viii) the gross amount payable excluding tax;

ix) the rate of any cash discount offered;

x)   the amount of tax chargeable at each rate;

xi) the total amount of tax chargeable.

Where a person provides an invoice containing the above which includes items which are exempt or zero-rated he must distinguish on the invoice between these supplies and state separately the gross total amount payable in   respect of each.

25

(1) <u>John Downs</u>
The turnover limit for VAT registration is (1988/89) £22,100. John is, therefore, not liable to be registered. Since it appears that all his customers are taxable persons, he will be in a less competitive position if he is not VAT registered. This is because his customers cannot recover that part of his charges which relates to the VAT he has suffered. John can, if he so wishes, apply for voluntary registration. This will mean that VAT will have to be added to his charges. However, he will be able to recover the VAT that he has suffered.

<u>On Comparison (Assuming VAT charged to him to be £1,500 (10% of 15,000))</u>

<u>If he does not register</u>, his total charges will be £16,500, leaving him with a net £15,000 after deducting the VAT that he has suffered. However, his customers will have no VAT recovery and will bear the full charge of £16,500.

If he does register, his total charges will be £17,250 (15,000 x VAT @ 15%). His customers will be able to recover the VAT of £2,250 as input tax, reducing their costs to £15,000. John will have to pay over as output tax £2,250, less input tax of £1,500, i.e. £750. His net position will, of course, be the same as before, i.e. £15,000 except he will be more competitive.

(2) Michael

His turnover is not expected to exceed £21,100 in the next year. He may, therefore, apply to Customs and Excise for his VAT registration to be cancelled.

(3) Julie

Julie will not be liable to register for VAT since she expects her turnover only to rise with inflation and be less than £22,100. Julie will not have to charge VAT to her residential guests.

(4) Adam and Sandra

Adam supplies only exempt goods and he is not liable to be registered for VAT. Adam, of course, will not be able to recover VAT charged to him except by increasing his prices to his customers. Zero-rated supplies are taxable supplies, so Sandra will be registered for VAT since her taxable turnover
exceeds £22,100 No VAT will be charged on the zero-rated supplies but Sandra will be able to recover any tax charged to her. Customs and Excise have discretion not to register a person whose taxable supplies are all zero-rated if that person does not wish to be registered. If such an exemption is granted it is conditional upon there being no loss to the Exchequer and the trader is required to notify Customs and Excise of any change in circumstances.

26

(a) Three calendar months is the standard period for VAT. Quarter dates do vary for different businesses according to their business classification. Often a trader will request that the return dates be amended to coincide with his accounting period. Monthly VAT accounting periods may be requested; however, the advantages must be weighed against the administrative burden of having to complete 12 returns a year. Where a business is taken over as a going concern, an application may be made to retain the tax periods of the previous business.

(b) A taxable person must keep records of all taxable goods and services, supplied or received, and including any taxable supplies and goods taken or used for non-business purposes. He must also keep records of any exempt supplies. The records must be of sufficient detail to enable the VAT liability to be correctly ascertained. The records will include copies of tax invoices and all invoices on which VAT input tax is claimed. Records for each tax period must be summarised in a detailed VAT account showing:

(1)   output tax (including that on goods for non-business use);

(2)   deductible input tax (including tax on imported goods and services from abroad);

(3)   any adjustments in respect of overpayments or underpayments made in previous returns.

All records and non-related documents must normally be kept for a six-year period (previously 3 years). The VAT account is summarised and the output or input tax returned on VAT Form 100 showing the net amount payable or repayable. If tax is payable then the amount must be forwarded with the return. Penalties may be imposed for late, incomplete or incorrect returns.